Repairing the Athlete's Image

Repairing the Athlete's Image

Studies in Sports Image Restoration

Edited by Joseph R. Blaney, Lance Lippert, and J. Scott Smith

LEXINGTON BOOKS
Lanham • Boulder • New York • Toronto • Plymouth, UK

Published by Lexington Books
A wholly owned subsidiary of The Rowman & Littlefield Publishing Group, Inc.
4501 Forbes Boulevard, Suite 200, Lanham, Maryland 20706
www.rowman.com

10 Thornbury Road, Plymouth PL6 7PP, United Kingdom

British Library Cataloguing in Publication Information Available

Library of Congress Cataloging-in-Publication Data

Repairing the athlete's image : studies in sports image restoration / edited by Joseph R. Blaney, Lance
Lippert, and J. Scott Smith.
p. cm.
Includes bibliographical references and index.
ISBN 978-0-7391-3896-0 (cloth : alk. paper) -- ISBN 978-0-7391-3899-1 (electronic)
1. Sports--Public relations. 2. Sports--Public opinion. 3. Sports in popular culture. I. Blaney, Joseph
R. II. Lippert, Lance R. III. Smith, J. Scott.
GV714.R47 2012
659.2'9796--dc23
2012027966

The paper used in this publication meets the minimum requirements of American
National Standard for Information Sciences Permanence of Paper for Printed Library
Materials, ANSI/NISO Z39.48-1992.

Printed in the United States of America

Contents

Introduction: Why Sports Image Restoration and How Shall We
    Proceed?   1
Joseph R. Blaney, Illinois State University

I: Drugs

  1 From the Mitchell Report to Brian McNamee: Roger Clemens's
     Image Repair Discourse   9
     J. Scott Smith, University of Missouri

  2 "Big Mac" with a Side of Steroids: The Image Repair Strategies
     of Mark McGwire   27
     John McGuire and Lori Melton McKinnon, Oklahoma State
     University, and Wayne Wanta, University of Florida

  3 Defense of an Anti-Hero: Barry Bonds's "State of the Great
     Address"   41
     J. Scott Smith, University of Missouri

  4 The Image Repair Media Interview as *Apologia* and
     Antapologia: Marion Jones on the *Oprah Winfrey Show*   59
     Michael R. Kramer, Saint Mary's College

  5 The Michael Phelps Saga: From Successful Olympian, to Pot
     Smoker Caught on Camera, to Renewed Role Model and Brand   71
     Rod L. Troester and Lindsay Johns, Penn State University Erie,
     The Behrend College

II: Marital Infidelity and Sexual Misconduct

  6 Tiger Woods's Image Repair: Could He Hit One Out of the Rough?   89
     William L. Benoit, Ohio University

 7 Power, Privilege, and the Surprising Absence of Repair: Kobe
    Bryant and Interest Convergence   97
    Rachel Alicia Griffin, Southern Illinois University

 8 Strategies of Silence: The John Terry Affair and the British Press 123
    John Huxford, Illinois State University

III: Social Deviance and Integrity

 9 Bad Newz Kennels: Michael Vick and Dogfighting   151
    J. Scott Smith, University of Missouri

10 The Failed Comedy of the NBA's Gilbert Arenas: Image
    Restoration in Context   169
    Theodore F. Sheckels, Randolph-Macon College

11 Plaxico Burress Takes His Best Shot   187
    Mark Glantz, St. Norbert College

12 In the Dark at Texas Tech: News Coverage Involving the Image
    Repair Discourse of Mike Leach and Adam James   203
    *Kevin A. Stein, Southern Utah University, Paul Turman, South
    Dakota Board of Regents, and Matthew Barton, Southern Utah
    University*

13 How Bobby Knight Changed His "Bad Boy" Image to Become a
    Media Darling   223
    Ric Jensen, Ashland University

IV: On-Field Actions

14 Belated Remorse: Serena Williams's Image Repair Rhetoric at
    the 2009 U.S. Open   239
    LeAnn M. Brazeal

15 Unsports(wo)manlike Conduct: An Image Repair Analysis of
    Elizabeth Lambert, the University of New Mexico, and the NCAA   253
    Jordan L. Compton, Ohio University

V: The Organizational Turn

16 No Pepper: Apologia and Image Repair in the 2002 Labor
    Negotiations Between Major League Baseball and the Players
    Association   267
    Kevin R. Meyer and Craig W. Cutbirth, Illinois State University

17 Giving Them the Ol' Misdirection: The NCAA and the Student-
    Athlete   283
    Mike Milford, Auburn University

18 A Death, a Family Feud, and a Merger: The Image Repair of
Teresa Earnhardt and Dale Earnhardt, Inc.   297
Angela M. Jerome, Western Kentucky University

19 The Puck Stops Here: The NHL's Image Repair Strategies
During the 2004-2005 Lockout   319
*James R. DiSanza, Nancy J. Legge, H. R. Allen, and James T.
Wilde, Idaho State University*

20 Celebrating Spectator Sports in America: The Centrality of
Press Conferences and Media Interviews to Sports Image Repair   359
*Peter M. Smudde and Jeffrey L. Courtright, Illinois State
University*

VI: Research in Brief

21 Reputation Differences between Mortification-Only and
Mortification/Corrective Action Strategies Following a
Transgression by a Professional Athlete   395
John Twork and Joseph Blaney, Illinois State University

Conclusion   401
Joseph R. Blaney

Index   403

About the Authors   411

Introduction:
Why Sports Image Restoration and How Shall We Proceed?

Joseph R. Blaney, Illinois State University

Public relations practitioners are responsible for coordinating communication between the public and the organizations or individuals they represent. When the organizations or individuals warrant positive publicity, public relations agents inform the public about organizational or individual accomplishments. However, when negative publicity becomes associated with a represented group or person, practitioners must implement a communication strategy designed to salvage the images of their clients. Image is defined as "the perception of a person (or group, or organization) held by the audience, shaped by the words and actions of that person, as well as by the discourse and behavior of other relevant actors" (Benoit, 1997, p. 251). The purpose of this book is to illuminate how athletes and their related organizations can respond to allegations of misdeeds for their own betterment and the integrity of their sports. Through case studies and other approaches, the collection of authors herein will offer insight into high-profile sports figures' attempts to repair image, and concomitantly, illuminate the field of sports communication. Toward this end, the essays are organized thematically into five book parts: (1) drugs, (2) marital infidelity and sexual misconduct, (3) social deviance and integrity, (4) on-field actions, and (5) the organizational turn. Finally, the essays are capped off with a "research-in-brief" test of a major assumption about image repair strategy combinations.

Image is of specific interest to public relations practitioners because it has a direct influence on the success or failure of an individual or organization within the public arena. If an image becomes damaged during a communication crisis, it must be restored in order to preserve the economic and social value of the individual or organization. In an effort to identify common, primary strategies utilized during the image restoration process, Benoit (1995) advanced his Image Restoration Theory (IRT). Now the gold standard for analyzing image repair discourse, many of the case studies in this book employ that approach. It is for that reason that this chapter offers a brief treatment of IRT, saving us from sundry reviews of literature in many of the chapters.

Although Benoit created IRT, it was influenced by Goffman's face-work research of the 1950s to 1970s. Benoit compared face-work to how "Threats to one's image often prompt image restoration discourse" (Benoit, 1997, p. 251). He also drew on Ware and Linkugel's (1973) notion of *Apologia*, Burke's (1969) *Purification*, and Scott and Lyman's (1968) *Accounts*, among other frameworks.

The image of an individual or organization is vital. A damaged image can cost an individual or corporation millions of dollars, which is why it is imperative to understand key image repair strategies. When applying Benoit's IRT to an organization or individual's damaged image, two initial qualifications must be met. First, the accused must be held responsible for an action. Second, the act must be considered offensive (Benoit, 1997).

With the first two qualifications achieved, IRT can be applied to the evaluation of crisis communication discourse using five broad categories of image repair strategies. The first strategy is *denial*, which is utilized when a firm simply denies an accusation, saying it is not responsible for the offensive act. This may also involve *shifting the blame* to another firm, claiming that "another person or organization is actually responsible for the offensive act" (Benoit, 1997, p. 180).

Second, evasion of responsibility consists of four options, which include provocation, defeasibility, accident, and good intention. *Provocation* transpires when a firm claims its act was in response to another's offensive act. *Defeasibility* transpires when a firm claims to have a lack of information and control over the offensive act. *Accident* describes when a firm tries to convince the public that the act in question occurred unintentionally. Finally, *good intentions* occur when a firm claims that the offensive act was an inadvertent result of behavior performed with the best of intentions (Benoit, 1997).

The third category of image repair strategies consists of reducing the offensiveness of the event. This can be accomplished through bolstering, minimization, differentiation, transcendence, attacking the accuser and compensation. First, *bolstering* occurs when a firm tries to offset negative feelings connected with the offensive act by enhancing the audience's positive feelings toward the offenders. Second, *minimization* occurs when a firm attempts to downplay the extent of damage caused by the offensive act. Third, *differentiation* transpires when a firm distinguishes its offensive act from other, similar, but even more offensive acts in an effort to mitigate the offensiveness of the act in question. Fourth, *transcendence* transpires when a firm tries to place the offensive act in a more favorable context by illustrating how the benefits of the act outweigh the drawbacks. Fifth, *attacking the accuser* describes when a firm that is accused of offensive behavior responds by accusing the accuser of equal or greater offensiveness. Finally, *compensation* occurs when a firm compensates those who are offended in order to improve the firm's image (Benoit, 1997, p. 181).

The final two categories of image repair strategies include corrective action and mortification. Unlike the first three strategies, these two do not include variants. *Corrective action* transpires when a firm corrects the problem that caused the offensive act. "This action can take the form of restoring the state of affairs existing before the offensive action, and/or promising to prevent the recurrence of the offensive act" (Benoit, 1997, p. 181). The fifth and final image repair strategy is *mortification*. This occurs when a firm confesses to the offensive act, and then asks for forgiveness (Benoit, 1997).

APPLYING IMAGE RESTORATION

As aforementioned, the majority of IRT research consists of critical content analyses, which provide descriptive insight into the effectiveness of specific IRT strategies in past cases. One of the first analyses to directly apply IRT focused on the image restoration efforts of figure skater Tonya Harding. Benoit and Hanczor (1994) identified athletics as being particularly relatable to IRT because, "as sports have become an increasingly important part of the American social fabric, athletes are often called upon to defend themselves" (1994, p. 428). They focused on allegations against Harding, which linked her to an attack on rival figure skater Nancy Kerrigan. While Kerrigan practiced on January 6, 1994, a man struck her above her right knee, and shortly thereafter, reports began to implicate Harding as a conspirator in the plot to eliminate her longstanding rival from the 1994 Winter Olympics (Benoit & Hanczor, 1994).

With her image in disrepair, Harding agreed to an interview with Connie Chung on the television program *Eye-to-Eye*. Benoit and Hanczor investigated Harding's dialogue in order to identify and evaluate her image repair discourse. Based on their analysis, Benoit and Hanczor found that Harding primarily utilized bolstering, denial and attacking the accuser tactics. Bolstering was exemplified by (1) claiming that she had a difficult childhood, (2) describing the hard work she had put in to accomplish her goal of competing at the Olympics, (3) expressing sympathy for Kerrigan, (4) embracing the simple idea of having children and making a better life for them, and (5) promising to donate financially to the Special Olympics (Benoit & Hanczor, 1994).

In regards to denial, Harding repeatedly denied wrongdoing. "She reiterated the claim that she had not violated the Olympic code of conduct. Furthermore, she asserted that she had no prior knowledge of the attack" (Benoit & Hanczor, 1994, p. 423). Harding also exemplified the "attacking the accuser" strategy by attempting to portray her primary accuser, ex-husband Jeff Gillooly, in a negative light. Harding not only charged Gillooly with lying about her involvement in the conspiracy, but she also accused him of abusing her and threatening her with violence if she spoke to the authorities about what she knew regarding the attack. "If she can make the audience dislike and not trust her accusers, the accusations may be undermined" (Benoit & Hanczor, 1994, p. 424).

Upon evaluating Harding's specific IRT strategies, Benoit and Hanczor found her tactics to be appropriately chosen, but not effectively executed. In conclusion, "The discourse created an impression that was inconsistent with the picture most people probably had of Harding, and thus was relatively ineffectual" (Benoit & Hanczor, 1994, p. 429). Dozens of similar content analyses have been subsequently published. However, most do not provide statistical evidence that supports the superiority of one IRT strategy over others. Therefore, the practical, day-to-day use of IRT by public relations practitioners has received minimal scholarly attention. Benoit and Hanczor (1994) may have offered the original IRT foray into sports image repair, but this approach has been applied many times to sports (Brazeal, 2008), corporations (Blaney, Benoit, and Brazeal, 2002; Benoit and Harthcock, 1999; King, 2006), entertainment (Benoit, 1997), religion (Blaney and Benoit, 1997; Blaney, 2001; Miller, 2002; Blaney, 2009) and politics (see Blaney and Benoit, 2001 for an exhaustive treatment; also Benoit, 2006; and Liu, 2008).

One attempt at empirically testing some assertions of the previous casework is Twork and Blaney's (2012) test of whether mortification plus defined corrective action (a promise to attend anger management therapy) received a better response to accusations of untoward on-field behavior of a hypothetical athlete than a simple expression of mortification. This study revealed no significant difference between athletes who merely apologized and those who apologized and offered corrective action. Still, claims of previous research that extolled the virtue of the "mortification-corrective action couplet" (e.g., Blaney and Benoit, 2001) should be considered tentative as Twork and Blaney (2012) failed to conduct a manipulation check of the experimental conditions of apologizing only and apologizing/promising to attend anger management counseling.

As stated above, many of the twenty case studies examined in the following chapters employ the IRT approach. Perilous situations for athletes are detailed and responsive texts were carefully chosen to represent the image repair discourse of these athletes. From there, our authors offer critical analysis of the IRT strategies and discuss their effectiveness or lack thereof. We hope that these case studies will illuminate the best routes to image repair for athletes faced with reputational disaster.

REFERENCES

Benoit, W. L. (1995). *Accounts, excuses, and apologies. A theory of image restoration discourse.* Albany: State University of New York Press.

Benoit, W. L. (1997). Hugh Grant's image restoration discourse: An actor apologizes. *Communication Quarterly*, 45, 251-267.

Benoit, W. L. (1997). Image restoration discourse and crisis communication. *Public Relations Review*, 23, 177-186.

Benoit, W. L., & Hanczor, R. (1994). The Tonya Harding controversy: An analysis of image repair strategies. *Communication Quarterly*, 42, 416-433.

Benoit, W. L., & Hartchcock, A. (1999). Attacking the tobacco industry: A rhetorical analysis of advertisements by the "Campaign for Tobacco Free Kids." *Southern Communication Journal, 65*, 66-81.

Blaney, J. R. (2009). The Vatican's response to the sexual abuse crisis in America: An image restoration study (pp. 199-210). In J.R. Blaney & J.P. Zompetti (Eds.), *The rhetoric of Pope John Paul II.* Lanham, MD: Lexington Books.

Blaney, J.R., Benoit, W. L., & Brazeal, L. M. (2002). Blowout!: Firestone's image restoration campaign. *Public Relations Review, 28*, 379-392.

Blaney, J. R. (2001). Restoring the juridical image: *Apologia* for *Ex Corde Ecclesiae. Journal of Communication and Religion, 23*, 94-109.

Blaney, J. R., & Benoit, W. L. (1997). The persuasive defense of Jesus in the Gospel According to John. *The Journal of Communication and Religion, 20*, 25-30.

Brinson, S., & Benoit, W. L. (1996). Dow Corning's image repair strategies in the breast implant crisis. *Communication Quarterly*, 44 , 29-41.

Burke, K. (1968). *A rhetoric of motives.* Berkeley: University of California Press.

Goffman, E. (1963). *Stigma.* London: Penguin.

Liu, B.F. (2008). From aspiring presidential candidate to accidental racist? An analysis of Senator George Allen's image repair during his 2006 reelection campaign. *Public Relations Review*, 34, 331-336.

Miller, B. A. (2002) *Divine apology: The discourse of religious image restoration.* Westport, CT: Greenwood Publishing.

Scott, M. B., & Lyman, S. M. (1968) Accounts. *American Sociological review, 33,* 46-62.

Twork, J., & Blaney, J. R. (2012). Reputation differences between mortification-only and mortification/corrective action strategies following a transgression by a professional athlete. A paper presented at the Fifth Summit on Communication and Sport. Peoria, IL.

Ware, B., & Linkugel, W. (1973). They spoke in defense of themselves: On the generic criticism of apologia. *Quarterly Journal of Speech*, 59, 273-283.

I

Drugs

Chapter One

From the Mitchell Report to Brian McNamee: Roger Clemens's Image Repair Discourse

J. Scott Smith, University of Missouri

After various accounts and allegations about rampant steroid use among baseball players, Major League Baseball decided to hire former US senator George Mitchell to conduct an independent investigation into MLB player steroid use (Curry, 2006b). Allegedly, the investigation arose after MLB commissioner Bud Selig read an advanced copy of the book, *A Game of Shadows: Barry Bonds, BALCO and the Steroids Scandal That Rocked Professional Sports*, during the weekend of March 25, 2006 (Chass, 2006). After reading *Game of Shadows*, Selig announced that former Senate majority leader George J. Mitchell would lead an investigation into MLB steroid use prior to the current MLB drug testing policy (Curry, 2006b). The independent investigation further promoted MLB's attempt to repair its image from the damage done by baseball's "Steroids Era."

After a twenty-month investigation by Senator Mitchell, the 409 page Mitchell Report was released on December 13, 2007. During the inquiry, Mitchell lacked subpoena power resulting in only two active players (Jason Giambi and Frank Thomas) talking to Mitchell investigators. While the lack of subpoena power limited the scope and vigor of the investigation, The Mitchell Report implicated 89 players, most notably seven-time Cy Young award winner Roger Clemens (Wilson & Schmidt, 2007). Because Clemens was the most dominant pitcher of his generation, he received the most media attention.

The Mitchell Report's primary source on Clemens was his former trainer, Brian McNamee, who provided Mitchell investigators with information implicating Clemens's steroid and human growth hormone (HGH) use (Curry,

2007). McNamee and Clemens started working together in 1998, when Toronto Blue Jays general manager Tim McCleary hired McNamee to be the Blue Jays strength and conditioning coach (Kovaleski, 2007). Clemens became a Blue Jay in December 1996, after Boston Red Sox GM Dan Duquette stated Clemens was in the "twilight" of his career (Silverman, 1996). McNamee told Mitchell investigators he introduced Clemens to steroids when they started working together in 1998 (Kovaleski, 2007). Mitchell (2007) stated,

> Toward the end of the road trip [June 8-10, 1998] which included the Marlins series, or shortly after the Blue Jays returned home to Toronto, Clemens approached McNamee and, for the first time, brought up the subject of using steroids. Clemens said he was not able to inject himself, and he asked for McNamee's help. (p. 217)

The Mitchell Report's allegations clearly placed Clemens's image under attack and he needed to defend his reputation. This chapter applies Benoit's (1995) theory of image restoration discourse to Clemens's defense discourse subsequent to allegations that he used steroids and other performance-enhancing substances. This chapter will analyze two primary texts, Roger Clemens's appearance on *60 Minutes* with Mike Wallace and his testimony before Congress. First, I will examine the background to the controversy surrounding the allegations against Clemens. Second, I will critically analyze Clemens's defensive discourse. Finally, implications for image repair will be discussed.

January 6, 2008

Mike Wallace interviewed Roger Clemens on the CBS news magazine show *60 Minutes* that aired on January 6, 2008. The interview marked Clemens's first public appearance since the release of Senator Mitchell's report. Wallace asked Clemens about McNamee's allegations in the Mitchell Report suggesting that Clemens used steroids and human growth hormone. During the interview, Clemens relied on the image restoration strategies of denial, bolstering, attacking the accuser, and to a lesser degree differentiation.

Denial

Clemens emphatically and repeatedly denied ever using steroids and human growth hormone during the interview. First, he denied the allegations that Brian McNamee injected him with steroids during the 1998 season with the Toronto Blue Jays and with the New York Yankees in the 2000 and 2001 seasons. Second, Clemens denied acquiring needles to inject himself with steroids. Finally, Clemens denied knowing McNamee injected Clemens's teammate and friend Andy Pettitte with human growth hormone.

Throughout the interview Clemens denied that he ever took steroids and any other performance-enhancing drugs. Wallace relied on excerpts from the Mitchell report to question Clemens. Wallace read from the Mitchell report, "McNamee injected Clemens approximately four times in the buttocks over a several week period, with needles that Clemens provided, each incident took place in Clemens's apartment" (Wallace, 2008). Clemens responded, "It never happened. Never happened" (Wallace, 2008). This statement unequivocally denied that Clemens ever injected steroids (either personally or by McNamee) during the 1998 season with the Toronto Blue Jays.

McNamee also told Mitchell investigators he injected Clemens with performance-enhancing drugs during his 2000 season with the New York Yankees. Wallace stated, "During the latter part of the regular season, McNamee injected Clemens in the buttocks four to six times with testosterone . . . also injected Clemens four to six times with human growth hormone." Clemens responded with, "My body never changed." One of the more salient arguments during the Steroids Era is the "eye test." Essentially, does it physically look like they've added exceeding amounts of muscle in a short amount of time? Various pre- and post pictures had been used by the media to illustrate the extensive muscle growth by alleged steroid users. Clemens's body had not undergone the type of dramatic change exemplified by homerun hitters Barry Bonds, Mark McGwire, and Sammy Sosa (all presumed to be steroid users). Yet, Clemens further argued that his body never changed in a more unrealistic manner, stating,

> If he's putting that stuff in my body, if what he's saying, which is totally false, if he's doing that to me, I should have a third ear coming out of my forehead, I should be pulling tractors with my teeth.

While this exaggerated characterization of how steroids would have affected him was unrealistic, the initial "my body never changed" argument seemed plausible and if accepted by his audience, might repair Clemens's image.

Wallace probed Clemens about the personal accomplishments he achieved during the years of alleged steroid use. "In two of the three years that McNamee claims that he injected you 98 and 2001 you won twenty games and Cy Young awards as the American League's best pitcher." Clemens responded with, "I won in 1997. I won the Cy Young award 2004 when he supposedly stated, I wasn't doing it." This statement offers plausible deniability for Clemens especially considering he did not start working with McNamee until the 1998 season. Clemens further denied the allegation through his durability. Clemens stated,

> Why didn't I keep doing it if it was so good for me? Why didn't I break down? Why didn't my tendons turn to dust? That's all it's good for. It's a quick fix. I don't believe in it, I don't do it.

Clemens stressed the physical harm associated with steroid abuse, which inherently denies any steroid use because of his durability. This statement suggested that Clemens's elbow ligaments and shoulder tendons would not endure the strain of steroid use.

Possibly the most damaging statement against Roger Clemens was by his friend and former New York Yankees and Houston Astros teammate, Andy Pettitte. On December 15, 2007, Pettitte publicly admitted McNamee injected him in 2002 with human growth hormone in an effort to expedite his recovery from injury (Schmidt, 2007). Wallace stated, "When Andy confirmed that McNamee had indeed told the truth about injecting him that gave McNamee credibility, made his claims about injecting you seem more believable." Clemens retorted, "I had no knowledge of what Andy was doing. . . . Had no idea about it." Clemens completely denied having any information about Pettitte's relationship with McNamee. But Pettitte's admitted use of human growth hormone bolstered McNamee's credibility while hurting Clemens's image.

Bolstering

Clemens relied on the image restoration strategy of bolstering in two instances during the interview with Wallace. First, Clemens discussed his grueling workout regimen. Second, he alluded to his toughness and desire to place his team and teammates before himself. Mike Wallace began the interview discussing the possibility of Clemens competing at a high level in Major League Baseball in his mid-forties. "People I talk to say, 'Come on. 45 years old? How does he still throw a ball and compete and so forth? It's impossible.'" Clemens responded, "It's not impossible. You do it with hard work. Ask any of my teammates. Ask anybody that's come here and done the work with me." In another Mitchell Report account, McNamee stated Clemens trained harder after starting a steroid program in 1998. Clemens denied the steroids program and stated, "Never, I've trained hard my entire career." These statements attempted to reduce the offensiveness of steroid allegations by focusing on Clemens's strong work ethic. These statements, if accepted by his audience, might explain his longevity and success rather than steroids.

Clemens denied steroid and human growth hormone use, but he admitted to using various painkillers allowing him to grit through games. He recounted a meeting with Joe Torre in a trainer's room before a World Series game where Torre noticed Clemens was injured and intended to scratch Clemens from his start. Clemens recalled,

> And I told Joe Torre that I'll be damned if 15 minutes before I'm gonna start a
> World Series game I'm gonna go out there and look my teammates in the eye
> and tell 'em I can't go. As long as the other team doesn't know that I'm
> hurting, I can get people out throwin' 85 without using my leg. And get you

six innings under my belt.' I'm gonna take this Toradol shot and hope it works. And mask some of this pain so I can get out there and do my job. That's the things I put my body through. And I'm not ashamed of that because I get paid a lotta money to go out and perform. And I appreciate that they put that kind of trust in me.

These comments portray Clemens as a selfless athlete, trying to do whatever he could to help his team. If accepted by the audience, Clemens's image would be enhanced through his toughness, an important trait for an athlete.

Attack Accuser

Clemens attacked McNamee's credibility by questioning his loyalty. Wallace asked, "Why would Brian McNamee want to betray you?" Clemens responded, "You know I don't know. I'm so upset about it. How I treated this man and took care of him." Later in the interview, Wallace suggested McNamee was probably watching *60 Minutes* and asked Clemens if he had anything to say to McNamee. "Yeah, I treated him fairly, I treated him great as anybody else, I helped him out." These statements displayed Clemens's surprise and dismay over McNamee's allegations. If Clemens's audience accepted his depiction of McNamee as disloyal, the damage to Clemens's image might be reduced.

Differentiation

Clemens differentiated his situation from Pettitte's in an effort for his audience to accept his denials. Clemens stated, "Andy's case is totally separate. I was shocked to learn about Andy's situation." Clemens further differentiated from Pettitte with the type of injections he received from McNamee. "Lidocaine and B-12. It's for my joints, and B-12 I still take today." Furthermore, Clemens describes the amount of shots for pain as commonplace. Clemens explained, "The number of shots that you get over the course of a season, which was many for me. Whether they be vitamins or for pain, Toradol. Pain shots. To go out and perform." These comments are clearly to reduce the offensiveness of the shots McNamee allegedly injected Clemens with. But more importantly, Clemens wanted to differentiate his situation from Pettitte's by describing it as less offensive because he was taking legal shots.

Clemens answered Wallace's questions with a clear and straightforward strategy: explicitly deny any steroid use, try to discredit Brian McNamee, bolster his image, and differentiate his situation from Pettitte's. While the *60 Minutes* interview allowed Clemens to promote his case without repercussions, Congress called Clemens (along with McNamee, Pettitte, and Chuck Knoblauch) to testify under oath (Wilson, 2008a). The substance of Congress's questions to Clemens would be similar to Wallace's, but Clemens would face perjury charges if he lied to Congress (Wilson, 2008b). Clemens's appearance before Congress forced him to continue to defend and repair his image, which was still under attack.

Second Phase: Congressional Hearings

Before examining Clemens's congressional testimony, a couple of events leading up to the hearings should be mentioned. The day after the *60 Minutes* interview aired, Clemens revealed a seventeen minute taped phone conversation between him and McNamee during a public press conference (Antonen, 2008). The decision to play the tape seemed puzzling as no new information emerged out of the conversation. What the tape did provide was a dishonest image of Clemens. Early in the conversation McNamee said, "I'm on a cell phone. And I understand that I don't expect—I can't open up to you the way I want to, and I know you can't. And you know how I feel about you." Clemens said, "I don't know who's on our lines or whatever." To which McNamee replied, "I got nobody on my line. I don't know." But Clemens was taping the private conversation, without McNamee's consent, and then played the tape to the general public. McNamee felt betrayed by Clemens, especially because information about his ill son was released. As a result, on January 10, 2008, McNamee turned over syringes, gauze, and vials allegedly containing performance-enhancing drugs to federal authorities. He said these items would produce a positive DNA match with Roger Clemens. More damaging than the possible incriminating evidence given to federal authorities was Clemens's dishonest approach to clearing his name (Schmidt & Wilson, 2008). In the battle for credibility between Clemens and McNamee, the only way secretly taping McNamee would be advisable is if McNamee admitted to lying. McNamee did not confess, which led to a dishonest image of Clemens.

Along with the taped phone conversation, Andy Pettitte gave a sworn deposition on February 4, 2008, corroborating McNamee's claims that he injected Pettitte with human growth hormone. This was significant because Pettitte was under oath and would face federal prosecution if he lied. Pettitte was viewed as the most truthful person involved in the Clemens-McNamee situation (Hohler, 2008). On page 31 of Pettitte's deposition, Michael Gordon, the Majority Senior Investigative Council for the Committee on Oversight and Government Reform, asked Pettitte if he ever discussed Clemens's steroid use with McNamee. Pettitte responded,

> Yes. . . . Well, we were—we were at my—we were at my house. You know we were in—and I have a gym. We were training in my gym. And I can just remember, you know, Mac telling me that Roger, you know, that he had gotten steroids for Roger. (Pettitte deposition, 2008)

Along with steroids, Pettitte recalled a conversation where Clemens admitted using human growth hormone. Pettitte stated, "I remember a conversation in 1999 where Roger had told me that he had taken HGH." Pettitte's sworn deposition damaged Clemens's image and credibility leading up to the February 13, 2008 congressional hearing.

February 13, 2008: The Congressional Hearing

The congressional hearing provided a different atmosphere than the interview with Mike Wallace, with US congresspersons questioning in a much more aggressive nature. Additionally, Clemens was under oath, pacing perjury charges if his responses were found to be untruthful. Representative John Tierney (D-MA) attacked Clemens's credibility by stating Clemens made claims in earlier testimony that were later found to be untruthful. Tierney stated,

> But we know that some of the things you told us with great earnestness appear to not be accurate. And this raises questions about your own credibility. . . . Mr. Clemens, you told the committee that you had had no conversations with Mr. McNamee about HGH. You did that three times in the early part of your deposition. But your own statements now showed that you had two specific and memorable conversations with him about HGH.

Representative Tierney's comments characterized the tone of many of the other Democrat congresspersons questioning Clemens. Furthermore, members of Congress believed Andy Pettitte gave a candid and truthful deposition. Representative Elijah Cummings (D-MD) stated that he believed Andy Pettitte to be truthful and asked Clemens if he agreed with this assessment. Clemens stated, "I would agree with that, yes, sir." While the initial reports from the Mitchell Report focused on Brian McNamee's statements and credibility issues, Pettitte's credibility was perceived to be much higher, which strengthened the attack on Clemens's image. During the congressional hearing, Clemens relied on the image restoration strategies of denial, bolstering, good intentions, shifting the blame, and defeasibility.

Denial

Clemens denied using performance enhancing drugs throughout the hearing. Representative Cummings asked Clemens, "In his deposition, Mr. Pettitte told the committee that he had a conversation with you in 1999 or 2000 in which you admitted that you used human growth hormones. Is this true?" Clemens responded, "It is not."

Along with denying human growth hormone use, Clemens denied ever telling Pettitte he used human growth hormone. Representative Cummings asked, "So you did not tell Mr. Pettitte at this time that you used human growth hormones?" Clemens retorted, "I did not." Even though Clemens agreed that Pettitte was a truthful person, Clemens argued Pettitte incorrectly recalled the conversation about human growth hormone. Clemens furthered, "I believe Andy has misheard, Mr. Congressman, on his comments about myself using HGH, which never happened." Furthermore, Clemens offered his own account of the conversation between him and Pettitte:

> The conversation that I can recall, that I had with Andy Pettitte, was at my house in Houston, while we were working out. And I had expressed to him about a TV show something that I have heard about three older men that were using HGH and getting back their quality of life from that.

This statement provided a different version of the conversation Pettitte recalled. Additionally, Clemens offered the closeness of his friendship as a means to enhance his denial:

> My problem with what Andy says, and why I think he misremembers, is that if Andy Pettitte knew that I had used HGH, or I had told Andy Pettitte that I had used HGH, before he would use the HGH, what have you, he would have come to me and asked me about it. That is how close our relationship was. And then when he did use it, I am sure he would have told me that he used it.

The close relationship Clemens and Pettitte had is well documented, especially with Clemens coming out of retirement to join Pettitte in Houston with the Astros. Also, Clemens recalled conversations about other supplements he and Pettitte had used:

> And I say that for the fact that we also used a product called Hydroxycut and ThermaCore. Andy and I talked openly about this product. And so there is no question in my mind that we would have talked, if he knew that I had tried or done HGH, which I did not, he would have come to me to ask me those questions.

During Representative Tierney's (D-MA) questioning, Clemens denied having any detailed conversations with McNamee about HGH. Clemens stated, "Mr. Congressman, again, I never had any detailed discussions with Brian McNamee about HGH."

But Mr. Clemens, come on, the questions early in the morning hadn't been prior to your wife. The questions were had you ever. You can see where that leaves us with some credibility issues here. You have three times said never and then only when somebody really presses you on a specific instance you have a recollection of two memorable conversations.

Clemens stated, "Again, prior to Mr. Congressman, we had no detailed discussion about HGH." Tierney fired back, "Prior to what?" Clemens stated, "During my testimony with the committee." Tierney continued to attack Clemens's credibility as he asked about his knowledge about HGH. Before going into the line of questioning, Tierney read an excerpt from Clemens's deposition. "'Did you do any research on your own about human growth hormone?' And you answered, 'No, I haven't. I've never researched it. I couldn't tell you the first thing about it.'"

Representative Stephen Lynch (D-MA) questioned Clemens about a mass on his right buttock that McNamee attributed to injecting the steroid Windstrol too quickly into Clemens. Clemens denied that charge, stating it could be from a muscle strain, a strained glute. Lynch obtained the MRI of the mass on Clemens's buttock and sent a copy to Dr. Mark Murphy, the chief of musculoskeletal radiology at the Armed Forces Institute of Pathology, for analysis. Lynch stated, "It says it was likely related to the patient's prior attempted intramuscular injections. He [Dr. Murphy] said that the MRI showed that the muscles of the buttocks showed no strain or trauma. So he concluded that the injury was not a strained muscle." Additionally, Lynch quoted Dr. Murphy, "'It is my opinion that the history and the MRI imaging descriptions are more compatible with a Windstrol injection, as the inflammatory component is prominent by report.'"

Representative William Clay (D-MO) asked Clemens about the authenticity of his career. "Can I look at my two children with a straight face and tell them that you, Roger Clemens, have always played the game with honesty and integrity?" Clemens responded, "Yes, sir. . . . Without a question. I took no shortcuts."

Representative Virginia Foxx (R-NC) discussed photos of Clemens from 1997 through the years he was accused of steroid use. After suggesting Clemens's body shape did not change, Representative Foxx asked Clemens about his rigorous workouts. Clemens stated,

Thank you, Congresswoman, yes. When all these false allegations came out about me, I told them to go talk to the trainers and the people around me that know me the best. My body didn't change. I didn't start throwing harder. The fact of the matter is, I started locating better as a pitcher.

Furthermore, Clemens discussed his past success as a means to deny McNamee's allegations.

And in that 1996 season when I was in the twilight of my career, I tied my own single season record of 20 strikeouts, I led the league in strikeouts that year. I was in the top 10 in innings pitched and ERA. And if I was in the twilight of my career, I doubt that the Toronto Blue Jays' ownership would have made me the highest paid pitcher in the game of baseball the following year. That following year, 1997, I won the Triple Crown award of baseball, which is pitch wins, ERA, and strikeouts.

Bolstering

Clemens bolstered his reputation through discussing his tough upbringing and diligent work ethic. He stated, "And I take a little offense to that for the fact that my father passed away when I was 9 years old. My mother—I was raised by great, strong women, my mother and my grandmother. They gave me my will and my determination." Clemens continued,

> I have had a great work ethic since I was in high school. I didn't have a car in high school. I ran home, which my condominium or town home was about 2 miles from my house. Somebody's tried to break my spirit in this room. They are not going to break my spirit. I am going to continue to go out and do the things that I love to do and try and be honest and genuine to every person I can be. It is the way I was brought up. It is what I know. But you can tell your boys that I did it the right way, and I worked my butt off to do it.

Clemens also bolstered himself as a patriotic American. He stated,

> When the Commissioner asked me to get myself together to go out there, and the league asked me to put USA on my chest and represent my team, my country, I did everything I could do to get ready. They pushed my date up to try get me ready sooner. I told them, I could shake hands and wave flags and sell tickets for you if you want me to do that, but if you want me on the field it is going to take longer to get this body going. And I did, and I went out there and I did the best I very—I could probably do. And I was proud to have the USA on my chest.

Good Intentions

Another aspect of the hearing involved Clemens's former nanny (the nanny's name was kept confidential). McNamee claimed the nanny was at José Canseco's party and that she could verify Clemens was at the party. When Clemens was informed by the committee they wanted to interview the nanny, Clemens met with the nanny even though he was instructed not to by the committee. Committee Chairman Representative Henry Waxman (D-CA) questioned Clemens's judgment insofar as meeting with the nanny after being told not to. Representative Waxman summed up his attack on Clemens by stating,

One option for you was to have given the committee the nanny's contact information and had no contact with her. Another option could have been to give her a heads-up that the committee would be calling her. But you chose, I think, the worst approach. That is my opinion.

Clemens responded, "Mr. Chairman, I believe that just like through this whole hearing, I was doing y'all a favor by finding a nanny that was— supposedly came in question, so." Here Clemens highlighted his previous and current cooperation with the committee through providing information and finding his former nanny. Clemens displayed his good intentions to find his former nanny. After Representative Waxman continued to press Clemens about why he felt he should talk to the nanny before the committee, Clemens stated, "Mr. Chairman, I hadn't talked to her in years. And I did everything I could to locate her to—if you guys had any questions for her. And I did tell her to answer truthfully." Clemens concluded with,

> Mr. Chairman, I was doing y'all a favor; and as far as I was concerned, I haven't seen this lady in a long time. She is a sweet lady, and I wanted her to get her to you as quick as possible, if you had any questions for her.

Again Clemens argues he was trying to find his former nanny so she would get in touch with the congressional committee. These utterances served to place Clemens in a more favorable light, suggesting that he had no intention of coaching the nanny, but rather reassuring the nanny that she should tell the truth.

Shift the Blame

Clemens shifted the blame when he was questioned about the mass in his buttocks. Clemens stated, "I got a B-12 shot and it obviously gave me some discomfort. I hate to get on Dr. Taylor who gave the shot, but if he gave me a bad shot, he gave me a bad shot. I don't know how to explain that." This statement served to shift the blame from Clemens's possible steroid use to a poor injection.

Defeasibility

Clemens relied on defeasibility as a strategy in defense of an alleged 2005 conversation between him and Pettitte. The conversation was the second Pettitte recalled having with Clemens about human growth hormone. Pettitte recalled asking Clemens what he would say if someone asked him about his human growth hormone use and Clemens told Pettitte that he never used human growth hormone, but his wife Debbie had. Congressman Cummings asked Clemens if he remembered this conversation and Clemens responded,

"I don't believe I had a conversation in 2005 with him in Kissimmee, Florida. We would have been with the Houston Astros at the time. But I don't remember that conversation whatsoever."

EVALUATION

Both phases of Clemens's image repair discourse will be evaluated with internal and external data. First, Clemens's discourse will be examined for internal consistency and plausibility. Second, commentary from the *New York Times* and ESPN's television program *Pardon the Interruption* will provide the media's opinion. Finally, relevant public opinion polls will be examined.

First Phase

Clemens's defense strategies on *60 Minutes* were partially successful. While primarily relying on denial, Clemens rightly pointed out his body type never changed. Other players accused of steroid use like Mark McGwire, Barry Bonds, and Sammy Sosa gained significant muscle mass later in their careers, unlike Clemens. But Clemens's argument that steroids are a detriment to a baseball player is contrary to admitted steroid users' accounts. The late Ken Caminiti stated in a June 3, 2002, *Sports Illustrated* article that steroids helped his performance that led to his 1996 unanimous MVP award (Verducci, Yaeger, Dohrmann, Llosa, & Munson, 2002). During the 1998 season, Mark McGwire used Androstenedione (Andro), once a legal performance-enhancing drug (now banned) that has steroid-like qualities, when he broke Roger Maris's single-season homerun record. Even more than these known uses of performance-enhancing drugs are the media and public perceptions that a majority of MLB players used steroids during what is now known as the "Steroids Era." Every new record accomplished during the Steroids Era faces major public scrutiny. For Clemens to assert that steroids possess a negative effect toward one's career is contrary to player performance and media opinions.

Clemens appropriately denied knowing Andy Pettitte was injected by McNamee. Additionally, Clemens properly differentiated his relationship with McNamee from Pettitte's as Clemens stated McNamee injected him with B-12 and Lidocaine, not steroids or HGH. However, Pettitte's admission of HGH use was particularly damaging because Pettitte is perceived as highly credible. Pettitte was one of Clemens's best friends and he admitted to his performance-enhancing drug use only two days after the Mitchell Report was released. The more Clemens and McNamee attacked each other, the more Pettitte's credibility grew.

Clemens's attempts at bolstering through his diligent training were partially effective as they coincided with his explanation that his body never changed. This provided a plausible explanation for Clemens' longevity and effectiveness into his mid-forties. Clemens's other attempts at bolstering were not as effective as they were not nearly as relevant. Being a tough competitor and placing his team before individual achievements are valued traits for an athlete, but the public already knew Clemens for his toughness and his initial trade to the New York Yankees occurred due to Clemens's desire to win a World Series.

The attacks on McNamee were also partially effective. Clemens's portrayal of McNamee being a poor friend and taking advantage of him could garner some sympathy for Clemens. One might understand that McNamee had to tell investigators what he knew because he faced prosecution if he lied, but Clemens told Wallace that McNamee did not warn him about the Mitchell Report allegations even though McNamee saw Clemens just days before the report was released. His excellent work ethic provided a plausible explanation for his success into his 40s. This coupled with the earlier playing of a taped phone conversation between he and McNamee, Clemens's attack on McNamee would garner some sympathy from his audience. But Clemens did not adequately counter Andy Pettitte's admission of HGH use. Pettitte's account bolstered McNamee's credibility leaving Clemens's audience with doubt about whom to believe.

Media's Opinion

Pardon the Interruption (*PTI*) hosts Michael Wilbon and Tony Kornheiser began their January 7, 2008, episode discussing Mike Wallace's interview of Roger Clemens (Rydholm, 2008a). Kornheiser asked, "Wilbon, are you starting to believe Clemens?" Wilbon responded,

> Tony, I still don't know what to believe, this tape is sort of fascinating. Look, this whole thing is he said, he said. There's no evidence or real concrete tangible evidence any of us are going to become privy to. So we're being asked to believe by McNamee first through George Mitchell and then by Roger Clemens, "believe me," "no believe me." Now this tape, this audio tape does some damage as far as I'm concerned where McNamee's voice, the person identified by the Clemens group as McNamee, he loses some credibility when he says, "I'm with you, I can't open up to you the way I want to, I thought I had no other choice." These sentences seem to me damage McNamee's credibility which would mean yes, I'm starting to believe Roger Clemens at least a little bit.

Kornheiser agreed with Wilbon that Clemens's situation was based on whether you believe Clemens or McNamee. However, Kornheiser referenced Andy Pettitte's admitted HGH use as damaging Clemens's credibility. Kornheiser stated, "I want to believe Roger Clemens, I was troubled and am troubled by the fact that McNamee was the same trainer for Andy Pettitte. And what he said about Andy Pettitte, Andy Pettitte confirmed." Kornheiser ended his comments about Clemens's situation by agreeing with Clemens's assertion that his reputation is damaged without sufficient evidence:

> What Clemens said last night on *60 Minutes* about not getting the benefit of the doubt anymore in America that's what happens to athletes with everything athletes have done, they are guilty until proven innocent and it's hard to repair your reputation.

The statements from Kornheiser and Wilbon displayed their inability to fully believe Clemens did not use steroids.

New York Times columnist George Vecsey held a stronger opinion than Wilbon and Kornheiser. He compared Clemens's discourse with that of President Richard Nixon's Checkers speech and President Bill Clinton's denial of an inappropriate relationship with White House intern Monica Lewinsky. Vecsey stated,

> Roger Clemens did not muster up a gift cocker spaniel named Checkers, the way Richard M. Nixon did in 1952, and he did not wag his finger at the nation the way President Bill Clinton did in 1998. All he could do was muscle up a fading fastball of what appeared to be false outrage Sunday night for *60 Minutes*. (Vecsey, 2008, p. D5)

Vecsey's contention was that Clemens's aggression was an indication of his guilt. Yet, at the end of this phase, there still appeared to be doubt about whether one should believe Clemens or McNamee.

Second Phase

Clemens's image repair efforts during the congressional hearing were not effective. Even though representatives Davis (R-VA), John Tierney (D-MA), Dan Burton (R-IN), Darrell Issa (D-CA), and Christopher Shays (R-CT) attacked and severely damaged McNamee's credibility and reputation, the nature of the attacks on Clemens changed. From the release of the Mitchell Report on December 13, 2007, until the Mike Wallace interview on January 6, 2008, Clemens was primarily attacked by the information McNamee provided Mitchell investigators. The congressional hearings provided Andy Pettitte's and Chuck Knoblauch's depositions that bolstered McNamee's credibility while attacking Clemens's. Pettitte's deposition damaged Clemens severely because unlike McNamee, the representatives praised Pettitte's courage and forthright responses. Clemens could not afford to attack Pettitte at this point because he affirmed his strong friendship since December 15, 2007, when Pettitte admitted his HGH use. Clemens's explanation that Pettitte "misremembered" the conversations they had about HGH was insufficient to repair the damage from Pettitte's deposition.

Additionally, Representative John Tierney's (D-MA) line of questioning pointed out the inconsistencies in Clemens's defense. After Clemens stated he had no conversations with McNamee about HGH and then later recalled a heated conversation about his wife's HGH use with McNamee, Clemens did not produce a viable explanation for how he could deny such conversations with McNamee and then describe a very vivid one later on. Tierney's line of questioning damaged Clemens's credibility and reputation

Finally, the questioning surrounding his former nanny was quite damaging. For whatever reason, Clemens thought it was necessary to meet with his former nanny before allowing Congress to interview her. Even if Clemens did not "coach" his former nanny into telling investigators Clemens was not at Canseco's June 8-10 party, Chairman Henry Waxman (D-CA) remarked, "The impression it leaves is terrible." And it was. Clemens should have allowed his lawyer Rusty Hardin or his investigators to meet with the nanny rather than Clemens himself. Clemens is a pitcher, not an attorney nor an investigator, so interviewing the nanny was unnecessary.

Media's Opinion

PTI hosts Michael Wilbon and Tony Kornheiser discussed the implications of the congressional hearings (Rydholm, 2008b). Kornheiser asked Wilbon at the start of the episode, "I have a very simple question, who do you believe?" Wilbon answered, "Tony, it's hard, they both have probably lied multiple times, in various capacities during the investigation and maybe even, somebody had to be lying of course in the room." Wilbon clearly did not believe Clemens or McNamee possessed a high level of credibility. Wilbon further stated,

> My opinion is I don't believe Roger Clemens anymore. I sat here yesterday and said "we may not know what to believe or who to believe" it's just that Clemens seemed to be caught in so many lies, the whole thing with the nanny and whether he was at Canseco's place it just seemed to me that was a Perry Mason moment where they trot out somebody you go "whoa" and on Perry Mason the person would have broke down on the stand crying and admitted to everything that wasn't going to happen there. I find it impossible now to believe Roger Clemens.

Kornheiser disagreed to a certain extent that Clemens supporters would probably still support him, but people on the fence would not be swayed. He stated,

> I think it is possible to still believe him and have that allegiance, just on the basis that McNamee was crushed, he was crushed and shown to be a liar time and time and time and time again. But Clemens got wounded, and he got wounded severely in this. And if you just draw a little circle to see what happened Knobloch admits I took this stuff from McNamee, Pettitte admits I took this stuff from McNamee. Now we find out Roger Clemens's wife concedes there's HGH there. And he tries to deny he ever talked about it ever knew about it, we find a lot of inconsistencies so I agree with you that you find it harder and harder to believe Roger Clemens.

The most interesting aspect of the congressional hearing is that Clemens wanted to appear before Congress. If Clemens had let the *60 Minutes* interview stand as his primary image repair discourse, his reputation would not have taken such a downturn. Clemens's reputation received major damage from the tape recording of McNamee, his interaction with his former nanny, and Pettitte's testimony.

Polling Data

A February 27, 2008, a *USA Today*/Gallup poll revealed most Americans thought Roger Clemens lied during the congressional hearings. Fifty-seven percent of respondents polled believed Clemens lied, while 31 percent believed he told the truth. Also, 45 percent of respondents had a favorable opinion of Clemens, with 37 percent having a negative opinion of him. However, 62 percent of people polled believed Clemens should be elected to the Hall of Fame (HOF), and only 29 percent said Clemens should not be elected. Fifty-one percent of fans who thought Clemens lied during the congressional hearings believed Clemens should be elected to the HOF, while 44 percent stated he should not be elected.

IMPLICATIONS

The major implication from this analysis is that a denial strategy is best used succinctly. Roger Clemens seemingly could not wait to tell, defiantly, any and everyone that he did not use steroids. However, the more he talked and tried to clear his name, the less believable he became. Clemens's major error was discussing his alleged steroid use after the *60 Minutes* interview. Brian McNamee's credibility was under a great deal of scrutiny and it appeared that he was not believable. Appearing before Congress was unwise because

Clemens could not clear his name by testifying. Before the congressional hearing the feeling was "we don't know who to believe." After the congressional hearings the feeling changed to "we don't believe either of them." Future research should examine other instances when a rhetor utilizes a denial strategy excessively.

CONCLUSION

Roger Clemens started his defense discourse with a prepared statement detailing the catch-22 scenario of an athlete accused of using performance-enhancing drugs:

> If I keep my emotions in check, then I am accused of not caring. When I kept quiet at the advice of my attorney until he could find out why in the world I was being accused of these things, I was accused of having something to hide, so I am guilty. When I did speak out, I was accused of protesting too much, so I am guilty.

Here Clemens aptly describes the situation of accused steroid users. There is a balancing act that one has to perform for the public to believe they did not use steroids. So far, no baseball player accused of steroid use has repaired his image. Clemens's prolonged denial strategy demonstrated that suggesting something more intensely and over a longer period of time does not make image repair efforts more effective. Much like in everyday conversation, the louder and longer someone talks, the less people hear.

REFERENCES

Antonen, M. (2008a, January 8). Trainer remorseful but doesn't recant statements on tape. *USA Today*, p. 11C.

Antonen, M. (2008b, February 27). Poll: Majority of fans think Clemens is lying. *USA Today*, p. 1C.

Araton, H. (2008, February 14). Politicians turn steroid hearing into a partisan squabble. *The New York Times*, p. D1.

Benoit, W. L. (1995). *Accounts, excuses, and apologies: A theory of image restoration strategies*. Albany: State University of New York Press.

Benoit, W. L. (1997). Hugh Grant's image restoration discourse: An actor apologizes. *Communication Quarterly*, *45*, 251-267.

Chass, M. (2006, March 29). Selig is poised to begin steroids inquiry. *The New York Times*, p. D1.

Curry, J. (2006a, March 8). Jealousy led Bonds to steroids, authors say. *The New York Times*, p. D1.

Curry, J. (2006b, March 31). Steroid investigation begins, but not without some concerns. *The New York Times*, p. D1.

Curry, J. (2007, December 14). Former trainer puts Yankees stars under microscope. *The New York Times*, D1.

Hohler, B. (2008, February 14). Clemens hit hard on the hill: Pitcher leaves self vulnerable as he denies steroid use to skeptical lawmakers. *The Boston Globe*, p. A1.

Kovaleski, S. F. (2007, December 15). A baseball lover from Queens, key to tarnishing a Yankee era. *The New York Times*, p. A1.

Mitchell, G. J. (2007, December 13). Report to the commissioner of baseball of an independent investigation into the illegal use of steroids and other performance enhancing substances by players in Major League Baseball. *DLA Piper US LLP*.

Nelson, J. (1984). The defense of Billie Jean King. *Western Journal of Speech Communication*, *48*, 92-102.

Rydholm, E. (Producer). (2008a, January 7). *Pardon the Interruption* [Television broadcast]. Washington, DC: Entertainment Sports Programming Network.

Rydholm, E. (Producer). (2008b, February 14). *Pardon the Interruption* [Television broadcast]. Washington, DC: Entertainment Sports Programming Network.

Sandomir, R. (2008, February 14). Quite a show, but with one crucial no-show. *The New York Times*, p. D3.

Schmidt, M. S. (2007, December 16). Pettitte confirms Mitchell report and says he used H.G.H. *The New York Times*, p. S1.

Say it ain't so, Roger, and Barry, and . . . (2007, December 14). *The New York Times*, p. A40.

Selig announces probe of BALCO allegations. (2006, March 30). Retrieved on May 3, 2009, from   http://mlb.mlb.com/news/press_releases/press_release.jsp?ymd=20060330&content_id=1 374459&vkey=pr_mlb&fext=.jsp&c_id=mlb.

Silverman, M. (1996, December 14). Baseball end of an era: No return fire from Sox brass tried to keep ace. *Boston Herald*, p. 40.

Vecsey, G. (2008, January 7). An unconvincing portrait of an angry victim. *The New York Times*, p. D5.

Verducci, T., Yaeger, D., Dohrmann, G., Llosa, L. F., & Munson, L. (2002, June 3). *Sports Illustrated*, *96*, 34-45.

Wallace, M. (2008, January 6). *60 Minutes* [Television broadcast].

Wise, M. (2008, February 14). Untruth be told. *The Washington Post*, p. E1.

Wilson, D. (2008a, January 5). Congress calls on Clemens and 4 others to testify. *The New York Times*, p. D1.

Wilson, D. (2008b, January 19). Clemens sets date to meet with committee. *The New York Times*, p. D1.

Wilson, D., & Schmidt, M. S. (2007, December 14). Report ties star players to baseball's "steroids era." *The New York Times*, A1.

Chapter Two

"Big Mac" with a Side of Steroids: The Image Repair Strategies of Mark McGwire

John McGuire and Lori Melton McKinnon,
Oklahoma State University, and
Wayne Wanta, University of Florida

Mark McGwire, nicknamed "Big Mac," ranks as one of the premier power hitters in Major League Baseball (MLB) history with 583 home runs. McGwire, who was a twelve-time All-Star, earned Rookie of the Year (1987) and Gold Glove (1990) honors during his career. But McGwire's most memorable baseball achievement came in 1998, when he shattered Roger Maris's single-season home run record. McGwire's 70 homers that season eclipsed Maris's mark of 61 set back in 1961. McGwire's hitting prowess helped him earn a place on *The Sporting News* "100 Greatest Baseball Players" list as well as Major League Baseball's All-Century Team named in 1999 (Baseball-reference.com, 2010).

Yet, despite his icon status, McGwire failed to win election into baseball's Hall of Fame in the 2000s. In fact, McGwire's vote totals have ranked well below the 75 percent threshold necessary to be admitted, receiving less than 25 percent of the votes needed in each of the first four years he was eligible for selection ("McGwire Apologizes," 2010). The reason? The once celebrated star was suspected of being among a group of players who used steroids to enhance on-field performance. In January 2010, McGwire finally admitted what many had suspected: He had indeed used steroids and human growth hormones during his major league career.

From a strategic communication perspective, it is important to look beyond short-term damage and to consider his long-term reputation. Thus, the question becomes, "How can McGwire's public reputation survive questions of steroid use surrounding his baseball accomplishments?" Image restoration is the attempt to compensate for or to undo damage to an image. This chapter examines two of McGwire's public statements about steroids using Benoit's image restoration theory (1995) as an analytical framework.

Hitting It Out of the Park: On and Off the Field

The Oakland Athletics drafted Mark McGwire in the first round of the 1986 baseball draft. In his first major league season, he set a rookie record by hitting 49 homers (Baseball-reference.com, 2010). During McGwire's time with the Athletics, he and teammate Jose Canseco, known as the "Bash Brothers," led the team to two American League titles and a World Series sweep in the 1989 "Earthquake Series."

Over the next few years, McGwire's batting average declined all the way to .201 in 1991 (Baseball-reference.com, 2010). In a *Sports Illustrated* interview, McGwire stated 1991 was the worst year of his life due to injuries and marital problems (Wulf, 1992). McGwire struggled through more injuries in 1993 and 1994 before returning to All-Star form in 1995 and 1996. The Athletics eventually traded McGwire at mid-season of 1997 to the St. Louis Cardinals. Between those two stops, McGwire smashed 58 home runs that year, which was a career high (Baseball-reference.com, 2010)

During the 1998 season, McGwire and Sammy Sosa of the Chicago Cubs raced to be crowned as reigning home run king, each with a shot of breaking Roger Maris's long-standing home run record. McGwire was the first to eclipse Maris, ironically hitting his record breaking sixty-second homer against Sosa and the Cubs. The historic home run chase ended with 70 homers for McGwire and 66 home runs for Sosa ("McGwire Apologizes," 2010). This ballpark battle in the summer of 1998 is considered by many to be one of the major factors in revitalizing baseball after the 1994 strike and cancellation of the World Series that year (McCarver, 1999). According to Spain (1999), as the level of fan and media interest grew, even post-game press conferences became major events. In fact, fans flocked to stadiums as attendance jumped from just over sixty-two million fans to more than seventy million fans (Sarte, 2010). MLB's marketing team worked with sponsors such as MasterCard International and McDonald's Corp. to extend interest and build goodwill for the game (Spain, 1999). Using existing footage, McGwire and Sosa appeared in a MasterCard International "Priceless" TV commercial (Friedman, 1999). McDonald's also announced national sponsorship deals with both McGwire and Sosa during the race. In the company's ads, the two sports legends endorsed the Big Mac sandwich (PRNewswire,

1998). Friedman (1999) noted that McGwire chose to take a more low-profile status with regard to marketing than Sosa. While Sosa sponsorships are estimated to have earned about $9 to $10 million in endorsements, McGwire endorsements generated only about $3 million above his $9 million annual salary from the Cardinals organization. McGwire opted for charity-type promotions and those with limited involvement on his part.

In the 1999 season, McGwire hit 65 home runs and led the league with 147 runs batted in on just 145 hits. Injuries over the two years, however, again derailed McGwire's seasons, as he saw his home runs totals decline (32 in 2000 and only 29 in 2001). McGwire finally retired after the 2001 season.

McGwire and Steroids

Even during the 1998 home run chase, McGwire started becoming mired in speculation that he and other major league players were using performance-enhancing substances to gain an advantage on the playing field. McGwire had admitted to an Associated Press reporter that he used "androstenedione, a steroid precursor that was legally available and didn't become a controlled substance until 2004" (Associated Press, 2010). Although MLB did not ban steroid use until a year after his retirement, McGwire's achievements were now being tainted by the steroids controversy in baseball.

In 2005, Jose Canseco released his book, *Juiced: Wild Times, Rampant 'Roids, Smash Hits, and How Baseball Got Big.* In this book, Canseco praised performance-enhancement drug use and its role in baseball. He wrote, "They wanted steroids in the game to make it more exciting, hoping they would be able to build its popularity back after the disastrous cancellation of the 1994 World Series. . . . Directly or indirectly, nearly everyone in baseball was complicit" (p. 4). Canseco chose to disclose names of alleged steroid users, including McGwire and Sosa ("McGwire Apologizes," 2010).

Canseco's allegations focused media attention on performance-enhancing drug use in the major leagues and led to a March 2005 U.S. House committee hearing on the subject. Although McGwire originally sought immunity from criminal prosecution as a condition to testify, he eventually agreed to appear without immunity. Instead of expressly referring to his Fifth Amendment privilege, McGwire followed his attorney's advice to neither confirm nor deny that he used steroids. McGwire repeatedly said that he "was not here to talk about the past." Unfortunately, as one writer observed, the congressional committee, the press, and millions of Americans watching the hearings live were interested in "the past" (McCann, 2010).

Image Management: Back in the Game?

Although McGwire didn't speak out in the court of law, he had been tried and convicted in the court of public opinion. For the most part, McGwire faded into the background. However, he remained quietly involved in baseball, privately training pro players and offering hitting lessons during the off-season.

On October 26, 2009, St. Louis Cardinals manager Tony LaRussa confirmed that McGwire would replace Hal McRae as the team's hitting coach. Although LaRussa knew that hiring McGwire would create a public relations stir, he felt confident in McGwire's abilities as a hitting coach (Gammons, 2010). LaRussa, McGwire's former manager in Oakland and St. Louis, had always been a strong supporter of McGwire. In an interview with Madden (2010), LaRussa admitted, "I'm aware of the fact that some people have said we can't win because this is going to be a distraction, and I take responsibility for that." With the prospect of being back in uniform with the steroids controversy looming over him, McGwire decided to go public about his steroid use. Part of McGwire's efforts included hiring Ari Fleischer Sports Communications (Fleischer was a former White House press secretary for George W. Bush) ("From Bush," 2010). According to Fleischer's website, his agency works with athletes to "identify and help fix problems" and to "sharpen messages and improve images" (fleischersports.com, 2010). McGwire then did a series of interviews in January 2010, including a chat with Major League Baseball Network's Bob Costas. Admitting that his steroid use was a mistake, he apologized to his family, friends, and fans. Although these interviews were meant to put the issue to rest, reporters continued questioning McGwire about his past steroid use.

As McGwire had already secured a return to professional baseball and expressed little interest in whether he ever reached the Hall of Fame ("Transcript," 2010), we identify the target of McGwire's image repair effort to be the general public and sports fans in particular. The researchers have chosen to examine two significant texts: McGwire's opening statement to a House committee in 2005 and McGwire's interview with Bob Costas in 2010. Thus, we pose the following research questions:

> RQ1: What image restoration strategies were employed by Mark McGwire during his 2005 testimony before the U.S. House?
> RQ2: What image restoration strategies were employed by Mark McGwire during his 2010 interview with Bob Costas?

MARK MCGWIRE TALKS ABOUT STEROIDS

2005: "I'm not here to talk about the past"

The first Mark McGwire text to be analyzed is his opening statement to the House Committee on Government Reform in 2005, which was taking up the steroids issue in baseball. Using C-Span video of the hearing, the opening text was transcribed by one of the researchers. We consider McGwire's opening statement given before the committee (and a national television audience on several cable networks) an opportunity to restore his image with a message that he could control. While McGwire's appearance is still best remembered for the former player repeatedly answering "I'm not here to talk about the past" when questioned about steroid use within the game, McGwire's opening statement combined several strategies that sought to repair his image with the public while being cautious of legal consequences from what he said under oath.

Evasion of responsibility

While McGwire acknowledged in his statement to the House panel that steroids were a problem within Major League Baseball, it was a problem no one had taken on during his playing days: "Like any sport, where there is pressure to perform at the highest level, and there has been no testing to control for performance enhancing drugs, problems develop" ("Steroid Use," 2005). The researchers coded this statement as use of defeasibility, a form of evading responsibility, as McGwire argued that as no formal testing procedures were in place to identify steroid users, there was no ability to control the problem while he played the sport. At the same time, McGwire employed defeasibility in communicating his unwillingness to say anything about the past to the House committee:

> Asking me or any other player to answer questions about who took steroids in front of television cameras will not solve the problem. If a player answers no, he will simply not be believed. If he answers yes, he risks public scorn and endless government investigations. My lawyers has *[sic]* advised me that I cannot answer these questions without jeopardizing my friends and my family and myself. ("Steroid Use," 2005)

McGwire is citing in this statement not only his inability to give complete answers for fear of prosecution, but his doubt about whether anyone would believe he was telling the truth, even while under oath.

Reducing offensiveness of event

McGwire used several forms of this strategy in his opening statement. For example, McGwire sought to bolster his own image by demonstrating his loyalty to baseball and those he played with: "I've always been a team player. I've never been a person who spreads rumors or said thing about teammates that could hurt them" ("Steroid Use," 2005). McGwire was, in his own way, citing the familiar athletic credo about the goings-on in a team's locker room as being the concern of only those who occupy that room. McGwire also sought to bolster his own image before the public by calling attention to his charitable works, including the establishment of a children's foundation with $3 million of his own money. McGwire used transcendence in talking about previous testimony before the committee given by families of amateur athletes who had suffered health complications related to steroid usage. McGwire urged that the hearings be more than seeking to identify professional players who had been cheating: "I admire the parents who had the courage to appear before the committee and warn of the dangers of steroid use. My heart goes out to them" ("Steroid Use," 2005). McGwire tried in this and subsequent statements to demonstrate his empathy for the families as well as shift the focus from past actions of himself and other players to the current problem of steroids in youth sports.

McGwire used the occasion of the House hearing to attack one former teammate. Using simple denial, McGwire rejected Jose Canseco's claims in his first book about steroids in baseball: "It should be, it should be enough that you consider the source of the statements in the book in that many inconsistencies and contradictions have already been raised" ("Steroid Use," 2005). The wording of McGwire's utterance sought to raise doubts about Canseco's motivations as well as Canseco himself, who had faced legal problems in the past.

Corrective action

McGwire identified corrective actions that should be taken about steroids at all levels of athletics. First, he pledged to refocus his foundation's efforts into educating children about the perils of steroids and other illegal substances. Second, McGwire also volunteered to be the face of this public campaign: "I will use whatever influence and popularity I have to discourage young athletes form taking any drug that is not recommended by a doctor" ("Steroid Use," 2005). These corrective actions tied into the strategies previously noted, that McGwire wanted to focus on the larger problem of steroids in athletics rather than addressing what did or should happen regarding the use of steroids by Major League Baseball players.

2010: "I was given this gift by the Man upstairs"

As noted above, McGwire did a number of interviews with reporters when he finally acknowledged his past use of steroids. The researchers analyzed McGwire's interview with Bob Costas of the Major League Baseball Network. In addition to having access to an interview transcript, the choice of interviewer was important. Bob Costas is a renowned sportscaster who had covered McGwire during the 1998 home run chase.

In our analysis, we found McGwire employed all five of Benoit's image repair strategies during the Costas interview in explaining why he used steroids and why he was coming forward five years removed from his House testimony. While McGwire utilized mortification in his interview, it is apparent the former All-Star also wanted to reduce the offensiveness of his actions and even evade some responsibility in his responses.

Mortification

In coming forward to acknowledge his use of steroids while a Major League Baseball player, McGwire expressed regret several times about what he had done: "The most important part is to come clean. . . . I hope they [the public] really see how truly sorry I am" ("Transcript," 2010). Later in the interview, McGwire identified specific targets for his apology, including his family, the family of the late Roger Maris, the game of Major League Baseball, and its commissioner, Bud Selig.

Reducing offensiveness of event

Several examples from Benoit's typology about reducing offensiveness can be found in this interview. For example, McGwire attacked his main accuser, Jose Canseco, and claims made in Canseco's book about McGwire's behavior as a teammate, explaining it all away by saying "He [Canseco] had to sell a book" ("Transcript," 2010). McGwire also sought to bolster his own image in the interview. For example, McGwire noted his refusal to use his record home run season to try and break the bank. An example McGwire cited was the potential income he declined from selling memorabilia collected during the season: "I don't have one thing from that '98 season. I didn't keep any of that stuff. I gave everything away to teammates, players, coaches, and umpires, people that came through. I just wanted them to have the mementos" ("Transcript," 2010). In this instance, McGwire is portraying himself as someone rising above the desire to make every possible dollar as fast as he could, a stereotype associated with the modern professional athlete.

McGwire also made several statements that can be classified as using transcendence by explaining current and past actions were done out of loyalty to his wife and family. For example, McGwire told Costas that his actions during the 2005 House hearing on steroids were done in part to spare his family media attention: "How the heck am I going to bring those people in for some stupid act I did?" ("Transcript," 2010). McGwire also pointed to his desire to start his own family that led to his retirement after the 2001 season, and not his concern about his past steroid use. In each of these cases, McGwire attempts to transcend his own mistakes by showing his concern about family.

One of McGwire's recurring arguments in the interview was that steroids, in the end, had no impact on his phenomenal home run seasons in the late 1990s. In this research study, we categorize this argument as McGwire using minimization, trying separate his use of steroids from his natural baseball skills. One of McGwire's first statements in the Costas interview was that he ". . . was given this gift by the Man upstairs" ("Transcript," 2010). McGwire was attempting to make a case that it was his God-given natural talent that allowed him to become one of the all-time great home run hitters and not the use of steroids. To back up his point, McGwire cited hitting a home run in his first Little League at-bat, followed by success hitting the long ball at all levels of the game, including his rookie season with Oakland ("Transcript," 2010). Later in the interview, McGwire also credited maturing as a hitter: "I just believed in my ability and my hand-eye coordination. And I believed in the strength of my mind. My mind was so strong, and I developed that on my own. No pill or no injection is going to do that" ("Transcript," 2010). Again, McGwire is attempting to minimize the importance of steroid use while calling attention to the other physical and mental attributes he brought to his major league career.

Evasion of responsibility

McGwire's responses caused Costas to premise multiple questions around McGwire's belief in his natural ability to hit a baseball, and ergo, why the slugger still decided to use steroids. McGwire's responses employed what we classified as good intentions, a form of evasion of responsibility. McGwire stated his use of steroids had an altruistic purpose; specifically, helping his body recover from injuries and get back on the field.

> I was using steroids, thinking it was going to help me. It was brought to my attention it was going to help me heal faster and make my body feel back to normal. I was a walking MASH unit. It doesn't feel good when you have teammates walking by saying "He's injured again." ("Transcript," 2010)

As McGwire had identified himself as a "team player" going all the way back to his 2005 House testimony, he was now making the same sort of argument in that getting back to the field superseded the ethical and potential health issues related to steroid use. The argument also supported McGwire's attempts to minimize the issue of taking steroids. McGwire saw his use of steroids as a way of returning his body to an optimal physical condition, allowing his natural playing skills (e.g., hand-eye coordination) to help him once again reach professional excellence. So while McGwire was using this interview to apologize for his actions, these image repair strategies sought to explain and perhaps even justify his faulty judgments related to using steroids.

Denial

While McGwire utilized forms of denial on only a couple of occasions during his interview with Costas, his first response to a question represented an effort to shift the blame. Asked when he first used steroids, McGwire suggested easy access to steroids was a greater reason than his desire to try them: "The gyms you worked out back in the day. It was really available. Guys at gyms talked about . . . I was given a couple weeks worth. I tried it, never thought anything of it, just moved on from it" (Transcript," 2010). McGwire was suggesting that his first steroids encounter was something, for the time and the culture, considered commonplace and pushed upon him by others. McGwire also utilized simple denials when he rejected claims made in Jose Canseco's book about steroid use while teammates with the Oakland Athletics as well as Costas's observation that McGwire's steroids confession was linked to the statute of limitations expiring related to the ballplayer's use of performance-enhancing drugs ("Transcript," 2010).

Corrective action

McGwire acknowledged he wanted to admit his steroid use before leaving for the start of baseball's spring training in Florida and his new job as hitting coach for the St. Louis Cardinals. It was through this new opportunity in baseball that McGwire sought to offer corrective action to alter his tarnished image through giving back to the game. McGwire suggested some of his corrective actions would be in the way that he approached his new position: "I want to be a really good hitting coach. I'll be there from sun up to sundown helping these guys" ("Transcript," 2010). In this statement, McGwire is promising that his dedication as the Cardinals' hitting coach will demonstrate his love of the game to Cardinals fans he had let down. We also classified McGwire as promising to use his return to baseball as a way of restoring his image with his own family: "The last visual people have of me is standing up with my right hand in Congress. So now my children can see me in uniform" ("Transcript," 2010). This again suggested McGwire saw his return to professional baseball and the way he approached his job as a way of repairing the damage he had done to his image as one of the game's greatest players.

DISCUSSION

An analysis of Mark McGwire's 2005 statement to a U.S. House Committee and his 2010 interview with Bob Costas using Benoit's image restoration theory suggests that he used a variety of strategies in hopes of repairing his image. In his 2005 statement to the House Oversight committee, we found McGwire employed defeasibility (a form of the strategy classified as evading responsibility) and multiple examples of reducing offensiveness (e.g., bolstering his image by discussing his philanthropic work).

McGwire also pledged corrective action to deal with the steroids problem in sports, which included volunteering to be a spokesman in messages targeting young athletes about the dangers of performance-enhancing substances. Just five years later, when McGwire finally admitted his personal use of steroids, he employed many of the same strategies. The major difference was McGwire's use of mortification to express his regret about ever having used steroids. At the same time, McGwire tried to reduce the offensiveness of his actions. In particular, McGwire employed minimization, stating that steroids did not enhance the physical skills he employed in hitting a baseball. He combined this strategy with that of citing good intentions (a form of evading responsibility). McGwire suggested his use of steroids was to help his body recover from injuries in order to display his natural baseball talents (e.g., hand-eye coordination). McGwire also utilized strategies of denial (e.g., rejecting claims made in Canseco's book) and corrective action (e.g., to succeed in his job with the Cardinals).

As the researchers identified McGwire's image repair efforts were aimed at the general public and sports fans in particular, it is necessary to examine results of both scientific and non-scientific opinion polls to judge success in both situations analyzed. The Gallup organization regularly asks about favorable or unfavorable opinions of prominent public figures. The survey asked about Mark McGwire on several occasions, including his home run record season in 1998. In December of that year, McGwire's favorable rating was measured at 87 percent, compared to 3 percent unfavorable. McGwire still remained quite popular in another survey taken in June 2000, with a favorable rating of 72 percent (only 6 percent unfavorable). But another Gallup survey taken after McGwire's congressional testimony in March 2005 found his favorable rating had declined to 53 percent while his unfavorable rating had quadrupled (25 percent) ("Favorability," 2010). Gallup noted that

McGwire's decline in his favorable rating (19 percent between the 2000 and 2005 questions) was the sixth largest decline in a public figure's favorable rating between measurements since the company started keeping such records ("John Edwards," 2009). As a result, we judge McGwire's image repair efforts that year as unsuccessful.

While no scientific polls could be found regarding McGwire's January 2010 confession of steroid use, several online sports sites conducted non-scientific opinion polls that suggested McGwire had generally failed to sway public opinion to him. An online poll on *The Washington Post*'s sports website showed 79 percent of respondents supported the idea of wiping McGwire's percent home run season from the baseball record books on account of his steroids admission (Westrick, 2010). Another poll on fox-sports.com, in which more than 335,000 people took part, showed 42 percent wanted McGwire's 1998 home run mark erased, while another 28 percent called for the mark to carry an asterisk in the record books ("McGwire Admits," 2010). Another national online sports publication asked its readers whether McGwire or golfer Tiger Woods would be forgiven first by the public (Woods had his public image damaged at by allegations of sexual liaisons outside of his marriage). Of nearly 2000 respondents, 52 percent said Woods would be forgiven first while only 48 percent said McGwire would ("Who Will," 2010).

Even in St. Louis, where McGwire had repeatedly made baseball history and helped the Cardinals make the playoffs, the city's most influential sports columnist had trouble reconciling statements made by McGwire to Costas and other reporters. *St. Louis Post-Dispatch* writer Bernie Miklasz said he and many other people were having trouble accepting McGwire's argument that his steroid use helped heal his body, but did not enhance his ability to hit home runs (Miklasz, 2010). There were other influential baseball figures who commended McGwire's admission, including former all-time home run champion Henry Aaron and baseball commissioner Bud Selig. Despite these endorsements, McGwire's level of support among the public had not significantly improved following his steroids admission. Ultimately, we judge McGwire's image repair effort in early 2010 as initially unsuccessful. We hesitate in making a more forceful claim due to an absence of scientific polling data and that McGwire's promised corrective actions (involving his return to baseball) had only commenced shortly after his January 2010 interview.

One of the conclusions as to why McGwire failed in his image repair attempts was a lack of mortification expressed in both situations. Benoit (1995) has identified mortification as a key part of successful image repair, regardless of whether it is an athlete, celebrity or politician. In his 2005 statement to the House, McGwire offered no mortification as he declined to discuss any involvement he previously had or knew of with steroids. While

McGwire offered an explanation for his lack of candor (concern about potential criminal prosecution), it is obvious that the public was disappointed with the former star's behavior before the committee. When McGwire did admit to steroid use five years later, his statements of mortification were accompanied by extensive explanations we coded as trying to reduce offensiveness and evading responsibility. McGwire's tortured explanation that steroids only healed his body and did not influence his physical ability to hit a baseball seemed to fail the sincerity test with the public, as online sports polls suggested. Brazeal (2008) found another star athlete, Terrell Owens, encountered similar problems when he tried to explain away his bad behavior instead of focusing on his mortification over his actions. This research study suggests McGwire would also have been better served by being unequivocal about being sorry for betraying the public's trust instead to trying to explain his steroid use.

A second conclusion about McGwire's inability to win back public support after his January 2010 admission of steroid use is that he was hampered by the loss of goodwill with his fans and the general public. Past research done on image repair has shown public figures considered to be celebrities or entertainers (like athletes) typically enjoy a reservoir of goodwill with the public. Benoit's study of actor Hugh Grant's image repair on *The Tonight Show* following his dalliance with a prostitute showed Grant's image repair succeeded because he had a pre-existing level of likability from his movie career. Thus, Grant had an easier time repairing the damage caused in this embarrassing incident than perhaps a politician or a businessman in need of image repair (Benoit, 1997). Mark McGwire once enjoyed a very high level of public support, as shown by the Gallup poll questions on favorability about the ballplayer from 1998 and 2000. But stories about steroids in baseball, as well as José Canseco's book alleging McGwire's use of steroids, started eroding away at this popularity. After McGwire appeared before the U.S. House committee investigating steroids in 2005 and his failure to substantially address his involvement at that time, the steep decline in McGwire's favorability became apparent. Still, McGwire's favorability number after that hearing was 53 percent, a majority of those polled. That another five years passed before McGwire publicly acknowledged his steroids use probably hurt the former ballplayer's popularity even more.

Thus, McGwire's delay in acknowledging his steroid use is the basis of a third conclusion in this research study. Mark McGwire's image repair strategy in 2010 (and even 2005) may have been hampered (or even doomed) by not addressing his steroid use on a timely basis. Twelve years passed between the time when McGwire was hailed as a hero for his home run power and the time when he admitted steroid use. Perhaps McGwire's image repair strategies would have been more successful had he been more forthright earlier. The time between the original offensive act and the time of the apology has rarely been considered in comparable studies, in part because the party that commits the offensive act typically understands the advantage in quickly addressing the offensive behavior. For past and current ball players who may yet be hiding their own steroid use, the analysis of McGwire's image repair efforts suggests that such admissions may be more effective if they are made sooner rather than later.

As noted above, we believe Mark McGwire's 2010 image repair effort to be initially unsuccessful, but still with the chance to ultimately be successful based on the corrective actions he is taking (McGwire's return to and involvement in Major League Baseball). Just as passage of time may have hampered McGwire's efforts to repair his image with the public, time (as well as future actions) may eventually help Mark McGwire achieve his goal of winning back the support of not just baseball fans, but people everywhere.

REFERENCES

Associated Press (2010, January 14). McGwire admits using steroids in 70-HR year. *NBC Sports.com.* Retrieved May 3, 2010, from http.nbcsports.msnbc.com/id/ 34809569.

Baseball-reference.com (2010). *Mark McGwire.* Retrieved May 2, 2010 from www.baseball-reference.com/players/m/mcgwima01.shtml.

Benoit, W. L. (1995). *Accounts, excuses, and apologies: A theory of image restoration strategies.* Albany: State University of New York Press.

Benoit, W. L. (1997). Hugh Grant's image restoration discourse: An actor apologizes. *Communication Quarterly, 45*(3), 251-267.

Brazeal, L. (2008) The image repair strategies of Terrell Owens. *Public Relations Review, 34*(2), 145-150.

Canseco, J. (2005). *Juiced: Wild Times, Rampant 'Roids, Smash Hits, and How Baseball Got Big.* New York: Harper Collins.

Favorability: People in the news. (2010, May 1). *Gallup.com.* Retrieved May 1, 2010 from http://www.gallup.com/poll/1618/favorability-people-news.aspx#4.

Fleischersports.com. (May 2010). Corporate website, www.fleischersports.com.

Friedman, W. (1999, July 5). Home run kings still, but not with ad deals: McGwire and Sosa fail to meet expectations for marketing dollars. *Advertising Age* [online]. http://adage.com

From Bush to Big Mac: PR man to polish steroid poster boy Mark McGwire's image. Bush press secretary Fleischer helps restart McGwire's baseball career (2010, February 17). *abcnews.com.* Retrieved May 3, 2010, from abc.news.go.com/politic/mark-mcgwire-spring.

Gammons, P. (2010, January 25). McGwire return a distraction: Cardinals brass will need a plan when spring training begins. *MLB.com.* Retrieved May 3, 2010 from http://mlb.mlb.com/news/print.jsp?myd-20100125&content_id=79s.

John Edwards, Sarah Palin both see favorable ratings slide. (2009, October 16). *Gallup.com.* Retrieved May 7, 2010, from http://www.gallup.com/poll/123698/ john-edwards-sarah-palin-favorable-ratings-slide.aspx.

Madden, B. (2010, February 19). Mark McGwire's steroid talks continue to hang over St. Louis Cardinals' spring training. *New York Daily News* [online edition]. Retrieved May 4, 2010 from http://www.nydailynews.com/fdcp?1272945807404.

McCann, M. (2010, January 12). Despite new confession, McGwire faces no perjury threat from 2005. *SI.com [sports law].* Retrieved May 3, 2010, from http://si.ptintthis. clickability.com.

McCarver, T., & Peary, D. (1999). *The perfect season: Why 1998 was baseball's greatest year.* New York: Random House.

McGwire admits to steroid use. (2010, January 12). *FoxSports.com.* Retrieved May 3, 2010, from http://msn.foxsports.com/mlb/story/mcgwire-admits-to-steroid-use?GT1=39002.

McGwire apologizes to LaRussa, Selig. (2010, January 11). *ESPN.com.* Retrieved May 3, 2010 from http://sports.espn.go.com/mlb/news/story?id=4816607.

Miklasz, B. (2010, January 12). Mark McGwire, the day after. *St. Louis Post-Dispatch* [online edition]. Retrieved May 6, 2010. from http://interact.stltoday.com/blogzone/bernies-extra-points/bernies-extra-points/bernies-5-minutes/2010/01/mark-mcgwire-the-day-after

PRNewswire (1998, May 4). McDonald's announces Mark McGwire and Sammy Sosa national sponsorship deals. Retrieved May 3, 2010, from www.encylopedia.com/doc/1G1-53068908.html.

Sarte, B. (2010, January 13). Mark McGwire: Has baseball's savior fallen? *Bleacher Report.com.* Retrieved May 3, 2010, from http://bleacherreport.com/articles/325272-mark-mcgwire.

Spain, W. (1999, June 28). Mark McGwire & Sammy Sosa: Paul Beeston. *Advertising Age* [online edition]. Retrieved May 3, 2010, from http:/adage.com

Steroid use in baseball: Players. (2005, March 17). *C-Span Video Library* [online]. Available at http://www.c-spanvideo.org/program/185904-2.

Transcript: McGwire interview. (2010, January 11). *San Jose Mercury News* [online edition]. Retrieved April 5, 2010, from http://www.mercurynews.com/ fdcp?1270489843765.

Westrick, J. (2010, January 11). Mark McGwire admits steroid use. *The Washington Post* [online edition]. Retrieved May 6, 2010, from http://views.washingtonpost.com/ post-user-polls/2010/01/mark-mcgwire-admits-steroid-use.html.

Who will be forgiven first, Tiger Woods or Mark McGwire? (2010, January 12). *Sportingnews.com.* Retrieved May 6, 2010, from http:www.sportingnews.com/mlb/article/2010-01-12/who-will-be-forgiven-first-tiger-woods-or-mark-mcgwire.

Wulf, S. (1992, June 1). Most happy fella. *Sports Illustrated* [online edition]. Retrieved May 6, 2010 from http://sportsillustrated.cnn.com/vault/article/magazine/ MAG1003839/1/index.htm.

Chapter Three

Defense of an Anti-Hero: Barry Bonds's "State of the Great Address"

J. Scott Smith, University of Missouri

On December 3, 2004, the *San Francisco Chronicle* reproduced sealed grand jury testimony from athletes associated with Bay Area Lab Co-operative (BALCO), which was charged with orchestrating one of the most elaborate sports doping scandals in U.S. history. Federal prosecutors asked Barry Bonds and other elite athletes about their involvement with steroids, particularly two undetectable steroids known as the "cream" and the "clear" (Williams & Fainaru-Wada, 2004). Troy Ellerman, the attorney for BALCO founder Victor Conte and vice president James Valente, leaked the grand jury testimony of Barry Bonds and other athletes during the BALCO trial to reporters Lance Williams and Mark Fainaru-Wada (Egelko, 2007).[1] On December 4, 2003, federal prosecutors questioned Bonds for three hours over material seized during a raid of Greg Anderson's home in September 2003. Anderson was Bonds's trainer and friend, who federal prosecutors contended was a middleman between Bonds and BALCO, buying and distributing steroids to Bonds. Federal prosecutors questioned Bonds about the evidence gathered from Anderson's home, which included calendars that suggested the cycling of steroids, billing information, and a long list of performance-enhancing drugs highlighted by the undetectable designer steroids known as "the cream" and "the clear" (Williams & Fainaru-Wada, 2004). Additionally, federal prosecutors informed Bonds that he could not be prosecuted for admitting crimes during his testimony, but warned Bonds that he would face perjury charges if prosecutors discovered he lied under oath (Williams & Fainaru-Wada, 2004). Bonds utilized the image repair strategies of denial and defeasibility during his testimony. He denied any involvement with doping calendars, knowingly taking performance-enhancing drugs, and he de-

41

nied talking to Anderson about the substances Anderson gave him. Bonds used a defeasibility strategy by stating, "I never asked Greg. . . . When he said it was flaxseed oil, I just said, 'Whatever'" (Williams & Fainaru-Wada, 2004, p. A1). Bonds's defeasibility strategy shifted the attention onto his trainer Greg Anderson, but he's continually refused to testify against Bonds. Illustrating his resolve, Anderson refused to testify during Bonds's 2011 perjury trial and was sent to prison for the fifth time for his involvement with BALCO (Swartz, 2011).[2]

Grand jury testimony from other MLB players enhanced federal prosecutors' assertions that Bonds used steroids. Then New York Yankees first baseman Jason Giambi and his brother Jeremy testified that they received steroids from Anderson, whom they sought out because of Bonds's on-field prowess. Yankees outfielder Gary Sheffield testified that he trained with Bonds before the 2002 season and Sheffield was taking "the cream" and "the clear" which were given to him by Anderson. Sheffield stated, "I know I've seen Greg give Barry the same thing I was taking. I didn't see him taking those red beans, but I seen him taking this (clear) and this cream here" (Williams & Fainaru-Wada, 2004, p. A1). Major League Baseball has been widely known for its ability to self-censor and avoid condemning statements about one another, so these statements from players damaged Bonds's image.

The *San Francisco Chronicle*'s article was printed in the middle of baseball's offseason, allowing Bonds to delay responding to questions about his alleged steroid use until spring training. Just before spring training began in 2005, *60 Minutes* reporter Mike Wallace interviewed Jose Canseco about the contents of his book, *Juiced*, on February 13, 2005 (*60 Minutes*, February 13, 2005). Canseco claimed that steroids were widely used in baseball, dramatically increased his performance, and that he personally injected Mark McGwire with steroids. Canseco targeted Bonds briefly in his book and concluded that after witnessing Bonds's weight gain and performance in 2001 that "Barry was definitely on steroids" (Canseco, 2005, p. 216). Canseco's interview brought more media attention to steroids in baseball and specifically to Bonds.

Canseco's new book created even more anticipation for Bonds's initial spring training press conference, which was an annual media event. *Associated Press* reporter Janie McCauley (2005) described the general anticipation of this event, "It's when the San Francisco Giants superstar holds his annual state-of-Barry address—and more often than not, it's the most he says to reporters all season." *San Francisco Chronicle* writer Ray Ratto called it "Tuesday's State of the Great Address" and Bonds did not disappoint while fielding fifty questions from reporters (Ratto, 2005, p. D1). The press conference was slated to have more than one hundred media members attend, but the media could only ask Bonds about issues that were not sealed as part of the BALCO investigation. The rules of the press conference forced the media to be creative with indirect questions about Bonds's alleged steroid use without directly involving his BALCO grand jury testimony. More than anything else on display at "The State of the Great Address" was Bonds's contentious relationship with reporters.

Historically, Barry Bonds has had a combative relationship with the media dating back to his tenure with the Pittsburgh Pirates. On March 4, 1991, Bonds had an infamous-obscenity laden argument with Pirates manager Jim Leyland stemming from Bonds's poor attitude throughout spring training because Bonds had not received a contract extension from the Pirates (Bodley, 1991). Bonds stated, "I wouldn't re-sign with Pittsburgh if they gave me $100 million" (Bodley, 1991, p. 1C). Bonds's strained relationship with his coaches led to Leyland vehemently criticizing Bonds on the field in front of a reporter. *Boston Globe* columnist Bob Ryan lambasted Bonds in his article, "Spoil system creates athletic ingrates the likes of Barry Bonds" (Ryan, 1991, p. 69). Ryan (1991) concluded, "What Barry Bonds needs is a good spanking. . . . I also felt there were too few people willing to tell these spoiled narcissists exactly where to go, which is why Jim Leyland is my new hero. Me, and many others" (p. 69). Bonds explained that he was misunderstood because he was not afforded a middle ground by reporters: "If I'm quiet and don't talk, then I'm called sulky or moody, but when I do say something, it's not written the way I say it, then all of a sudden it's said that I'm talking too much" (Smith, 1991, p. D23). Bonds further explained that he did not have bad intentions: "I don't wake up in the morning and say, 'Oh, boy, this is a good day to be a total ass,' or 'this is a great day to tick people off,'" (Smith, 1991, p. D23). After the incident, Bonds began to get booed off the field by fans so consistently that Leyland even commented, "I think the booing has really gotten a little unfair. He damn sure doesn't deserve what he's getting. That stuff is getting pretty old now" (Sports News, 2005).

By 1996 Bonds was already a three-time MVP and had grown tired of being ridiculed by the media and fans. His frustration led to additional altercations with the media, most notably shoving *USA Today* reporter Rod Beaton in the locker room before a May 9, 1996, game (Georgatos, 2005). Although he was urged by Giants executive Larry Baer to be more cordial with reporters, Bonds decided to restrict his access to the media and fans. He stated, "I'm not going to allow the media to bother me anymore. I'm not going to allow the fans to bother me or get to me anymore" (Georgatos, 2005). Bonds offered his personal interpretation of his negative persona: "Barry Bonds' bad-boy image came from the newspaper. It didn't come from anywhere else. Once you're stamped as a bad boy in the press, there's no way out" (Georgatos, 2005). Bonds argued that he's only portrayed as a villain, even in instances with umpires. "All they see is, 'Barry Bonds flew off the handle.' That's what is in the newspaper. 'Barry Bonds gets fined'" (Georgatos, 2005). One of the best indicators of Bonds's strained relationship with the media and fans was his omission from Major League Baseball's All-Century team in 1999 (All-century team, 1999). Fans voted for the best players at each position and the Baseball Writers Association of America (BBWAA) voted to complete the roster. Before facing any steroid allegation, Bonds was neither a media nor fan favorite.

Bonds's negative reputation with the media is an important component to understanding his image repair efforts because his image was already damaged substantially before being accused of using steroids. This chapter argues that evaluating Bonds's image repair strategies is best understood through the lens of the American sports anti-hero, an athlete with supreme ability and performance without being beloved by the media or fans.

ANTI-HERO

Before detailing the image repair strategies Bonds utilized in his press conference, examining his statements as an anti-hero is important for contextualizing Bonds's defense discourse. Generally found in literary characters, an anti-hero is someone who "lacks the attributes of the traditional protagonist or hero. The anti-hero's lack of courage, honesty, or grace, his weaknesses and confusion, often reflect modern man's ambivalence toward traditional moral and social virtues" ("Anti-hero," 2011). Anti-heroes are subversive characters that do not adhere to the dominant ideology. Anti-hero characters were popularized in 1960s novels during an anti-establishment movement prompted by the Vietnam War. They have the ability to be heroes, yet choose not to be (Simmons, 2008). Particularly with Bonds, he was one of the greatest players in baseball history, yet his contentious relationship and subsequent actions with reporters created his "bad boy" persona.

Bonds's on-field achievements represent those of an American sports hero, much like the other two faces of the Steroid Era: Mark McGwire and Roger Clemens. Bonds's career achievements are unparalleled. He won a record seven MVP titles in his career, including four straight during his alleged steroid use ("Barry Bonds statistics," 2008).[3] Yet, Bonds was not revered for his achievements, but rather reviled for his surly demeanor with the media, fans, coaches, and teammates. Bonds had the unique ability to help the San Francisco Giants win games and concurrently receive negative attention due to his unaccommodating demeanor.[4] Warsaw Sports Marketing Center executive director Rick Burton stated,

> Barry has not been loved by the media and hence by the fans, so some of what he's been getting is the residual impact of his relationship with the media. They have been much less likely to write the puff pieces they did in McGwire's year. (Gloster, 2001)

As previously mentioned, Bonds thought his negative persona was cemented in the media, leading him to make few attempts to repair his negative image.

Bonds's defense discourse presents a unique contribution to our understanding of image repair research because his case problematizes one of the assumptions that Benoit's (1995) theory of image restoration is founded on. Benoit (1995) argues, "Maintaining a positive reputation is one of the central goals of communication" (p. 63). This chapter will argue that Bonds did not have a positive reputation prior to accusations that he used performance-enhancing drugs. Yet, not having a positive image does not preclude him from wanting to keep his reputation from further damage. I will argue that Bonds's role as an anti-hero made certain image repair strategies (e.g., attack accuser and denial) more appropriate in his case because he did not have a positive reputation prior to the December 3, 2004, *San Francisco Chronicle* article. In a sense, Bonds had less to lose than other players accused of steroid use like Mark McGwire and Roger Clemens because they had positive reputations before being attacked.

Bonds alluded to his status as an anti-hero in three instances during his "State of the Great Address." The first anti-hero attribute Bonds displayed during the "State of the Great Address" is his lack of grace. When asked about Jose Canseco's comments on *60 Minutes* that Bonds used steroids, Bonds quipped:

> I was better than Jose now and I've been better than Jose his whole career. So I don't have anything to talk about Jose. If he wants to go make money, go make money. You had the Bash Boys, you had one of the best lineups in baseball that's second to some of the Yankees lineups or you can go on. For somebody that brags about what he did, I don't see any of your records.

Along with his lack of grace, Bonds departs from the established American sports hero model. Generally, the best player on a team becomes the "face of the franchise." The prime example in baseball is New York Yankees captain Derek Jeter. He knows his responsibility is more than just performing on the field, he is the first player the media talks to when there's positive or negative news concerning the Yankees. Jeter handles that responsibility elegantly; he accommodates reporters, praises teammates, and chooses his public comments carefully. During the "State of the Great Address" Bonds conveys that he's never been interested in that role:

> I just wanted to do my job and go home. I made my choice. It may not have been the right choice. It may not have been the choice of what America wants or what the people want, but that's my choice, that's my decision. But it doesn't make me a bad person. It doesn't make me an evil person. It doesn't make me that you know I'm some different person or I'm separating myself from anyone else. I am just—I want to go to work.

Bonds later added,

> I think it's because I haven't given you guys what you wanted, that's all. I just chose that road. It wasn't—it wasn't for any bad reason, it was for my own personal reasons, my own safety net as you could say, just to play the game. I don't—I don't care about the other parts of it. I just care about the game and playing the game. I mean, I guess if I would have given you guys what you wanted, smiled all the time and did everything, I'd have endorsement deals and the whole nine yards, but that wasn't the road that I wanted because that's not what I really care about.

These statements are important for this analysis because Bonds appears to be content with his negative reputation. However, Bonds's grand jury testimony demonstrates that he cares about his records and his place in baseball history. So while his reputation with the media and fans might not be important to Bonds, he wanted to protect his records from being tainted and discounted because of his alleged steroid use.

CRITICAL ANALYSIS OF BONDS'S "STATE OF THE GREAT ADDRESS"

Barry Bonds came to his annual spring training press conference in an aggressive manner that prompted *San Francisco Chronicle* writer Ray Ratto (2005) to describe Bonds as "even more of himself than he usually is" (p. D1). This analysis focuses on the February 22, 2005, "State of the Great Address," a full text version of which the *San Francisco Chronicle* provided on their website ("Transcript of Bonds," 2005). This text was chosen not only because it was Bonds's first response to the leaked BALCO grand jury testimony, but it also represented an anticipated annual event where Bonds carefully planned his responses to reporters' artfully crafted questions. For instance, the moderator began the press conference stating, "Barry is here to answer any questions except for, he can't answer questions on BALCO because it's a legal matter and also any personal questions. But baseball related, how his knee is doing, anything like that. First question?" To which the first question was, "Can you explain over the last four or five years your amazing production, your tremendous growth in muscle strength getting stronger as you get older?" Throughout the press conference, Bonds faced questions indirectly related to his presumed steroid use, which, in turn, he answered indirectly. During the "State of the Great Address" Bonds relied primarily on attack accuser and denial, and to a lesser degree transcendence and bolstering.

Attack Accuser

Bonds attacked the media in three different ways during his press conference. First, he attacked the media for repeating the same stories and beats about his grand jury testimony, which they were not allowed to question him about. Second, Bonds attacked the integrity of journalists, questioning their motives and methods. Third, he attacked the media in a chiding way to seemingly his own amusement. To a lesser extent, Bonds attacked Jose Canseco and his book.

Bonds attacked the media's credibility, by referring to their actions as outright lies or as merely tabloid journalism. His most direct attack occurred during the middle of the press conference when he was asked, "What's going to be your approach to repair it [his reputation] from here on out? [Do] you expect other people to come clean and move forward?" Bonds attacked vehemently:

> We just need to go out there and do our jobs, just as you professionals do your job. All you guys lied. All of y'all and the story or whatever have lied. Should you have asterisk behind your name? All of you lied. All of you have said something wrong. All of you have dirt. All of you. When your closet's clean, then come clean somebody else's. But clean yours first, ok.

He also attacked the reporters' motives, declaring, "Are y'all going to be good people or are you all going to be who you are and make the game or sports what it is? It's become 'Hard Copy' all day long. Are you guys jealous? Upset? Disappointed? What?" This statement functioned to label the media's questioning as second-rate journalism, which would undermine the media's attacks on Bonds. He furthered his attack, stating,

> It's just sad that, you know, this is where sports has become a spectacle now. It's not –it's become comical and it's sad, because we're not—we're not trying to make it comical because we're not writing the stories. You know, we're just trying to go out there as human beings and do our job.

This direct attack on the media illustrates his combination of attack accuser and transcendence strategies. Bonds utilizes a victimage strategy, suggesting that there is a media circus surrounding the details from the December 3, 2004, *San Francisco Chronicle* article, but also couches his statement in a larger context as just "human beings" and trying to "do our job."

Bonds's most frequent response to questions about steroids was to attack reporters for recycling the same stories. Through a calculated and peculiar analogy, Bonds likened the continued questions about steroids to reruns of *Sanford and Son*. Bonds stated, "You guys are like rerun stories. This is just—this is old stuff. I mean, it's like watching *Sanford and Son*, you know, you just, rerun after rerun after rerun." Later Bonds suggested the media move forward from the steroid issue to covering MLB's new drug testing program. He stated, "Y'all stop watching Red Foxx in rerun shows and let's go and let the program work and allow us to do our job." When Bonds was pressed about Jason Giambi providing an apology, he attacked the media again. "I'm just sorry that we're even going through all this rerun stuff. . . . But what's your purpose and what you're doing it for, rewriting it, writing it over and over and over again, what's your reasoning? What are you going to apologize for when you're wrong?" These statements questioned the legitimacy of the media's constant questioning of Bonds's presumed steroid use that could not be answered (due to the BALCO investigation) or had been previously denied by Bonds.

Another way Bonds attacked reporters was though biting sarcasm. Ratto (2005) characterized Bonds as "more combative, more dismissive, more rambling, more defiant and yet stingingly accurate on some points. What he was not, was compliant" (p. D1). His jokes toward reporters were chiding, starting with his phone ringing at the beginning of the press conference. "Let me turn that off. I don't want y'all to see that. That's a little too high-tech." When asked "Have you lied about anything?" Bonds replied, "Yeah, I lied to my parents when I was growing up. Lied to my friends." Clearly this was not the context the reporter meant the question in, so the reporter redirected, "Baseball." Bonds again evaded the questioner's intentions, stating, "Have I lied about baseball? Yeah, I told a couple of stories that I hit a couple of balls a couple of places that I really didn't, yeah. That's about the extent of it." At another point during the press conference, a reporter's question, "What are we moving forward from?" agitated Bonds, which led to him stating, "Ok. Strike one, ball one, one out, cheer, boo, yeah, game over, let's go home. I mean, what else do you want to talk about?" Bonds's approach was to irritate the media members on hand, instead of answering their questions willingly, he provided abstract answers that evaded the questions.

Bonds also attacked Jose Canseco (who claimed in his book *Juiced* that Bonds used steroids) when reporters asked about his reaction to Canseco's book. Bonds attacked, "You know, to me, Canseco, you've got to come with a whole lot more than what you're talking about, and fiction, man. There's a whole bunch of those books and stories out there, basically, you know, it's just to make a buck. That's all it is, it's about making money." This statement sought to reduce Canseco's credibility just trying to profit off of the public interest surrounding steroid use in baseball. This statements sought to damage Canseco's credibility and mitigate the impact of the accusations against Bonds.

Denial

Bonds never explicitly denied using steroids, but he made several implicit denials. The first question of the February 22, 2005, press conference asked about Bonds's unprecedented production over the past five years: "Can you finally put to rest . . ." Bonds sharply interrupted the reporter, saying, "Can I? Hard work that's about it. Now it's to rest." Even though Bonds does not blatantly state he never used steroids, his response was firm and absolute. Later in the press conference a reporter asked, "Jason Giambi felt the need to make an apology. Is there anything that you need to apologize for?" Bonds responded with, "What did I do?" Here the rules of the press conference are clearly demonstrated, as the reporter's roundabout question is about Bonds's BALCO testimony, but Bonds brushed the question aside by stating there was nothing to apologize for, implicitly denying he used steroids.

Another way Bonds implicitly denied using steroids was through stonewalling or evading the question altogether. When asked about Jason Giambi's apology, Bonds rambled to evade the question, stating,

> I'm sorry that, you know, this fiction all stuff and maybe some facts, who knows, but I'm sorry that, you know—we're all sorry about this. None of us want to go through this. None of us want to deal with this stuff. We want to go out and do our job.

This stonewalling instance demonstrates Bonds's desire to deny his steroid use. The denial is very abstract with "this fiction all stuff and maybe some facts" suggesting that the stories about his steroid use are untrue. Moreover though, the response represents his desire to evade the intention of the question, which was, does he want to apologize for using steroids like Jason Giambi did?

Near the end of the "State of the Great Address," Bonds also denied steroids would help baseball performance: "I don't know if steroids is going to help you in baseball. I just don't believe it. I don't believe steroids can help you, eye/hand coordination, technically hit a baseball, I just don't believe it and that's my opinion." This is the only instance Bonds actually used the word "steroid" during the entire press conference, and these statements perform as an implicit denial. Bonds argued he does not believe steroids would increase one's performance, which implied that Bonds did not use steroids. If the public accepted Bonds's claim that he thought steroids would not improve performance, then it might have strengthened his denial strategy and reputation.

Transcendence

Bonds used the image repair strategy of transcendence in two different ways. First, he framed steroids in the larger drug context. Second, he attempted to place baseball's "Steroids Era" into a larger sports context.

Bonds utilized transcendence in an effort to place steroid use in baseball in a larger drug context. Even though Bonds never mentioned "steroids" in these utterances, the comparison was implied as he declared, "I mean, we've got alcohol that's the number one killer in America and we legalize that to buy in the store. You've got, you know, you've got tobacco number two, three killer in America, we legalize that." Later, Bonds was asked if the drug testing program was "long overdue," to which Bonds replied, "Alcohol is long overdue that we should ban that. There's a lot of things we should ban and get out of here." Bonds is trying to get his audience to examine steroids through a wider drug context. This appears to be an appropriate strategy when steroids are viewed in the larger drug context; they neither kill more than legal drugs nor are perceived any worse than other illegal drugs.

Bonds also attempted to place baseball in a larger sports scandal context. He qualified his stance on letting the drug testing program work instead of concentrating on the past by declaring, "If that's the case [investigating the "Steroids Era"], we're going to go way back into 19th, 18th centuries in rehashing the past and we'll crush a lot of things in a lot of sports if that's what you guys want. If you just want a lot of things out of the sports world, then we can go back into the 1800s and basically asterisk a lot of sports if that's what you choose and that's what you want to do." Even if the public only referred to baseball's own scandals, one would find a history of corked bats, nail files, foreign substances, spit balls, sharpened spikes, stealing signs, and other actions to enhance performance.

Bolstering

Bonds utilized bolstering in two instances. First, he bolstered his image as a self-sacrificing player, willing to do anything for his team. Second, he bolstered his image by supporting MLB's drug testing program.

Bonds bolstered his image by arguing he was a good teammate that just wanted to enjoy the game. "I put my body through a lot in 147 games last year. I played more games than anyone on my team, and [I'm] the oldest and I'm still trying to recover from that." Here, Bonds bolstered his image as a sacrificing player, putting his body through significant punishment for his team. He echoed these statements later when he stated, "The sad part about it [all the media scrutiny about passing Babe Ruth on the all-time homerun list] man, I just really want to go play baseball. The record thing, I don't really care about as much as just going out there and playing a game and being the best and that's what I tell my kids." Bonds bolsters his image by suggesting the joy of the game is his primary motive, which he strengthens by linking his play to his children.

Bonds bolstered his image by supporting MLB and Commissioner Bud Selig for implementing baseball's drug testing program. Bonds praised MLB's drug testing program. "I commend Bud Selig and the Players' Union and all of the players for trying to put together a testing program that supposed to satisfy everyone. I cannot say enough for what Bud has come out and stated." His support for the baseball establishment bolstered Bonds's image as a company man and as someone concerned with the health of baseball. Although Bonds is perceived as a loner, he states, "there's a code in baseball: Respect your peers regardless of whatever." Canseco was harshly criticized by baseball insiders because his book *Juiced* discussed locker-room behavior, so Bonds rightly praised baseball's actions. These statements also strive to enhance his denials of steroid use because the testing program would provide a "clean" game.

EVALUATION

Bonds's February 22, 2005, "State of the Great Address" presented a unique rhetorical situation. Although Bonds was not the first player accused of steroid use, he was widely the most unpopular, and yet, the most accomplished. Overall, I believe Bonds's image restoration efforts were partially effective when viewing his discourse as an anti-hero. Before ever being accused of using steroids, Bonds represented the player media and fans alike loved to hate. One might suggest that Bonds had an advantage over players with positive reputations accused of steroid use because their reputations could fall further than his. For Bonds, "image restoration" or "image repair" did not mean getting himself back into the good graces of the media and the public, rather it meant not becoming the scapegoat of baseball's Steroid Era. To this end, Bonds was successful.

Bonds's heavy utilization of attack accuser was not surprising considering two members of the media sought out and published sealed grand jury testimony, along with his combative history with sports reporters. One of Bonds's primary goals was to keep the status quo with concern to his presumed steroid use. He achieved this by attacking the credibility of reporters. His most direct attack on reporters stating, "All you guys lied. All of y'all and the story or whatever have lied" questioned the objectivity of reporters, without which, journalists lose all credibility. This strategy was appropriate to remain consistent with his previous strained relationship with reporters, as noted by Saltzman (2003), who quoted an anonymous reporter stating Bonds "basically views reporters as cockroaches who have invaded his throne room." Bonds's goal was to make the "State of the Great Address" about anything other than his steroid use, which he was successful in doing. Again, a successful defense for Bonds was maintaining the status quo of his already negative reputation, while avoiding any direct questions about his alleged steroid use.

Beyond that direct attack, Bonds deflected attention through other, more sarcastic attacks, which were effective. Most notably, the analogy to *Sanford and Son* reruns was a planned attack that deflected the attention away from his alleged steroid use and toward his combative relationship with reporters. Additionally, his sometimes rambling and chiding of reporters deflected attention away from his alleged steroid use and toward his responses instead. Bonds's frustrated response, "Ok. Strike one, ball one, one out, cheer, boo, yeah, game over, let's go home. I mean, what else do you want to talk about?" demonstrated Bonds's predetermined plan to avoid discussing his alleged steroid use by attacking reporters. Overall, Bonds's attacks dominated the "State of the Great Address" which provided interesting quotes for reporters, yet little substantive material about his presumed steroid use.

Second, Bonds's use of denial was partially effective. The initial exchange during the press conference exemplified Bonds's denial strategy. When asked about how he could explain his gains in strength and performance he stated, "Can I? Hard work that's about it. Now it's to rest." The initial question "Can I?" demonstrates Bonds's acknowledgment of the strained relationship between him and reporters. Even if he unequivocally denied using steroids, the questions would continue to come. This lackluster answer for reporters was an effective denial for Bonds simply because it was lackluster. His refusal to answer definitively did not allow reporters to extrapolate further.

However, Bonds's other denials were not as effective. Bonds elaborated at times when he should not have, particularly when asked if he wanted to make an apology like Jason Giambi did. Bonds's statements were abstract and unclear as noted by the statement, "this fiction all stuff and maybe some facts." This response provided room for interpretation by reporters where Bonds would have been better off holding his comments after his initial statement, "What did I do?" Additionally, his denial that steroids would not help performance was not effective. Bonds utilized the hand/eye coordination argument, which was a salient argument about steroid use in baseball during the late 1990s and early 2000s before reporters and the general public possessed greater knowledge about steroid use. The naïve stage of steroids helping performance was gone by 2005 and steroid use was acknowledged by former MVPs Ken Caminati and Jose Canseco to have helped their performance tremendously. Steroids may not help one's hand/eye coordination, but steroids turn fly-ball outs into homeruns, which is what hitters from the Steroid Era benefited from, and reporters were keenly aware of this fact by 2005.

Third, Bonds's use of transcendence was not effective. The context of sports provides a sense of the non-serious that is rarely acknowledged publicly, but is always present. With this in mind, Bonds's attempt to contextualize steroids in the larger context of alcohol was not effective. Additionally, alcohol is not comparable to steroids because it does not help one with job performance. Second, the insistence that the use of performance-enhancing drugs has clouded sports for centuries was an appropriate strategy, but also probably not effective. Twentieth-century pharmacology and technology are much more advanced than that of the nineteenth and eighteenth centuries and the impact of steroids in baseball was tremendous, particularly with homeruns.

Finally, Bonds's attempt at bolstering his image was not effective. Bonds's claims of being a good teammate were probably not believed as that was completely counter to his reputation. The general public's disdain for steroids prompted MLB's players union to agree to a performance-enhancing testing policy. Bonds appropriately supported this policy, but his statements were clouded with his stance that reporters should let the testing program work. This insinuates looking forward, rather than into the past to see who used steroids and how their production changed through performance-enhancing drugs. Viewed from this perspective, Bonds' position could be thought of as self-serving, as Bonds's records during the Steroids Era would be protected.

Overall, I evaluate Bonds's image repair efforts during the "State of the Great Address" as effective. When viewing his discourse through the lens of the anti-hero, the measure of a successful defense changes. Bonds knew he could not achieve a positive reputation through his discourse, but he could preserve his reputation without it being further damaged. Bonds utilized his negative reputation with the media through aggressive and continuous attacks at reporters. To demonstrate the effectiveness of his attacks, neither the titles ("Bonds angrily avoids steroids issue"; "Barry's in midseason form") nor the leads of the *Associated Press* or *San Francisco Chronicle*'s coverage of Bonds's "State of the Great Address" focused on Bonds' presumed innocence or guilt with regard to steroids. The focus of the stories was on his surly demeanor and attacks on reporters, not whether he was guilty of using steroids.

Media Opinion

The March 17, 2005 congressional hearing displayed the strong swing of
media opinion in light of Mark McGwire's "I'm not here to talk about the
past" answer about whether he used steroids. The *Associated Press* polled
155 of the 516 members of the Baseball Writers Association of America
(BBWAA) from March 18 to 23 and found that writers were much more
likely to vote for Bonds than McGwire to be elected to baseball's Hall of
Fame (Blum, 2005). Only 65 voters stated they would vote for McGwire, 58
said no, and 38 were undecided. If these voting percentages stayed consistent
throughout all 516 voters, McGwire would be short almost 20 percent (55.6
percent) of the 75 percent necessary to become inducted into the Hall of
Fame. Contrary to McGwire, 105 voters stated they would induct Bonds into
the Hall, 25 said no, and 25 were undecided. With 80.8 percent of the vote,
Bonds would be elected into the Hall of Fame despite the steroids allegations.

The BBWAA voter poll is particularly illuminating about the media's
relationship with players they believed were steroid users. McGwire, the
gentle giant who co-produced the jovial 1998 summer homerun race that
"saved baseball," could not come close to garnering the votes to get into the
Hall of Fame. Baseball reporters turned on McGwire, abandoning the 1998
hero and making him the prominent face of the Steroids Era in 2005. Additionally, the BBWAA voter poll provided further insight into the voters'
relationship with Bonds. Even though Bonds continued a contentious relationship with the media, they revered his prowess on the field of play, voting
for Bonds constantly, as noted by his seven MVP awards.

IMPLICATIONS

Several implications for image repair efforts can be derived from this analysis. First, the criteria for a successful image repair effort change when viewed
from the perspective of an anti-hero. When the second assumption of the
theory of image restoration is violated, the criteria for evaluating a successful
defense change as well. Bonds's primary defense tactic of attack accuser is
not a particularly useful strategy when trying to repair a previously positive
reputation, but Bonds did not have a positive persona. Bonds successfully
made the coverage of his "State of the Great Address" about his attacks on
reporters and not on his alleged steroid use. Bonds's contentious relationship
was actually an asset to his defense because he only needed to preserve his
negative reputation. The goal for Bonds was to not become the scapegoat of
the Steroids Era, which Mark McGwire became just weeks later at the March
17, 2005 congressional hearing with his infamous "I'm not here to talk about

the past" statement. Had Bonds provided similar ambiguous statements without chiding reporters he, along with McGwire, would have become a face of the Steroids Era. Future image repair research should examine other possible image repair attempts when the second assumption of the theory of image restoration is violated.

Second, the utility of the image repair strategy of transcendence should be examined with regard to the context of sports. When examining Bonds's discourse, his attempt to place steroids in the larger drug context of alcohol was not effective. However, his statements were accurate; alcohol is a legal drug that harms Americans much more than steroids. The ineffectiveness of his statement is due to the trivial nature of sports, which only becomes apparent when compared to other aspects of life. Sports concurrently provide Americans a passion to associate with that becomes part of their communities and identities, but are not allowed to be thought of as "serious." The moment sports are placed into a larger context, the assertion becomes that sports are not that important. Possibly beyond the scope of image repair research, future studies should examine why sports can become such a large part of one's identity, yet not be considered a serious subject matter.

CONCLUSION

This chapter applied the theory of image restoration to Barry Bonds's "State of the Great Address" discourse through the lens of an anti-hero. This analysis revealed that Bonds's defense strategy of attack accuser and denial were effective as they maintained his negative reputation without him becoming a face of the Steroids Era. Unfortunately for Bonds, this would not remain the case. On March 8, 2006, *Sports Illustrated*'s cover story provided an excerpt from *San Francisco Chronicle* reporters Mark Fainaru-Wada and Lance Williams's book *Game of Shadows*, which described, in great detail, Bonds's performance-enhancing drug use. Since the release of *Game of Shadows*, Bonds, along with Roger Clemens and Mark McGwire, has become a face of the Steroids Era. The detailed nature of the book left little doubt in most people's minds that Bonds used steroids, which led to his federal indictment on perjury charges. One might suggest that Bonds would have been better off had he come "clean" at the "State of the Great Address" by admitting his steroid use and utilizing mortification. However, with his negative reputation preceding him, Bonds might not have been forgiven by the public. His "State of the Great Address" performance provided Bonds a year's reprieve from becoming the face of the Steroids Era. Even though *Game of Shadows* provided an insurmountable attack on Bonds's image, his "State of the Great Address" provides a unique image repair instance where Bonds utilized his negative reputation to protect his image from further damage. Sure, the "State of the Great Address" makes Bonds look like a jerk, but that's precisely the point.

NOTES

1. Leaking grand jury testimony is a federal offense and Ellerman was sentenced to two and a half years in prison on July 12, 2007.
2. On April 14, 2011, a 12-person jury found Bonds guilty of obstruction of justice, but U.S. District Judge Susan Illston declared a mistrial on the three perjury charges. The jury voted to acquit Bonds of lying about steroid use (8-4 vote) and HGH use (9-3 vote). The panel voted to convict Bonds of getting an injection from someone other than his doctor, but one juror held out (11-1 vote) where a unanimous vote is required to convict ("Barry Bonds found guilty of obstruction," 2011).
3. Bonds's 2001-2004 production is only rivaled by Babe Ruth's 1920-1923 span in baseball history. Not only did Bonds set the single-season homerun record of 73, but he eclipsed two records that were deemed unsurpassable. Bonds (.609) shattered Ted Williams's (.553) 1941 single-season record for on-base percentage in 2004. Bonds (.863) also passed Babe Ruth's (.847) 1920 single-season record for slugging percentage in 2001.
4. Bonds was instrumental in leading the Giants to the 2002 World Series where he batted .471 with 4 homeruns in 7 games.

REFERENCES

Barry Bonds found guilty of obstruction. (2011, April 14). Retrieved on January 3, 2012 from http://sports.espn.go.com/mlb/news/story?id=6347014.

Barry Bonds statistics. (2008). Retrieved on October 29, 2011, from http://www.baseball-reference.com/b/bondsba01.shtml.

Benoit, W. L. (1997). Hugh Grant's image restoration discourse: An actor apologizes. *Communication Quarterly*, *47*, 251-267.

Blum, R. (2005, March 24). AP exclusive: McGwire falling short, Bonds getting by with Hall voters, AP survey shows. *The Associated Press.*

Bodley, H. (1991, March 5). Hot words fly between Bonds, manager. *USA Today*, p. 1C.

Canseco, J. (2005). *Juiced: Wild times, rampant 'roids, smash hits, and how baseball got big.* New York: HarperCollins.

Coile, Z. (2006, April 15). Poll: Public thinks Bonds cheated. *The San Francisco Chronicle*, p. D1.

Egelko, B. (2007a, February 15). Lawyer admits leaking BALCO testimony; He agrees to plead guilty; prosecutors say they'll drop bid to jail Chronicle reporters. *The San Francisco Chronicle*, p. A1.

Egelko, B. (2007b, July 13). The BALCO case; Judge sends leaker to slammer, chides Bush. *The San Francisco Chronicle*, p. B4.

Fainaru-Wada, M., & Williams, L. (2006).The truth about Barry Bonds and steroids.*Sports Illustrated*, *104*, 38-51.

Georgatos, D. (1996, June 2). Bonds still loves the game—It's the other stuff he can't stand. *The Associated Press.*

Gloster, R. (2001, September 29). Gloster on baseball: America lukewarm as Bonds chases McGwire. *The Associated Press.*

McCauley, J. (2005, February 21). Bonds' arrival at spring training sure to be crazy.*The Associated Press.*

Ratto, R. (2005, February 23). Barry's in midseason form. *The San Francisco Chronicle*, p. D1.

Ryan, B. (1991, March 7). Spoil system creates athletic ingrates the likes of Barry Bonds. *The Boston Globe*, p. 69.

Saltzman, J. (2003, January). The anticelebrity, the media, and the public. *USA Today Magazine, 131*, 35.

Schmaltz, J.(2003, June). The king of swing: What fuels baseball super hitter Barry Bonds? *Muscle & Fitness*.

Schulman, H. (2005, March 5). Barry mania; Bonds says there are far worse things than steroids, such as cocaine and heroin. *The San Francisco Chronicle*, p. D1.

Simmons, D. (2008). The anti-hero in the American novel: From Joseph Heller to Kurt Vonnegut. New York: Palgrave MacMillan.

Smith, C. (1991, March 6). Baseball; Bonds says he's puzzled by bad-guy image. *The New York Times*, p. D23.

Sports News. (1991, March 17). The Associated Press.

Swartz, J. (2011, March 23). Bonds' trainer remains silent. *USA Today*, p. 1C.

Transcript of Barry Bonds' training camp news conference. (2005, February 23). Retrieved on April 25, 2009 from http://www.sfgate.com/cgi- bin/article.cgi?file=/c/a/2005/02/23/TRANSCRIPT.TMP

Williams, L., & Fainaru-Wada, M. (2004, December 3). What Bonds told BALCO grand jury. *The San Francisco Chronicle*, p. A1.

Chapter Four

The Image Repair Media Interview as *Apologia* and *Antapologia*: Marion Jones on the *Oprah Winfrey Show*

Michael R. Kramer, Saint Mary's College

After years of denying doping allegations, 2000 Olympic gold medalist Marion Jones admitted using steroids while training for the summer games. She pled guilty to lying to federal investigators about her steroid use and received a six-month prison sentence. Like many professional athletes caught in misconduct, Jones attempted to repair her image through public discourse. Prior to her incarceration, the runner appeared on the *Oprah Winfrey Show* to discuss the scandal. This essay will analyze both Jones's primary image repair strategies and Winfrey's responses (*antapologia*) to Jones's self-defense. I argue that the interview format facilitated Winfrey's *immediate antapologia*, which undermined and impacted the substance of Jones's image repair effort. The analysis then discusses the implications for athletes using image repair media interviews.

> Seemingly blessed with super human talent, Marion Jones looked like she had it all, poise, beauty, and a smile that could light up the stands. But for the fastest woman in the world, the fall has been slow and painful . . .

With these words, talk show host Oprah Winfrey introduced track star Marion Jones as a guest on her January 16, 2008, program. What precipitated Jones's "fall" is all too familiar in the sports world of the twenty-first century. The world-famous runner, winner of three gold and two bronze medals at the 2000 Summer Olympics, used steroids and would be going to prison for lying about it to federal agents. During the past five years, a steady stream of athletes, many at the highest level in their respective sports, have faced allegations regarding steroids, performance-enhancing substances, or other drugs. Doping scandals have generated, and will continue to generate, a significant amount of image repair discourse in professional and Olympic sports.

This essay will analyze the image repair strategies used by Marion Jones during her pre-incarceration appearance on the *Oprah Winfrey Show*. Applying Benoit's (1995) work on image repair, I demonstrate how Jones employs multiple strategies, primarily bolstering, differentiation, and transcendence. In the next section, Winfrey's reactions, in which she actively undermines the image repair effort of her guest, are examined. I argue that Winfrey engages in *immediate antapologia*. Kevin A. Stein (2008) argues that *antapologia*, a response to image repair discourse, "has been virtually ignored by researchers" (p. 20). This chapter helps fill that gap in the research. Moreover, commentators have lamented the dearth of apologia and image repair scholarship involving women. This analysis also addresses that need.

The first section of this essay provides some background information on the Jones doping scandal. Next, I discuss two pieces of scholarly literature that form the analytical foundation for my essay. In the analysis section, image repair and *antapologia* concepts are applied to the Winfrey-Jones interview and I demonstrate how Winfrey's *immediate antapologia* simultaneously undermines and influences the substance of Jones's image repair effort. The conclusion discusses the implications of the study and suggests avenues for further research.

BACKGROUND ON THE SCANDAL

After winning five medals (three gold and two bronze), track star Marion Jones became known as "America's darling at the 2000 Summer Olympics" and, to many, "the greatest female athlete in the world" (Shipley, 2007). However, unknown to her legions of admirers, Jones, while training for the Sydney games, used the anabolic steroid tetrahydrogestrinone (more commonly known as THG or "the clear"). Federal agents opened an investigation of the Bay Area Laboratory Co-operative (BALCO), a nutritional supplements company associated with providing athletes with "the clear." In 2003, when investigators questioned Jones about her ties to BALCO, she knowingly lied about both her previous steroid use and her connection to an unrelated bank fraud case (Shipley 2007). The International Olympic Committee initiated a probe in December 2004 into whether Jones had used steroids. Throughout this period, the speedster "publicly insisted she never used performance-enhancing drugs" (Schmidt & Wilson, 2008).

The charade ended on October 5, 2007, when Marion Jones appeared in U.S. District Court to plead guilty to lying to federal agents about her steroid use and involvement in the bank fraud case. As a result, she surrendered her Olympic medals. On January 11, 2008, a federal judge sentenced Jones to a six-month prison term, two years of probation, and 400 hours of community service. In his sentencing remarks, the judge "was not convinced that [Jones] had come clean about her knowledge of the drugs that she was taking" (Schmidt & Wilson, 2008).

Five days after her sentencing, the athlete appeared on the *Oprah Winfrey Show*. The appearance was promoted as an "exclusive" since it was Jones's first interview since her sentencing. In addition to being watched by Winfrey's vast audience, the interview garnered extensive media coverage. In light of her prior admission of guilt, her pending imprisonment, and the sentencing judge's public skepticism about Jones's candor, the interview occurred at a time when Jones's public image had plummeted. Jones would be imprisoned soon, and the interview represented her best chance for achieving high-profile image repair before incarceration.

METHOD

This analysis will use William L. Benoit's image repair strategies as described earlier in the volume. Also, it is worth noting that image repair discourse found in media interviews has received scant scholarly attention. In one study, Benoit (2006) critiqued President George W. Bush's performance during a February 2004 interview with Tim Russert on NBC's *Meet the Press*. Benoit argues that media interviews, like the ones in which Bush and Marion Jones participated, are perilous venues for image repair rhetoric. Unlike apologia delivered as a public speech, the accused cedes control over critical aspects of an interview. Benoit explains the risks in the context of the Bush-Russert exchange:

> Tim Russert could ask about topics the president would rather avoid; he could phrase questions in ways that are less favorable to Bush; and he could use follow-up questions to press if the president appeared to be evading the issue. (p. 291)

Benoit concludes that image repair discourse offered during a media interview was "quite different from and more risky than the more traditional image repair speech" (p. 291). This essay aims to build on Benoit's claim and address some of the differences and risks faced by the accused interviewee.

My analysis of the Jones-Winfrey interview also draws on and extends Kevin A. Stein's concept of *antapologia*. Building on Halford Ross Ryan's work on *kategoria* (accusation) and *apologia* (self-defense), Stein (2008) argues that image repair scholars should study *antapologia*, or responses to *apologia*. Stein offers a useful distinction between *antapologia* and *kategoria*:

> What distinguishes *antapologia* from simply a follow-up instance of *kategoria* is the fact that the former is designed to be a response to the apologetic discourse and the latter is designed to be a response to the initial harmful act perpetrated by the accused. When the discourse addresses the account of the act, it constitutes an instance of *antapologia*. (pp. 19-20)

Through an analysis of the Soviet Union's *antapologia* in response to U.S. self-defense discourse in the wake of the U-2 incident, the author identifies eight *antapologia* strategies aimed at either strengthening the original accusation or weakening the initial *apologia*. These strategies are: (1) identifying concessions in the apologia, (2) refining the attack based on the apologia, (3) portions of the apologia are false, (4) the accused has contradicted previous apologia strategies, (5) apologia does not take responsibility, (6) apologia reflects character flaws of the accused, (7) defense against attacks made in the apologia, and (8) harm will come from the apologia itself (p. 23). Stein concludes that the Soviet response to the U.S. *apologia* was persuasive to Soviet citizens.

The concept of *antapologia* offers additional utility when studying image repair media interviews. As Benoit (2006) noted, such self-defense efforts present unique risks to the accused. Those risks emerge from the opportunity of the interviewer to respond, not just to the original accusation but to the *apologia* discourse as well. The media interviewer often has the ability and incentive to engage in *antapologia* and, therefore, self-defense media interviews could be analyzed using Stein's framework. However, temporality becomes a more prominent factor in the interview scenario. In Stein's U-2 case study, the Soviet *antapologia* discourse responding to U.S. explanations for the spy plane emerged over the course of several weeks. During a one-on-one, freewheeling question-and-answer session, the interviewer's *antapologia* can be immediate. The accused has no idea whether or when the interviewer will respond directly to a particular element of the image repair effort. A response can come with no warning, and the interviewee has little to no time to prepare a counter-response to rehabilitate the self-defense. These temporal challenges have the potential to wreak havoc on the execution and overall effectiveness of the accused's *apologia*, as demonstrated in the next section.

ANALYSIS

I will analyze Oprah Winfrey's interview with Marion Jones first as an artifact of image repair. Then Winfrey's responses will be studied as an example of *immediate antapologia*. All page references are to the official interview transcript obtained from the *Oprah Winfrey Show*.

Jones's Use of Image Repair Strategies

During her interview with Oprah Winfrey, Marion Jones presents numerous image repair strategies. The following section identifies and analyzes three key strategies: bolstering, differentiation, and transcendence.

Bolstering

Jones engages in multiple instances of bolstering by attempting to connect herself to positive attributes and associations. First, she portrays herself as a concerned and loving mother who strives to teach her children moral conduct. When Winfrey asks whether Jones had informed her children about her upcoming incarceration, the athlete responds in the negative and explains:

> We're talking about a 4-year-old who was upset this morning that I couldn't drop him off at school, you know? It's—so it is gonna be challenging. He loves mommy. But we teach our kids that to do the right thing and that when they make mistakes, you know, they're to step up to the plate, tell mommy and daddy what you did and let's move forward. (p. 3)

In her answer, Jones conveys that not only is she a loving mother, but also a *loved* mother by her young son. The desire to shield him from the harsh reality of her jail term would be viewed positively by many viewers. This passage goes further in its bolstering effect, however. Here, Jones is not a detached celebrity who delegates child care to a live-in nanny; she is a sensitive, active, hands-on parent who participates in her children's daily lives and moral education.

Marion Jones also offers herself to the public as a religious person who believes in and relies upon God during times of challenge. The interview is peppered with seven religious references, including direct references to God, prayers, and being "blessed." For example, her first response states that ". . . prayers have really allowed me to get through [the scandal] and to be strong" (p. 2) and she ends the interview with optimism in her faith, believing that ". . . with the grace of God, we'll get through it and come out even better at the other end" (p. 6). While her faith strengthens her, it also motivates Jones to perform positive actions following her jail term as a way to repay God for her good fortune. At one point, she informs Winfrey, "once I'm able to return

home that, you know, I can use what God has given me, you know, to help
people. I have been blessed with so much . . ." (p. 4). Jones offers no details
as to what form this future service may take and more specifics would fortify
the strategy. Nevertheless, she acknowledges both a gift and a debt to God
that reinforces an impression of Jones as a true woman of faith.

Jones's religious bolstering is less persuasive at other times during the
interview. When Winfrey presses her about when she decided to admit her
drug use, Jones explains:

> I have been blessed with a super amount of talent, but I cannot go on anymore
> with this baggage, lying to the world, lying to God. And, you know, I realize
> that, I realize that, you know, people might not forgive me, but God forgives.
> (p. 4)

Jones credits God for her athletic ability while seeking his forgiveness. Such
expressions of thankfulness and contrition can be effective for an accused.
However, in this passage, Jones undermines the bolstering effort in two
ways. First, her description of her athletic skills is rather immodest and may
be disagreeable to the audience. Second, Jones's admission of "lying to God"
could strike some as odd in the sense that someone who truly believed in an
all-knowing God would realize that such deception was impossible.

A third strain of bolstering defense can be found in Jones's attempts to
present herself as a respectful person deferential to the popular Winfrey. In
her first response, she attempts to establish this tone: "I just, first of all,
wanna thank you, Oprah, for allowing me this opportunity to briefly share
with the people who have supported me and who have loved me throughout
all of this" (p. 2). Although Winfrey is benefiting from booking the exclusive
interview with Jones, the athlete thanks the host for "allowing" her to appear
on the program. Also, Jones expects to be allotted only enough time to
"briefly" address the audience. She does not present herself as a celebrity
who graciously accepted an invitation to come to Winfrey's studio and regale
the audience with lengthy tales of athletic success. Rather, Winfrey is "giving" Jones an "opportunity" to speak (p. 2). Finally, in several instances,
Jones refers to her interviewer as "ma'am." Jones's bolstering strategies had
potential. If she succeeds in persuading the audience that she is a devout,
humble mother, the public should view her more favorably.

Differentiation

Jones engages, at least implicitly, in the image repair strategy of differentiation, the favorable comparison of the accused's conduct to more offensive
behavior. At different points during the interview, the speedster characterized
her actions as a "mistake" rather than intentional deception or illegality. In
fact, early in the interview, Jones expresses no regrets for pleading guilty and

"admitting to the world that I lied, Oprah, that I've made mistakes" (p. 2). That passage is the *only* instance in the entire dialogue where she explicitly acknowledged that she had lied. However, Jones immediately pivots to the less damning admission that she's "made mistakes." She never addresses specifically or explains her use of steroids. After introducing her differentiation strategy, Jones, in the very next comment, underscores the importance she places on this aspect of her image repair. She justifies her appearance by stating ". . . that is the *main reason* [italics added] I agreed to even speak today. And I want people to understand that, you know, everybody makes mistakes" (p. 2). This strategy is then maintained as Jones equates misconduct with "mistake" six separate times throughout the conversation. The argument that "everyone makes mistakes" is hardly novel, but, if conveyed convincingly, can resonate with most audience members. This framing also sets the stage for her use of transcendence.

Transcendence

In transcendence, the accused justifies transgressions by drawing the audience's attention to more important values. Jones engages in transcendence as an extension of her differentiation strategy discussed above. The critical aspect of the scandal, from her perspective, is the transgressor's ability and willingness to move from denial to admission and then to share with others the wisdom that comes from that journey. She explains this point to Winfrey:

> I truly think that a person's character is determined by their admission of their mistakes and then, beyond that, what do I do about it, you know? How can I change the lives of people? How can I use my story to change the lives of a young person? And to me, now, it's really about looking forward, looking to the future. (p. 2)

Here, Jones posits that lying to federal investigators is not the most important component of her situation, or of her character. One's character cannot be defined by a single act but is rather a process of mistake, admission, mentoring. Clearly, in her mind, the final two steps of that process should be the focus of Winfrey and the audience judging her. In particular, the idea of the accused as a youth mentor is most transcendent in that process as Jones spends most of the above passage "looking to the future" rather than explaining her drug use and deception. In fact, Jones explicitly affirms that what the appearance is "really about" is her "story," her journey toward making future societal contributions and ultimately achieving redemption. The plan probably sounds commendable to many viewers in that people generally want criminals to learn from and do something positive in response to their behavior. Such transcendence is an appealing strategy because it puts the accused in a positive light and shifts the audience's attention away from the present misconduct and toward an unknowable and malleable future.

Winfrey's Discourse as Antapologia

Oprah Winfrey was hardly a sympathetic ear during her exchange with Jones. The talk show host challenged the athlete and expressed skepticism about many of her comments. In so doing, Winfrey engaged in *immediate antapologia* for all three of Jones's primary image repair strategies.

Response to Bolstering Strategy

As discussed above, one of Jones's most pervasive bolstering strategies involved religious references regarding God's forgiveness, her God-given talents, and the importance of prayer. These types of statements are common in athlete-media discourse and often are not addressed by the interviewer at all. Winfrey, however, does not take this usual tack. After Jones notes how "blessed" she is, Winfrey interrupts her, asking, "But have you always been a believer in God, 'cause it always gets me when people are in trouble and they just find God. Did you just find God, or have you always been a believer in God?" (p. 5). This statement is potentially devastating to Jones's image repair. First, a highly regarded media personality and trusted cultural icon is, in effect, casting doubt upon Jones's faith by suggesting that she only recently became a believer in God. In addition, the alleged recent conversion emerged not from a genuine spiritual awakening but rather, Winfrey implied, as a rhetorical strategy. As a result, Jones is compelled to address explicitly her faith history *after* she had already used several religious references. She responds, "I've always believed in God, but everybody strays . . ." (p. 5). This refutation seems oddly underdeveloped considering the critical point at issue. The weak response suggests that Jones did not anticipate Winfrey's use of *antapologia* regarding her religious beliefs.

This *antapologia* strategy falls somewhere in between Stein's "portions of the *apologia* are false" and "*apologia* reflects character flaws" strategies. This finding also supports the utility of adding to Stein's typology an additional strategy called "the *apologia* is disingenuous/cynical" in order to deal more precisely with this type of situation. This textual analysis provides evidence of the effectiveness of Winfrey's strategy in undermining Jones's image repair. Of the nine total religious references employed by the athlete during the interview, seven occurred *before* Winfrey's challenge. The instances of religious bolstering decreased significantly after the *antapologia*.

As discussed above, Jones, in framing the event and addressing her host, seeks to associate herself with the positive qualities of respect and deference. The runner addresses Winfrey as "ma'am," until the latter puts an end to it during the following exchange:

> WINFREY: You knew you were lying, right?
> JONES: Yes, ma'am.
> WINFREY: Yeah. You don't have to call me ma'am, Marion. Really, it's okay. It's okay. I know I'm getting old but okay. You call me, ma'am. I'm gonna call you ma'am back, okay?
> JONES: Okay. All right. (p. 3)

Here, the host appears non-receptive to Jones's attempts at deference and, in fact, responds, albeit humorously, in a manner that conveys to the audience the impression that Jones is not being deferential, but rather is drawing attention to Winfrey's age. Later in the interview, when Jones lets slip another "ma'am," Winfrey does not let it pass unnoticed, and she makes good on her prior warning:

> WINFREY: Did you just find God, or have you always been a believer in God?
> JONES: No, ma'am.
> WINFREY: Okay. Okay, ma'am.
> JONES: I've always—sorry, Oprah.
> WINFREY: Okay. (p. 5)

The running joke continues until the very end of the segment when Winfrey refers to Jones as "ma'am" and the latter replies with "Have a good afternoon, ma'am" (p. 6). In these exchanges, Jones's attempts to win favor with Winfrey and her audience through respectful language are first challenged by the host and ultimately trivialized as comic banter.

Response to Differentiation Strategy

Jones uses differentiation when she repeatedly characterizes her misconduct as a "mistake" rather than a legal, ethical, or moral violation. In the middle of the interview, when Jones is engaged in the bolstering strategy of associating herself with moral parenting, Winfrey interrupts and turns her attention back to the differentiation strategy so that the host can offer the following *antapologia*:

> Yeah, this is the thing, I know we have a short amount of time so I wanna just be able to get a few questions in here. You were saying that, obviously, we all make mistakes and there isn't a person watching you who hasn't made some in

their own lives. When you see yourself on that tape and saying and denying
adamantly that you were not using drugs, what were you thinking at the time,
because you knew at that—at that time, you knew you were lying, right? (p. 3)

First, Winfrey's initial tone suggests that Jones is not answering the host's
questions as directly as she would like, reinforcing an overall skepticism that
undermines the athlete's self-defense efforts. Second, although she acknowledges Jones's point that mistakes are a common human experience, Winfrey
labels the argument "obvious" and implies that it adds little new to the
discussion of the scandal. Finally, Winfrey pivots away from "mistakes" and
refocuses the characterization of Jones's initial misconduct as illegal and
unethical ("using drugs") and her deception as intentional ("denying adamantly," "you knew you were lying"). Both of these characterizations are
generally viewed much more negatively than simply making a mistake, and
Winfrey seems intent on challenging and weakening her guest's differentiation argument. Winfrey's *antapologia* here has elements of Stein's "apologia
does not take responsibility" and "apologia reflects character flaws of the
accused," but also suggests the additional strategy of "the apologia is eva-
sive/incomplete."

As with her use of religious references as bolstering, Jones reduces her
reliance on the misconduct-as-mistake differentiation *after* Winfrey provides
the above response. Of the six total "mistake" references, only two occurred
after Winfrey confronts her on the issue. Therefore, the interviewer's ability
to engage in *immediate antapologia* appears to have altered the trajectory of
the image repair effort.

Response to Transcendence Strategy

Expanding on her differentiation defense, Jones argues that admitting her
"mistake" and using her experience someday to help others is the most important aspect of the scandal, more important than her drug use, cheating, and
lying. In doing so, the track star employed the strategy of transcendence.
Jones introduces this strategy early in the interview when she reveals her
intent to use her "story" to "change the lives of a young person" (p. 2). That
statement leads to the following exchange:

JONES: And to me, now, it's really about looking forward, looking to the
future. How can I make this wrong a right?
WINFREY: Well, the future right now looks like you're gonna be going to jail
and . . .
JONES: That's the immediate future. (p. 2)

While Jones wants to keep the audience focused on an ambiguous future that makes her story of redemption an inevitability, Winfrey deflates the move from the outset. The only future she is concerned about is the very concrete prospect of incarceration that awaits the athlete. This blunt retort characterizes Jones not as a misunderstood celebrity destined for absolution, but as, simply put, a criminal. Coming from a public figure as esteemed as Oprah Winfrey, the remark is devastating to Jones's image repair. Jones tries to respond by relegating her prison term to the "immediate future" but the damage is done. Although later in the speech she does make two references to trying "to help people" (p. 4) upon her release from prison, Jones no longer emphasized that goal as the most critical element of her misconduct. It was no longer transcendent. Also, the host never asked for specific details of Jones's future redemptive activities, notwithstanding potential audience interest in such follow-up. Through this *immediate antapologia*, which also falls under the strategy of "the apologia is evasive/incomplete," Winfrey effectively undermines the accused's transcendence strategy. The conclusion will discuss the implications of the above analysis.

CONCLUSION

This essay supports Stein's argument that image repair and apologia criticism can be studied usefully as a three-component speech set of *kategoria, apologia,* and *antapologia* and that "*antapologia* is an important feature of the apologetic situation" (Stein, 2008, p. 19). The examination of the Oprah Winfrey-Marion Jones interview demonstrates how the concept of *antapologia* can be particularly salient when studying image repair in the context of a media interview. The temporal proximity of self-defense to response in a question-and-answer session strengthens the fusion of *apologia* and *antapologia* as an image repair speech set. The possibility of what is called here *immediate antapologia* creates both risks and opportunities for interviewers and interviewees alike.

   In the Winfrey-Jones exchange, Jones selects potentially helpful image repair strategies, primarily bolstering, differentiation, and transcendence, but her execution of the strategies often comes across as inconsistent or underdeveloped. In addition, Winfrey's reactions articulated and criticized the flaws of the image repair effort with an immediacy not possible when self-defense is presented as a unilateral public statement. Moreover, Winfrey's *immediate antapologia* appears to have affected the substance of the image repair itself, as Jones reduces her reliance upon the very strategies that Winfrey challenges. This finding further supports Stein's inclusion of *antapologia* as a third component in the self-defense speech set. Further study of media interviews is needed to increase our understanding of the role of *immediate antapologia* in image repair and to expand on Stein's typology of *antapologia* strategies, such as the strategies of "the apologia is disingenuous/cynical" and "the apologia is evasive/incomplete" found in the above analysis. Such research provides guidance for both the invention and criticism of image repair discourse.

Increasing our understanding of image repair media interviews is particularly important in the context of sports scandals. Some traditional elements of sports and sports journalism make the image repair interview attractive to the accused athlete. Interviews offer the opportunity for a "one-on-one performance" that may appeal to an athlete's competitive instincts. Also, athletes may favor the interview, a familiar and comfortable staple of sports coverage, over a traditional public speech. Third, they often encounter deference and sycophancy in their dealings with sports journalists who covet access to prized players. Therefore, the star quarterback, pitcher, or point guard may sit down for an interview expecting little scrutiny or challenge in terms of their image repair strategies. As seen in this analysis, exploring the interplay between image repair, athletes, and sports journalism can generate valuable insights and strategies for image-conscious athletes and a watchdog media.

REFERENCES

Benoit, W. (2006). President Bush's image repair effort on *Meet the Press*: The complexities of defeasibility. *Journal of Applied Communication Research, 34*(3), 285-306.

Exclusive: Marion Jones' first interview. (2008, January 16). The *Oprah Winfrey Show* [Transcript].

Schmidt, M. & Wilson, D. (2008, January 12). Marion Jones sentenced to six months in prison. *New York Times*. Retrieved May 20, 2010, from http://www.nytimes.com.

Shipley, A. (2007, October 5). Marion Jones admits to steroid use. *Washington Post*. Retrieved May 20, 2010, from http://www.washingtonpost.com.

Stein, K. (2008). *Apologia, Antapologia*, and the 1960 Soviet U-2 incident. *Communication Studies, 59*(1), 19-34.

Chapter Five

The Michael Phelps Saga: From Successful Olympian, to Pot Smoker Caught on Camera, to Renewed Role Model and Brand

Rod L. Troester and Lindsay Johns, Penn State University Erie, The Behrend College

ABSTRACT

The career of twenty-two-time Olympic medalist Michael Phelps presents an interesting case study in how a successful athlete can go from amazing achievements in the pool, through an embarrassing online posting of alleged illegal behavior, to recovering professional and commercial opportunities. In the 2004 and 2008 Olympic Games, Phelps was one of the stars in the pool. Then, in February 2009, a photo published online showed Phelps apparently smoking marijuana. The hero of the Olympic pool was then the embarrassed "bad-boy" engaging in illegal activities. This case study will trace the development of Phelps's career, seeking support for the premise that image repair can best be accomplished when the "accused" actively seeks to manage the fallout from an embarrassing incident with honesty and openness. The theoretical approaches of Burke and Benoit inform this analysis. Adding to these perspectives is what we refer to as the "band-aid approach," suggesting that not only is the content of image management strategies important, but also the timeliness of response to threats to image and reputation. Michael Phelps's situation is contrasted with that of Tiger Woods to illustrate the importance of such a timely response. These analyses are placed in the context of our twenty-first century, 24/7, technologically driven media and news cycle, as well as the lessons to be learned from these two cases.

INTRODUCTION: THE IMPORTANCE OF IMAGE AND REPUTATION

Image, identity, and reputation are important to everyone. We all see ourselves in a certain way, we generally care what others think of us, and we try to shape and protect our reputations as an integral part of who we are and how we function in society. Communication scholars have long known that image, identity, and reputation are, in large part, shaped by those around us—how others react to what we do and what we say. As Benoit (1997) observes, "Image is the perception of a person (or group, or organization) held by the audience, shaped by the words and actions of that person, as well as by the discourse and behavior of other relevant actors" (p. 251). All this is true for people in general, but it is even more significant for those in the public spotlight including celebrities, entertainers, politicians, and sports figures. This essay examines the plight of one such public figure, Michael Phelps, whose sports accomplishments made him a household name, a role model to thousands of young people, as well as a valuable commercial brand sought after for product endorsements. Specifically, this essay will explore the increasingly important role that sports play in American culture and society, the saga of a young athlete whose triumphs in Olympic competition were nearly overshadowed by what could be called a "youthful indiscretion," and how the communication strategies employed were instrumental in recovering his reputation and salvaging lucrative commercial endorsements.

THE IMPORTANCE OF SPORTS IN AMERICAN SOCIETY—AND THE OLYMPICS IN PARTICULAR

Amateur and professional sports are woven into the fabric of American life. Starting in elementary school, through high school, into college sports, and leading into the professional ranks, we are a nation that values and encourages sports competition for all ages. We spend millions of dollars in support of our favorite sports as participants and/or spectators, and we admire and respect those who rise to the top of their respective games. Additionally, those who reach the top of their games can "cash in" on their success through product endorsements and sponsorships.

Every four years the world's best athletes gather for the summer and winter Olympic Games, respectively, to determine who are the very best at their respective sports. The Olympic Games and Olympic athletes have become popular spectator events and valuable commercial properties. For example, the 2008 Olympic Games earned an estimated 146 million dollars in profit (Lei, 2009).

The 2004 and 2008 Summer Olympic Games in Athens and Beijing were both popular with spectators and profitable for athletes. A 2008 *USA Today/Gallup* poll (Jones, 2008) found that 56 percent of Americans planned to watch a great deal or fair amount of the media coverage, and for 27 percent of the respondents, swimming was named as their favorite sport in the games. At both the 2004 and 2008 Olympic Games, swimming became a focus of attention as Michael Phelps broke records and achieved unprecedented medal success.

Michael Phelps can easily be considered one of the world's best athletes. The whole world watched as he broke the record for most gold medals won in a single Olympic games in 2008. The Olympics were not a new venue for Phelps. He competed in his first Olympic Games in 2000 as the youngest American male swimmer in sixty-eight years. While he did not medal in his 2000 Olympic debut, he quickly became an "up and comer" in the competitive swimming community. In the 2004 Olympic Games Phelps tied the record for most medals won in a single Olympic games. After his record in the 2004 Olympic Games, Phelps cemented himself as a world class athlete and role model for young children by winning a record eight gold medals at the 2008 Beijing Games. He was selected as the U.S. Olympic Committee's sportsman of the year and the Associated Press's male athlete of the year.

THE INCIDENT AND THE AFTERMATH

Against the backdrop of this unprecedented success, Phelps's career and brand were nearly destroyed by the publication of a controversial photograph. The weekly British tabloid *News of the World* (owned by Rupert Murdoch's News Corp) published a photo of someone who appeared to be Michael Phelps smoking from a glass bong pipe on February 1, 2009. *News of the World* published the photo under the headline "What a Dope." (The story and photo can be accessed at: http://www.newsoftheworld.co.uk/news/150832/14-times-Olympic-gold-medal-winner-Michael-Phelps-caught-with-bong-cannabis-pipe.html.) The photograph was reportedly taken with a cell phone camera during an off-campus party near the University of South Carolina sometime around Thanksgiving 2008. How the photo made it into the hands of the British tabloid is unclear. An unnamed witness to the event is quoted by the tabloid as saying, "He (Phelps) was out of control from the moment he got there (the party). If he continues to party like that I'd be amazed if he ever won any more medals again" (Dickinson, 2009). Georgina Dickinson (2009), who authored the article, claims "Phelps' aides went into a panic over the story and offered us a raft of extraordinary incentives not to run the picture."

Given the tabloid nature of the publication, the veracity of the claims, quotes, and overall story may be suspect. However, in an era of 24/7 news cycles and instantaneous Internet access to incredible amounts of information, it is not surprising that the picture and story spread quickly beyond the tabloid press to the mainstream media including prominent newspapers and nightly network and cable newscasts. If we assume, as the tabloid alleges, that they told Phelps in advance of their intention to publish the picture, Phelps and his representatives had time to reflect, decide, and plan how best to react to the publication of the photo. This effort was reportedly coordinated through the marketing and sports management company Octagon, which is a subsidiary the Interpublic Group of Companies—one of the largest global advertising holding companies (see Octagon.com).

On Sunday February 1, 2009—the same day the photo was published—Phelps released a short apology statement through Octagon. In the statement Phelps stated:

> I engaged in behavior which was regrettable and demonstrated bad judgment. I'm 23-years-old, and despite the successes I have had in the pool, I acted in a youthful and inappropriate way, not in a manner that people have come to expect from me. For this, I am sorry. I promise my fans and the public—it will not happen again. (Shipley, 2009)

This statement, along with the photo, was carried by numerous media outlets—including *News of the World.*

It is worth noting that this incident is not Phelps's first encounter with having to explain a "youthful indiscretion." In 2004, Phelps pled guilty to drunk driving and served eighteen months probation. Following that incident Phelps reportedly said, "Getting into a car after anything to drink is wrong. It's dangerous and unacceptable" ("Other Driver Caused," 2009).

THE FALLOUT, SPONSOR REACTIONS, AND PREDICTIONS OF PHELPS'S DEMISE

In the days that followed the incident there were many differing opinions on how Phelps's sponsors would react. Given his success in the 2008 Olympic Games, he had reached a whole new level of role model status and commercial potential. Understandably, his sponsors would be hesitant to come out in support of him because marijuana is, after all, illegal. However, many experts commented on the situation. For example, Bob Dorfman of Baker Street Advertising is quoted as saying, "I think consumers and marketers will cut him some slack because it's 'only' marijuana, something that it seems like other professional athletes get arrested for every five minutes—not that that condones it" (Michaelis, 2009). Bill Mallon, an Olympic historian, had a somewhat different view. "He probably will take some hits with this. Corporations, sponsors, a lot of those put behavior clauses in contracts. . . . Our president smoked it. Clinton smoked it. It's not the worst drug in the world" (Shipley, 2009).

Speedo, Omega, and Subway were just a few of the sponsors that made statements in support of Phelps. Speedo's announcement stated that Phelps was "a valued member of the Speedo team and a great champion" (Vranica & Steele, 2009). Omega, the Swiss watch company, said in a statement, "The current story in the press involves Michael Phelps' private life and is, as far as Omega is concerned, a nonissue" (Harris, 2009). Subway's declaration said, "Like most Americans, and Michael Phelps himself, we were disappointed in his behavior. Also like most Americans we strongly accept his apology. Moving forward, he remains in our plans" (York, 2009). Not all sponsors were so understanding and accommodating. Kellogg's was the only company to not retain Michael Phelps as a sponsor, hesitant to have "the Phelps image" on cereal boxes targeted at young children. Phelps's contract with Kellogg's was set to expire at the end of February 2009. The company decided not to renew the contract because the photo was "not consistent with the image of Kellogg's" (Snead, 2009; "Michael Phelps' contract"; Bryson-York, 2009a).

Importantly, Phelps did not break anti-doping rules because he was not using the substance during the time of competition, and therefore he did not receive any sanction from anti-doping authorities in the swimming world. The U.S. Olympic Committee came out with a statement that said:

> We are disappointed in the behavior recently exhibited by Michael Phelps. Michael is a role model, and he is well aware of the responsibilities and accountability that come with setting a positive example for others, particularly young people. In this instance, regrettably, he failed to fulfill those responsibilities. Michael has acknowledged that he made a mistake and apologized for his actions. We are confident that going forward, Michael will consistently set the type of example we all expect from a great Olympic champion. (Shipley, 2009)

While the U.S. Olympic Committee was willing to work with Phelps to avoid a repeat incident, the USA Swimming Organization was looking to send a stronger message. They suspended Phelps for three months and also withdrew financial support during his suspension. "We decided to send a strong message to Michael because he disappointed so many people, particularly the hundreds of thousands of USA Swimming member kids who look up to him as role model and hero," said the USA Swimming Organization (Macur, 2009).

While the Michael Phelps brand did have some serious obstacles to overcome, he landed a new sponsor just four months after the release of the photo. H2O Audio announced in June 2009 that they were planning to use Phelps in a summer ad campaign. The H2O Audio Company has a line of waterproof headphones and accessories (McCarthy, 2009).

In the aftermath of the publication of the photo, the statement released by Phelps along with comments from analysts and commentators sought to salvage, repair, and begin to rebuild the image and reputation of Michael Phelps the Olympian, and Michael Phelps the brand. The strategies used, whether intentional or not on the part of Phelps, illustrate the successful use of image management strategies.

METHODS: THREE ANALYSES OF THE RHETORICAL STRATEGIES USED BY PHELPS

Considerable research by communication scholars and others informs the process of image management and reputation repair, recovery, and restoration. Kenneth Burke's approach to image restoration discourse provides two broad strategies. Another prominent body of research is the work of William Benoit in his 1995 book *Accounts, Excuses, and Apologies: A Theory of Image Restoration Strategies*. A final means of analysis, the band-aid approach, suggests a focus on taking either a proactive or reactive approach to image restoration emphasizing the immediacy of response in addition to the content of response. Each of these will be used as methodologies for the analysis of the discourse used by Michael Phelps in his attempts to manage and recover his image and reputation.

Here is the statement made by Phelps that will be used for analysis:

> I engaged in behavior which was regrettable and demonstrated bad judgment. I'm 23-years-old, and despite the successes I have had in the pool, I acted in a youthful and inappropriate way, not in a manner that people have come to expect from me. For this, I am sorry. I promise my fans and the public—it will not happen again (Shipley, 2009).

Burke

Kenneth Burke's idea of the Rhetoric of Rebirth involves three steps: pollution, purification and redemption (Foss, Foss, & Trapp, 1985). Pollution is the original state of being guilty. Purification is the action taken in cleansing the guilty party. Redemption is the new state or reputation that is achieved after the first two steps are completed.

In the first step, pollution, there is an action that results in guilt. "Guilt, is Burke's term for original sin, an offense that cannot be avoided or a condition in which all people share" (Foss, Foss, & Trapp, 1985, p. 178). Burke says that guilt arises in the environment of hierarchy that is embedded in our language system. In these various hierarchies that are created through language there are hundreds of "thou shalt nots" and no one is capable of following them all. When a person violates one of these rules they feel a sense of guilt (Foss, Foss, & Trapp, 1985).

Michael Phelps is higher up in the social hierarchy system than your average person because of his celebrity status. When a photograph of him smoking out of a water bong was published, he felt guilty and perhaps the public perceived him to be guilty. Smoking marijuana is illegal and therefore no matter where a person is on the hierarchical scale, they are subject to punishment. This led to the next step in the process of the Rhetoric of Rebirth.

The second step, purification, requires some reaction to be taken to cleanse the person of the guilt resulting from the pollution. The guilty party can take two "paths" toward purification: victimage, which is shifting the blame onto someone else, and mortification, which is admitting the offense and asking for forgiveness (Foss, Foss, & Trapp, 1985). Victimage consists of reassigning the blame onto a "vessel" other than the person who was originally charged. This person then becomes the victim. If this approach is successful, as the rhetor shifts the blame to the victim, the rhetor's reputation is cleansed. Mortification involves self-sacrifice and an admission of wrongdoing, a sincere apology, and asking for forgiveness which can purge the offender's guilt and restore his/her image (Foss, Foss, & Trapp, 1985).

In the case of Michael Phelps, he followed the mortification strategy. He almost immediately released an apology statement and requested forgiveness. The statement was short and to the point. Phelps did not try to rationalize his behavior or blame the other partygoers. In his statement Phelps pointed out that he was young and made a mistake. This was probably his best strategy for image restoration.

Most people understand that young people often do things without considering the full consequences of their actions. Had Phelps tried the victimage approach, he and his image would likely have suffered. It is hard to pin the fault on a third party when there is photographic evidence of the offending act. By victimizing another person, Phelps would have appeared to be avoiding the situation and responsibility, or possibly that he felt he was better than the other people at the party. Had he attempted to use a scapegoat, it may have seemed like he felt he was above punishment for his actions, while the others at the party should be punished for their actions.

The final step of redemption is evidence that "a change has taken place within the rhetor; the rhetor's self has been purified and redeemed" (Foss, Foss, & Trapp, 1985, pp. 181-182). For Phelps, evidence of his public redemption came when he received his first new sponsor and endorsement contract following the offending act. H20 Audio was seemingly willing to forgive and overlook Phelps's act and offered him an endorsement deal (McCarthy, 2009). Phelps, who is often seen listening to music during practice and before competitions, was a logical endorsement choice for the organization. This was the act that may have signaled that at least as a commercial brand, Michael Phelps's redemption was complete.

Benoit's Theory of Image Restoration

Taking an approach that draws heavily on rhetorical theory, including Burke, Benoit (1995) reviews the existing literature on image restoration and reputation recovery/repair and proposes a theory of image restoration. His theory includes five specific rhetorical strategies available to those seeking to repair and recover their image and reputation. This body of work is reviewed elsewhere in this volume. Benoit's theory of image restoration (1995) suggests a five-strategy typology for those accused of wrongdoing or needing to defend attacks on their reputations including: denial, evading responsibility, reducing offensiveness, corrective action, and mortification.

Given the statement released to the press by Phelps's agent, denial and evading responsibility were clearly not considered viable options. However, Phelps could have employed denial and claimed that the photograph was a fake or a fabrication of some sort. This could have allowed him to argue that it was not him in the photograph. Had Phelps denied or challenged the authenticity of the photograph, he would then have had to come up with a reasonable and plausible explanation for the photograph or essentially generate an alibi that established his presence elsewhere when the photograph was taken. Both of these strategies would have further complicated rather than helped to resolve his situation.

Short of being able to deny the authenticity of the photograph, Phelps could have tried to evade responsibility by suggesting he was provoked or lacked control of the situation. He could have argued that he was forced to engage in the behavior, claimed it was an accident, or suggested good or harmless intentions or motives for his actions. This strategy and its variants would have also complicated rather than resolved the situation. All of these strategies are the means suggested by Benoit for evading responsibility (1995, pp. 76-77). One reading of Phelps's statement could be taken as evading responsibility in that he essentially argues that his youth in part explains or is responsible for his actions. In his statement he says, "I acted in a youthful and inappropriate way." He seems to offer this statement more as explanation rather than an excuse for his behavior.

In fact, Phelps's statement and subsequent comments do not deny the authenticity of the photograph and the behavior it displays, but rather he takes responsibility for his actions. Both Burke and Benoit describe this strategy as mortification, or admitting responsibility and asking for understanding and forgiveness. The Phelps statement says, "I engaged in behavior which was regrettable. . ." This phrase fulfills the first requirement for mortification, taking responsibility. Phelps concludes the statement by saying, "For this [behavior], I am sorry. I promise my fans and the public—it will not happen again." Clearly with these final sentences Phelps is satisfying the second requirement for mortification, asking for forgiveness and understanding from the public.

This strategy is consistent with Phelps's previous brush with the law in his 2004 DUI and his more recent involvement in a 2009 auto accident. At the time of the 2004 DUI, Phelps accepted responsibility and characterized his behavior by saying, "Getting into a car after anything to drink is wrong. It's dangerous and unacceptable" ("Other Driver Caused," 2009). In other statements reportedly made by Phelps in 2004 he says, "I've let a lot of people down, including myself. It is definitely an honor to be a role model for kids, and I hope to still be one and to have fans out there. This is a mistake that I made, and I'm going to have to live with this for the rest of my life" (cited by Brennan, 2009). Once again, Phelps clearly accepts responsibility for his behavior, even though he does not explicitly ask forgiveness.

In August 2009, Phelps was again involved in an auto accident. While he was not at fault in the accident, he was cited for driving without a valid license and admitted to Baltimore police that he had consumed a beer about an hour before the accident ("Other Driver Caused," 2009). One could argue that while Phelps is good at accepting responsibility, his ability to change his behavior remains a problem, possibly questioning the sincerity of his apologies. As Brennan (2009) observed in *USA Today*: "You want to believe him, of course, because he's Michael Phelps. But, sadly, now, you do have to wonder."

A final strategy deserves mention not because it was employed by Phelps so much as mentioned by media commentators and analysts following publication of the photo. Benoit writes that those accused can seek to reduce the offensiveness of their act or behavior in several ways, for example bolstering and minimizing the act (1995, pp. 77-78). According to Benoit, "Bolstering may be used to mitigate the negative effects of the act on the actor by strengthening the audience's positive affect for the rhetor" (1995, p. 77). The Speedo Corporation, one of Phelps's key sponsors, issued a statement saying "Speedo would like to make it clear that it does not condone such behavior and we know that Michael truly regrets his actions. Michael Phelps is a valued member of the Speedo team and a great champion. We will do all that we can to support him and his family" (cited by Vranica & Steel, 2009). This statement suggests that while Phelps's behavior is clearly wrong, he is nonetheless both a great champion, and no less important from Speedo's perspective, literally a valued member of the team. Likewise, Subway Corporation, another of Phelps's sponsors, issued a statement saying: "Like most Americans, and like Michael Phelps himself, we were disappointed in his behavior. Also like most Americans, we accept his apology. Moving forward he remains in our plans" (Byson-York, 2009b). In the same publication, Phelps is quoted as saying: "I am heartened by the strong show of support from my many sponsors. My focus now is on the pool and on practice." Again, there is tacit acknowledgment of the incident, and an attempt to shift attention back to the pool and the positive aspects of Phelps's accomplishments and potential, both athletically and commercially.

In the days following the publication of the photograph, at least one advertising executive and an Olympic historian's comments sought to minimize the negativity of the act. Bob Dorfman of Baker Street Advertising, and author of *The Sports Marketer's Scouting Report,* is quoted as saying: "I think consumers and marketers will cut him some slack because it's 'only' marijuana, something that it seems like other professional athletes get arrested for every five minutes—not that that condones it" (Michaelis, 2009, p. C13). Bill Mallon, an Olympic historian, said, "He probably will take some hits with this. Corporations, sponsors, a lot of those put behavior clauses in contracts. . . . Our president smoked it. Clinton smoked it. It's not the worst drug in the world" (cited by Michaelis, 2009, p. C13). While these commentators are not speaking for Phelps, they are perhaps reflecting a part of public sentiment in that while marijuana is illegal, its use may not be perceived as negatively as other "hard drugs." In fact, according the Pew Research Center for People and the Press, public opinion over the past twenty years continues to shift toward legalizing marijuana, from 16 percent favoring legalization in 1980, to 35 percent in 2008 and 41 percent in 2010 ("Survey Reports," 2010). If professional athletes and a former president of the United States have used marijuana, and public opinion seems to be shifting toward legalization, perhaps it is not so bad that Michael Phelps was photographed "just smoking pot."

In terms of the content of Michael Phelps's statement following the publication of the embarrassing photograph, he and his agents clearly employed strategies that effectively sought to repair and recover his reputation. Through mortification and the taking of corrective action, Phelps's statement provided an apology, accepted responsibility for his behavior, and sought to reassure the public and his sponsors that such behavior would not happen again. The statements from commentators and analysis may have inadvertently sought to bolster Phelps's reputation in statements that minimized the seriousness of his offense and served to remind the public of his many accomplishments.

THE "BAND-AID" APPROACH: TAKE IT SLOW OR RIP IT OFF

From early childhood on, anyone who has ever experienced a cut or injury requiring a bandage faces the decision of whether to eventually remove said bandage slowly or quickly. As we have all discovered, slow removal risks prolonged pain as the adhesive pulls at each small hair on the arm, while quick removal may involve the same amount of pain, but for a shorter period of time. Similar reasoning can be used to understand the decision faced by those whose image and reputations are threatened by a negative story or publicity. A slow response to a potentially embarrassing incident risks prolonged pain, while a timely response involves pain but the discomfort passes more quickly. Essentially the argument being made is that those engaged in controversy requiring image management strategies are best advised to take a proactive strategy of attempting to manage and positively shape news coverage early on, rather than assume a reactive strategy of responding to the often negative news coverage. Therefore, in addition to using effective image management communication strategies, the "band-aid" approach suggests the timing of the use of these strategies becomes critical.

A useful example is to briefly compare and contrast how Michael Phelps proactively managed the controversy surrounding publication of the photo with how professional golfer Tiger Woods reactively responded to media reports following his traffic accident and the subsequent disclosure of alleged marital difficulties. As we have suggested in this essay, Michael Phelps and his agents quickly responded to the publication of the photo with a well-crafted statement expressing regret, an apology, and a promise to change. By doing so, his statements became a part of the story and perhaps helped to shape the story and subsequent coverage in a more favorable light.

On November 27, 2009, Tiger Woods crashed his sport utility vehicle into a utility pole and suffered minor injuries ("Tiger Woods Injured," 2009). Several days passed before Woods agreed to speak with authorities about the details of the accident ("Police: Woods, wife unavailable for interview," 2009, p. 10C). In the interim, media speculation was rampant regarding the causes of the accident and possible marital problems. As the story unfolded over the next days and weeks, numerous suspected affairs were reported and several alleged mistresses came forward. Finally, on February 19, 2010, Tiger Woods carefully orchestrated a news conference to explain and apologize for the incident and the disclosure of marital problems (Anthony, 2010, p. 3A).

Granted, there are key differences between these two examples. While both Phelps and Woods are world-class athletes, Woods's dominance in professional golf is of longer standing than Phelps's success in the Olympic pool. Woods is also clearly the more valuable commercial brand. Finally, there may be differences in their perceived and reported offending behaviors. The photo of Phelps depicting his alleged smoking of an illegal substance may or may not be perceived by the public as different and therefore more serious than Woods's alleged infidelity.

Following the logic of the band-aid approach, Michael Phelps ripped off the bandage, suffered the immediate short-term pain, and moved forward by proactively seeking to manage the situation through his timely statement. In contrast, Tiger Woods's delayed response and prolonged silence allowed the bandage on his alleged marital difficulties to be slowly and painfully removed with each new revelation and each new self-proclaimed former mistress who claimed a relationship with Woods. As Woods chose not to react to the allegations as they occurred, the pain and uncertainly lingered. In the information vacuum created by his lack of response, the media and commentators filled the void with continued speculation and reports of new affairs.

While we will never know how things might have developed differently for both Phelps and Woods had they managed their respective difficulties differently, it is possible to speculate that the outcomes might have been different. As we have suggested, Phelps could have denied the authenticity of the photo and challenged the motives of those who took and provided the photo to the media. The media's motivation in publishing the photo could also have been questioned. Doing so might have turned public opinion toward his accusers and the ever-intrusive media that published the photo. Woods could have issued a timely statement explaining the automobile crash and responded to media speculation of marital problems. He could have requested that the public and the press respect his privacy as he dealt with his personal and family problems. No doubt the same self-proclaimed mistresses would have come forward, but they would have done so after a well-respected world-class athlete had requested privacy in dealing with his personal life.

An anonymous quotation suggests, "If a person tells the truth, it becomes part of his/her past. If a person tells a lie it becomes part of her/his future." The wisdom of this quote informs the present analysis. By proactively seeking to manage the photo story and respond to it in a timely and calculated way, Michael Phelps sought to put the controversy behind him and move on with his career. By failing to respond and choosing to remain silent for so long, Tiger Woods allowed the story to be a continuing part of his future. Carefully crafted and timely responses to public controversy appear to be vital to image repair and restoration.

THE 24/7 NEWS CYCLE AND THE IMPORTANCE OF NEW MEDIA

In the past, it may have been possible for someone of Phelps's stature to simply ignore negative media attention and hope that it would go away. The instantaneous access to, and the ready availability of news and information in the twenty-first century made such an option impossible and even unwise. The 24/7 news cycle will be fed by whatever information and comment are available. In the era of social networking technologies like Facebook, MySpace, and Twitter, and web-enabled cell phones, cell phone cameras with video capability, and many other new personal and media technologies, those with the technology and Internet access can both make and help to report the news. These technologies make the careful and timely response of those involved in public controversies all the more important. In fact, the same technologies that facilitate the media's attention to celebrity behavior can be used by the savvy celebrity to respond, manage, and shape potentially negative stories.

It is understandable and perhaps commendable that Phelps and his agents seized the opportunity to shape the story rather than be shaped by the story. It is conceivable to propose that Phelps could have engaged in a strategy of denial—claiming that the photo in question had somehow been altered or "photoshopped" as a tactic to ruin his reputation. The technology certainly exists to make such an argument possible and plausible. As we have suggested, following such a strategy would have likely prolonged the story and controversy and would ultimately have likely failed. Had he insisted on denying the authenticity of the photo, the media would likely have found the partygoer who took the picture, gathered additional possibly more embarrassing photos and quotes, and added the information to the next news cycle. This, in turn, would have necessitated further comment and denial on the part of Phelps.

Given his success in the pool, Michael Phelps could have shunned the spotlight and lucrative endorsement contracts and focused exclusively on his swimming. Clearly this was not the path he chose. As Brennan (2009) observes in *USA Today,* he " . . . instead chose a path that guaranteed his every move would be photographed and monitored by every cell phone in every room he entered." Clearly the technologies that feed the 24/7 news cycle have changed news reporting and how celebrities must respond to the news.

LESSONS TO BE LEARNED FROM THE PHELPS SAGA

Image and reputation are important to all of us, but are critically important to those who find themselves in the public eye. Given the prominence of sports in American life, it is not surprising that we enjoy being spectators, we look to successful athletes as role models, and we respond to athlete endorsements for the products we buy. When these athletes stumble in their personal lives, the media brings the story to us "warts and all." How prominent athletes choose to manage media attention and their images and reputations will likely be an arena of continued and intensive study.

The rhetorical strategies suggested by Burke and Benoit, and the "band-aid" approach to the timely response to controversial media coverage provide valuable lessons for future athletes caught up in the sometimes negative glare of the media spotlight. As a case study, Michael Phelps's response to the publication of a potentially career-ending photograph is particularly instructive. "Fessing up," coming clean, and apologizing seem to be valuable communicative strategies suggested by the writing of both Burke and Benoit. Whether intentionally or intuitively followed by Phelps and his agents, these strategies seem to have provided a means for him to account for his behavior and positively manage and repair his image and reputation. The public seems to have accepted his account as have those who continue to want us to purchase products carrying his endorsement and likeness. Granted, he suffered some losses, but the damage could arguably have been much worse.

The contrast between how Michael Phelps and Tiger Woods responded or chose not to respond to being thrust into the public eye is also instructive. An immediate and proactive approach to image management, using the communicative strategies suggested by Burke and Benoit, seems to have advantages over what might be characterized as a reactive stone-walling approach. As many of us learned in our youth and following the logic of the "band-aid" approach, getting a negative experience behind us is often preferable to prolonging the pain and negativity.

The role of new technologies and 24/7 media attention and news cycles cannot be emphasized enough. Our private lives are increasingly becoming public. Sometimes this is by choice. In the case of celebrities and public figures, these technologies may threaten to make anyone with a cell phone and Internet access not only an intruder in their private lives but a contributor to the frenzy that has become the 24/7 news industry. Clearly, we can all manage our behavior in public and seek to shape a positive image and reputation, celebrities included. In the twenty-first-century technology and media environment, celebrities will increasingly need to be vigilant of their behavior and savvy as to the use and potential abuse these technologies and media afford.

REFERENCES

Anthony, T. (2010, February 20). Wood's carefully staged apology clouded its sincerity, Mea culpa obscured. *Erie Times-News* [Associated Press story], p. 3A.

Benoit, W. L. (1997). Hugh Grant's image restoration discourse: An actor apologizes. *Communication Quarterly*, 45 (3), 251-268.

Brennan, C. (2009, February 2). A sad day for Phelps' fan club. *USA Today*,p. C.13. Retrieved February 8, 2010, from ProQuest National Newspapers Premier. (Document ID: 1637706651).

Bryson-York, E. (2009a, February 5). Kellogg's to drop Olympian Phelps. *Advertising Age.* Retrieved from http://adage.com/article?article_id=134363.

Bryson-York, E. (2009b, February 9). Phelps brand takes a hit. *Advertising age* (Midwest Region Edition). Chicago: 80 (5).

Dickinson, G. (2009, February 2). What a dope. *News of the World.* Retrieved from http://www.newsoftheworld.co.uk.

Foss, S, Foss, K, & Trapp, R. (1985). *Contemporary perspectives on rhetoric.* Prospect Heights, IL: Waveland Press.

Harris, R. (2009, February 2). Phelps backed by sponsors after marijuana photo. *Spartanburg Herald—Journal.* Retrieved February 8, 2010, from ABI/INFORM Dateline. (Document ID: 1637412421).

Jones, J. M. (2008, August 7). Swimming tops track as public's favorite Olympic event. Retrieved from: http://www.gallup.com/poll/109321/Swimming-Tops-Track-Publics-Favorite-Olympic-Event.aspx.

Lei, Lei (2009, June 6). Beijing Olympic earnings hit $146m. *China Daily.* Retrieved from http://www.chinadaily.com.cn/china/2009-06/20/content_8304725.htm.

Macur, J. (2009, February 5). Phelps disciplined over marijuana pipe incident. *The New York Times.* Retrieved from www.nytimes.com/2009/02/06/sports/othersports/06phelps.html.

McCarthy, M. (2009, June 16). Phelps lands first sponsor since infamous bong photo. *USA Today.* Retrieved from http://www.usatoday.com/sports/olympics/2009-06-15-phelps-waterproof-headphones_N.htm.

Michaelis, V. (2009, February 2). Phelps fallout: Small setback. *USA Today.* Retrieved from ProQuest National Newspapers Premier (Document ID: 1637706661).

Newberry, P. (2009, February 1). Phelps acknowledges photo using pot pipe. *Spartanburg Herald - Journal.* Retrieved from ABI/INFORM Dateline (Document ID: 1636681351).

Other driver caused wreck with Phelps. (2009, August 13). Retrieved from http://sports.espn.go.com/oly/swimming/news/story?id=4398254.

Michael Phelps' contract with Kellogg Co. will not be renewed. (2009, February 6). *USA Today.* Retrieved from http://www.usatoday.com/sports/olympics/2009-02-05-phelps-kellogg_N.htm.

Police: Woods, wife unavailable for interview. (2009, November 29). *Erie Times-News,* p. 10C.

Shipley, A. (2009, February 2). Phelps will not face any sanctions: Photo appears to show drug use. *The Washington Post.* Retrieved from ProQuest National Newspapers Premier (Document ID: 1636628111).

Snead, E. (2009, February 5). Kellogg's dumps Michael Phelps for smoking pot! The Dish Rag. Retrieved from blog.zap2it.com/the dishrag/2009/02/kelloggs-dumps-m.html.

Survey reports: Broad public support for legalizing medical marijuana. (2010, April 1). The Pew Research Center for People and the Press. Retrieved from http://people-press.org/report/602/marijuana/

Tiger Woods injured in minor car accident. CNN.com. Retrieved from http://www.cnn.com/2009/US/11/27/tiger.woods/index.html.

Vranica, S. & Steel, E. (2009, February 3). Phelps image as hero hurt by photos. *Wall Street Journal* (Eastern Edition). Retrieved from ABI/INFORM Global (Document ID: 1637337311).

II

Marital Infidelity and Sexual Misconduct

Chapter Six

Tiger Woods's Image Repair: Could He Hit One Out of the Rough?

William L. Benoit, Ohio University

Tiger Woods was on top of his game in 2009 when a shocking scandal emerged: He had engaged in affairs for years with multiple women. He withdrew from golf and checked into a clinic for sex addiction treatment. He posted two brief statements on his webpage in December 2009 and gave a televised speech of apology in February 2010. This chapter applies the theory of image repair discourse to Tiger Woods's image repair efforts. His discourse emphasized mortification and also employed transcendence (arguing that he has a right to privacy) and corrective action. Of course, his behavior was too offensive for some to overlook, but his image repair effort is evaluated as generally well developed.

Key Terms: Tiger Woods, affair, image repair, mortification, corrective action

INTRODUCTION

On November 27, 2009, golfer Tiger Woods was involved in an automobile accident. Elin Nordegren, Woods's wife, broke one of the car's windows with a golf club. Presumably she was reacting to news of his repeated infidelity; it certainly attracted attention to the golfer's personal life. Jaimee Grubbs, a waitress, reported that she had engaged in an affair with Woods for thirty-one months. Within a week, ten other women claimed to have been in relationships with the golfer—and more emerged later. The *Vancouver Sun* (2010), quoting the *National Enquirer*, reported that Woods admitted to his wife that he had engaged in affairs with 120 women. It also claimed that he had cheated with their neighbor. Of course, the *National Enquirer* is hardly a reputable source, but this illustrates the tenor of the many rumors swirling about Woods. Given his squeaky-clean image, this news was very shocking. Most people were aware of this scandal (in March, only 6 percent reported that they had not heard about it; Pew, 2010a); about half had an unfavorable opinion of Woods (CNN, 2009). A study concluded that his sponsors "lost a collective $5 to $12 billion in the wake of the scandal involving his extramarital affairs" (UC Davis News & Information, 2009). Not surprisingly, companies using Woods in advertising began dropping him like hotcakes: Gatorade, Accenture, Gillette, and AT&T (ESPN, 2010). Woods's image was threatened: He took a break from golf and posted two statements on his webpage. He entered a clinic in January 2010 (ESPN, 2010). He made a public statement in February; over half of the public had heard "a lot" about his televised apology (Pew, 2010b). This chapter analyzes his image repair discourse concerning this scandal.

METHOD: RHETORICAL CRITICISM USING IMAGE REPAIR THEORY

The task of understanding persuasive messages employed to repair a tarnished image has occupied many critics and theorists (see, e.g., Coombs, 1995; Hearitt, 1994; Rowland & Jerome, 2004; Seeger, Sellnow, & Ulmer, 2003; Ware & Linkugel, 1973). The literature acknowledges that face, image, or reputation can be extremely important, that threats to image arise throughout human affairs, and that persuasive messages can help repair damage done to a reputation from accusations or suspicions of wrongdoing. Relying on previous scholarship in the area (e.g., Burke, 1970; Scott & Lyman, 1968; Ware & Linkugel, 1973), Benoit identified a variety of potential image repair strategies grouped under five general strategies (1995a, 1997b, 2000; see also Blaney & Benoit, 2001; and the critique by Burns & Bruner, 2000). Image repair theory has been employed to understand persuasive discourse in several different contexts: political (Benoit, 2006a, 2006b; Benoit, Gullifor, & Panici, 1991; Benoit & Henson, 2009; Benoit & McHale, 1999; Benoit & Nill, 1988a; Blaney & Benoit, 2001; Kennedy & Benoit, 1997; Len-Rios & Benoit, 2004; Zhang & Benoit, 2009), corporate (Benoit, 1995b; Benoit & Brinson, 1994; Benoit & Czerwinski, 1997; Brinson & Benoit, 1996; Blaney, Benoit, & Brazeal, 2002), countries (Drumheller & Benoit, 2004; Zhang & Benoit, 2004), sports (Benoit & Hanczor, 1994; Wen, Yu, & Benoit, 2009) and other realms (Benoit, 1997a; Benoit & Anderson, 1996; Benoit & Brinson, 1999; Benoit & Nill 1988b).

Threats to an image have two components: blame or responsibility, and offensiveness; the image repair strategies attempt to deal with these two elements (Benoit, 1995a, 1997b). Five general categories of image repair strategies are identified (denial, evading responsibility, reducing offensiveness, corrective action, and mortification), three of which with sub-categories, fourteen distinct image repair strategies. Denial has two variants: One may use simple denial to deny committing the offensive act or shift blame to the "true" culprit. A rhetor can try to evade responsibility for the wrongful act by pleading provocation (the deed in question was a reasonable act to an earlier wrong committed against the rhetor), defeasibility (lack of information or power to control events), accident (inadvertent harms), or good intentions (events went awry despite trying to do the right thing).

The accused can also attempt to reduce the offensiveness of the act. Bolstering attempts to improve the audience's positive affect for the rhetor to outweigh or counterbalance the offensiveness of the wrongful action. Minimization argues that the wrongful act was less offensive that it appears. Differentiation suggests that the act performed by the accused was less offensive than it seems (e.g., I did not *steal* your car; I *borrowed* it without asking first). Transcendence claims the rhetor was motivated by other, more important, concerns. Attacking one's accuser may diminish the credibility of the accusations (and if the accuser is the victim, attacking the accuser could create the impression that the victim deserved what he or she got). Compensation offers something of worth to the victim to redress the loss. Corrective action promises to repair the damage caused and/or prevent its recurrence. Mortification admits blame for the offense and requests forgiveness.

RHETORICAL ANALYSIS OF WOODS'S IMAGE REPAIR EFFORTS

Woods released two statements on his webpage, one on December 2 (2009a) and one on December 11 (2009b). He explicitly used mortification in both statements. In his first message, he wrote: "I have let my family down and I regret those transgressions with all of my heart. I have not been true to my values and the behavior my family deserves. I am not without faults and I am far short of perfect" (2009a). His second statement was more specific about his offense: "I am deeply aware of the disappointment and hurt that my infidelity has caused so many people, most of all my wife and children. I want to say again to everyone that I am profoundly sorry and that I ask for forgiveness" (2009b). In my experience, instances of mortification are often vague. Woods acknowledged his infidelity, said he was sorry, and explicitly asked to be forgiven. These utterances clearly illustrate mortification.

The two statements on Tiger Woods's webpage also employed transcendence. In his first message, he wrote, "I am dealing with my behavior and personal failings behind closed doors with my family. These feelings should be shared by us alone" (2009a). He also requested "privacy for my family" and argued that "What's most important now is that my family has the time, privacy, and safe haven we will need for personal healing" (2009). So, Woods argued that his—and his family's—need for privacy was a more important value that the news' prurient interest, adding that he and his "family have been hounded to expose intimate details of our personal life" (2009a), also suggestive of attacking his accusers in the press.

Woods's initial image repair efforts also employed corrective action. He declared that "I will strive to be a better person and the husband and father that my family deserves" (2009a). In the second message, he acknowledged that he wanted to "repair the damage I've done," if possible, and that "I need to focus my attention on being a better husband, father, and person" (2009b). So, Woods's first two image repair discourses mentioned corrective action. They were vague, talking about his goals rather than explaining what he would do to help.

On February 19, 2010, Tiger Woods gave a televised speech of apology (over 13 minutes long). Mortification was the primary strategy, one he used almost twenty times. "I am deeply sorry for my irresponsible and selfish behavior," "I have let you down," "For all that I have done, I am so sorry." Again, he explicitly identified his offensive behavior, not pulling any punches: "The issue involved here was my repeated irresponsible behavior. I was unfaithful. I had affairs. I cheated." Woods also explicitly accepted personal responsibility for his misbehavior: "I am the only person to blame. . . . I knew my actions were wrong. . . . I never thought about who I was hurting. . . . I was wrong. I was foolish. I don't get to play by different rules" (2010). As in his first two image repair messages, Woods admits that he was wrong and says he is worry. Mortification was used more extensively in his speech than in his two initial statements, although he did not actually ask for forgiveness in the third message.

Corrective action is also developed more fully in his speech than it was in his two web statements. Woods noted that "It's now up to me to make amends and that starts by never repeating the mistakes I've made." Woods reported that "for 45 days . . . I was in inpatient therapy receiving guidance for the issues I'm facing. I have a long way to go, but I've taken my first steps in the right direction." He also explained that "Starting tomorrow, I will leave for more treatment and more therapy" (2010). These statements all function to describe his attempts to deal with his offensive behavior, providing more detail than was available in his previous messages.

His speech also revisits his use of transcendence to argue for his and his family's privacy: What he and his wife "say to each other will remain between the two of us." He also declares that "I still believe it is right to shield my family from the public spotlight" and one passage again attacks the news media: "My behavior doesn't make it right for the media to follow my two-and-a-half-year-old daughter to school and report the school's location. They staked out my wife and they pursued my mom . . . please leave my family alone" (2010). So, Woods again employed transcendence and his speech attacked accusers. The speech repeated the themes employed in Woods's initial webpage statements, elaborating the defense he outlined there (that is, it introduced no new strategies but did provide greater development of his initial image repair strategies).

EVALUATION

Mortification and corrective action were the right strategies to employ. Woods had clearly behaved in a way that would offend most people. He had not a single affair but at least ten, repeatedly committing infidelity. The public believed he had engaged in a pattern of offensive behavior over time and it was important to admit it and apologize. A minor criticism of his speech is that it would not have hurt to have asked for forgiveness in the speech.

His use of transcendence and attacking the accuser may have helped a bit. Most people probably believe that celebrities deserve scrutiny, but their families deserve some protection. He stressed the need for privacy for his family. However, given the fact that the unwanted media attention to Woods's family was driven by his own behavior probably mitigated the benefits from these strategies.

Woods may have been prompted, in part, to give the speech because a large group of people (40 percent) believed he should address this issue publicly (ABC News, 2010; poll conducted February 11-14, 2010). A poll taken after his speech reported that 55 percent were "personally ready to forgive" Woods; 28 percent apparently accepted his transcendence argument, believing it was not their business (ABC News/ESPN, 2010). Fifty-four percent stated that companies should use Woods in endorsements again (31 percent disagreed; ABC News/ESPN, 2010). It is clear that everyone had not forgiven Woods; after all, his offensive act was completely voluntary and he had affairs for years. Nevertheless, his image repair efforts appear to have helped matters. It did not succeed at preventing his divorce (Canning & Netter, 2010). In 2010 Woods returned to golf in the Masters Tournament in April, where he tied for fourth place.

CONCLUSION

Tiger Woods's personal behavior was offensive. His behavior, when it came to light, damaged his public image. However, his image repair messages helped to repair that image. Use of mortification and corrective action in particular were good choices. Unfortunately, he was not successful at saving his marriage and it is clear that his golf career suffered a major setback from this scandal.

REFERENCES

ABC News Poll (2010). Retrieved September 11, 2010 from the iPOLL Databank, The Roper Center for Public Opinion Research, University of Connecticut. http://proxy.mul.missouri.edu:3097/data_access/ipoll/ipoll.html.

ABC News/ESPN Poll (2010). Retrieved September 11, 2010 from the iPOLL Databank, The Roper Center for Public Opinion Research, University of Connecticut. http://proxy.mul.missouri.edu:3097/data_access/ipoll/ipoll.html.

Benoit, W. L. (1995a). *Accounts, excuses, apologies: A theory of image restoration strategies.* Albany: State University of New York Press.

Benoit, W. L. (1995b). Sears' repair of its auto service image: Image restoration discourse in the corporate sector. *Communication Studies, 46,* 89-105.

Benoit, W. L. (1997a). Hugh Grant's image restoration discourse: An actor apologizes. *Communication Quarterly, 45,* 251-267.

Benoit, W. L. (1997b). Image repair discourse and crisis communication. *Public Relations Review, 23,* 177-186.

Benoit, W. L. (2000). Another visit to the theory of image restoration strategies. *Communication Quarterly, 48,* 40-44.

Benoit, W. L. (2006a). Image repair in President Bush's April 2004 news conference. *Public Relations Review, 32,* 137-143.

Benoit, W. L. (2006b). President Bush's image repair effort on *Meet the Press*: The complexities of defeasability. *Journal of Applied Communication Research, 34,* 285-306.

Benoit, W. L., & Anderson, K. K. (1996). Blending politics and entertainment: Dan Quayle versus Murphy Brown. *Southern Communication Journal, 62,* 73-85.

Benoit, W. L., & Brinson, S. L, (1994). AT&T: Apologies are not enough. *Communication Quarterly, 42,* 75-88.

Benoit, W. L., & Brinson, S. L. (1999). Queen Elizabeth's image repair discourse: Insensitive royal or compassionate Queen? *Public Relations Review, 25,* 145-156.

Benoit, W. L., & Czerwinski, A. (1997). A critical analysis of USAir's image repair discourse. *Business Communication Quarterly, 60,* 38-57.

Benoit, W. L., Gullifor, P., & Panici, D. A. (1991). President Reagan's defensive discourse on the Iran-Contra affair. *Communication Studies, 42,* 272-294.

Benoit, W. L., & Hanczor, R. S. (1994). The Tonya Harding controversy: An analysis of image repair strategies. *Communication Quarterly, 42,* 416-433.

Benoit, W. L., & Henson, J. R. (2009). President Bush's image repair discourse on Hurricane Katrina. *Public Relations Review, 35,* 40-46.

Benoit, W. L., & McHale, J. P. (1999). Kenneth Starr's image repair discourse viewed in *20/20*. *Communication Quarterly, 47,* 265-280.

Benoit, W. L., & Nill, D. M. (1998a). A critical analysis of Judge Clarence Thomas's statement before the Senate Judiciary Committee. *Communication Studies, 49,* 179-195.

Benoit, W. L., & Nill, D. M. (1998b).Oliver Stone's defense of *JFK*. *Communication Quarterly, 46*, 127-143.

Blaney, J. R., & Benoit, W. L. (2001). *The Clinton scandals and the politics of image restoration*. Westport, CT: Praeger.

Blaney, J. R., Benoit, W. L., & Brazeal, L. M. (2002). Blowout! Firestone's image restoration campaign. *Public Relations Review, 28*, 379-392.

Brinson, S. L., & Benoit, W. L. (1996). Dow Corning's image repair strategies in the breast implant crisis. *Communication Quarterly, 44*, 29-41.

Burke, K. (1970). *The rhetoric of religion*. Berkeley: University of California Press.

Burns, J. P., & Bruner, M. S. (2000). Revisiting the theory of image restoration. *Communication Quarterly, 48*, 27-39.

Canning, A., & Netter, S. (2010, August 24). Tiger Woods divorce: Golf phenom already getting propositions. *ABC News*. Accessed 9/11/2010: http://abcnews.go.com/Entertainment/tiger-woods-divorce-golf-phenom-propositioned/story?id=11466507.

CNN/Opinion Research Corporation Poll, Dec, 2009. Retrieved May 1, 2010 from the iPOLL Databank, The Roper Center for Public Opinion Research, University of Connecticut. http://proxy.mul.missouri.edu:3097/data_access/ipoll/ipoll.html.

Coombs, W. T. (1995). Choosing the right words: The development of guidelines for the selection of the "appropriate" response strategies. *Management Communication Quarterly, 8*, 447-475.

Drumheller, K., & Benoit, W. L. (2004). USS *Greeneville* collides with Japan's *Ehime Maru*: Cultural issues in image repair discourse. *Public Relations Review, 30*, 177-185.

ESPN. (2010). Tiger Woods event timeline. Accessed 9/10/10: http://sports.espn.go.com/golf/news/story?id=4922436

Hearit, K. M. (1994). From "we didn't do it" to "it's not our fault": The use of *apologia* in public relations crises. In W. Elwood (Ed.), *Public relations inquiry as rhetorical criticism: Case studies of corporate discourse and social influence* (pp. 117-131). Westport, CT: Praeger.

Kennedy, K. A., & Benoit, W. L. (1997). Newt Gingrich's book deal: A case study in self-defense rhetoric. *Southern Communication Journal, 63*, 197-216.

Len-Rios, M., & Benoit, W. L. (2004). Gary Condit's image repair strategies: Squandering a golden opportunity. *Public Relations Review, 50*, 95-106.

Ling, D. A. (1970). A pentadic analysis of Senator Edward Kennedy's address to the people of Massachusetts, July 25, 1969. *Central States Speech Journal, 21*, 81-86.

Memmott, M. (2011, January 8). NPR CEO apologizes for "psychiatrist" remark. http://www.npr.org/blogs/thetwo-way/2010/10/21/130728202/npr-ceo-williams-views-of-muslims-should-stay-between-himself-and-his-psychiatrist.

Pew Weekly News Interest Index Poll. (2010). Retrieved May 1, 2010 from the iPOLL Databank, The Roper Center for Public Opinion Research, University of Connecticut. http://proxy.mul.missouri.edu:3097/data_access/ipoll/ipoll.html.

Pew Weekly News Interest Index Poll. (2010b). Retrieved May 1, 2010 from the iPOLL Databank, The Roper Center for Public Opinion Research, University of Connecticut. http://proxy.mul.missouri.edu:3097/data_access/ipoll/ipoll.html.

Rowland, R. R., & Jerome, A. M. (2004). On organizational *apologia*: A reconceptualization. *Communication Theory, 14*, 191-211.

Scott, M. S., & Lyman, S. M. (1968). Accounts. *American Sociological Review, 33*, 46-62.

Seeger, M. W., Sellnow, T. L., & Ulmer, R. R. (2003). *Communication and organizational crisis*. Westport, CT: Praeger.

Tiger Woods confessed to cheating with 120 women while married: Report. (2010, April 30). *Vancouver Sun*. http://www.vancouversun.com/sports/Golf+Tiger+Woods+reportedly+confessed+cheating+with+women+while+married/2967214/story.html.

UC Davis News & Information (2009, December 28). Tiger Woods Scandal Cost Shareholders up to $12 Billion. http://www.news.ucdavis.edu/search/printable_news.lasso?id=9352&table=news

Ware, B. L., & Linkugel, W. A. (1973). They spoke in defense of themselves: On the generic criticism of *apologia*. *Quarterly Journal of Speech, 59*, 273-283.

Wen, J., Yu, J., & Benoit, W. L. (2009). Our hero can't be wrong: A case study of collectivist image repair in Taiwan. *Chinese Journal of Communication, 2*, 174-192.

Woods, T. (2009a, December 2). Tiger comments on current events. Retrieved January 7, 2010, from http://web.tigerwoods.com/news/article/200912027740572/news/

Woods, T. (2009b, December 11). Tiger Woods taking hiatus from golf. Retrieved January 7, 2010, from http://web.tigerwoods.com/news/article/200912117801012/news/

Woods, T. (2010, February 19). Tiger's public statement. Retrieved January 7, 2010, from http://web.tigerwoods.com/news/article/201002198096934/news/. Video available on YouTube: http://www.youtube.com/watch?v=Xs8nseNP4s0.

Zhang, J., & Benoit, W. L. (2004). Message strategies of Saudi Arabia's image restoration campaign after 9/11.*Public Relations Review, 30*, 161-167.

Zhang, W., & Benoit, W. L. (2009). Former Minister Zhang's discourse on SARS: Government's image restoration or destruction? *Public Relations Review, 35*, 240-246.

Chapter Seven

Power, Privilege, and the Surprising Absence of Repair: Kobe Bryant and Interest Convergence

Rachel Alicia Griffin, Southern Illinois University

The purpose of this chapter is to examine the public discourse surrounding Kobe Bryant and the sexual assault charges that were brought against him in 2003. The author contends that Bryant's access to class and celebrity privilege, embodiment of an "acceptable" Black male subject position, and affirmation of patriarchy fueled the public's willingness to support his assertion of innocence. Focusing on dominant notions of Black masculinity and interracial sexual contact, a critique driven by interest convergence (Bell, 1980a) and public pedagogy (Giroux, 2000; Giroux, 2004) reveals that Bryant serves as an indication of the omnipresent of the matrix of domination (Collins, 2000). Furthermore, the public reaction to Bryant being accused, charged, and investigated indicates blatant disregard toward gender violence as a serious and culturally sanctioned issue.

INTRODUCTION

In U.S. culture, talented professional athletes are often admired and honored as cultural heroes. The general public—whether one identifies as a fan or not—has access to not only their professional careers but also elements of their personal lives. For example, there has been ample media coverage of Ricky Williams's spiritual departure and return to the NFL; Shaquille O'Neal's divorce; David Beckham's family; and LeBron James's roots in

Akron, Ohio (Abrams, 2010; Hammel, 2007; Jackson, 2010; *USA Today*, 2004). Given the constant media coverage dedicated to professional sports, many star athletes are hypervisible in the public eye and subsequently vulnerable to public scrutiny when their behavior is regarded negatively. Take Tiger Woods as a recent example; his private life was rendered exceptionally public when his infidelity became national and international news (Araton, 2010; Randhawa, 2010). Given the cultural significance of sports figures combined with the hypervisibility of sport celebrities, sport serves as a cultural text that offers a rich space for analysis (Hoberman, 1997; McDonald & Birrell, 1999; Miller, 2001). Highlighting the pedagogical nature of sport, Andrews and Jackson (2001) position sports celebrities as public figures who inform private experience. Building upon scholarly work that signifies the cultural relevance of sport, the pedagogical nature of sport narratives, and the ways that sport media can reproduce and/or contest dominant ideologies (Brown, 2005; Butterworth, 2007; Delgado, 1997; Delgado, 2005; Hoberman, 1997; Miller, 2001; Oates, 2007; Trujillo, 1991); this chapter positions the 2003 sexual assault charges brought against professional basketball player Kobe Bryant at the center of inquiry. As such, the purpose of this chapter is to problematize the public discourse surrounding the incident and subsequently theorize what the sparse call for Bryant to repair his public image teaches us about gender violence. More explicitly, at the intersections of race and gender, I am especially curious why Bryant, as a Black man accused of raping a White woman, was not discursively positioned at the mercy of the "Black male as an insatiable beast" stereotype.[1]

As a biracial (African American and White) Black[2] female who identifies as a critical scholar and gender violence activist, my curiosity regarding Bryant was initially sparked by the public reaction to the accusations, charges, and investigation. I was shocked because the overarching dominant discourse of U.S. society that positioned and continues to position Black men as dangerous and hypersexual (especially toward White women as the embodiment of virtue, purity, and innocence) did not run rampant via the media. This is not to say that Bryant should have been positioned as the "Black male as an insatiable beast" or that he should have been assumed to be guilty because he is a strong, muscular Black man. Rather, it is to acknowledge what the grand narrative of U.S. history tells us about men of color who are accused or even suspected of hurting White women. Consider for instance Charlie Jackson 1910; Scottsboro 1931; Emmett Till 1955; the Stuart Case in Boston 1989; Susan Smith in South Carolina 1994; and Iowa State 2001.[3] The theme throughout all of the aforementioned cases is that Black males were assumed to be guilty and subsequently sought after and/or punished with little consideration of their possible innocence. In addition, many of these cases resulted in numerous Black males being harassed and accosted as possible suspects with little to no evidence of actual guilt (Boser, 2002;

Patton & Snyder-Yuly, 2007; Terry, 1994). As such, Black males are rarely afforded the benefit of the doubt *and* able to emerge largely unscathed in the aftermath of being accused of violent crimes against Whites in general and White women in particular. In this context, this project is guided by two overarching questions:

As a Black man accused of raping a White woman, why didn't Kobe Bryant fall from grace?[4]

Whose interests were served when the charges against Bryant were dropped and seemingly forgotten?

To embody self-reflexive research Alexander (2006a) calls for scholars to bring our identities, desires, and assumptions to the forefront of our work rather than masking our positionalities with the illusion of objectivity. In answer to his call, it is vital for me to acknowledge the perspectives that I arrive to this project with. First, although I believe that it is an important conversation to have, for the purpose of this project I am not concerned with Bryant's innocence or guilt.[5] In addition, to mark my feminist inclination to respect survivor-friendly practices, I will not refer to the woman who came forward by name.[6] Last, I believe that academics have a responsibility to generate critical dialogue about the complexity of privilege and marginalization when they collide in the context of social issues, such as gender violence, that impact everyday lives. Therefore, I engage this critique as a means to examine what the public discourse surrounding Bryant as a professional athlete accused of rape teaches us about systems of privilege, oppression, and gender violence.

THE RAPE INVESTIGATION

The woman who came forward filed a report with the Eagle County Sheriff on July 1, 2003, in Eagle County, Colorado, indicating that she had been sexually assaulted by Bryant on June 30, 2003 (Corliss, 2003). As with the majority of date rape cases, the issue was not whether or not sex occurred on June 30, 2003, at the Cordillera Lodge and Spa where Bryant was staying and the woman worked. Rather, as a she said/he said case, their narratives differ with regard to consent and/or the use of force (Corliss, 2003; Shapiro & Stevens, 2003). When initially questioned by the police, Bryant's first response was that he had not had sex with her (Samuels, 2003). However, he later admitted to police that he had had consensual sex with her but was fearful of admitting that he had cheated on his wife (Shapiro & Stevens, 2003). Two weeks after the initial report was made to police, Bryant was formally charged with one count of felony sexual assault (CNN, 2003). Consistent with she said/he said cases, Bryant reiterated time and time again that he was guilty of adultery but not rape. For example, at a press conference held the day the charges were filed, he said, "I'm innocent . . . I didn't force her to do anything against her will. I'm innocent. I sit here in front of you guys furious at myself. Disgusted at myself for making a mistake of adultery" (CNN, 2003). His wife, Vanessa Bryant, released a similar statement making the same distinction. She said, "I know that my husband has made a mistake—the mistake of adultery. He and I will have to deal with that within our marriage, and we will do so. He is not a criminal" (CNN, 2003). Following the investigation, the formal charges against Bryant were dropped on September 1, 2004 (ESPN, 2004a). The district attorney, Mark Hurlbert, rooted his decision to drop the charges in the woman's decision not to testify[7] but also offered, "This decision is not based upon a lack of belief in the victim—she is extremely credible and an extremely brave young woman" (ESPN, 2004a).

Although the charges were dropped and the case has since been settled via a civil suit (Sarche, 2005), my curiosity as a critical scholar has intensified. Time and time again, I find myself intrigued as to why Bryant, a Black man who stands 6'7" tall and weighs approximately 200 lbs, was not widely criminalized for being charged with sexually assaulting a White woman described as "girlish-looking" (Samuels, 2003) with long blond hair and blue eyes (Shapiro & Stevens, 2003).

DOMINANT NOTIONS OF BLACK MASCULINITY

In U.S. society dominant understandings of Blackness, juxtaposed against meanings of Whiteness, are rooted in chattel slavery (Jackson, 2006; Marable, 2000; Wilson, 1965).[8] According to Saint-Aubin (2002), racist ideological discourses during slavery "became a conscious effort to articulate, to justify, and to propagate a universal White supremacy based on the notion of an inherent Black corporal, intellectual, and moral inferiority" (p. 255). Via the circulation of White supremacist ideologies, Whiteness became symbolic of cleanliness, innocence, peace, security, beauty, intelligence, and power (Baynton, 2001; Fanon, 1967; Hecht, Jackson, & Ribeau, 2003). By comparison, Blackness was characterized as a social contaminant to the purity of the White race. The Black body was inscribed with negative marks of character including amorality, menace, disease, guilt, sin, and devilish desire (Baynton, 2001; Black, 1997; Fanon, 1967; Hecht et al., 2003; Jackson, 2006; Staples, 1980). For Black men in particular, the dominant White belief system created pathological subject positions for Black men as violent, dangerous, animalistic, and uncontrollably sexual (Davis, 1985; Hodes, 1997; Jackson & Dangerfield, 2002). In the context of masculinity, Black men were not worthy of or entitled to the respect, dignity, or security afforded to White men. According to Marable (1998), there were three overarching beliefs that White men held in regard to Black men during the era of slavery. Black males were considered naturally less intelligent than White males; politically threatening to White power; and dangerous sexual predators who were unable to control their lust for White women (Marable, 1998).

Contemporary notions of Black masculinity remain bolstered by dominant historical ideologies that position Black males as dangerous and inferior. As it stands, the discursive locations largely available to Black males are severely limited to: (a) athlete, (b) criminal, (c) hip-hop star, or a combination thereof (Jackson, 2006).[9] These discursive positions circulate widely in public discourse representative of the commonsensical roles (according to dominant ideologies of Whiteness) that Black males are ready, willing, and able to fulfill. Therefore, Black males most often remain entrapped in dominant notions of Black masculinity and as such do not have access to the same privileges that White males do. Mutua's (2006) conceptualization of gendered racism offers a means to mark the stigmatization that Black males encounter as simultaneously raced and gendered beings. One particular context in which Black men have experienced oftentimes deadly stigmatization is when they have been suspected and/or accused of having sexual contact with White females.

BLACK MALE/WHITE FEMALE INTERRACIAL SEXUAL CONTACT

Sexual contact between Black men and White women has been criminalized and stigmatized as inappropriate, offensive, and threatening throughout U.S. history (Boser, 2002; Dorr, 2001; Hodes, 1997; Kennedy, 2002; Mann & Selva, 1979; Wriggins, 1983). As a result, Black men accused of raping White women (oftentimes regardless of evidence and/or an admission of sexual contact) have been overwhelmingly found guilty in the eyes of the public and the law (Dorr, 2001). Hence although a woman's word has rarely if ever been enough for allegations of rape to be taken seriously (Smith, 2001), historically when White women accused Black men of rape, the assumption of guilt was rooted in the notion that hypersexual Black men lust after honorable and pure White women (Brownmiller, 1975; Marable, 1998) and "that no white woman would consent to sexual relations with a black man" (Dorr, 2001, p. 250). According to Dorr (2001), "Unlike cases in which women accused members of their own races of assault, white legal authorities usually accepted white women's accusations of rape against black men, regardless of other evidence" (p. 247). In practice, the juxtaposition of ani-malistic Black males against virtuous White females has resulted in thou-sands of Black men being arrested, charged, convicted, harassed, and mur-dered regardless of evidence of rape, evidence of the intent to rape, or con-sent (Boser, 2002; Brownmiller, 1975; Patton & Snyder-Yuly, 2007).

Several historical narratives indicate the dominant assumption that Black males desire and intend to sexually violate White females. For instance, in 1910 Charlie Jackson was murdered after being falsely accused of assaulting a White woman (Boser, 2002). Perhaps the most notorious example are the nine Scottsboro Boys, who served a combined total of 104 years behind bars between 1931 and 1950 before having their convictions for raping two White women overturned (Goodman, 1994; Norris & Washington, 1979). Also commonly noted is the murder of Emmett Till in 1955, whose body was found in the Tallahatchie River after he whistled at a White woman (Metress, 2002). Voicing the perceptions of Black male deviance and the need to protect the virtue of White women, in 1964 "the Georgia Supreme Court described the rape of a white woman by a Black man as 'a crime more horrible than death[,] . . . the forcible sexual invasion of her body, the temple of her soul,' which 'soil[ed] for life her purity, the most precious attribute of all mankind'" (*Sims v. Balkcom*, 1964, as cited in Wriggins, 1983).

Shifting into a discussion of more recent instances where Black male bodies have been coded as dangerous to Whites in general and White females in particular, we can look to the Stuart case in Boston in 1989, Susan Smith in South Carolina in 1994, Iowa State in 2001, and Carl Chatman in 2002. Both Charles Stuart and Susan Smith falsely named Black men as the assai-lants in crimes against their loved ones, Charles Stuart for the murder of his pregnant wife, Carol, and Susan Smith for carjacking and the subsequent kidnapping of her young sons who were later found drowned (Boser, 2002; Butterfield, 1992; Terry, 1994).[10] Reflecting on Smith's false allegations that a Black man committed the crime after she confessed to murdering her children, Tyrone Mason asserted, "I guess she figured if she said a black man did it people would believe her no matter what kind of story she came up with. . . . That's what hurts. As long as it's allegedly a black man involved, America will fall for anything" (as quoted in Terry, 1994). Similarly in 2001, a White female student at Iowa State University accused four Black men of kidnapping and rape. Immediately after her report, the local community re-acted supportively and a manhunt for the Black men she described ensued. According to Patton and Snyder-Yuly (2007), the accuser's narrative reignit-ed the myth of the Black animalistic brute raping the virginal White woman. Highlighting the relevance of gendered racism in the context of sexual vio-lence, the woman herself said in an apology: "I wish I could take it all back or make everyone understand or I wish I could have said the guy was white . . ." (Frierson, 2002, as cited in Patten & Snyder-Yuly, 2007, p. 869). Last, the *Chicago Sun-Times* (Mitchell, 2007), reflecting on the 2002 trial of Carl Chatman, a poor Black man who was tried for raping a White woman, reported:

> It took jurors just 30 minutes to find him guilty beyond a reasonable doubt even though there was no saliva, no semen, no blood and no hair found on the victim. His sentence totaled one year for every minute the jury deliberated.

Given both historical and contemporary discourse surrounding sexual contact between Black males and White females, it is clear that Black male bodies have been scripted to reflect sexual danger (Jackson, 2006). While there are White men and men of color who hurt women of all races and ethnicities, here I would like to focus on the overarching presumption of guilt that Black men endure and why Kobe Bryant was not held to the same (albeit racist) presumption. Thus, despite the offensive assumption of Black males as dangerous rapists, dominant ideological understandings of sexual contact between Black men and White women position the assumption of Bryant as the quintessential rapist as legitimate. Further indicative of the overarching sentiment toward Black men who are accused of raping White women, 85 percent of those exonerated of a rape conviction have been Black men accused of assaulting White women (Innocence Project, 2007). Offering his interpretation of this statistic, Peter J. Neufield says, "What it says to me is that, ultimately, if you are a black man charged with sexually assaulting a white woman, the likelihood that you will be convicted, even if you are stone-cold innocent, is much, much higher" (Fears, 2007).

    In specific relation to Bryant as a man accused, the Louisiana judge who wore "Blackface, a prison jumpsuit, and handcuffs as part of his Kobe Halloween costume" (Simpson, 2003, as cited in Leonard, 2004, p. 307) and the Eagle County sheriffs who ordered T-shirts with an image of a hangman on the front and Bryant's jersey number on the back (Bucher, 2003; Henson, 2003, as cited in Leonard, 2004) also illustrate the presence of tumultuous racial histories and the presumption of Bryant's vulnerable culpability. Heightening the likelihood of the general public blocking Bryant's return to iconic status is that even if most believe that the sex was consensual, sexual contact between Black men and White women remains stigmatized by society in general and detested by many Whites in particular.[11] Even his defense lawyer, Pamela Mackey, called forth the undeniable histories of interracial sexual contact between Black men and White women when she said, "There is lots of history about black men being falsely accused of this crime by white women" (Luzadder & Martinez, 2004). Although I don't agree with her defense tactics, I do believe that it is important to remember that Black men have been castrated, flogged, lynched, whipped, murdered, or at the sheer minimum jailed for having sexual contact with White women without the question being raised as to whether or not the sex was consensual. Given that Kobe Bryant is clearly an anomaly, I will rely upon interest convergence, a tenet of critical race theory, to theorize why he did not fall from grace.

INTEREST CONVERGENCE AND PUBLIC PEDAGOGY

Critical race theory (CRT) was created in legal studies to critique the laws and policies that uphold White supremacy in the United States (Crenshaw Gotanda, Peller, & Thomas, 1995). Although birthed by legal scholars, CRT has since been utilized in multiple disciplines, including education (Dixson & Rousseau, 2005; Ladson-Billings, 1998; Tate, 1997), gender studies (Boris, 1994; Wing, 1997), and sport analysis (Davis, 1995; Donnor, 2005; Hylton, 2005). Seven tenets that most CRT scholars adhere to include: (a) interest convergence, (b) racism as an everyday reality for people of color, (c) colorblindness as insufficient, (d) race as a socially constructed phenomenon, (e) whiteness as property, (f) racialized realities as dynamic and contextual and (g) racially marginalized narratives as a means for resistance (Chapman, 2005; Crenshaw et al., 1995; Delgado, 2000; Delgado & Stefancic, 2001; Harris, 1995; Tate, 1997).

To examine the public reaction to Bryant being arrested and charged as a Black man for sexually assaulting a White woman, interest convergence will be employed to read the public pedagogy of sport discourse critically. Coined by Bell (1980a) in the context of U.S. race relations, interest convergence contends that only the interests of Blacks that "secure, advance, or at least not harm" (p. 22) the interests of Whites will be fulfilled. Relying on *Brown v. Board of Education* (1954) as an example, Bell (1980a) argues that the Supreme Court voted to desegregate schools not out of the desire to serve the best interests of Black schoolchildren, but rather to assuage the United States' negative international image.[12] Contextualizing the federal decision to desegregate schools both Bell (1980a) and later Dudziak (2000) explain that the Black interest in quality education provided a means for Whites in power to appease the international criticism that racism generated. Armed with justifiable suspicion, both offer crucial insights as to why the Supreme Court, which had historically ruled against equality for African Americans,[13] came to a unanimous consensus in favor of desegregation (Bell, 1980a; Dudziak, 2000). More specifically, Bell (1980a) and Dudziak (2000) argue that those in power (i.e., Whites) had more to gain from desegregation than from maintaining segregation (Bell, 1980a; Dudziak, 2000). Therefore, although cloaked as a symbol of racial progress, the *Brown* decision was politically utilized to: (a) promote democracy in opposition to communism, (b) gain support for democracy from Third World countries that had significant populations of people of color, (c) placate and silence protests for African American equality, [14] and (d) claim that racial progress was being made (Bell, 1980a; Delgado, 2006; Dudziak, 2000). [15]

Scholars have applied interest convergence in a variety of contexts, including affirmative action (Taylor, 2000), coalition building (Cashin, 2005), college football (Davis, 1995; Donnor, 2005), Latina/o equality (Delgado, 2006), Native Americans and higher education (Castagno & Stacey, 2007), and school desegregation in the Ohio Valley (Leigh, 2003), to reveal how White interests play a role in whether or not the interests of people of color are addressed and met. Inspired by this research, I contend that interest convergence is exceptionally relevant to understanding why Bryant, as a Black man accused of raping a White woman, was not vilified in accordance with U.S. racial history. In the aftermath of the charges and the investigation, I argue that Bryant benefited from the vested interest that upper-class White males have not only in his professional success, but also in the maintenance of sexism, classism, and racism. As such, the support that has sustained his image as an upstanding and valuable basketball player can be examined as a means to inadvertently uphold the status quo.

Coupling interest convergence and public pedagogy together, the overwhelming public support of Bryant and the discursive messages broadcasted by the support he received can be simultaneously problematized since public pedagogy highlights the significance of public discourse (Giroux, 2004; Giroux, 2000). Sandlin describes public pedagogy as "the education provided by popular culture; popular culture teaches audiences and participants through the ways it represents people and issues and the kinds of discourses it creates and disseminates" (2007, p. 76). Illustrating the strength of the media coverage of the Bryant case and corroborating a critique of the media discourse as pedagogical, the Associated Press (2003) chose Bryant's rape case as "the story of the year" based on its notoriety. Noting the influential power of sports media, McDonald and Birrell (1999) encourage critical readings of sport and sports celebrities as texts that "offer unique points of access to the constitutive meanings and power relations of the larger worlds we inhabit" (p. 283). Working from their insights, in this chapter I will engage interest convergence to illuminate how Bryant's appeals to: (1) class and celebrity privilege, (2) characteristics of "good" Black men, and (3) patriarchy positioned him as a rare exception to societal rules rooted in dominant understandings of sexual contact (consensual and nonconsensual) between Black men and White women. Taken together, these three interdependent reasons contextualize why Bryant as a Black man accused of raping a White women did not fall from grace.

KOBE BRYANT AND INTEREST CONVERGENCE

Class and Celebrity Privilege

Without question, Kobe Bryant has access to an extreme level of class and celebrity privilege. Indicative of his upper-class status, his salary during the 2002-2003 season was $12,375,000, with a six-year contract valued at $70.9 million (*USA Today*, 2003) and his endorsement contracts totaled millions as well (Associated Press, 2009). Indicative of his fame, at the time that the accusations surfaced he had won three championships with the Lakers, played in five All-Star games, and his jersey was a recurring leader in NBA jersey sales (Gittrich, 2003; NBA, 2010; Nelson, 2009). Given his wealth, Bryant was able to surround himself with a highly skilled team of defense lawyers, private investigators, and a security detail. In addition, it is quite possible that his wealth and fame played a strong role in police and court records being sealed, a gag order being issued by Judge Gannett, and a rigorous, arguably illegal, according to Colorado's Rape Shield laws, investigation into the life of the woman who came forward (CNN, 2003; Luzadder & Martinez, 2004; Samuels, 2003).

Boldly signifying the strength of his status as an acclaimed celebrity athlete was the standing ovation and fan support he received at the opening exhibition Lakers-Clippers pre-season game on October 23, 2003, while charged with sexual assault (Dilbeck, 2003; Moore, 2003). Among the 18,298 NBA fans in attendance, Youngman (2003) and Moore (2003) reported that there were several adults and children wearing Bryant's jersey, chanting his name, and holding up signs that read "Kobe We Love You" and "No. 8 is still No. 1." According to Dilbeck (2003), "if there were any boos, they were drowned out by the loud ovation." Beckstaff (2003) described the crowd's roar as "intense" when Kobe was introduced, "Whatever the public at large may think of Bryant's character, there wasn't a hint of animosity in the building on Thursday." Possibly the most appalling display of support for Bryant from a gender violence standpoint was convicted rapist Mike Tyson who, like others in the audience, held up a sign that read "Free Kobe" (Beckstaff, 2003).

Taking class and celebrity status into consideration as contextual elements of Bryant's experiences as a man charged with rape and then having the charges dropped, it becomes apparent that his class and celebrity privilege served him well throughout the investigation and pretrial hearings. Thus, Bryant was able to successfully navigate the legal system and garner public support—both of which are rarely afforded to Black men who are accused of hurting White women. Likewise, he was able to stress his innocence to a mass audience that was not only willing to listen but also supported his claim. Looking to past high-profile sexual assault cases, the 1991 Patricia

Bowman and William Kennedy Smith trial also involved a male with access to exorbitant wealth and fame while the woman had far less access to class and celebrity status. Reflecting on the ways that Kennedy benefited from class and celebrity privilege, Freeman (1993) offers:

> education, family background, and class militate against him being the kind of man who rapes. He does not need to, one is tempted to think, since he is a young, attractive, well-bred, professional young man. The notion of needing to rape implies that men are driven to it by unsatisfied desire, that is, by women who deny them access, which would clearly not be Smith's problem. (p. 532)

Extending her critical insight to Bryant, embedded in the public's willingness to accept his innocence are his appeals to wealth and fame, which when fused with rape myths also lead to the assumption that he wouldn't have to rape a woman since numerous women would be willing to have sex with him. Bolstering the public's disbelief of Bryant's guilt despite the prediction that "there are going to be many parents who will never, never, never buy a Kobe Bryant jersey for their children, even if he turns out to be innocent" (Purdy, 2003) is the reality that Bryant's jersey was ranked seventh among the top twenty-five best-selling player jerseys in 2004 (NBA, 2004) and first during both the 2006-2007 and 2008-2009 seasons (Nelson, 2009). Even more staggering, less than five years after the charges were filed, Bryant's endorsement income was estimated at $16 million; he ranked second in the NBA after LeBron James (Arango, 2007).

Importantly, Bryant's best interests aren't the only interests that were satisfied via his access to class and celebrity privilege. In particular, the NBA had a vested interest in preserving Bryant as a player since his phenomenal talent clearly appeals to the predominantly White fan base that is willing to spend their money on tickets to see him play and apparel that displays his team and jersey. From a critical standpoint guided by interest convergence, if Bryant's six-year contract is worth $70.9 million (*USA Today*, 2003) then it is almost unimaginable how much money the league, owners, and investors earn off of his popularity. Referring to the ongoing sexual assault case against Bryant, Mark Cuban, the owner of the Dallas Mavericks, highlighted the publicity that scandal attracts to the league. He said, "From a business perspective, it's great for the NBA. It's reality television, people love train-wreck television and you hate to admit it, but that is the truth, that's the reality today" (ABC, 2003). Revisiting his thoughts later in *USA Today*, Cuban offered, "Notoriety sells in this day and age. . . . I can't think of anyone who is going through a legal problem who doesn't get high attention. Is that cold-blooded? Yeah. But it is bottom-line reality" (Meyer, 2003). Cuban's comments although admittedly "cold-blooded" underscore the benefits that the league stood to gain. This is not to say that a star player like

Bryant being convicted of rape would benefit the league, but rather to note how the NBA benefited not only from the publicity brought forth (i.e., the public tuning in to watch him play in the midst of the scandal) but also when the charges were dropped and Bryant returned to the Lakers.

Performing the "Good" Black Man

Closely tied to Bryant's class and celebrity privilege is his relationship to what numerous scholars have explored as the binary juxtaposition between "good" Black men versus "bad" Black men (Alexander, 2004; Bogle, 1996; Collins, 2006; Richardson, 2007). Rooted in slavery, this socially constructed dichotomy positions "good niggers" as those who are complicit in the face of power and aim to please Whites (Bogle, 1996). "Good" Black men are apolitical, domesticated, and emasculated (Collins, 2006; Richardson, 2007). By comparison, "bad niggers" resist oppression and speak truth to power as brutes in need of authority (Bogle, 1996; Brookes, 2002). "Bad" Black men appeal to Whiteness only in the context that they can be controlled and subsequently rendered less threatening. In the context of sport, "good" Black men are discursively constructed as those who are surprisingly civilized while "bad" Black men in need of discipline and supervision are the rule (rather than the exception). Noting the negative implications of this "fixed" binary, Ferber (2007) argues that the "division between the good guys who have been tamed and know their place versus the bad boys who refuse to submit to control reflects the historical and ongoing construction of black masculinity in dominant discourses and limits the ways in which Black men are now seen in our culture" (p. 22). Offering a sharp critique of the weakness inherent in both discursive positions of "good" and "bad," Collins (2006) says:

> Virtually all representations of black masculinity pivot on questions of weakness, whether it is a weakness associated with an inability to control violent impulses, sexual urges, or their black female heterosexual partners or a weakness attributed to men whose lack of education, employment patterns, and criminal records relegate them to inferior social spaces. . . . These images equate black male strength with wildness and suggest that an allegedly natural black male strength must be tamed by family, civilization, and, if all else fails, the military or the National Basketball Association. (p. 75)

Perceived as safe and admirable by Whites before the rape charges were filed, Bryant was clearly positioned as a "good" Black man. Highlighting Bryant's appeals to the embodiment of a palatable (and profitable) embodiment of Black masculinity,[16] previous to the charges being filed he was described as having a "pristine" image, embodying a "mature" demeanor, and being "the quintessential good guy" (Shapiro & Stevens, 2003, p. 21).

He was also referred to as the "single-minded basketball puritan" (Kawaka-mi, 2003), and Gittrich (2003) described him as "an athlete with a choirboy image who once told teammates, 'I would never get into trouble like Mike Tyson'" (p. 3). Drawing upon a comparison between Tyson and Bryant, Purdy (2003) offers:

> We know that, without making an immense leap, you can draw some parallels here to Mike Tyson's 1992 rape trial in Indianapolis. Just as Bryant did with his alleged victim, Tyson invited a young woman, still in her teens, to his hotel room. And the case more or less came down to he-said, she-said testimony. We know that, in the Tyson case, a jury found the boxer guilty. . . . The difference, of course, is that Bryant has a far more positive image than Tyson. That should help Bryant's credibility.

Further emblematic of Bryant's reputation as a "good" Black man are his childhood, character, and life experiences. Bryant grew up in Italy from ages six to twelve while his father, Joe Bryant, played professional basketball for the European leagues (Shapiro & Stevens, 2003). Much of the public praise for Bryant mentions his ability to speak fluent Italian, his respect for past players, his intelligence, and his preference for a private rather than flashy lifestyle (Shapiro & Stevens, 2004). Explicitly marking Bryant as "good" in an article entitled "Say it Ain't So Kobe," Zollo said, "Where Allen Iverson's been the bad boy, Kobe has been the pretty boy" (as quoted in Corliss, 2003).[17] Even the contrasting critiques of Bryant as "aloof," "self-absorbed," and "socially stunted" (Samuels, 2003; Smith, 2003) mark him as non-threatening, which sets him apart from the subject position of "bad" Black man. In addition to being situated as "good" via the media, Bryant also outwardly contradicted being positioned as a "bad" Black man during the investigation. For example, he cried in public, expressed concern for his family, openly admitted to being "terrified," and did exactly what he was told (Corliss, 2003; Purdy, 2003; Shapiro & Stevens, 2004; *Washington Post*, 2003).

Speaking to notions of "good" and "bad" Black masculinity, Leonard (2004) asserts, "In a single year, Kobe Bryant has gone from the next Michael Jordan to yet another Black athlete. Allegations have transformed him from an Uncle Tom to a dangerous Black brute" (p. 307). However, taking a critical account of the outpour of public support coupled with the suspicious absence of severe damage to his reputation, I disagree. In a similar vein, Katz (2006), reflecting on Bryant's assumed innocence as a man being falsely accused, says that Bryant was granted "honorary white citizenship" (p. 140), read critically as a pardon for embodying a performance of Black masculinity deemed acceptable in White eyes. Miller (2001) describes this phenomenon among Black professional athletes as a "black passport to white status" that is "always revocable" (p. 82), which necessitates the continued exploration of why Bryant's "honorary" "passport" into the protective embrace of "white supremacist capitalist patriarchy" (hooks, 2000) did not become an irate chokehold when he was accused, charged, and investigated. While this gesture of camaraderie with Whites may seem progressive on the surface, via interest convergence we can bear witness to the ways that "honorary white citizenship" (Jackson, 2006, p. 140) marks the convenience of Whites to act as gatekeepers in their own best interest.

Looking deeply at the layered complexity of racism guided by interest convergence reveals the public support for Black athletes in general and Bryant in particular as a means for Whites to claim colorblindness (Leonard, 2004). According to Leonard (2004), "Whites demonstrate their colorblindness through their pocketbooks (tickets, gear, and jerseys), hero worship, and love for players regardless of race" (p. 289). However, since colorblindness discursively functions to strengthen White supremacy rather than bespeak racial progress (Bonilla-Silva, 2003), in this context Bryant becomes a tokenistic symbol of racial progress that has yet to be made. From a critical standpoint, Bryant and other Black celebrity athletes such as Michael Jordan and Tiger Woods do not transcend race (i.e., meaning that race does not matter) rather they entice Whites to make racialized exceptions (i.e., meaning that race does not matter enough). Although the bipolar disposition toward Black men as "good" or "bad" is essentialist in nature by failing to recognize the diversity among Black men and relegating Black men to "stereotypically pathologized" positions (Alexander, 2006b, p. 74) as "sell outs" (i.e., good niggers) or "deviants" (i.e., bad niggers); it is also clear that Bryant's marked status as a "good" Black athlete appealed to those in positions of power and privilege. Thus had Bryant's image previous to the allegations not appealed to the social location of "good" Black man, his ability to protect his reputation via the claim of innocence would have been drastically diminished.

A Salute to Patriarchy

In addition to Bryant having access to class and celebrity privilege combined with his embodiment of an acceptable Black masculine identity, his recovery in the eyes of the public also serves as a salute to patriarchal understandings of violence against women. It has long been argued that sexual violence toward women is overlooked, dismissed, and encouraged in U.S. society (Brownmiller, 1972; Katz, 2006; Meyers, 1997). The rare exceptions are typically when a sexual violation meets the patriarchal standards of "real rape" (Estrich, 1987), which requires that the survivor be considered "rapable" (Freeman, 1993). "Real rape" according to Estrich (1987) occurs when a woman explicitly says "no," a stranger (rather than an acquaintance) has sex with her against her will, and she fights back during the attack. In addition, Freeman (1993) asserts that a woman must be "rapable" to be believed, which requires that the sexual violation of her body be considered a crime and called rape. If the sexual violation is not in accordance with "real rape" (Estrich, 1987), then "people are likely to employ one or more rape myths to explain away the assault" (Franuik et al., 2008). Grounded in patriarchal culture, rape myths function to dismiss the seriousness and likelihood of sexual assault (Burt, 1980; Katz, 2006). Oftentimes these myths manifest with indications that only certain types of women can be raped, most women ask for it and subsequently deserve to be raped, and men can't help themselves if a woman "leads" them on (Burt, 1980; Franuik et al., 2008). In this context, females are rarely afforded the assumption of honesty when they come forward and males are rarely held accountable for sexually violating women.

As previously discussed, the common exception to the patriarchal strength of rape myths has been when Black men have been suspected or accused of raping White women given the potency of racism (Brownmiller, 1972; Dorr, 2001; Mann & Selva, 1979; Wriggins, 1983). However, with regard to Bryant, the deployment of rape myths in his defense surprisingly remained steadfast despite the overwhelming tendency to criminalize any sexual contact between Black males and White females. Illustrating how patriarchal rape myths worked in Bryant's favor, Franuik et al. (2008) note the prevalence of assertions via media coverage that the woman was lying, that she actually wanted to have sex with Bryant, and that Bryant would not commit the crime of rape. More specifically, only 35 percent of the news articles analyzed did not contain rape myths (Franuik et al., 2008). Overall, the authors conclude that journalists were statistically more likely to write positively about Bryant as a person and negatively about the woman's character and reputation (Franuik et al., 2008). The representation of rape in the media is profoundly consequential in terms of the information the general public learns about the incident, the people involved, and how those involved are regarded and responded to. In the context of the allegations against Bryant, we must consider the public pedagogy of the press coverage. For example, while the woman was met most often with hostility and disbelief, Bryant was met with support and advocacy. While she was accused of trying to destroy and exploit the career of a famous athlete, he was positioned as a man who made a mistake. While she was depicted as an emotionally unstable, promiscuous, and money-hungry woman, Bryant attended the ESPY's and won "favorite male athlete" at the Teen Choice Awards (Harris, 2003). While she was plastered on the cover of the *Globe* with the headline "Kobe's Accuser: Did She Really Say No?" (Rodack, 2003) he was depicted in the media as a serious and sorrowful athlete struggling to save his family and his career. As a result, the media offered women who are victimized by gender violence a harsh lesson: come forward and risk public defamation.

Given the drastic differences in the discursive reaction toward the woman who came forward and Bryant, U.S. society as a male-dominated, male-centered, and male-identified culture (Johnson, 2004) becomes exceptionally clear. Consequently, Bryant's declaration that he was guilty of only adultery (CNN, 2003) was afforded much more credibility than the woman's indication that she had not been a willing participant in the sexual activity that occurred. Here we are reminded by gender violence research that rape myths function in patriarchal culture to relieve males of sexual responsibility, question the credibility of women, and blame survivors of sexual assault for having been assaulted (Burt, 1980; Franuik et al., 2008; Meyers, 1997). Additionally, accounting for interest convergence bolsters Dorr's (2001) assertion that after World War II White men ". . . became distrustful, not of their willingness to accuse black men falsely, but rather of their willingness to accuse *any* man of rape at all . . . as white women faced scrutiny of their motives, characters, and truthfulness, black men received a small, but real, share in the gender privileges white men held" [emphasis original] (p. 248). Extending Dorr's critical insight, Wriggins (1983) says:

> . . . since the tolerance of coerced sex has been the rule rather than the exception, it is clear that the rape of white women by black men has been treated seriously not because it is coerced sex and thus damaging to women, but because it is threatening to white men's power over both "their" women and black men. (p. 116)

Stemming from the ideological justification of violence against women and the willingness of Whites in particular and contrived instances to grant Black men more access to patriarchal privilege is the harsh reality that *all* men have a shared interest in the dehumanization of women. Working on behalf of Bryant, rape myths functioned to bolster the general public's opinion that he was innocent of rape while his accuser was discounted as an unreliable and greedy woman (Franuik et al., 2008). The conceptual insights of interest convergence reveal how Bryant via patriarchal commitments to the dehumanization of women becomes a tokenistic exemplar of hegemony at its best. Thus, those with a vested interest in protecting the oppressive foundation of U.S. society benefited on multiple fronts when Bryant was able to retain his cultural status as an iconic, professional basketball player. More specifically, in the aftermath of the media circus surrounding the case, violence against women remains indiscernible as a serious systemic issue allowing sexism to remain intact; colorblindness can be claimed allowing racism to remain unchallenged; and the billions in revenue the NBA and corporate sponsors generate as long as Bryant plays basketball keep the machination of capitalism lucrative.

THE IMPLICATIONS OF SYSTEMIC OPPRESSION

In reflection upon public discourse, it is vital to note that the majority of rapes are never mentioned in the media (Meyers, 1997). The cases that do garner media attention are likely to involve women who come forward as victims of famous males, which evidently validates the worth of rape as a news story. Illuminating the media's disingenuous coverage of violence against women as a severe and culturally sanctioned issue, more often than not women who come forward are vilified, demeaned, and blamed (Los & Chamard, 1997; Jiwani & Young, 2006; Meyers, 1997). Given that the women most commonly believed are White women who name a Black male as their attacker, I contend that the only force strong enough in U.S. society to prevent Bryant's fall from grace is the matrix of domination (Collins, 2000). In essence, sexism, racism, and classism were intentionally orchestrated to shield Bryant from the raced and gendered blows that easily could have been unleashed to shred his character, destroy his career, and remembering the diabolical past, even take his life.[18] Although those in power are laboriously dedicated to maintaining the invisibility of these systems, evidence of their strength arrived in my mailbox in February 2008 when Kobe Bryant appeared on the cover of *SLAM* magazine with the U.S. flag draped over his head and around his shoulders. The imagery of the draped flag brings forth that of a nun's veil. From beneath the flag, his face exudes focus and determination while the headline across his chest in large bold black print reads, "KOBE AGAINST THE WORLD" (*SLAM*, 2008). Although the cover story is dedicated to Bryant's role on Team USA which makes the U.S. flag a rational symbolic choice for the photo shoot, from a critical standpoint Bryant draped in the flag and *SLAM* choosing to display the image on the cover tells me that the allegations of rape made against Bryant have been essentially forgiven and forgotten.

Remembering interest convergence, the treatment of Bryant is not understood as an indication of the decriminalization of Black men in general or his individual ability to transcend race as a famous athlete. Rather, Bryant's ability to maintain his iconic status and continue to profit implies that the power structure is more committed to upholding patriarchy and profit than racism. For instance, marking the league's corporate decision to distance itself from the case, NBA commissioner David Stern said, "As with all allegations of a criminal nature, the NBA's policy is to await the outcome of a judicial proceeding before taking any action. We do not anticipate making further comments during the pendency of the judicial process" (CNN, 2003). A critical interpretation of the league's decisive action (or lack thereof) indicates that those in positions of power were more committed to protecting their investments than addressing rape as a social issue or entertaining the possibility that Bryant was in fact a rapist who deserved to be punished. Therefore, dominant systems did not turn toward race consciousness as some may be tempted to believe; in actuality they turned toward the maintenance of capitalistic profit and patriarchy. Simply stated, Kobe Bryant had enough to offer people with power in exchange for his freedom and livelihood. Given this outcome, it is clear that Bryant as a Black male who could have easily been criminalized beyond recovery is worth far more out of jail than he is in jail.

As a term of the agreement made between the prosecutors and the defense when the charges were dropped on September 1, 2004, Bryant made the following apology:

> First, I want to apologize directly to the young woman involved in this incident. I want to apologize to her for my behavior that night and for the consequences she has suffered in the past year. Although this year has been incredibly difficult for me personally, I can only imagine the pain she has had to endure. I also want to apologize to her parents and family members, and to my family and friends and supporters, and to the citizens of Eagle, Colorado.
>
> I also want to make it clear that I do not question the motives of this young woman. No money has been paid to this woman. She has agreed that this statement will not be used against me in the civil case. Although I truly believe this encounter between us was consensual, I recognize now that she did not and does not view this incident the same way I did. After months of reviewing discovery, listening to her attorney, and even her testimony in person, I now understand how she feels that she did not consent to this encounter. (ESPN, 2004b)

In the context of his apology, Bryant ironically became one of the few people reported in the media to express sorrow for the woman who named him as her attacker. Housed within this apology, likely crafted by Bryant's expensive legal team, he acknowledges her pain, refutes accusations that she was motivated by money, and albeit oddly, concedes that from her perspective she did not consent to sex. [19] Crystallizing our understanding of the case as is and subsequently Bryant's access to systemic privilege, the civil case was settled for an undisclosed amount in March 2005 (Sarche, 2005). Sparse information regarding the settlement released to the media was accompanied by a statement from Bryant's attorneys that read, "The parties and their attorneys have agreed that no further comments about the matter can or will be made" (Sarche, 2005).

CONCLUSION

In closing, whether you believe in the innocence or guilt of Bryant and the long list of professional athletes who have been accused, charged and/or tried for gender violence, including O. J. Simpson, Mike Tyson, Sean Burke, Patrick Roy, Christian Peter, and most recently Ben Roethlisberger; of importance to remember is that public discourse informs private consciousness. With regard to the public discourse surrounding Bryant, I am particularly concerned with how easily and conveniently rape myths were deployed to protect him in accordance with dominant interests. More pointedly, the general public, under the influence of the media, has continually blamed women who come forward and often forgiven, if not rewarded, the men they accuse time and time again. Consider Anita Hill, Patricia Bowman, and Desiree Washington—all of whom were defamed for accusing powerful men of sexual offenses before Bryant's accuser was largely damned by the press and the public. Mirroring my grave concerns regarding the public pedagogy of high-profile rape cases such as Bryant's, Sharon Carbine, an alumni of Lower Merion High School where Bryant was a star basketball player, said, "My impression is that Kobe has done phenomenal harm to women. . . . I am seriously concerned that other women who have been raped in the future will be afraid to report the rape due to what they saw happen to this young woman" (Blanchard, Mastrull, & Schogol, 2004). In reflection on the lessons offered with regard to Bryant's seeming avoidance of a fall from grace, critically I must ask, when will men who can reap the benefits of privilege be consistently held accountable for hurting women both legally and socially regardless of their public image? Likewise, when will women be afforded respect and public concern regardless of who the accused may be? As it stands, the blind idolization of celebrity athletes comes at a cost and in the context of gender violence those who pay the highest price are the one billion women in the world who will be bruised, beaten, and raped in their lifetime (United Nations, 2006). As such, we must question the ways that gender violence is normalized, ignored, and excused on a daily basis. Likewise, we must situate sport and media as pedagogical forms of popular culture rather than innocent entertainment. In closing, I leave you with a quote from a reporter whose words left me quite humble in a state of self-reflection on the Bryant case: "Something bad happened. Two lives will never be the same. Shame on us for treating it as entertainment" (Lincicome, 2003).

NOTES

1. This is not to insinuate that Bryant should have been assumed to be guilty as a Black man accused of raping a White woman. Nor do I wish to imply that the stereotypical assumption of Black males as insatiable beasts is fair, appropriate, or acceptable. However, the strength of this cultural stereotype has been well documented by numerous scholars (Mann & Selva, 1979; Marable, 2000; Saint-Aubin, 2002; Wriggins, 1983), which renders the instances in which it does not take hold rich for examination.

2. I choose to identify as a biracial Black woman to mark both avowal and ascription in regard to identity performance. Hence, I identify myself as biracial to mark both my African American and White cultural roots, however, my body is often read solely as Black.

3. Each of these cases will be briefly described in the section entitled "Black Male/White Female Interracial Sexual Contact."

4. The wording of this question was inspired by a news article entitled "Bryant's Fall from Grace Irreparable" (Lincicome, 2003).

5. Although I am not focusing on his innocence or guilt, I do position the improbability of any woman filing a false report as contextually important. As it stands, the false report rate for rape is comparable to that of other serious crimes and ranges between 2 to 8 percent (Lonsway, Archambault, & Lisak, 2009); this means that approximately 92 percent of the time women who come forward are telling the truth.

6. The woman who came forward to file charges against Bryant had her name released to the public in violation of Colorado's rape shield laws by Bryant's defense lawyer, radio talk shows, tabloids, and websites (Haddad, 2005). Therefore although her name is known, out of respect for her privacy and rape shield laws, I will not use her name.

7. It is important to recognize that the woman's decision not to testify does not mean that she recanted her story. Rather it means that she did not wish to take the stand and recount her experiences in court. Equally as important to recognize is that because the case did not go to trial, neither Bryant or the woman testified under oath.

8. To avoid essentialism, it is important to recognize that not all Whites endorsed slavery or were racist. However, categories of race were created and maintained for the benefit of people who could identify or pass as White (Harris, 1995).

9. As notions of U.S. society as "post-racial" circulate now that Barack Obama has been elected as the first African American president, some might advocate to add "president" to the list of subject positions largely available to Black males. However, I am quite cautious in doing so since most Black men will never be assumed to be president or assumed to have the potential to be president whereas most Black men will be assumed to identify as athletes, criminals, and/ or hip-hop stars at some point in their lifetimes. For rich discussions of the impact of President Obama's campaign and presidency on discourses concerning race and racism, see Bonilla-Silva and Ray (2009) and Terrill (2009).

10. See Patton and Snyder-Yuly (2007) for a detailed discussion of both of these cases.

11. Childs (2005) offers insight as to how interracial relationships have historically been perceived as a cultural taboo that few welcome and many seem to hope will deteriorate, disappear, or at least not appear in their own families and neighborhoods. In addition, Leonard (2004) offers lucid examples of White supremacist reactions to Bryant being charged with raping a White woman.

12. During the Cold War, racism in the United States received a great deal of negative international attention. Take, for example, Jimmy Wilson who in 1958 was sentenced to the electric chair for stealing $1.95; not only was he sentenced but his conviction was upheld by the Alabama Supreme Court (Dudziak, 2000). This case in particular resulted in international outrage from countries including but not limited to Australia, Africa, Canada, England, Italy, Jamaica, Israel, and Norway; see Dudziak (2000) for further discussion. Also, see Clark and Pearlman (1948) and Dudziak (2000) for additional examples.

13. Take for example, *Roberts v. City of Boston* (1849), *Dred Scott v. Sandford* (1857), and *Plessy v. Ferguson* (1896). See Bell (1980b), Browne-Marshall (2007), and Delgado (2002) for further discussion.

14. African Americans such as Josephine Baker, W. E. B. DuBois, and Paul Robeson who were well known nationally and internationally were exceptionally vocal regarding the racist treatment of Blacks in the United States, especially during the Cold War. Internationally, the United States viewed this as a potential crisis, especially when outspoken Blacks began advocating in favor of Communism abroad (Bell, 1980a; Delgado, 2002; Dudziak, 2000). In addition, hundreds of Blacks had fought in the Vietnam war and the likelihood of them acquiescing to racist treatment upon their return to the U.S. was slim (Dudziak, 2000).

15. This is not to say that all Whites who were in favor of Black equality acted out of self-interest but rather to note that at this time in U.S. history, progressive Whites had not been able to secure such large measures in favor of Black equality based solely on appeals to democratic humanity (Bell, 1980a).

16. It is essential to recognize that those who embody notions of "good" Black men are regarded positively according to the White status quo (Alexander, 2006b).

17. See Brown (2005) for a rich critique of the ways that media discourse positions Allen Iverson as a "bad" Black man.

18. This not to say that Bryant himself or his family, financial earnings, and reputation did not endure any negative consequences whatsoever; he noted his own embarrassment and humiliation, apologized for the suffering of his family, lost some endorsements, and was occasionally booed (Associated Press, 2006; CNN, 2003). However, it is important to recognize that not only was he able to regain his popularity but it is also questionable as to whether he ever truly lost his popularity given the outpour of public support. More specifically, given that his jersey never fell from among the top ten sellers and that major corporations such as Nike kept him under contract it seems that he avoided the public admonishment that the majority of Black men accused of raping White women have endured.

19. Arguably detracting from any reading of sincerity in Bryant's apology were his defense lawyers Pamela Mackey and Hal Haddon, who said, "Kobe was facing life in prison for a crime he did not commit. The accuser insisted on that statement as the price for his freedom. That statement doesn't change the facts: Kobe is innocent and now he is free" (ESPN, 2004).

REFERENCES

ABC News. (2003). Cuban: Kobe scandal "Great Business for NBA": Dallas Mavericks owner says Bryant rape allegations will boost ratings. ABC News. Retrieved from http://abcnews.go.com.

Abrams, J. (2010, May 2). Heading home to celebrate. *New York Times*. Retrieved from http://www.nytimes.com.

Alexander, B. K. (2004). Passing, cultural performance, and individual agency: Performative reflections on Black masculine identity. *Cultural Studies/Critical Methodologies, 4*(3), 377-404.

Alexander, B. K. (2006a). Performance ethnography: The reenacting and inciting of culture. In D. S. Madison & J. Hamera (Eds.), *The Sage handbook of performance studies* (pp. 411-441). Thousand Oaks, CA: Sage Publications.

Alexander, B. K. (2006). *Performing black masculinity: Race, culture, and queer identity.* Lanham, MD: AltaMira Press.

Andrews, D. L., & Jackson, S. J. (Eds.). (2001). *Sport stars: The cultural politics of sporting celebrity.* New York: Routledge.

Arango, T. (2007, December 10). LeBron Inc. *Fortune*, pp. 100-108.

Araton, H. (2010, February 20). Apologizing, Woods sets no date for return to golf. *New York Times*. Retrieved from http://www.nytimes.com.

Associated Press. (2003, December 31). Bryant rape case named story of year. Retrieved from http://nbcsports.msnbc.com.

Associated Press. (2006, February 9). After 2½ years, Kobe's first Nike ad airs. Retrieved from http://nbcsports.msnbc.com.

Baynton, D. C. (2001). Disability and the justification of inequality in American history. In P. Longmore & L. Umanski (Eds.), *The new disability history: American perspectives* (pp. 33-57). New York: New York University Press.

Beckstaff, H. (2003, October 24). Kobe at ease and effective in Lakers loss. *San Bernardino Sun.* Retrieved from http://www.lexisnexis.com.

Bell, D. (1980a). *Brown v. Board of Education* and the interest convergence dilemma. *Harvard Law Review, 93*(3), 518-533.

Bell, D. (1980b). *Civil rights: Leading cases.* Boston: Little, Brown.

Black, D. P. (1997). *Dismantling black manhood: Studies in African American history and culture.* New York: Garland Publishers.

Blanchard, M. P., Mastrull, D., & Schogol, M. (2004, September 2). Reaction mixed at Kobe Bryant's alma matter; At Lower Merion High School's freshman orientation, students cheered. Parents and alumni, however, hedged. *Philadelphia Inquirer*, B01.

Bogle, D. (1996). *Toms, coons, mulattoes, mammies, and bucks: An interpretive history of blacks in American films* (4th ed.). New York: Continuum.

Bonilla-Silva, E. (2003). *Racism without racists: Color-blind racism and the persistence of racial inequality in the United States.* Lanham, MD: Rowman & Littlefield.

Bonilla-Silva, E., & Ray, V. (2009). When Whites love a Black leader: Race matters in Obamaerica. *Journal of African American Studies, 13*, 176-183.

Boris, E. (1994). Gender, race, and rights: Listening to Critical Race Theory. *Journal of Women's History, 6*(2), 111-124.

Boser, U. (2002, August 26/September 2). The black man's burden: The Scottsboro travesty of 1931 did not end scapegoating of African-Americans. *U.S. News & World Report*, 50-51.

Brookes, R. (2002). *Representing sport.* New York: Oxford University Press.

Browne-Marshall, G. J. (2007). *Race, law, and American society: 1607 to present.* New York: Routledge.

Brownmiller, S. (1975). *Against our will: Men, women, and rape.* New York, NY: Fawcett Columbine.

Brown, T. J. (2005). Allan Iverson as America's most wanted: Black masculinity as a cultural site of struggle. *Journal of Intercultural Communication Research, 34*(1), 65-87.

Bucher, R. (2003). Error in Eagle County sheriff's judgment. ESPN. Retrieved from http://sports.espn.go.com.

Burt, M. R. (1980). Cultural myths and support for rape. *Journal of Personality and Social Psychology, 38*, 217-230.

Butterfield, F. (1992, November 1). Trial to begin in 1989 slaying case in Boston. *New York Times.* Retrieved from http://www.nytimes.com.

Butterworth, M. L. (2007). Race in "the race": Mark McGwire, Sammy Sosa, and the heroic construction of Whiteness. *Critical Studies in Media Communication, 24*, 228-244.

Cashin, S. D. (2005). Shall we overcome? Transcending race, class, and ideology through interest convergence. *St. John's Law Review, 79*, 253-291.

Castagno, A. E., & Lee, S. J. (2007). Native mascots and ethnic fraud in higher education: Using tribal critical race theory and the interest convergence principle as an analytic tool. *Equity and Excellence in Education, 40*, 3-13.

Chapman, T. K. (2005). Expressions of "voice" in portraiture. *Qualitative Inquiry, 11*(1), 27-51.

Chattanooga Times Free Press. (2003, October 4). Friend says accuser attempted suicide. Retrieved from http://www.lexisnexis.com.

Childs, E. C. (2005). *Navigating interracial borders: Black-White couples and their social worlds.* New Brunswick, NJ: Rutgers University Press.

Clark, T. C., & Perlman, P. B. (1948). *Prejudice and property: An historic brief against racial covenants.* Washington: Public Affairs Press.

CNN. (2003). Kobe Bryant charged with sexual assault. Retrieved from http://www.cnn.com.

Collins, P. H. (2000). *Black feminist thought: Knowledge, consciousness, and the politics of empowerment.* (2nd ed.). New York: Routledge.

Collins, P. H. (2006). A telling difference: Dominance, strength, and Black masculinities. In A. D. Mutua (Ed.). *Progressive Black masculinities* (pp.73-97). New York: Routledge.

Corliss, R. (2003, July 28). Say it ain't so, Kobe. *Time, 162*(4). Retrieved from www.time.com.

Crenshaw, K., Gotanda, N., Peller, G., and Thomas, K. (Eds.). (1995). *Critical race theory: The key writings that formed the movement.* New York: The New York Press.

Crenshaw, K. W. (1995). Mapping the margins: Intersectionality, identity politics, and violence against women of color. In D. Danielson and K. Engle (Eds.), *After identity: A reader in law and culture* (pp.332-354). New York: Routledge.

Davis, A. (1985). *Violence against women and the ongoing challenge to racism.* Latham, NY: Kitchen Table Press.

Davis, T. (1995). The myth of the superspade: The persistence of racism in college athletics. *Fordham Urban Law Journal, 22*(3), 615-698.

Delgado, F. P. (1997). Major league soccer: The return of the foreign sport. *Journal of Sport and Social Issues, 21*, 287-299.

Delgado, F. P. (2005). Golden but not brown: Oscar de la Hoya and the complications of culture, manhood, and boxing. *International Journal of the History of Sport 22*, 194-210.

Delgado, R. (2000). Story-telling for oppositionalists and others: A plea for narrative. In R. Delgado & J, Stefancic (Eds.), *Critical race theory: The cutting edge* (2nd ed.) (pp. 60-70). Philadelphia: Temple University Press.

Delgado, R. (2002). Explaining the rise and fall of African American fortunes—Interest convergence and Civil Rights gains. *Harvard Law Review, 37*, 369-387.

Delgado, R. (2006). Rodrigo's roundelay: *Hernandez v. Texas* and the Interest-convergence dilemma. *Harvard Law Review, 41*, 23-65.

Delgado, R., & Stefancic, J. (2001). *Critical race theory: An introduction.* New York: New York University Press.

Dilbeck, S. (2003, October 24). For Bryant, nerves not an issue on court. *Daily News of Los Angeles*, pp. S1.

Dixson, A. D., & Rousseau, C. K. (2005). And we still are not saved: Critical race theory in education ten years later. *Race Ethnicity and Education, 8*(1), 7-27.

Donnor, J. K. (2005). Towards an interest-convergence in the education of African-American football student athletes in major college sports. *Race Ethnicity and Education, 8*(1), 45-67.

Dorr, L. L. (2001). "Another Negro-Did-It Crime": Black-on-White rape and protest in Virginia, 1945-1960. In M. D. Smith (Ed.), *Sex without consent: Rape and sexual coercion in America* (pp.247-264). New York: New York University Press.

Dudziak, M. L. (2000). *Cold War Civil Rights: Race and the image of American democracy.* Princeton, NJ: Princeton University Press.

ESPN. (2004a). Case will not be retried, but civil trial pending. Retrieved from http://sports. espn.go.com.

ESPN. (2004b). Kobe Bryant's apology. Retrieved from http://sports.espn.go.com.

Estrich, S. (1987). *Real rape.* Cambridge, MA: Harvard University Press.

Fanon, F. (1967). *Black skin, White masks.* New York: Grove Press.

Fears, D. (2007, May 3). Exonerations change how justice system builds a prosecution: DNA tests have cleared 200 convicts. *Washington Post*. Retrieved from http://www. washingtonpost.com.

Ferber, A. L. (2007). The construction of black masculinity: White supremacy now and then. *Journal of Sport and Social Issues, 31*(1), 11-24.

Franuik, R., Seefelt, J. L., Cepress, S. L., & Vandello, J. A. (2008). Prevalence and effects of rape myths in print journalism. *Violence Against Women, 14*(3), 287-309.

Freeman, J. (1993). The disciplinary function of rape's representation: Lessons from the Kennedy Smith and Tyson trials. *Law and Social Inquiry, 18*(3), 517-546.

Giroux, H. A. (2004). Cultural studies, public pedagogy, and the responsibility of intellectuals. *Communication and Critical/Cultural Studies, 1*(1), 59-79.

Giroux, H. (2000). Public pedagogy as cultural politics: Stuart Hall and the "crisis" of culture. *Cultural Studies, 14*(2), 341-360.

Gittrich, G. (2003, October 6). Fear of split sickened Kobe's wife. *Daily News*, 3.

Goodman, J. (1994). *Stories of Scottsboro: The rape case that shocked 1930's America and revived the struggle for equality.* New York: Pantheon Books.

Haddad, R. I. (2005). Shield or sleeve? *People v. Bryant* and the rape shield law in high-profile cases. *Columbia Journal of Law and Social Problems, 39*, 185-221.

Hammel, S. (2007, September 5). Shaquille O'Neal files for divorce. *People*. Retrieved from http://www.people.com/people/article/0,,20054672,00.html

Harris, C. (1995). Whiteness as property. In K. Crenshaw, N. Gotanda, G. Peller, & Thomas, K. (Eds.). *Critical race theory: The key writings that formed the movement.* (pp.276-291). New York: The New York Press.

Harris, D. (2003, August 7). PR is key for Kobe Bryant. ABC News. Retrieved from http://abcnews.go.com.

Hecht, M. L., Jackson, R. L., & Ribeau, S. A. (2003). *African American communication: Exploring identity and culture.* (2nd ed.). Mahwah, NJ: Lawrence Erlbaum Associates.

Hoberman, J. N. (1997). *Darwin's athletes: How sport has damaged Black America and preserved the myth of race.* Boston: Houghton Mifflin.

Hodes, M. (1997). *White women, Black men: Illicit sex in the nineteenth-century South.* New Haven, CT: Yale University Press.

hooks, b. (1981). *Ain't I a Woman: Black women and feminism.* Boston: South End Press.

hooks, b. (2000). *Where we stand: Class matters.* New York: Routledge.

Hylton, K. (2005). "Race," sport and leisure: Lessons from critical race theory. *Leisure Studies, 24*(1), 81-98.

Jackson, B. (2010, April 27). Documentary provides insight into Miami Dolphins' Ricky Williams. *Miami Herald*. Retrieved from http://www.miamiherald.com

Jackson, R. L. (2006). *Scripting the black male body: Identity discourse, and racial politics in popular media.* New York: State University of New York Press.

Jackson, R. L., & Dangerfield, C. (2002). Defining black masculinity as cultural property: Toward an identity negotiation paradigm. In L. Samovar & R. Porter (Eds.), *Intercultural communication: A reader* (10th ed.) (pp. 120-130). Belmont, CA: Thomson Wadsworth.

Jiwani, Y., & Young, M. L. (2006). Missing and murdered women: Reproducing marginality in news discourse. *Canadian Journal of Communication, 31*, 895-917.

Johnson, A. (2004). Patriarchy. In P. S. Rothenburg (Ed.), *Race, class and gender in the United States.* (6th ed.) (pp.165-174). New York: Worth Publishers.

Katz, J. (2006). *The macho paradox: Why some men hurt women and how all men can help.* Naperville, FL: Sourcebooks.

Kawakami, T. (2003, October 9). In Bryant, shades of Mike Tyson; His life come unhinged, star faces fight alone. *San Jose Mercury News*, 1D.

Kennedy, R. (2002). Interracial intimacy. *Atlantic Monthly*, 103-110.

Ladson-Billings, G. (2004). New directions for multicultural education: Complexities, boundaries, and critical race theory. In J. A. Banks & M. C. A. Banks (Eds.), *Handbook of research on multicultural education* (2nd ed.) (pp. 50-65). San Francisco: Jossey Bass.

Leigh, P. R. (2003). Interest convergence and desegregation in the Ohio Valley. *Journal of Negro Education, 72*(3), 269-296.

Leonard, D. J. (2004). The next M.J. or the next O.J.? Kobe Bryant, race, and the absurdity of colorblind rhetoric. *The Journal of Sport and Social Issues, 28*(3), 284-313. doi: 10.1177/0193723504267546.

Lincicome, B. (2003, October 11). Bryant's fall from grace irreparable. *Seattle Post*, D2.

Lonsway, K. A., Archambault, J., & Lisak, D. (2009). False reports: Moving beyond the issue to successfully investigate and prosecute non-stranger sexual assault. *Voice, 3*(1), 1-12.

Los, M., & Chamard, S. E. (1997). Selling newspapers or educating the public? Sexual violence in the media. *Canadian Journal of Criminology, 39*, 293-328.

Luzadder, D., & Martinez, J. (2004, January 24). Team Kobe raises race as issue. *Daily News*. Retrieved from http://www.lexisnexis.com

Mann, C. R., & Selva, L. H. (1979). The sexualization of racism: The Black rapist and White justice. *Western Journal of Black Studies, 3*(3), 168-176.

Marable, M. (1998). The Black male: Searching beyond stereotypes. In M. S. Kimmel & M. A. Messner, *Men's lives* (4th ed.) (pp. 18-24). Boston: Allyn & Bacon.

Marable, M. (2000). *How capitalism underdeveloped black America.* Boston: South End Press.

McDonald, M. G., & Birrell, S. (1999). Reading sport critically: A methodology for interrogating power. *Sociology of Sport Journal, 16*, 283-300.

Metress, C. (Ed.). (2002). *The lynching of Emmett Till: A documentary narrative.* University of Virginia Press.

Meyer, D. (2003, August 6). Cuban on Kobe: Scandal sells. CBS News. Retrieved from http://www.cbsnews.com.

Meyers, M. (1997). *News coverage of violence against women: Engendering blame.* Thousand Oaks, CA: Sage Publications.

Moore, D. L. (2003, October 24). Crowd warms to Bryant in his return to Lakers. *USA Today,* 10C.

Miller, T. (2001). *Sportsex.* Philadelphia: Temple University Press.

Mitchell, M. (2007, June 17). He raped a White woman—or did he?—too many red flags in '02 trial of poor, Black man. *Chicago Sun-Times.* Retrieved from http://0-infoweb.newsbank.com.bianca.penlib.du.edu.

Mutua, A. D. (2006). Theorizing progressive Black masculinities. In A. D. Mutua (Ed.). *Progressive Black masculinities* (pp.3-42). New York: Routledge.

NBA. (2004). Shaq, T-Mac lead most popular jersey list. Retrieved from http://www.nba.com.

NBA. (2010). NBA Finals: All-time champions. Retrieved from www.NBA.com.

Nelson, R. (2009). Kobe tops NBA jersey sales, again. Retrieved from www.slamonline.com.

Norris, C., & Washington, S. (1979). *The last of the Scottsboro boys.* New York: Putnam.

Oates, T. P. (2007). The erotic gaze in the NFL draft. *Communication and Critical/Cultural Studies, 4*(1), 74-90.

Patton, T. O., & Snyder-Yuly, J. (2007). Any four Black men will do: Rape, race, and the ultimate scapegoat. *Journal of Black Studies, 37*(6), 859-895.

Purdy, M. (2003, October 10). Bryant case so far: Ugh; What we've learned doesn't bode well. *San Jose Mercury News,* 1D.

Randhawa, K. (2010, February 19). Tiger Woods today made an emotional apology to the world as he said: "I had affairs, I cheated." *London Evening Standard.* Retrieved from http://www.thisislondon.co.uk.

Richardson, R. (2007). *Black masculinity and the U.S. South: From Uncle Tom to gangsta.* Athens: University of Georgia Press.

Rodack, J. (2003). *Globe* defends decision to publish photo, name of Kobe accuser. The Poynter Institute. Retrieved from http://www.poynter.org/content/content_print.asp?id=53516.

Saint-Aubin, A. F. (2002). A grammar of black masculinity: A body of science. *The Journal of Men's Studies, 10*(3), 247-270.

Samuels, A. (2003, October 13). Kobe off the court. *Newsweek.* Retrieved from http://0-find.galegroup.com.bianca.penlib.du.edu.

Sarche, J. (2005, March 5). Kobe Bryant, rape accuser settle civil suit. *San Diego Union Tribune.* Retrieved from http://signonsandiego.com.

Sandlin, J. A. (2007). Popular culture, cultural resistance, and anticonsumption activism: An explanation of culture jamming as critical adult education. *New Directions for Adult and Continuing Adult Education, 115,* 73-82.

Shapiro, J., Stevens, J. (2004). *Kobe Bryant: The game of his life.* New York: Revolution Publishing.

SLAM. (2008, February). A man apart. *SLAM.* pp. 70-75.

Smith, D. M. (2001). Introduction: Studying rape in American history. In M. D. Smith (Ed.), *Sex without consent: Rape and sexual coercion in America* (pp.1-9). New York: New York University Press.

Smith, S. A. (2003, October 12). Kobe has family that's failed him. *Philadelphia Inquirer,* D01.

Staples, R. (1980). *Black masculinity: The Black male's role in American society.* San Francisco: Black Scholar Press.

Tate, W. F. (1997). Critical race theory and education: History, theory, and implications. *Review of Research, 22,* 195-247.

Taylor, E. (2000). Critical race theory and interest convergence in the backlash against Affirmative Action: Washington State Initiative 200. *Teachers College Record, 102*(3), 539-560.

Terrill, R. E. (2009). Unity and duality in Barack Obama's "A More Perfect Union." *Quarterly Journal of Speech, 95*(4)363-386. doi: 10.1080/00335630903296192.

Terry, D. (1994, November 6). A woman's false accusation pains many Blacks. *New York Times*. Retrieved from http://www.nytimes.com.

Trujillo, N. (1991). Hegemonic masculinity at the mound: Media representations of Nolan Ryan and American sports culture. *Critical Studies in Mass Communication 8*, 290-308.

USA Today. (2003, March 18). 2002-2003 NBA salaries—Western Conference. Retrieved from www.usatoday.com.

USA Today. (2004, April 6). Posh Spice confident about her marriage. Retrieved from www.usatoday.com.

Washington Post. (2003, October 5). Bryant "terrified" upon his return to the Lakers. *The Washington Post*. pp.E03.

Wilson, T. B. (1965). *The black codes of the South*. Birmingham: University of Alabama Press.

Wing, A. K. (1997). Introduction. In A. K. Wing (Ed.), *Critical race feminism: A reader*. (pp. 1-18) New York: New York University Press.

Wriggins, J. (1983). Rape, racism, and the law. *Harvard Women's Law Review, 6*, 103-141.

Youngman, R. (2003, October 25). A not so fabulous debut for Lakers. *Orange County Register*. Retrieved from http://www.lexisnexis.com.

Chapter Eight

Strategies of Silence: The John Terry Affair and the British Press

John Huxford, Illinois State University

"John Terry wants to become England's forgotten man," the *Sun*, Britain's most popular and populist tabloid, told readers on March 5, 2010. After five weeks of "scandal and sleaze, of tawdry revelations and scurrilous tales, of humiliation and loathing" (Smith, 2010, p. 7), the media storm surrounding Chelsea footballer Terry's affair with a teammate's partner had begun to subside—much to the relief of the man at its center. "It's important we forget this now and forget about me," Terry told reporters. "We just need to concentrate on winning the World Cup. . . . I certainly hope we can draw a line under everything now" (Jiggins, 2010, p. 82).

Branded "a liar, a cheat, a disgrace" (Evans & Tetteh, 2010, 4-5), a "laughing stock" (White & Pyatt, 2010, p. 4-5), and a "drinker and womanizer" (Pendlebury, 2010, p. 24), Terry's future looked bleak after the removal of a court injunction allowed journalists to trumpet his failings to the world. Yet despite a painful mauling in the media, Terry had emerged from the experience with his career largely intact and with a public image which, if tattered, remained serviceable. And this without the footballer ever issuing the sort of public apology that had been the mainstay of the defense of fellow sports sinner Tiger Woods.

The John Terry controversy offers an intriguing perspective on celebrity impression management. Coming on the heels of a campaign to rebrand the soccer star as a sponsor-friendly "family man," the scandal was met by Terry and his image makers with careful strategies of silence, absence and realignment, tactics that continued to echo in that final plea in March for national amnesia.

In exploring the Terry case study, this chapter brings together two important bodies of communication thought: the group of interrelated concepts known collectively as the "dramaturgical model" or "facework," and perspectives broadly categorized as the "narrative "paradigm" or "narrative theory."

The dramaturgical approach, originally and most famously pursued by sociologist Irving Goffman (1959, 1967) but extended by others (e.g., Cupach & Metts, 1994; Welsh, 1990; Benford & Hunt, 1992) regards communication as a series of performances, with the individual sliding from persona to persona in an on-going campaign of impression management. Key concepts arising from the theory include the difference between impressions deliberately given and those less consciously "given off" to audiences, the distinction between front and back stage, and the division of performance into such essential components as "setting" and "scene" (Goffman, 1959).

Yet for all of Goffman's reliance on theatrical metaphors, the dramaturgical model he offers stops short of regarding the subject as performing within the parameters of a given narrative. In the theatre, performances are seldom ad hoc or discrete, but rather exist within the context of an unfolding storyline. If all the world is indeed a stage and all its people merely players, as Shakespeare and Goffman would have it, then we are engaged not only in performance, but also in the quintessentially human activity of sense-making through storytelling (Porter, Larson, Harthcock, & Nellis, 2002; Fisher, 1984). Regarded by Fisher as an all-encompassing lens for communication (Fisher, 1984), narrative is seen as crucial to the cultural and social matrix that shapes individuals' lives (Rodden, 2008), a structuring framework influencing such diverse disciplines as psychology (Sarbin, 1986), education (Lyle, 2000) and journalism (Darnton, 1975; Campbell, 1991).

Applying textual analysis to a sample of national British newspapers,[1] this study explores the way in which performance and narrativization played out across coverage of the Terry scandal. I argue that, faced with public and commercial disaster, Terry—or perhaps more credibly, the image makers with whom he was surrounded[2]—utilized not only techniques of facework, but also diverse strategies of silence and absence, and directed narrativization, in a concerted attempt to salvage and reconstitute Terry's public image.

Performed within the semiotic space carved out by Terry's silence on the affair, these narratives of heroic quest, betrayal and confrontation, and emotional reunion centered around a trio of expressive displays that marked and shaped press coverage, discussed here as The Armband, The Handshake and The Kiss.

Each of these performances was disseminated and, to varying degrees, supported in the pages of the press both pictorially and textually, casting Terry in a specific persona, acting out particular scenes within a given narrative, with each carried to a mass audience.

In part one, I offer background on the history and influence of football in Britain, as well as discussing briefly John Terry's checkered career prior to the scandal of 2010. In the second section, I turn to an analysis of news coverage of the scandal, and a discussion of its implications for image management.

PART ONE: BACKGROUND

"The People's Game"

If sport is a key institution in the constitution of national identity (Smart, 2005, 13), human drama "at its finest" (Jackson & Andrews, 2005, 10) and a crucial component in the national and global economy (Mason, 1989; Kuper, 2003), then soccer stands as its most favored son.

Association football—or soccer as it is better known in the United States—can legitimately claim to be the world's most popular game. A survey conducted by FIFA (Fédération Internationale de Football Association), the sport's international ruling body, found that more than 240 million people are actively involved in playing the game today, roughly one out of every twenty-five of the world's population. At the same time, soccer's showpiece tournament—the World Cup—attracts the largest audience of any televised event. In 2006 it aired across 214 countries and territories, garnering 26 billion viewers (FIFA.com). The 2010 competition aimed to draw even larger numbers (SouthAfrica.info).

Historically, the roots of football run deep. Ancient China, Greece and Rome all engaged in ball games of varying styles and complexities, but it is medieval England that can be said to have truly invented the game (Dunning and Sheard, 1979; Rooney and Davidson, 1995). Traditionally played on Saints Days and other religious holidays, "folk" football matches sprang up across England from 800 BC onward, early examples being recorded in Derby, Atherstone, Sedgefield, Ashbourne, Twickenham and Teddington, among others (Malcolmson, 1973, 37). Light on rules and heavy on physical contact, these games could involve more than a thousand participants, range from one end of a town to another and last for days, occasionally turning into full-blown riots (Malcolmson, 1973; Dunning and Sheard, 1979; Bowden, 1995). It would not be until the nineteenth century that football developed into its recognizable form, with the first professional football league being established in 1888 (Dunning and Sheard, 1979; Home et al., 1999).

Rooted in working-class sensibilities, and most strongly associated with the north of England, the sport initially trailed the more middle-to-upper class English pastimes of tennis and cricket in both popularity and prestige, with the latter most likely to be regarded as the national sport (Holt, 1996).

While more prominent than its alternate variation—rugby football—the association game only truly began to broaden its appeal to include a professional and middle-class audience in the second half of the twentieth century. While the aftermath of war heightened the popularity for sport as an affordable form of mass entertainment (Smart, 2005; Mason, 1996), a collision of factors in the 1960s transformed football: the loosening of rules that limited the transfer of players between clubs, the ending of maximum wage limits and the advent of television all serving to change the nature and scope of the game (Mason, 1996). Although audience figures fluctuated over the next two decades, football had become the only credible contender for the title of "the people's game" (Walvin, 1994).

It was the growth of international soccer that would finally cement the sport's status in its mother country. In particular, the staging of the World Cup in England in 1966—and the national team's eventual triumph in a final watched by 400 million people worldwide—turned the team into a cultural icon and transformed football into something approaching a national obsession (Tibballs, 2003). By this time, soccer had become a weekly fixture on television, with the BBC's highlight show *Match of the Day* starting two years earlier. However much audiences at the grounds might rise and fall, television coverage would ensure football retained its hold on the nation, while also leading the sport deeper into the perilous realm of corporate sponsorship.

Football Celebrities

In terms of celebrity, footballers had found it difficult to match their cricketing counterparts. While a handful of players—including Stanley Matthews and Billy Wright—had transcended local notoriety to become national figures, the televised 1966 World Cup final brought a new level of stardom, with hat-trick hero Geoff Hurst, Captain Bobby Moore and Bobby Charlton becoming household names (Tibballs, 2003). The combination of television's ubiquity and the status of the national side made celebrity an increasingly important part of the sport. At the same time, a focus on football and its stars became central to the circulation wars being fought between Britain's burgeoning tabloid newspapers, extending and refining the phenomenon (Whannel, 2001).

However, it was with George Best that football entered the modern heights—and lows—of soccer superstardom. As controversial off the pitch as he was gifted on, the Manchester United striker demonstrated that, for the first time, "footballers could provide regular front page as well as back page copy" (Smart, 2005, p. 72). The division between private and public—a distinction already compromised in other areas of entertainment since the 1950s (Braudy, 1986; Gamson, 1994)—began to collapse as Best's drunken binges and sexual flings made headline news (Parkinson, 1975). Others would follow Best into the tabloid annals of soccer celebrity. Most notably, players in England's national squad, including Kevin Keagan and Paul Gascoigne, began to grasp the commercial opportunities a celebrity profile provided. But the perfect marriage of soccer, celebrity and commercial acumen came with the emergence of David Beckham.

Beckham, buoyed by high-profile performances with Manchester United and England and with a former Spice Girl spouse[3] who helped bridge the gap between sport and showbusiness, has become one of a small number of hyper-celebrities, global brands in their own right. Regarded as one of the most famous faces in the world (Wahl, 2009), Beckham has come to epitomize a combination of sports skill and marketing savvy once reserved for such U.S. stars as Michael Jordan and Tiger Woods.

In 2003, shortly before his transfer from Manchester United to Real Madrid, David Beckham was said to be earning in excess of £4.5 million per year from his club, around £1 million of which was reported to be for the use of his image. Total annual income from endorsements was in excess of £11.5 million (O'Connor, 2003). Much of Beckham's fame and commercial attraction might be traced to his role as a captain of England during World Cup campaign of 2006. With the final stages of the 2010 tournament on the horizon, another England captain—John Terry—seemed to be positioning himself to achieve similar success.

"Mr. Chelsea"

John George Terry was born in Barking, east London, in December 1980, joining the Premier League club Chelsea at fourteen after a spell in West Ham United's youth organization. Playing as a central defender, Terry established himself in Chelsea's first team in the 2000-2001 season, taking over the captain's role for the first time in December 2001 (Derbyshire, 2006). The past decade has proved to be the most successful period in Chelsea's long history, capped by the club winning Premier League titles in 2005 and 2006, reaching their first UEFA Champions Final in 2008, and emerging winners of England's prestigious Football Association Challenge Cup (commonly known as the FA Cup) in 2007 and 2009. The early months of 2010 saw the team at the top of the Premier table, while also on course for another FA Cup final (chelseafc.com; Worrall, Barker & Johnstone, 2009).

Despite bouts of injury, Terry has been widely acknowledged as a key factor in Chelsea's success, with the player picking up a slew of honors in his own right. In 2005 Terry was voted the Professional Football Association's Player of the Year, as well as best defender in the Champions League for 2005, 2008 and 2009. He was selected for the World XI for five years running at the FIFpro (Fédération Internationale des Associations de Footballeurs Professionnels) awards, a team chosen by football professionals from some forty nations (chelseafc.com; Worrall, Barker & Johnstone, 2009).

Yet for all his successes, the mercurial Chelsea star has been dogged by an equally lengthy string of controversies and scandals. His engagement to longtime girlfriend Toni Poole notwithstanding, Terry made front-page news for a series of ill-judged love affairs in 2004 and 2005 (Singh & Moriarty, 2010, p. 5) as well as being exposed as having an alleged gambling problem (Kay, 2005, p. 4-5). At the same time, controversy has surrounded members of his family, with both his parents running afoul of the law.

At the turn of 2010, Terry seemed intent on putting this storied past behind him, with the player—perhaps mindful of the financial opportunity offered by captaincy in the coming World Cup tournament—appearing to be repositioning himself with a persona that would be more attractive to sponsors.

A Branded Man

In 2010, Terry was reported to be one of the best paid players in English football, earning an estimated £7.8 million annually. In addition, he was involved in a £4 million sponsorship deal with Umbro, a British sportswear and equipment supplier (Sawer, 2010, p. 15).

Yet despite this, there was a sense that the player had been unable to fully capitalize on the fame that his performances with Chelsea and the national team had brought. "It is striking, given his profile, how few endorsements Terry has; evidence perhaps that his previous off-field troubles may [be] a factor," wrote Paul Kelso for the *Daily Telegraph*. "Umbro is his only personal sponsor . . . a deal with King of Shaves expired in 2008." (2010, p. 4).

There was every reason to believe that a more family-friendly image and the potential of glory in the coming World Cup would tip the balance, perhaps propelling Terry into the upper echelons of stardom achieved by Beckham.

In the words of one marketing professional: "Companies had not made much use of Terry in marketing terms . . . but the potential was there given the prospect of the World Cup this summer. Previous England captains have all earned significant sums" (Orvice, 2010, p. 88).

The key to this lucrative future appeared to lie in reconfiguring Terry's sometime salacious image into one more family friendly. It has long been argued that personal identity consists of a series of personas or "masks," with facework taking each of these as a basis for performances of varying intents before differing audiences. To quote Robert Park:

> It is probably no mere historical accident that the word person, in its first meaning, is a mask. It is rather recognition of the fact that everyone is always and everywhere, more or less consciously, playing a role. . . . It is in these roles that we know each other; it is in these roles that we know ourselves. (Park, 1950: 249, quoted in Goffman, 1959: 19).

For Terry, commercial success seemed to demand a division of personas that allowed for contrasting personal qualities to be highlighted across public and private spheres. The footballer had built his public reputation on a front that represented the attitudes and behaviors of hegemonic masculinity—including aggression, extreme competitiveness, and a rejection of effeminacy—with which male team sports are traditionally associated (Parker, 2001; Schacht, 1996). On the pitch Terry was "a warrior, a fighter, a player who puts his heart and soul into every encounter" (Burt, 2010, p. 11).

Yet at the same time, sponsorship seemed, for Terry, to lie in reconfiguring these alpha-male qualities into the softer traits of attentive spouse and caring father in the private sphere—or to be more precise, within the news-mediated public *performance* of the private sphere.

This stark division of fronts and the corresponding appropriateness of contrasting personality traits is neatly illustrated by differing reactions to Terry's (in)famous penalty miss in the Champions League final of 2008. After Terry was pictured weeping at the miss—a behavior later attacked in some parts of the press (Woods, 2008, p. 17), England team-mate Frank Lampard was quick to repair and consolidate Terry's masculine front with a public assurance that his captain was a "man's man" (McIntosh, 2008, p. 25).

Yet in a home setting this vulnerability had consonance, opening the door to a need for the support of a loving family unit. In an interview published in *Exclusively Surrey* magazine in December 2009, Terry was happy to discuss how "his wife and family supported him" after the missed penalty:

> It was a massive blow, but that's when the family came to the fore. Toni was very supportive and I had the rest of my family on my side. Having a close, loving family helped a great deal. (quoted by Haywood, 2010: 5)

Terry had acquired a useful sign resource in 2008, when he was named "Dad of the Year" in a national survey. It was no coincidence that this achievement was later referenced prominently in an e-mail sent by Riviera Entertainment Limited apprising potential sponsors that John Terry was available: "to create effective brand awareness and endorse products and services globally" (*Daily Mail*, 2010).

At the same time, in publicity grounded in a contrast between the moral dissolution of the city and the supposed stable values of the countryside, newspapers carried the story that Terry was raising money for a move to a country mansion. An unnamed source told reporters, "John and his wife want a complete change of lifestyle. He'll be living the life of a genuine English country gentleman" (Flynn & Syson, 2010, p. 5). A few weeks later, the *Exclusively Surrey* magazine article took the public into the comfort of the Terrys' current home, where the Chelsea player allowed his blossoming family persona full rein, the couple talking about their hobbies, ambitions, and hopes for the future, including their twin daughters, Georgie and Summer.

PART TWO: SCANDAL

By the close of 2009, Terry's attempts to reconfigure his "private" persona had already stumbled. Undercover reporters from the *News of the World* had exposed the player for organizing a "secret tour" of Chelsea's training ground, apparently in exchange for a hefty cash payment (Palmer, 2009, p. 16-17).

However, there were ominous signs that an altogether more violent storm was about to break. On Friday, January 29, a "super-injunction" granted to Terry the previous week was lifted in the High Court. Within hours, the *Sun*'s web edition had broken the story that the footballer had engaged in an extra-marital affair with the girlfriend of Wayne Bridge, Terry's former Chelsea teammate, "best pal," and a colleague in the national side (The Sun Online, 2010).

Further revelations followed. By the weekend, the Sunday newspapers were alleging that Terry had made Bridge's girlfriend, Vanessa Perroncel, pregnant and had subsequently paid for the girl to have an abortion "to keep the scandal under wraps"(Sunday Mirror, 2010, p. 4-5).

The story was a gift to a British press eager to find their own national sports scandal to rival that of the ongoing, copy-producing Tiger Woods saga in the United States. Following the initial story on Friday, the *Sun* allotted ten pages of its Saturday edition to the scandal, the marathon coverage stretching across news, sports, and feature sections to include both front and back pages and the top slot of the day's editorial comment.

Righteous indignation flowed from the editorial pulpits of the national press. The *Daily Mail* opined that "even by the skewed moral standards of today's professional football, John Terry is in a class of his own," with the newspaper accusing the fallen soccer star of not only "serial philandering," but also "public drunkenness and urination, brawling, . . . and other regular displays of boorishness" (Pendlebury, 2010, p. 24). Similarly the *Daily Mirror*, in highlighting "the shame of John Terry's betrayal," dismissed the footballer as a "liar, a cheat, a disgrace" for having "done the dirty on his mate" (Evans & Tetteh, 2010, p. 4-5).

Inevitably, the breaking scandal derailed Terry's attempts to reconfigure his public image. Yet the division of self that facework posits, and that the processes of TV may encourage (Andrews, 1998: p. 200), would continue to be put to work by Terry and his PR team.

What followed was, if anything, an escalation of the division of personas across domains, these being guided by three general narratives: heroic quest, betrayal and confrontation, and emotional reunion. These storylines, in their turn, coalesced around a trio of expressive performances that marked and shaped press coverage, discussed here as The Armband, The Handshake, and The Kiss. Each cast Terry in a specific persona, acting in a specific scene within a given narrative. And each was performed within the space that Terry's insistent silence left open.

Silence

From the outset, strategies of silence—of *absence* of communication—characterized Terry's response to the uncovering of the scandal, even though some of these approaches were markedly less successful than others. Unsurprisingly, the Chelsea player's initial reaction to the threat of scandal was an attempt to enforce silence, primarily on the media through an injunction but also, allegedly, by attempting to bribe other participants in the drama (Perthern, Callagher, Chapman & Millbank, 2010).

It would have been clear to Terry that this news would undermine—indeed, invalidate the reality of—the "family man" persona he had been so assiduously cultivating, with potentially dire implications for both his England captaincy and future sponsorship deals. The "super injunction" he initially obtained was, in effect, a double gag on the news media, prohibiting the disclosure of the existence of the order itself as well as silencing the information that it protected (libelreform.org). The logic behind its adoption in the High Court rested squarely on the concept of there being a clear distinction between the world of sport, the public sphere and the private sphere, as disclosure to the general public would, it was argued, breach Terry's right to a "private and family life." However, the attempt floundered at a second hearing a week later due, in no small part, to the judge's recognition that the sports industry overlapped with the public realm—the information could be deemed, already, to be "in wide circulation amongst those involved in the sport in question, including agents and others, and not just amongst those directly engaged in the sport" (The Sun Online, 2010). At the same time, issues surrounding the central role of sponsorship presented a threat to the cultivated reality that hopes of such sponsorship had motivated in the first place.

The Political Economy of Sport

Professional sport, corporate sponsorship and television are said to form an economic "golden triangle," existing in a symbiotic relationship which reaps rich financial benefits (Aris, 1990). By the same token, soccer, at its highest level, has become increasingly a "commodified product" (Sugden and Tomlinson, 1998, p. 98), with football and other team sports offering an ideal vehicle for capturing "massive and/or committed audiences with consumption profiles attractive to advertisers/sponsors" (Arundel and Roche, 1998, p. 54).

Sport has the ability to cross cultural and spatial divides while offering a highly effective means for establishing a distinctive "set of emotional meanings and values around products" that could contribute to the process of "'brand building,' if not enhancement of 'brand value'" (Nixon, 2003, p. 40). In an age of hypersignification (Goldman and Papson, 1994) the result of this commercialization is evident to the most casual of observers. It is writ large across the length and breadth of football in a flurry of commodity signs, from the shirts, brands and company logos that players wear, to the commercial breaks that punctuate the televisual experience.

However, this process and its high level of visibility has led, for some, to a feeling that sport has been fatally compromised, with superstar figures such as Michael Jordan having been transformed from athletes competing for the love of sport to "commodity(s) signs and . . . multi and intertextual promotional construct(s)" (Andrews, 1998, p. 202) created to make money for their sponsors, their clubs—and themselves.

Given this sense of unease, it was perhaps unsurprising that the High Court judge, Mr. Justice Tugendhat, felt that Terry's real concern in seeking an injunction was not familial harmony so much as "the effect of publication upon the sponsorship business" (The Sun Online, 2010). It would be a suspicion that motivated press cynicism throughout coverage of the scandal, with sponsorship surfacing time and again to explain the distance between Terry's "family man" mask and his duplicitous "true" self (e.g., Dunn, 2010, p. 72; Alderson, 2010, p. 8).

Ironically, far from protecting Terry's secret, his application for an injunction may have led ultimately to public exposure, as "by rushing to court, the lawyers put Fleet Street on notice about the scandal" (*Sunday Mirror*, 2010, p. 4-5).

A more productive silence, however, surrounded Terry's public reaction to news coverage, as the player sought to protect his captaincy of the national team.

The Armband

A number of researchers have commented on the news media's penchant for fixing individual blame and focusing on punishment (e.g., Gitlin, 1980). Certainly the *Sun* was quick to link the scandal with Terry's captaincy of England, its earliest story suggesting that manager Fabio Capello would "now face pressure to strip Terry of his captaincy following the revelations," a statement which bore the recursive stamp of self-fulfilling prophecy given that the *Sun*'s own stance was part of that "pressure." It was a theme taken up immediately across the columns of press, even if some argued that Terry should retain the cherished armband (e.g., Fitzmaurice, 2010, p. 10; Curtis & McGarry, 2010, p. 55-56).

The armband has symbolic potency in soccer, representing not merely the role of captain but also—through the processes mapped out in symbolic interactionism (Herbert Blumer, 1969), indicating that its wearer possesses certain qualities integral to the role. To be stripped of the armband signifies both a fall in status and, in a sense, the loss of those individual qualities—the leadership persona—associated with the position.

On a more practical note, for Terry, the loss of the England captaincy would mean missing out on the £250,000 captain's bonus from the team's sponsorship cash share-out, as well as the commercial interest that would come from leading the national team into the World Cup (Orvice, 2010, p. 88)

It was here Terry's most persistent act of silence was performed. At no point in the scandal did the player offer an apology for—or indeed, an admission of—his actions.

While newspaper stories following a brief public statement reported that the footballer was "'keeping his own counsel' over the allegations about his private life" (The Sun Online, 2010), this was an extrapolation on the part of journalists. In fact, the statement had been careful to avoid all mention of the scandal, dealing exclusively with its potential implications. Spokesman Phil Hall had told reporters that: "John Terry asked me to make it clear that he has made absolutely no statement about his future as England captain." It was, in effect, a comment that no comment was being made, with Terry himself absent from the press call.

This was a markedly different approach to that taken by Tiger Woods, the superstar golfer caught in a similar situation, and a strategy that would inevitably lead to criticism. For Woods's American public, an apology was the least to be expected, just as those engaged in facework analysis argue that a rule violation is likely to raise expectations of this type of verbal redress being offered by the guilty party (Cupach & Metts, 1994). Moreover, such a response becomes increasingly predictable as the stakes are raised. As an individual's responsibility for an act and the negative nature of that act increase, offenders are more likely to offer more explicit and elaborate apologies, often accompanied by explanatory accounts (Cupach & Metts, 1992; Fraser, 1981). And for the most part, it is an approach that bears fruit, more elaborate apologies being shown to usually produce less blame, more forgiveness, perceptions of greater remorse and on occasions, less punishment (Cupach & Metts, 1994; Darby & Schlenker, 1982, 1989). Terry's decision not to make a public apology to those he was seen to have wronged—his wife, his managers, his former friend Bridge and, more inclusively, the sport's legions of supporters—was equated with a lack of contrition by some commentators. Similarly, Terry's failure to "say sorry" was cited as the reason Bridge later ruled himself out of the England squad. Bridge was unwilling to play on the same team as his "betrayer" (Lawton, 2010; Sanderson & Herbert, 2010, p. 4-5).

The press and the public's hunger for an apology surfaced in disguised forms over the following weeks. The *Sun*, for example, offered a guide entitled, "How to say sorry and do it successfully for just about anything," and included a postscript that John Terry should "take note" (Watkins, 2010, p. 39). A number of newspapers also covered a "prank" in which two autograph hunters attempted, unsuccessfully, to trick Terry into putting his name to an apology written out to Bridge (Lawton, Chadwick, and Tozer, 2010; The Sun Online, 2010). However, surprisingly, more overt calls for an apology from Terry were relatively rare, especially from the *Sun*, the newspaper perhaps most obsessed with the story.

It may be that the British public has never had the appetite for what Goffman labels the "cult of confession" of modern celebrity (1959, p. 205) to the extent of its U.S. counterpart. The reaction in Britain to Tiger Woods's apology, for example, was mixed at best, with a number of commentators across the media deploring what they regarded as a show of corporate crocodile tears. Dismissed as "the biggest con in sport" by the *Telegraph*, (White, 2010, p. 14), it was given an equally cynical reception by the *Daily Mail*:

> Yes, we understand. He let down his wife, his children, his fans, his friends, his family, his business partners. Oh, those poor business partners. Won't nobody think of the business partners? (Samuel, 2/20/10)

Terry's silence on the scandal allowed him to imply, and to stage, a strict division between his private, "sinful" persona and the performing self of professional football—the two being offered as discrete selves that should not be allowed to impact one upon the other. Thus, Terry's public comments continued to focus exclusively on issues of his professional role with Chelsea and England.

One particularly illuminating statement sought to limit and define the front on which he should be weighed, with Terry telling reporters: "I firmly believe fans want to judge me on the one thing I expect to be judged on—my football—and that's all I could ever ask for." In the same interview, accusations that Terry had failed to live up to his obligations as a role model were adroitly deflected from the personal sphere into the professional: "People talk about setting an example—and believe me, out on the pitch, that's all I want to do, whether it's for Chelsea or England." It was "on the pitch," not in his private life, that Terry was willing to serve as such a model (Dillon, 2010, p. 53).

While Terry did lose the captaincy of the national side (Armstrong, 2010, p 1, 4-5; Kelso & Burt, 2010, p. 2, 3), he retained both his place in the England team and possession of the captain's armband for Chelsea. Moreover, the demand for a public response to being stripped of the England leadership gave Terry the opportunity to cast himself in a decidedly heroic role. On Saturday, February 6, the front page of the tabloid which had been the most heavily involved in covering the scandal carried a tagline announcing an "exclusive": "Axed England captain John Terry confesses to the Sun."

However, the "confession" that emerged was not the long-anticipated admission of guilt, but rather a declaration that Terry had been "hurt" by the loss of the England captaincy and was now vowing to "fight back." "If there's a one per cent chance of being World Cup captain, I will fight for it tooth and nail," Terry insisted, an intention confirmed in an "overheard remark" during training: "I have fought all my life and I'm not going to stop now" (Custis, 2010, p. 1, 4-5).

The narrative being primed was both stirring and potentially redemptive—the hero's quest of the wounded warrior, struggling against all odds, to recapture his former glory. It was a theme perfectly suited to Terry's on-stage persona of tireless soccer "bulldog."

While the narrative faced resistance in some areas of the press, it was also influential. In reports on matches on league-leaders Chelsea and for the national team, the Terry scandal was reconfigured from "shameful" transgression to personal challenge: the underlying question being repeatedly whether the footballer could overcome his troubles and maintain his winning form on the pitch. Paradoxically, given the source of the stress Terry was under, the key attribute in this challenge came to be identified as "character."

The term echoed, article upon article. "He's shown his character. . . . He is a very strong character." (McGarry, 2010, p. 88); "he has shown great mental strength to come through such a stiff test of his character," (Anderson, 2010, p. 57). Often, it was an attribute directly linked to dramatic performance. Even in a *Telegraph* story otherwise highly critical of the footballer, its author felt obliged to note:

John Terry's venomous headed goal at Burnley was a demonstration of the
character required to excel at sport, of the attributes needed to win a World
Cup, to buy the unconditional support of fans. (Garside, 2010, p. 9)

Authenticity

In fact, grounding his bid for image repair in the bedrock of performance was
an astute move on Terry's part. In discussing the vagaries of celebrity, a
number of analysts have singled out sport as having a unique "authenticity"—the touchstone of performance granting a sense of validity that other
arenas of fame lack.

Celebrity is defined by Boorstin as the hollow "human pseudo-event," a
person "known for his well-knownness" (1961, p. 57). While by no means a
purely modern phenomenon (see Braudy, 1986), it is argued that television
and hypercommercialization have accelerated and accentuated the process,
leading many to confuse the "hero" with the showbiz star, "the Big Name
with the Big Man" (Gamson, 1994, p. 9).

However, for all its commodification in recent decades, sport is seen to
have retained a substantial degree of authenticity. As Barry Smart points out,
the qualities associated with outstanding sporting performance—including
skill, technique, speed, power, grace, motivation, courage, discipline and
success—have the credibility that comes from being displayed in front of
spectators and on live television, performed within strictly-enforced parameters:

> Professional sporting performances are subject to measurement and adjudica-
> tion. Standards reached and results achieved are carefully monitored and re-
> corded by governing bodies. Press reports and television coverage provide
> additional cultural records of sport performances. (Smart, 2005, p. 195)

In part, this coupling of performance and authenticity points to what Goffman terms "dramatic realization." Before an audience, the professional individual "infuses his activity with signs which dramatically highlight and portray confirmatory facts that might otherwise remain unapparent or ob-
scure. . . . He must mobilize his activity so that it will express during the
interaction what he wishes to convey" (Goffman, 1959, p. 30).

While this dramatization—the matching of surface activity to the ultimate
goal of the enterprise—may be difficult to achieve in many professions,
sports is one domain that allows for "so much dramatic self-expression that
exemplary practitioners . . . become famous and are given a special place in
the commercially organized fantasies of the nation" (1959, p. 31).

For Terry, eschewing any attempt at a verbal account served to focus—by
its very absence—attention back on professional performance. This allowed
the footballer to highlight the "dramatic realization" of his play, affording

him a degree of control over events. Indeed, such was the success of the strategy in directing attention to the performing body that the *Sun* felt compelled to recruit a body language expert to assess whether the "hidden stresses" of Terry's situation were surfacing in tell-tale gestures and expressions. (*Sun*, 2010, p. 7).

The Handshake

As already suggested, male team sports have been said to foster a traditional, even retrosexual, image of masculinity, providing the "final bastion" of traditional male values against the "feminization" of society (Kimmel, 1987; Messner, 1987, 1992). As such, these sports— soccer included—also stood accused of being unashamedly patriarchal (Boslooper and Hayes, 1973; Hargreaves, 1994), a domain in which, almost uniformly, women are treated as "lesser" (Hargreaves, 2000; Curry, 1991; Kane & Disch, 1993).

This bias may account for an unusual feature of early coverage in the Terry scandal. While initial stories of the scandal were strongly informed by notions of betrayal, the focus of this opening barrage was not the plight of cheated wife Toni, but rather the perfidy shown to Terry's former team-mate and best friend, Wayne Bridge. It was an angle made explicit in the opening paragraph of Saturday's leading article in the *Sun*: "Soccer love cheat John Terry's betrayal of team-mate Wayne Bridge came like a stab in the back for the player who was his best pal" (White, West, & O'Shea, 2010, p. 4-5). Similarly it was not Toni Terry or the couple's young twins, but Bridge who was said to be "in bits" after the revelations, both in the *Sun* and elsewhere (e.g., Evans & Tetteh, 2010, p. 4-5; *Daily Telegraph*, 2010, p. 10).

This focus played out pictorially as well as textually. Toni Terry did not appear on the *Sun*'s front page. Instead this was dominated by an image that illustrated the camaraderie between Terry and Bridge, the latter shown with his arm draped around Terry's shoulder and a hand placed affectionately on the teammate's chest (and over his heart). Unsurprisingly, perhaps, it took a woman to point out the discrepancy in this initial coverage, with columnist Karren Brady suggesting:

> It's a male, male world we live in, that's for sure. While Wayne Bridge is attracting all kinds of "how could he do it to his best pal" sympathy, John Terry's trouble-and-strife (wife) doesn't merit even a newsprint kiss and cuddle.

Far from a textual "cuddle," a thematic undercurrent in the news seemed to imply that the mother of two was getting no more than she deserved. Frequently, Toni Terry was dismissed as a WAG,[4] who had "wanted the trappings of being the wife of a millionaire footballer so much she'd do any-thing" (Martel Maxwell, 2010, p. 31). The price of such gold-digging, it was suggested, "was the loss of her right to public sympathy" (ibid.).

If outrage over Toni Terry's predicament was at first muted, the story of the betrayal of Bridge struck a nerve with fans and press alike. Painted in Othello-like hues in both the news and sports pages, the act was seen to have broken an unspoken code that existed between teammates. "His team-mates are willing to turn a blind eye to most indiscretions. However, there is a code of honor among players, as there is elsewhere that there are some things you just don't do," opinioned sports commentator Ian McGarry (2010, p. 88-89).

Such sentiments nod to chivalric codes of honor, extending the military metaphors that invariably frame male sports to the mores of group behavior. Yet, such team spirit may arise to fulfill a more pragmatic necessity. Goff-man points to the interdependence of any such grouping, since a "teammate" is someone whose dramaturgical co-operation one is dependent upon in fos-tering a given definition of the situation (1959, p. 83). Just as personal trans-gressions may threaten the team as a performing unit, "turning a blind eye" protects the impression being projected by the team as a whole. Thus any team has "something of the character of a secret society," its members "held together by a bond no member of the audience shares" (p. 104).

Tensions surrounding Terry's breach of football's "code of honor" be-came encapsulated in a narrative that owed much not only to Othello, but also to the genre clichés of the Western, where gunslinging protagonists live and die by unwritten codes, and a man, famously, if tautologically, is obliged to "have to do what a man has to do." As such, the narrative built to a convenient climax in February when Terry and Bridge met in what the *Daily Mail* described as a "High Noon" confrontation (Williamson, 2010).

It seemed appropriate that the showdown should come in the most ritual-ized moments of the match; the ceremonial handshake before kick-off. Such ritual creates a robust sense of group identity and preserves and propagates shared values and moral codes (Shils, 1975; Bell, 1997), while also offering "a message of pattern and predictability" in all areas of uncertainty, anxiety and potential disorder (Myerhoff, 1984, p. 150).

There were some suggestions made to the press that, alarmingly, Bridge should seek revenge on the pitch through an over-the-top tackle (Sweet, 2010, p. 84). But the matter could be settled more symbolically—and more safely—within the confines of ritual already built into the sport. The "Fair Play Handshake" between the competing teams signifies a tacit agreement that the forthcoming hostilities will be played within the spirit of the sporting occasion, although it was apparently the overlapping message of "mutual respect" that was uppermost in the mind of Wayne Bridge on the eve of the match. According to a "pal" quoted in the *Sun*, "Wayne kept saying 'the handshake is all about respect and I have no respect for him'" (ibid.).

Thus the betrayal and confrontation narrative crystallized around the instant the two former friends would stand face to face in the opening ceremony. The public nature of the spectacle was highlighted in reports, with the uncertainty of whether or not Bridge would signal his forgiveness by taking Terry's hand adding dramatic suspense to the scene. In the event:

> Football fans across the globe saw betrayed Bridge, 29, pull away his hand as former England skipper Terry offered his during the Fair Play Handshake. . . . Millions saw the Man City ace pointedly carry out his vow to ignore love rival Terry's outstretched hand during Saturday's pre-match formalities. (Peake, 2010, p. 4-5).

In fact, while Terry was delivered a public "snub" in the ritual, in the long term the incident worked to his advantage. The handshake confrontation and the Chelsea defeat that followed seemed to provide narrative closure to this aspect of the scandal. At the same time, Terry was widely seen as having given the ritual its due in proffering his hand (albeit grudgingly, according to the *Sun*'s watching body language expert) (ibid.).

The Kiss

We have seen that the relationship between Terry and his wife was not the initial focus of press coverage. Yet this was to change, especially as Terry—while remaining publicly silent on his indiscretions—began to follow a deliberate course of narrativized action.

The saga of "parted/reconciled lovers" is the most basic of narratives, one of the fundamental themes to which folktales across centuries and nations may be reduced (see Propp, 1984). It is also a staple of the modern soap opera, performed within a trope of "stormy relationships," where illicit affairs and acrimonious break-ups are often capped by equally passionate reunions (Blumenthal, 1997; Williams, 1992). Indeed, one of Britain's best known soaps at this time, *Footballers Wives*, laid the groundwork for just this species of narrative in the Terry affair, the similarity between soap and scandal being suggested by a number of journalists (e.g. Brady, 2010, p. 4; Mullock, 2010, p. 4-5).

However, the reconciliation storyline was most directly prefigured on February 10, when tabloid "Agony Aunt" Deidre Sanders—in suggesting that "most marriages survive one instance of cheating"—chose to direct her advice specifically toward the wayward Chelsea star: "The person who has done the cheating—are you listening JT—must woo their partner all over again" (Sanders, 2010, p. 44).

Once again, the *Sun* played a key role in this narrative. After breaking the scandal, the tabloid had committed a good deal of time, effort, manpower and column inches to its coverage. This was by no means surprising—the story's heady mix of sex, soccer and betrayal made it natural fodder for its tabloid tastes (and for those of its target audience). At the same time, the *Sun* had a special, if ambiguous, relationship with Terry. While the Chelsea footballer was the target of the *Sun*'s revelations, it was also a newspaper to which Terry occasionally contributed as a columnist.

With wife Toni having "fled" to Dubai days after the scandal broke (Wells, 2010, p. 1, 4-5), what was branded Terry's "make-or-break mission to rescue his marriage" was followed every step of the way by the *Sun*, although this interest was no means exclusive. To varying degrees, the tabloid press corps as a whole shadowed the story, from the footballer's request to take "compassionate leave" from Chelsea to undertake the trip (Millard, Pollard, & Crick, 2010, p. 1, 4) to the departure from Heathrow (Crick, 2010, p. 5; Moyes, 2010, p. 7) the landing in Dubai (Crick, 2010, p. 4; Evans, 2010, p. 7) through to the eventual, triumphant reconciliation (Crick, 2010, p. 1, 4-5, 9; Moyes, 2010, p. 1, 4-5).

In between, readers were updated by journalists in Dubai, who reported, ahead of Terry's arrival, the actions and state of mind of the "heartbroken" wife as she waited "lonely and saddened" with her children (Crick & Syson, 2010, p. 4-5; Moyes, 2010, p. 1, 4-5). Even allegations that Terry had "bedded" a second player's wife (Fricker, 2010, p. 1, 4-5; *Daily Mail*, 2010) could not seriously derail the narrative.

Setting and Semiotic Resources

In Goffman's terms, the setting of the reunion was rich in semiotic resources, from the glamour of the Le Royal Meridien hotel—a "sun-drenched five-star bolt hole" complete with "mega plush five-star penthouse suites" (Crick, 2010, p. 1, 4-5)—to the natural beauty of the resort itself, and the *Sun* waxing lyrical about Toni Terry sunbathing in the "tranquil spot, as the crystal clear sea lapped at her feet" (Crick, 2010, p. 1, 4-5).

Equally, press reports offered lavish descriptions of the clothes and accessories—articles of "personal front" (Goffman, 1959)—involved in the narrative. Toni sported "a jewel-encrusted black bikini" (Crick, 2010, p. 1, 4-5), while the disgraced husband was resplendent in "Chelsea blue-colored Abercrombie and Fitch designer swim shorts" (Crick, 2010, p. 1, 4-5). Even the timing of the romantic "mission" was propitious, with Terry flying out to stage the reconciliation over Valentine's Day weekend.

Set and semiotic equipment aside, it was to the codes of melodrama that the narrative most closely adhered. From Terry's performed persona of stricken lover on a "3,000 mile mission to save his marriage," the plot line reflected the logic and sensibilities of the TV soap. The story even came with the suspense-building plot reversals that are prerequisite for such melodrama (Landy, 1991). These included an angry exchange by phone on the beach between Terry and his wife before the husband flew out, and Terry's arrival at the airport in Dubai to find, to his dismay, that his wife was not there to greet him—each scene performed with a level of public visibility to rival the publicity shot.

The Terrys' children, too, proved useful props in scenes that were no less high profile. A "sad" Summer was reported to be "sobbing at the hotel poolside as she asked for (her father)," while the couple let it be known that "the reaction of the children would play a big part in Toni's decision whether to take him back." (Crick, 2010, p. 1, 4-5).

It was perhaps no surprise that, these reversals aside, the reconciliation was ultimately as swift as it was complete. By the morning following his arrival, Terry and his wife "hugged and kissed" in the sand for cameramen. With Toni having agreed to "make one final go of their marriage" the two announced that they were "stronger than ever as a couple . . . so in love." That done, "the then loved-up looking couple took a romantic stroll down the ultra luxurious complex's private beach" (Crick, 2010, p. 1, 4-5).

"Pictures Say More"

The world has taken, in the words of W. J. T. Mitchell, a "pictorial turn" (1992), with the language of images . . . everywhere" (Boorstin, 1963, p. 188). Photography has pushed ever more relentlessly toward the "publicizing of surfaces" (Gamson, 1994, p. 21), with most effective public images not only "vivid" but "simplified" (Boorstin, 1963, p. 190; Smart, 2005, p. 15).

While the melodrama of Terry's romantic mission was often conveyed in the tabloids through the sort of florid description one might expect of romantic fiction, it was primarily *pictures* that told the tale. Each step of the enterprise was faithfully recorded for public consumption, from Terry's departure and arrival in Dubai to the photograph of Toni lying in skimpy bathing suits on the beach, cell-phone in hand for the call from her wayward husband. A collage of images that mimicked the episodic visual narrative of the TV soap, it offered readers a near omniscient view as it built to its predicable climax.

Yet the narrative was most readily captured in the image of The Kiss that sealed the Terrys' reconciliation. It was at once a public performance, a ritualized symbol of romance and, in the indexical veracity granted to the camera (Messaris, 1997), an artifact of visual evidence that all was now well in the Terry household. Inevitably, The Kiss was the image most heavily reproduced across the British news media in the days that followed.

Intriguingly, even the linguistic construction of the scene, as offered in the *Sun*, nodded to its visual and performative nature, with the reporter suggesting that the happy couple "wasted no time in showing the world their three-year marriage was back on."

Similarly, Terry was also quick to underscore the power of the visual in a way that offered the sacrifice of surface to the public sphere, while privileging and reserving the spoken word for the intimacy of the private. "The pictures say more than words can say about how we are as a couple," the Chelsea player told reporters. Terry continued, "What me and Toni speak about, no one will ever know. No one will ever get close to knowing about how our life is" (Crick, 2010, p. 1, 4-5).

"We are private people," he insisted, as the cameras clicked.

"Zero to Hero?"

It had taken just five weeks for "Britain's sense of moral outrage to subside, for a crisis treated as though it threatened the very fabric of society to blow over" (Smith, 2010, p. 7)—a little longer perhaps than the twelve days that the *Telegraph* had suggested in February, but still a surprisingly brief period of time for a scandal that raised such interest among press and public alike.

In part, this can be accounted for by the impatience of the news media to move on to the latest sensation. But beyond this, a number of factors conspired to pinch off coverage after February 5. Not least of these were the maneuverings of Terry and his image makers, who had ultimately wrested a surprising amount of control of the saga into their own hands.

In any unfolding news story, it is an open question how much of what is reported is the choice of the journalists themselves, and how far coverage can be manipulated by others. Performer Nia Peeples argues that "you can pump the public full of an image" (quoted in Gamson, 1994, 75), with much of a publicist's activity geared towards controlling both the visual and verbal portrayal of their celebrity clients (Levine, 2003; Andrews, 1998).

News and marketing collide in a no man's land of unstable, shifting influences. The result, according to Gamson, is most commonly "a compromise on the part of entertainment-reporting organizations" (1994, 8), with the power capable of blocking journalists' access to investigation, and impeding the possibilities of writing a textured or nuanced story (p. 92).

Yet, in fact, journalists and publicists—for all their differences—enjoy a shared objective in capturing and holding their audience's attention. And often the "semifictional texts" (Gamson, 1998, p. 75) employed by the celebrity's publicity team can fit easily with the framework of popular narratives that are part and parcel of modern journalism (see Darnton, 1975; Campbell, 1991; Zelizer, 1992). However contrived it may have been, Terry's "love mission" was perfect copy for the British tabloids and their readers.

For all the uproar that the scandal created, the tactics of those seeking to exert damage control succeeded rather more than one might have expected. While Terry's initial attempt to impose silence through the courts proved counterproductive, other strategies of silence and absence were markedly more effective. The footballer's refusal to publicly acknowledge, let alone apologize, for the affair allowed him to imply and stage a strict division between his private, "sinful" persona and the performing self of professional sport—in effect, to rely on dramatic realization to "let his football do the talking." In this way, Terry took at least partial control of how he might be judged by his critics, and in a season where he would ultimately lead his club to victory in both the Premier League and the FA Cup, it was a test he could hardly be said to have failed.

Patriotism, too, could be marshaled to promote silence and squeeze this strand of the scandal to a close. To continue to criticize Terry, it was suggested ever more frequently as summer neared, was to risk disrupting England's preparations for, and thus chances in, the World Cup (Samuel, 2010; Winter, 2010, p. 5). Intriguingly, this argument was played out in microcosm in England's warm-up match against Egypt in March, when both the England manager and striker Wayne Rooney appealed for silence from fans—in the form of not jeering Terry—on the grounds that such dissent affected the whole team (Custis, 2010, p. 67-68).

On another narrative front, the shadow of the World Cup and footballing patriotism took the edge off the "moral outrage" felt over the betrayal of Wayne Bridge, whose decision to rule himself out of the England squad became increasingly comprehensible to fans and commentators, especially after the Manchester City player had been seen to make his point in the handshake "snub."

Meanwhile, on a third and final stage, a carefully choreographed reconciliation between Terry and his estranged wife fed directly into its audience's familiarity with TV melodrama, offering a series of glamorous photo-ops for its tabloid storytellers. This reporting was not without its cynicism in terms of the perceived phoniness of the scenes being enacted—the *Daily Mirror*, for example, writing scathingly that "disgraced John Terry turned in one of his most impressive performances yesterday—as he publicly played the besotted husband to perfection" (Moyes, 2010, p. 1, 4-5). Yet it was noticeable that such sentiments continued to be mixed with typically glamorous descriptions of both the couple and the setting, and surrounded with the photographs that "said more" than words. Whatever the transparency of the performance, the narrative was both familiar and beguiling enough to speed this section of the story to (relative) closure.

When the scandal broke at the end of January, the *Daily Record* asserted that the actions of love-rat Terry had taken him from "hero to zero" overnight (Nash, 2010, p. 1). There was a pleasing symmetry, perhaps, to the fact that five weeks later, another British tabloid was reporting the suggestion that the reverse trajectory was now a distinct possibility (Self, 2010, p. 74). According to football manager Tony Pulis, the Chelsea defender needed only a successful run in the World Cup to go from "zero to hero" in the hearts of a sometimes fickle nation.

NOTES

1. Note that the Lexis-Nexis database does not give page numbers for the *Daily Mail*.

2. This study examines a selection of national newspapers from Britain. The method of analysis is exegetical, offering a theoretically unified yet empirically eclectic perspective directed toward examining characteristic features of selected but representative texts (news reports). This is perhaps the most common method of qualitative research and the basis of a large body of seminal work, utilizing what Glaser and Strauss (1967) call "strategically-chosen examples" to illuminate theoretical concepts.

A basket of newspapers was drawn from various sections of the British national press. While all of the sample are "mainstream" publications and function as such, each is aimed at a specific market based on perceived class, income bracket, level of education and professional standing in a more defined manner than most American news publications. To simplify somewhat, the *Sun* and *Daily Mirror* (along with the *Sun*'s Sunday stablemate, the *News of the World,* and the *Daily Record*, the *Mirror*'s Scottish counterpart) are generally aimed at a working-class audience, and were perhaps the most energetic in covering the Terry scandal. The *Daily Telegraph* and its weekend counterpart, the *Sunday Telegraph* is directed at an upper-class or lower-upper-class readership. The *Daily Mail* and *Mail on Sunday* occupy a mid-market position between these, aimed at Britain's professional upper middle classes (or at least those who perceive themselves to be in this bracket). The sample, taken from the Lexis Nexis database, spans a two-month period, covering the outset and subsequent fading of the scandal between the end of January and March 2010.

3. Victoria Beckham (born Victoria Adams) is known for her role as Posh Spice, one-fifth of the British girl-band, the Spice Girls.

4. "WAG" is a faintly derogatory term for the Wives And Girlfriends of sports stars.

REFERENCES

Andrews, D. (1998). Excavating Michael Jordan: Notes on a Critical Pedagogy of Sporting Representation. In G. Rail (Ed.), *Sport and Postmodern Times* (pp.185-219). Albany, NY: State University of New York Press.

Aris, S. (1990). *Sportsbiz: Inside the Sports Business*. London: Hutchinson.

Arundel, J. & Roche, M. (1998). Media, Sport and Local Identity: British Rugby League and Sky TV. In M. Roche (Ed.),*Sport, Popular Culture and Identity* (pp.57-92). Verlag, Aachen: Meyer & Meyer.

Bell, C. (1997). *Ritual: Perspectives and Dimensions.* New York: Oxford University Press.

Benford, S., & Hunt, S. (1992). Dramaturgy and Social Movements: The Social Construction and Communication of Power. *Sociological Inquiry* (2) 1, 36-55.

Blumenthal, D. (1997). *Women and Soap Opera: A Cultural Feminist Perspective.* Westport, CT and London: Praeger.

Blumer, H. (1969). *Symbolic Interactionism: Perspective and Method*. Upper Saddle River, NJ: Prentice Hall.

Boorstin, D. J. (1961). *The Image: A Guide to Pseudo-Events in America.* London: Harper.

Boslooper, T. & Hayes. M. (1973). *The Femininity Game.* New York: Skein & Day.

Bowden (1995). Soccer. In K.B. Raitz (Ed.), *The Theater of Sports.* Baltimore, M.L: John Hopkins University Press.

Braudy, L. (1986). *The Frenzy of Renown.* New York: Oxford University Press.

Campbell, R (1991). *60 Minutes and the News: A Mythology for Middle America.* Urbana: University of Illinois Press.

chelseafc.com, downloaded 25/5/10.

Cupach, W. R., & Metts, S. (1992). The Effects of Type of Predicament and Embarrassability on Remedial Responses to Embarrassing Situations. *Communication Quarterly, 40,* 149-161.

Cupach, W. R., & Metts, S. (1994). *Facework (Sage Series on Close Relationships).*London/ Thousand Oaks/New Delhi: Sage Publications.

Curry, T. J. (1991). Fraternal Bonding in the Locker Room: A Feminist Analysis of Talk about Competition and Women. *Sociology of Sport Journal,*8, 119-135.

Darby, B. W. & Schlenker, B.R. (1982). Children's Reactions to Apologies. *Journal of Personality and Social Psychology,* 43, (4), 742-753.

Darby, B. W. & Schlenker, B.R. (1989). Children's Reactions to Transgressions: Effects of the Actor's Apology, Reputation and Remorse.*British Journal of Social Psychology,* 28, 353-364.

Darnton, R. (1975). Writing News and Telling Stories. *Daedalus,* Spring, 175-94.

Derbyshire, O. (2006). *John Terry: Captain Marvel.* London: John Blake.

Dunning, E. & Sheard, K. (1979). *Barbarians, Gentlemen and Players: A Sociological Study of Rugby Football.*New York: New York University Press.

Fisher, W. R. (1984). Narration as a Human Communication Paradigm: The Case of Public Moral Argument. *Communication Monographs, 52,* 347-367.

Fisher, W. R. (1987). *Human Communication as a Narration: Toward a Philosophy of Reason, Value, and Action.* Columbia: University of South Carolina Press.

Fraser, B. (1981). On Apologizing. In F. Coulmas (Ed.), *Conversational Routine: Explorations in Standardized Communication Situations and Pre-patterned Speech.* (pp. 259-271). New York: Mouton.

Fulton, H. E., Huisman, R., Murphet, J. & Dunn, A. (2006). *Narrative and Media.* Cambridge & New York: Cambridge University Press.

Gamson, J. (1994). *Claims to Fame: Celebrity in Contemporary America.* Berkeley/Los Angeles/London: University of California Press.

Gitlin, T. (1980). *The Whole World Is Watching.* Berkeley:University of California Press.

Glaser, B., & Strauss, A. (1967) *The Discovery of Grounded Theory.* New York: Aldine.

Goffman, E. (1959). *The Presentation of Self in Everyday Life.* New York: Doubleday.

Goffman, E. (1967). *Interaction Ritual: Essays on Face-to-Face Behavior.* New York: Anchor Books.

Goldman, R. & Papson, S. (1994). Advertising in the Age of Hypersignification. *Theory, Culture& Society,*11, (3), 23-53.

Hargreaves, J. (1994). *Sporting Females: Critical Issues in the History and Sociology of Women's Sports.* London: Routledge.

Hargreaves, J. (2000). *Heroines of Sport: The Politics of Difference and Identity.* London: Routledge.

Holt, R. (1996) Cricket and Englishness: The Batsman as Hero. *International Journal of the History of Sport.* 13, (1), 48-70.

Horne, J., Tomlinson A. & Whannel, G. (1999). *Understanding Sport: An introduction to the Sociological and Cultural Analysis of Sport.* London: Taylor & Francis.

Jackson, S. & Andrews, D. (Eds.) (2005). *Sport, Culture and Advertising: Identities, Commodities and the Politics of Representation.*London & New York: Routledge.

Kane, M. J. & Disch,L.J. (1993). Sexual Violence and the Reproduction of Male Power in the Locker Room: The Lisa Olson Incident.*Sociology of Sport Journal* 10, (4), 331-352.

Kimmel, M. (1987). *Changing Men: New Directions in Research on Men and Masculinity.* Newbury Park, CA: Sage.

Kuper, S. (2003). *Ajax, the Dutch, the War: Football in Europe During the Second World War.* London: Orion.

Landy, M. (Ed.) (1991). *Imitations of Life: A Reader of Film and Television Melodrama.* Detroit, MI: Wayne State University Press.

Levine, M. (2003). *A Branded World: Adventures in Public Relations and the Creation of Superbrands*. Hoboken, NJ: John Wiley & Sons.

Lyle, S. (2000). Narrative Understanding: Developing a Theoretical Context for Understanding How Children Make Meaning in Classroom Settings. *Journal of Curriculum Studies, 32*, (1), 45-63.

Malcolmson, R. (1973). *Popular Recreations in English Society: 1700-1850*. Cambridge and New York: Cambridge University Press.

Mason, T. (1989). *Sport in Britain: A Social History.*Cambridge & New York: Cambridge University Press.

Messaris, P. (1997). *Visual Persuasion: The Role of Images in Advertising*. Thousand Oaks, CA&London: Sage.

Messner, M. (1987). The Life of a Man's Seasons: Male Identity in the Life-Course of a Jock. In M. Kimmel (Ed.), *Changing Men: New Directions in Research on Men and Masculinity* (pp. 193-209). Newbury Park, CA: Sage.

Messner, M. (1992). *Power at Play: Sports and the Problem of Masculinity*. Boston: Beacon Press.

Mitchell, W. J. T. (1994). *Picture Theory: Essays on Visual and Verbal Representation*. Chicago &London: University of Chicago Press.

Myerhoff, B. G. (1984). A Death in Time: Construction of Self and Culture in Ritual Drama. In J. J. MacAloon (Ed.), *Rite, Drama, Festival, Spectacle: Rehearsals Toward a Theory of Cultural Performance* (pp. 149-178). Philadelphia: Institute for the Study of Human Issues (ISHI).

Nixon, S. (2003). *Advertising Cultures: Gender Commerce, Creativity*. London:Sage.

Park, R. (1950). *Race and Culture*. Glencoe, IL: The Free Press.

Parker, A. (2001). Soccer, Servitude and Sub-Cultural Identity: Football Traineeship and Masculine Construction.*Soccer and Society*, 2, (1), 59-80.

Parkinson, M. (1975). *Best: An Intimate Biography*. London: Hutchinson.

Porter, M. J., Larson, D. L., Harthcock, A., & Nellis, K. B. (2002). Re (de)fining Narrative Events: Examining Television's Narrative Structure.*Journal of Popular Film & Television, 30*, (1), 23-30.

Propp, V. (1984). *Theory and History of Folklore*. A. Liberman (Ed.) Minneapolis: University of Minnesota Press.

Rodden, J. (2008). How Do Stories Convince Us? Notes Towards a Rhetoric of Narrative. *College Literature*, 35, 148-173.

Rooney, J. F. & Davidson, A. B. (1995). Football. In K.B. Raitz (Ed.),*The Theater of Sports.*Baltimore, MD: Johns Hopkins University Press.

Sarbin, T. R. (1986). *Narrative Psychology: The Storied Nature of Human Conduct.*Westport, CT: Praeger.

Schacht, S. P. (1996). Misogyny On and Off the 'Pitch': The Gendered World of Male Rugby Players. *Gender & Society*, 10, 550-565.

Shils, E. (1975). *Center and Periphery.*Chicago & London: University of Chicago Press.

Smart, B. (2005). *The Sport Star: Modern Sport and the Cultural Economy of Sporting Celebrity*. London/Thousand Oaks/New Delhi: Sage.

SouthAfrica.info, downloaded 5/12/10.

Sugden, J., & Tomlinson, A. (1998). *FIFA and the Contest for World Football—Who Rules the Peoples' Game?* Cambridge:Polity Press.

Tibballs, G. (2003). *Great Football Heroes*. London: O'Mara.

Wahl, G. (2009).*The Beckham Experiment: How the World's Most Famous Athlete Tried to Conquer America*. New York:Crown Books.

Walvin, J. (1994). *The People's Game: History of Football Revisited*. Edinburgh:Mainstream.

Welsh, J. (1990). *Dramaturgical Analysis and Societal Critique*. Piscataway, NJ:Transaction Publishers.

Whannel, G. (2001). Punishment, Redemption and Celebration in the Popular Press: The Case of David Beckham. In D.L. Andrews & S. J. Jackson (Ed.),*Sports Stars: The Cultural Politics of Sporting*(pp. 138-150). London: Routledge.

Williams, C. T. (1992). *It's Time for My Story: Soap Opera Sources, Structure and Response.* Westport, CT and London: Praeger.

Worrall, M., Barker, K. & Johnstone, D. (2009). *Chelsea Here, Chelsea There.* London: Gate 17.

Newspapers

Alderson, A. "Has Captain Terry Crossed the Line?" *Sunday Telegraph*, 1/31/10, 8.

Anderson, D. "Off the Pitch, His Private Life is in Disarray. On The Pitch it's Business as Usual for JT." *Daily Mirror*, 2/1/10, 57.

Armstrong, J. "Finished in 12 mins; The John Terry Affair -Captain Gets Sack." *Daily Mirror*, 2/6/10,4-5.

Brady, K. "Super Goals." *The Sun*, 3/6/10, 4.

Brady, K. "The First Lady of Football." *The Sun,* 2/6/10, 2.

Burt, J. "Mr. Chelsea Has Now Lost The Air of Invincibility." *Daily Telegraph*, 1/30/10, Sport, 11.

Crick, A. "JT's Got Wahey With It; Wife Kisses Cheat Terry." *The Sun*, 2/13/10, 1, 4-5, 9.

Crick, A. "Don't Worry, Daddy is Coming Tomorrow." *The Sun*, 2/11/10, 5.

Crick, A. & Syson, N. "Terry's Wife Opens Her Heart . . . And His Wallet." *The Sun*, 2/4/10, 8-9.

Crick, A. "J.T. Flies in to See His Wife." *The Sun*, 2/12/10, 4.

Curtis, S. & McGarry, I. "England Stars Back JT." *The Sun*, 2/2/10, 55-56.

Custis, S., & West, A. "Axed Love Cheat Terry's pain." *The Sun*, 2/6/10, 6-7.

Custis, S. "Don't Boo JT." *The Sun*, 3/2/10, 67-68.

Daily Telegraph, Staff Writer, 1/30/10: "Affair with French model." Sport, 10.

Dillon, A. "JT: I'm On a Mission and Nothing Will Distract Me." *The Sun*, 2/24/10. 53.

Dunn, A. "Untenable! JT's a Figure of Ridicule and Vilification." *News of the World*, 1/31/10, 72.

Evans R. & Tetteh S. "A Liar, a Cheat, a Disgrace; Shame of England Captain Terry's Betrayal." *Daily Mirror*, 1/30/10, 4-5.

Evans, R. "I Will Fix It; Terry Vows to Sort Out Marriage in Dubai Showdown with Toni." *Daily Mirror*, 2/12/10, 7.

Fitzmaurice, M. "Terryble Behaviour But We Can't Judge." *Daily Mirror*, 2/3/10, 10.

Flynn, B. & Syson, N. "J.T. to Gentry." *The Sun*, 1/20/10, 3.

Fricker, M. "Terry's Fling With Second Player's Girl." *Daily Mirror*, 2/4/10, 1, 4-5.

Garside, K. "Where John Terry Differs From Tiger Woods is in The Absence of Shame." *Daily Telegraph*, 2/1/10, Sport, 9.

Haywood, L. "His Cosy Chat With Mag Hid The Truth." *The Sun*, 2/3/10, 5.

Jiggins, P. "JT: Time to Forget It." *The Sun*, 3/5/10, 82.

Kay, J. "Terry's £5,000 a Week Bets." *The Sun*, 12/2/05, 4-5.

Kelso, P. "Troubles Grow for Terry and Advisers." *Daily Telegraph*, 2/3/10, Sport, 4

Kelso, P. & Burt J. "Capello Sacked His Captain for Betraying Team Unity." *Daily Telegraph*, 2/6/10, Sport, 2-3.

Lawton, M. "No Apology So No World Cup." *Daily Mail*, 2/26/10.

Lawton, M., Chadwick G.,and Tozer, J. "How Did Two of the Most Notorious Pranksters in the Country Get into England's Team Hotel?" *Daily Mail*, 3/11/10.

Lawton, M., "So, isn't £170k a Week Enough?" *Daily Mail*, 11/27/09.

Mansey, K. "John Was There for Me—John Terry the Love Cheat." *Sunday Mirror*, 1/31/10, 4-5.

Maxwell, M. "Toni's a WAG's WAG, No Self Respect and No Right to Sympathy." *The Sun,* 2/3/10, 31.

McGarry, I. "He Will Always Be Skip; Carlo." *The Sun*, 2/6/10, 86, 88.

McGarry, I. "Chelsea's Code of Honour States: Some Things You Just Don't Do!" *The Sun*, 1/30/10, 88-89.

McIntosh, F. "Come On You Boo-Hoos." *Sunday Mirror*, 5/25/08, 25.

Millard, N., Pollard, C. & Crick, A. "Love Cheat's Dubai Trip Valentine's Day Reunion With Wife." *The Sun*, 2/2/10, 1, 4.

Moyes, S. "Toni the Lonely." *Daily Mirror*, 2/3/10, 1, 4-5.

Moyes, S. "Terry Heads for Reunion With Family; Marriage." *Daily Mirror*, 2/11/10, 7.

Moyes, S. "And Here's Some of Me When John Came Back After His Affair With That French Girl."*Daily Mirror*, 2/13/10, 1, 4-5.

Nash, E. "Terry Slept With Team-Mate's Girlfriend: Hero to Zero." *Daily Record,* 1/30/10, 1, 7.

O'Connor, A. "Is Beckham a Pawn in the Game?" *The Times*, 6/12/03, T2, 4-5.

Orvice, V. "£20M; That's How Much Terry Could Lose After Capello Strips Him of Captaincy." *The Sun*, 2/6/10, 88.

Palmer, A. "Terry's All Sold." *News of the World,* 12/20/09, 16-17.

Peake, A. "The Winner Shakes It All; Love-Split Coles' Pain as Wayne Bounces Back." *The Sun*, 3/1/10, 4-5.

Pendlebury, R. "A Seedy Serial Brawler, Drinker and Womaniser. How Can He Keep The Captaincy That He Has So Besmirched?" *Daily Mail*, 1/30/10.

Perthern, A., Callagher, I., Chapman, A., & J., Millbank, J. "England Captain Made Team-Mate's Girlfriend Pregnant—And Then Arranged For Abortion." *Mail onSunday*, 1/31/10.

Samuel, M. "Martin Samuel Column." *Daily Mail*, 3/3/10.

Samuel, M. "Brand Tiger is Out of a Hole, Now Let The Cash Tills Ring." *Daily Mail,* 2/20/10.

Sanders, D. "My View," *The Sun*, 2/10/10, 44.

Sawer, P. "Top of the Big Money Leagues." *Sunday Telegraph*, 3/28/10, News, 15.

Self, J. "Terry Will Be AHero, Says Tony." *The Sun*, 3/6/10, 74.

Singh, R. & Moriarty, R., "Series of Romps by Blues Ace." *The Sun*, 1/30/10, 5.

Smith, R. "Relief at Last for John Terry as England's Sense of Scandal Starts to Subside." *Daily Telegraph*, 2/11/10, News, 7.

The Sun "How the pressure showed." 3/4/10, 19.

The Sun online, Staff Reporter, "Terry Silent Over His Captaincy."2/3/10—downloaded 5/12/10.

The Sun online, Staff Reporter, "Terry Wound-Up by Joking Autograph Hunters." 3/5/10—downloaded 5/12/10.

The Sun online, Staff Reporter, "Legal Gag on John Terry Affair Lifted."1/29/10.

Sweet, G. "JT, You Deserve a Kickin." *The Sun*, 2/27/10, 84.

Watkins, N. "How to Make Apology Work." *The Sun*, 4/6/10, 39.

Wells, T. "Dubai Bye Terry; Soccer Love Rat Ditched." *The Sun*, 2/1/10, 1, 4-5.

White, J. "Welcome to Woods' One-Man Show, The Biggest Con in Sport." *Daily Telegraph*, 2/19/10, Sport, 14.

White, R., West, A., & O'Shea, G. "Betrayed By His Captain and Best Pal; Bridge 'In Bits' Over JT's Fling With His Beauty." *The Sun*, 1/30/10, 4-5.

Williamson, L. "Head to Head at High Noon." *Daily Mail*, 2/27/10.

Winter, H. "Wembley Crowd on Dangerous Ground if They Jeer Terry." *Daily Telegraph*, 3/2/10, Sport, 5.

Woods, J. "Please Save Us from the Boo-Hoo Boys." *Daily Telegraph*, 8/5/07, News, 17.

Social Deviance and Integrity

Chapter Nine

Bad Newz Kennels: Michael Vick and Dogfighting

J. Scott Smith, University of Missouri

On April 20, 2007, Michael Vick's cousin Davon Boddie was arrested outside of a Hampton nightclub and charged with possession of marijuana with intent to sell (Drug probe leads, 2007; Wyche, 2007). Boddie listed his current address as 1915 Moonlight Road, Smithfield, Virginia, a property Vick owned but did not reside in. On April 25, 2007, Vick's Moonlight Road property was raided by the Virginia State Police and Drug Task Force. "Evidence of dogfighting, including 66 dogs, treadmills, sticks to pry open dogs' locked jaws, a blood-stained pit and medical supplies were found, according to the Virginia Animal Fighting Task Force" (Wyche & Ledbetter, 2007, p. 2E). The raid on Vick's property prompted attacks from animal rights groups and national media exposure.

On April 26, 2007, the president and CEO of the Humane Society, Wayne Pacelle, released a statement declaring the investigation at Vick's Virginia property validated their reports that Vick was involved with dogfighting (Drug probe leads, 2007). The People for the Ethical Treatment of Animals (PETA) called for Falcons owner Arthur Blank to suspend Vick during the investigation and "to kick him off the team if it is found that dogs on Vick's property were neglected or used for fighting" (Drug probe leads, 2007). The charges leveled against Vick clearly illustrated that he needed to defend himself.

Prior to 2007, Michael Vick was one of the darlings of the National Football League (NFL). He was the first African American quarterback to be taken with the first overall selection in the 2001 draft and became a franchise player (Myers, 2001). Vick led the Atlanta Falcons over the Green Bay Packers 27-7 in the 2003 (2002 season) wild card game, which was the

Packers' first home playoff loss in franchise history (Newberry, 2003). Nationally, Vick had the highest selling jersey, so his popularity was widespread. Vick's exciting style of play was rewarded with a $130 million contract after the 2004 season (Sugiura, 2004). Vick lived up to the expectations in the 2004 season, leading the Falcons to an 11-5 record and a playoff berth.

After the 2004 season, Vick's professional and personal life slid downhill. The Falcons missed the playoffs two years in a row, going 8-8 in 2005 and 7-9 in 2006. On November 26, 2006, the Falcons lost at home to the New Orleans Saints, 31-13, and upon hearing boos from the Atlanta crowd as he exited the field, Vick flicked the crowd off with both middle fingers (Wyche, 2006). Along with his football disappointments, Vick had various personal issues. In March 2005, former girlfriend Sonia Elliot sued Vick because she said he knowingly gave her genital herpes (Sugiura, 2005). Possibly more embarrassing than the suit was the alias "Ron Mexico" that Vick used at various clinics while receiving treatment. Fans began custom-ordering Vick jerseys with "Mexico" on the back until the NFL stepped in to stop "Mexico" jerseys from being purchased (Sugiura, 2005). Also, just months before the dogfighting allegations surfaced, Vick was under investigation by TSA authorities when he tried to take a water bottle with a secret compartment through airport security (Wyche, 2007). Although the initial reports stated there were trace elements of marijuana in the bottle, lab results were inconclusive and Vick was not charged. Regardless, Vick's image had taken a significant hit on and off the field since beating the Packers in the 2003 playoffs.

These incidences led to media criticism, most notably *Atlanta Journal Constitution* columnist Jeff Schultz's column, "Enough! Time for Falcons to Punt Vick" (Schultz, 2007, p. 1H). Calls for Vick to be traded were made and it appeared Falcons management was fed up with the constant incidents. The seemingly clean image of Vick was taking a significant hit in the media and questions about his personal life started to surface. Those questions increased significantly when Vick's Moonlight Road property was raided.

CRITICAL ANALYSIS OF VICK'S IMAGE REPAIR DISCOURSE

Benoit's (1995) method will be applied to Vick's discourse in three subsets: (1) the attacks on Vick from the initial warrant and search of his Virginia property on April 25, 2007, (2) the discourse applied in response to the July 17, 2007 indictment, and (3) the discourse applied after agreeing to a plea deal on August 24, 2007.

First Response: April 27, 2007

Vick was in New York for the upcoming April 28, 2007, NFL draft and answered questions from reporters at a news conference where he announced his participation in the upcoming NFL quarterback challenge (Knobler & Wyche, 2007). After the initial reports of dogfighting, at Vick's Virginia property Vick relied on the image restoration strategies of denial, shift the blame, and corrective action.

Denial

Vick made explicit and implicit denials during his April 27, 2007, press conference. First, Vick adamantly denied that he ever spent time at his Virginia property. Vick stated, "I'm never there. I'm never at the house" (Knobler & Wyche, 2007, p. 2D). This denial represents a two-part denial. First, he explicitly denies ever being at the house, which implicitly denies his possible involvement in dogfighting. However, Vick did not directly deny the charge that he was involved in dogfighting. Forcefully denying the allegation that he had any involvement in a dogfighting ring might have been appropriate. These simple denials reject the accusation that Vick frequented his Virginia property and participated in dogfighting.

Defeasibility

Along with denying his presence at his Virginia property, Vick utilized the image restoration strategy of defeasibility. Vick wanted to evade responsibility for the situation by pleading a lack of information. Vick stated, "If I'm not there, I don't know what's going on" (Knobler & Wyche, 2007, p. 2D). If Vick was not at his Virginia property then he could not know what activities were being performed at the house. Here Vick de-emphasized his ownership of the house and shifted the focus toward his family members, who inhabited the house.

Shift the Blame

Vick used shift the blame to refocus the allegations away from himself and toward his family and friends. He stated, "I left the house with my family members and my cousin. They just haven't been doing the right thing" (Knobler & Wyche, 2007, p. 2D). This statement clearly denies any involvement in dogfighting and squarely places blame on his family members. Vick further shifts the blame: "When it all boils down, people will try to take advantage of you and leave you out to dry. Lesson learned for me" (Knobler & Wyche, 2007, p. 2D). Here, Vick suggested he was the victim, someone who was trying to help family members, but was taken advantage of. This statement aimed to shift the blame away from Vick and portray himself as a victim of his own generosity.

Corrective Action

Further examination of Vick's discourse revealed the image restoration strategy of corrective action. If the allegations were caused by Vick's family members taking advantage of his generosity, then an appropriate measure would be to stop helping them. When someone feels they were betrayed, taking corrective steps to avoid similar problems appears logical. Vick stated, "It's a call for me to really tighten down on who I'm trying to take care of" (Knobler & Wyche, 2007, p. 2D). This strategy aims to continue placing Vick in the role of the victim. Vick calls on himself to be more selective with the people he helps and this will alleviate his association with the negative allegations at his Virginia property. This comment continued to finger his family members as the root of the illegal actions and illuminated Vick's assurances that the problems were with the people he was helping rather than himself.

The Second Response: July 30, 2007

Before Vick's second statement, the public became aware of a federal investigation on June 8, 2007, when federal investigators produced a warrant to search Vick's Moonlight Road property (Wyche, 2007f). Until then, the investigation had been a state of Virginia matter and Surry County Commonwealth attorney Gerald Poindexter stated on May 16, 2007, that Vick was not under investigation (Wyche, 2007b). But when Poindexter was asked on June 8, 2007, who federal investigators would be interested in he responded, "Michael Vick, is he the target? Who else would be?" (Wyche, 2007f, p. 1H). When the federal government became involved, the investigation changed dramatically. Poindexter opined, "Obviously if the feds come in, the jurisdictional basis is some sort of interstate violation. We don't know what it is—the training of dogs, gambling, racketeering, whatever they want to call it" (Wyche, 2007f, p. 1H). This altered the severity of the allegations from a state of Virginia investigation focusing on Vick's family to a federal investigation against Michael Vick.

The federal government's focus on Vick became apparent on July 17, 2007, when Vick and his associates were indicted on charges of "Conspiracy to Travel in Interstate Commerce in Aid of Unlawful Activities and to Sponsor a Dog in an Animal Fighting Venture" ("United States of America," 2007). The indictment detailed an illegal dogfighting ring called "Bad Newz Kennels" bankrolled by Vick (aka "Ookie") and run principally by Purnell Peace (aka "P-Funk"), Tony Taylor (aka "T") and Quanis Phillips (aka "Q").

Specifically, the indictment chronicled the activities of the group from May 2001 to April 2007. The group tested or "rolled" pit bulls and executed those that performed poorly by means of shooting, electrocuting, drowning, hanging, and slamming. Bad Newz Kennels (primarily Peace, Taylor, and Phillips, with Vick attending fewer fights) traveled from Virginia to North Carolina, Maryland, New Jersey, and South Carolina to fight pit bulls from other kennels with prize purses ranging from $1,000 to $26,000. The indictment against the four men was particularly damaging for Vick because he was accused of not only bankrolling and partaking in dogfighting, but also participating in killing pit bulls that performed poorly in testing sessions.

The indictment provided animal rights groups the tangible evidence to support their earlier attacks on Vick. John Goodwin of the Humane Society stated,

> Some of the grisly details in these filings shocked even me, and I'm a person who faces this stuff every day. I was surprised to see that they were killing dogs by hanging them and one dog was killed by slamming it to the ground. Those are extremely violent methods of execution—they're unnecessary and just sick. ("Falcons' Vick indicted," 2007)

The indictment's detailed accounts of how the group executed pit bulls increased the attack on Vick's image as the cruelty to the dogs during testing was worse than the actual dogfighting.

Along with animal rights groups weighing in publicly on the indictment, the media responded as well. ESPN's nationally syndicated program *Pardon the Interruption* (*PTI*) hosted David Cornwell, who formerly provided the NFL with legal counsel and currently works as a legal representative for NFL players on their segment "5 good minutes" (Cohen, 2007). *PTI* co-host Michael Wilbon asked Cornwell how serious the indictment was for Vick. Cornwell responded,

> It's very serious. The seriousness arises out of the conspiracy charge. A conspiracy is an agreement, the government has to prove that there was an agreement, and one act in furtherance of the agreement, and then all co-conspirators are held liable for each others actions. So even if Vick wasn't at a dogfight or even if he didn't kill a dog, he would be responsible for the action of another co-conspirator, very, very serious. (Cohen, 2007)

The indictment identified the attack against Vick, providing graphic accounts of how dogs were executed in combination with the conspiracy charge. Vick's image was clearly under serious attack and required a response.

July 26, 2007

Michael Vick's arraignment occurred on July 26, 2007, at the United States District Court in Richmond, Virginia. After pleading innocent to the charges, Vick released a statement through his lawyer Billy Martin that relied on the image restoration strategies of denial and bolstering.

Denial

Vick continued to deny charges that he was involved in an illegal dogfighting ring. "Today in court I pleaded innocent to the allegations made against me. I take these charges very seriously and look forward to clearing my good name" ("Text of Vick's statement," 2007). Here, Vick denied the charges, yet did not reference dogfighting or gambling. Changing from his initial response, he decided not to continue to shift the blame to his co-defendants or other family members.

Bolstering

Martin bolstered Vick's image by displaying concern about those impacted by the indictment and the media attention it brought his family and team-mates. Martin stated,

> Above all I would like to say to my mom I'm sorry for what she has had to go through in this most trying of times. It has caused pain to my family and I apologize to my family. I also want to apologize to my Falcon teammates for not being with them at the beginning of spring training. ("Text of Vick's statement," 2007)

Although this statement clearly denies the charges and apologizes to Vick's mother and teammates, the statement was read by Martin rather than Vick. With such a short statement (102 words), the need for Martin to read it appears peculiar. Did Martin and his litigation team decide that it was better for Vick to not give the short statement? The decision for Vick not to speak appeared odder when on July 30, 2007, he participated in an interview with WVEE-FM in Atlanta by V-103 DJ Porsche Fox (Wyche, 2007b).

Vick granted WVEE-FM the first public interview since he was indicted on July 17, 2007. V-103 DJ Porsche Fox was given specific instructions by Vick's legal team not to ask questions directly related to the case. Vick primarily relied on the image restoration strategy of bolstering. Vick's interview with Porsche Fox bolstered his reputation in three ways. First, he praised his devoted fans for their continual support during the dogfighting allegations. Second, Vick presented the role of religion in his life. Finally, he expressed concern for the damage the allegations caused the city of Atlanta and Falcons owner Arthur Blank. These strategies aimed to bolster Vick's reputation with his audience.

Vick's legal counsel constrained Fox from asking any questions related to the case, which limited the type of responses Vick could provide. Due to the restrictiveness of the interview, Vick bolstered himself by thanking his fans, "I just want to thank all my fans and all my support and all the people that are praying for Mike Vick and are in my corner right now" (Wyche, 2007b, p. 1C). This statement appropriately thanked his fans, who continued to support him through serious allegations. Although this strategy would probably not gain support from those already having a negative opinion of Vick, maintaining the fans who still supported him was important.

Vick further bolstered himself through his belief in God. He stated,

> It's a crisis situation for me, but I'm going to get through it and I feel, by the grace of God, that's the only way. I believe in the outcome at the end, and that's why I put my faith in the man upstairs. (Wyche, 2007a, p. 1C)

The belief that one should put their faith in God is an important moral distinction in American life. Vick might garner support by stating that he, first, believes in God and second, places his fate in the hands of God. The image of Vick as a religious individual contrasts with the brutal acts detailed in the indictment. This strategy combined with his July 26, 2007, denial of the charges illustrates an attempt to present Vick as a pious man.

He also bolstered his image by expressing remorse for the situation he placed the city of Atlanta and team owner Arthur Blank in. "I know I put the city through a lot, my owner, Arthur Blank, who I love sincerely; I put him through a lot. It hurts me to put him through this situation" (Wyche, 2007b, p. 1C). The acknowledgment of damaging the reputation of the Atlanta Falcons, the city of Atlanta, and owner Arthur Blank illustrates Vick's concern for others. If the audience accepted Vick's distinction that he was legitimately concerned about the Falcons and the city of Atlanta, his reputation would be enhanced. Vick's responses after the indictment was issued were much more contrite and he did not shift the blame on his family or friends.

Phase 3: Mortification

Between the July 18, 2007, indictment and Vick's plea deal on August 27, 2007, Vick's accomplices agreed to plead guilty and cooperate with federal investigators. On July 30, 2007, Tony Taylor was the first member of Bad Newz Kennels to plead guilty, agreeing to the summary of facts that stated he helped start the dogfighting ring with Vick, Peace, and Phillips and that Vick almost exclusively funded the operation (Markon, 2007). On August 17, 2007, Peace and Phillips also agreed to plea deals with the government and faced maximum penalties of $250,000 in fines and up to five years in prison (Schmidt & Battista, 2007). With all other co-defendants agreeing to plea deals, Vick's attorneys urged Vick to agree to a plea deal.

With pressure and evidence building against Vick, he finally agreed to a plea deal on August 24, 2007 (Markon & Maske, 2007). Vick agreed to the statement of facts that detailed his involvement with Bad Newz Kennels starting in 2001 and had activity as recently as April 2007, just before the first raid on the Moonlight Road property. The statement of facts had two important distinctions for Vick: First, he did not admit killing dogs (even though he admitted being present during killings) and second, he denied ever betting on the fights or taking any of the winnings (Markon & Maske, 2007). Denying any gambling involvement was directed at Commissioner Roger Goodell because the NFL has a gambling policy within the collective bargaining agreement. Goodell was not impressed by the well-crafted documents, as Vick was suspended by the NFL immediately and indefinitely. Goodell wrote to Vick,

> Your admitted conduct was not only illegal, but also cruel and reprehensible. Your team, the NFL, and NFL fans have all been hurt by your actions. Your plea agreement . . . demonstrate[s] your significant involvement in illegal gambling. Even if you personally did not place bets, as you contend, your actions in funding the betting and your association with illegal gambling both violate the terms of your NFL Player Contract and expose you to corrupting influences in derogation of one of the most fundamental responsibilities of an NFL player. (Markon & Maske, 2007, p. E1)

Vick's admission to running an illegal dogfighting ring, after months of denying any involvement, required a rhetorical response.

On August 27, 2007, Michael Vick's plea agreement was accepted by United States District Judge Henry E. Hudson. Immediately after pleading guilty, Vick held his first press conference outside of the courthouse, speaking extemporaneously (Redmon, 2007). Vick primarily relied on mortification and bolstering, while using corrective action to a lesser degree.

Mortification

After denying the allegations of dogfighting for nearly four months, Vick signed a plea deal and apologized fully and unconditionally. Vick stated, "I take full responsibility for my actions. Not for one second will I sit right here and point the finger and try to blame anybody else for my actions or what I've done" (Text of Vick apology, 2007). This statement is essential for his apology because of his prolonged contention that he was innocent. Furthermore, this apology could not be fully accepted by his audience unless Vick condemned dogfighting. Vick stated, "Dog fighting is a terrible thing, and I did reject it" (Text of Vick apology, 2007). Even though "I did reject it" was an awkward phrase, denouncing dogfighting as a horrible crime was necessary for mortification to be a successful strategy.

Vick then apologized to NFL commissioner Roger Goodell, Falcons owner Arthur Blank, Falcons head coach Bobby Petrino, and his Falcons teammates.

> I want to personally apologize to Commissioner Goodell, Arthur Blank, coach Bobby Petrino, my Atlanta Falcons' teammates, you know, for our—for our previous discussions that we had. And I was not honest and forthright in our discussions, and, you know, I was ashamed and totally disappointed in myself to say the least. (Text of Vick apology, 2007).

This apology to the commissioner, owner, coach, and players is an attempt to assuage the damage done from his personal denials to each audience. In two instances, Vick had personal meetings with Goodell and Blank where he lied to both of them about his involvement with dogfighting. Vick's apology to both men is intrinsically linked to his ability to possibly play in the NFL again. Rather ironically, the gambling charges against Vick might hold more weight against him playing football again than the dogfighting. O'Dell (2007) stated, "The NFL suspended him indefinitely and without pay Friday after his plea agreement was filed. Merely associating with gamblers can trigger a lifetime ban under the league's personal conduct policy." Goodell has the authority to continue his indefinite suspension when he is released from prison and Blank will still own the rights to Vick when he is released.

Another instance of mortification came in apologizing to his young fans. Vick stated, "I want to apologize to all the young kids out there for my immature acts and, you know, what I did was, what I did was very immature so that means I need to grow up" (Text of Vick apology, 2007). Vick was an amazingly popular player in the city of Atlanta and apologizing to that fan base was appropriate.

Bolstering

Vick utilized bolstering in his statement in an effort to repair his image. Vick started his statement by saying,

> For most of my life, I've been a football player, not a public speaker, so, you know, I really don't know, you know, how to say what I really want to say. You know, I understand it's—it's important or not important, you know, as far as what you say but how you say things. So, you know, I take this opportunity just to speak from the heart. (Text of Vick apology, 2007)

This initial statement bolstered Vick as someone who was trying to convey a very contrite message. He affirmed this statement by not using note cards, having a lawyer speak on his behalf, or using a prepared message by an attorney.

Vick continued to bolster himself by stating he found religion through this experience. "I'm upset with myself, and, you know, through this situation I found Jesus and asked him for forgiveness and turned my life over to God. And I think that's the right thing to do as of right now" (Text of Vick apology, 2007). America is comprised of a Christian majority among its citizens and appealing to those sensibilities appears appropriate.

Corrective Action

Vick applied corrective action to a lesser degree than mortification and bolstering. Vick stated, "And I will redeem myself. I have to. So I got a lot of down time, a lot of time to think about my actions and what I've done and how to make Michael Vick a better person" (Text of Vick apology, 2007). Although Vick does not label specifically how he will "redeem" himself, he does promise that he will. He stated, "Dogfighting is a terrible thing, and I did reject it" (Text of Vick apology, 2007). This use of corrective action that he has stopped dogfighting is important for his audiences to be assured that this type of behavior is behind him.

EVALUATION

This section will evaluate Vick's image repair discourse for consistency and success. Due to Vick's plea deal, his specific involvement in Bad Newz Kennels remains unclear. However, what is clear is the public perception and response to Vick's image repair efforts. Furthermore, it is important to take each phase within its own context because information about the case changed and subsequently Vick's discourse changed.

First Phase

During the first phase, Vick relied on denial, defeasibility, shift the blame, and corrective action. These strategies were not surprising because an inhumane act like dogfighting produces strong negative attention from the media and general public. As such, Vick's use of denial was not surprising because he wanted to disassociate himself from an illegal and immoral act. In the short term, this was an appropriate strategy because Vick did not live at the property, so denying he had any involvement in the dogfighting ring seemed plausible. Furthermore, Vick's associates had criminal records, so while

Vick himself had never been convicted of a crime, Tony Taylor, Quanis Phillips, and Purnell Peace all were convicted or indicted on drug charges before the dogfighting investigation (Roberts, 2007). Denying he had any involvement in a dogfighting ring probably had little impact repairing his image due to his other instances of recent questionable behavior. The two aforementioned major incidents were when Vick gave Atlanta Falcons fans double middle fingers after a loss to the New Orleans Saints and the water bottle incident at the Miami airport. The public probably did not afford Vick the credibility he once had before these incidents.

Once the federal investigation was underway, Vick's use of denial was inappropriate. Vick missed the opportunity to cooperate with investigators in Virginia and admit his role in an illegal dogfighting ring. Vick might have used mortification in the early stages of the investigation (combined with cooperating with Virginia authorities), which would have probably reduced some of the damage to his image. Specifically, the graphic details listed in the July 17, 2007 indictment and August 24, 2007 statement of facts probably would not have become public had he cooperated with investigators. Also, Vick would not have lied to Commissioner Roger Goodell or Falcons owner Arthur Blank had he accepted responsibility for his actions and cooperated earlier.

Vick's use of defeasibility provided a logistical answer to allegations of training dogs for fighting and actual dogfighting taking place at his property. By stating he was not physically present at the Moonlight Road property, he could not know illegal activity was taking place. Again, while this image restoration strategy might have repaired his image before the federal investigation, his use of defeasibility was detrimental in the long term. The federal indictment provided evidence that Vick was involved in a criminal conspiracy and he no doubt knew of the operation at his Moonlight Road property.

Along with his use of denial and defeasibility, Vick utilized shifting the blame and corrective action. Vick portrayed himself as the victim in the situation and that he needed to select better friends in the future. The combination of these strategies might have repaired his image slightly because Taylor, Phillips, and Peace had criminal records. Even though shifting the blame to his associates probably lessened the initial attacks against Vick, his later acknowledgment of being part of Bad Newz Kennels further damaged his image. Vick shifted the blame to his accomplices who could not have developed the dogfighting ring without Vick. He funded the entire operation; he bought the Moonlight Road property and bankrolled all of the fights, so Vick's involvement was necessary for the ring to exist. Shifting the blame to the other members of Bad Newz Kennels was overall an ineffective strategy as Vick was the leader of the group, even if he did not oversee day-to-day operations.

For whatever reason, Vick must have believed that his fame and fortune would keep him from being implicated in a dogfighting ring during the initial phase of the investigation. His use of denial, defeasibility, and shift the blame were strategies consistent with the assumption that he could avoid prosecution. Even though these strategies probably mitigated the damage from immediate attacks, Vick's early discourse was severely detrimental to his image as the federal investigation detailed his involvement with Bad Newz Kennels.

Phase 2

Vick pleaded innocent at his July 26, 2007 arraignment, presenting the opportunity to make a statement. The V-103 interview presented a much different type of discourse than the initial statement on April 27, 2007. Vick's reliance on bolstering and corrective action in this interview were not appropriate for the charges he was facing. When Vick pleaded innocent to charges in court, the chance to continually shift the blame to others was still available. By continuing to deny the charges by pleading innocent, Vick could keep shifting the blame to the other co-defendants.

The reason this discourse was ineffective is not due to poor choices in strategies, but rather the channel of communication he chose. Facing a felony indictment is a very serious situation for anyone. If Vick was willing to speak publicly on July 30, 2007, why did he choose not to speak on July 26, 2007, after his arraignment rather than have his attorney Billy Martin read his statement? Vick limited the audience size by choosing to speak on a local Atlanta radio station rather than at his earlier press conference, which would have reached a national audience.

Furthermore, the questions that V-103 DJ Porsche Fox was allowed to ask were peculiar as well. If one is willing to deny charges legally in court (by pleading innocent to the charges at the arraignment) it would appear appropriate to also deny those charges publicly. Vick did not deny the charges in the interview, which questions the decision to have the interview.

Commentary

Mason-Dixon Polling and Research conducted a telephone poll for the *Atlanta Journal-Constitution* on July 23 and 24, 2007 (Vejnoska, 2007). Ninety-seven percent of respondents said they were aware of the dogfighting allegations surrounding Vick. The poll asked respondents if Vick was convicted of dogfighting should he be allowed to play again in the NFL. Sixty-five percent of respondents said he should be banned from football, 22 percent said he should not be banned, and 13 percent said they were unsure (Vejnoska, 2007). This poll illustrates that people clearly believed Vick was involved in dogfighting and his punishment should be severe.

Note that no scientific polling data were available after Billy Martin's statements or Vick's V-103 interview. This could be due to various factors: First, the first utterance was by Vick's lawyer Billy Martin rather than Vick himself. Although Martin spoke for him, an attorney speaking for a client does not produce the same effect as the rhetor under attack. Second, Martin's statement was extremely brief (only 102 words, a paragraph's worth) and did not promote a strong response from the audience. Similarly, the V-103 interview provided a small, limited audience rather than a larger media event. Both rhetorical situations did not provide the gravity necessary to invoke a scientific poll.

Phase 3

Evaluation of Vick's discourse from the August 27, 2007, press conference suggests his image restoration discourse was partially effective. Of course once Vick pled guilty to federal charges of conspiracy to travel in interstate commerce, the chances of gaining support from various audiences appeared minimal. Even though Vick's discourse appeared well-conceived, the timing of the apology and severity of the charges he now agreed to damaged his image immensely.

After admitting to dogfighting and gambling on dogfighting, Vick relied heavily on mortification. One could argue that Vick had no other recourse but to apologize at this point, but the manner in which Vick apologized was well-advised. Vick's apology was complete, taking full responsibility for his actions. He further apologized to his various audiences, his fans, teammates, Commissioner Roger Goodell, and Falcons owner Arthur Blank. But this apology only occured after months of denial, including personal meetings with Goodell and Blank when he lied to them. Although Vick appeared contrite during the press conference, it could not repair the trust broken with Goodell and Blank.

Additionally, the severity of the dogfighting charges he agreed to in the statement of facts was very damaging. Dogfighting in and of itself is cruel and unusual. The ghastly description of Vick partaking in the electrocuting, slamming, hanging, drowning, and shooting of dogs represents a horrific image. Even the full apology Vick made is not enough to restore his image when he agreed to the gory details in the statement of facts.

Along with the graphic details of the statement of facts, Vick's constant rebuttal that he took no part in dogfighting and was innocent of the charges against him for nearly four months limited the effectiveness of a full apology. This prolonged denial could have led to a loss in credibility. For instance, Vick condemned dogfighting, which is essential for his mortification to be accepted by his audiences. However, he was involved in dogfighting for nearly seven years (that we know of) and he denied any involvement for four months. Vick also lied to owner Arthur Blank and Commissioner Roger Goodell, so if he lied to them, why should his audiences believe him now?

Even though the horrific details of dogfighting rightfully take the full attention of audiences, the gambling charge provides the major roadblock for Vick to return to the NFL. The NFL collective bargaining agreement provides a player conduct code, so the NFL could ban Vick from playing in the league for life if it chose to. By not addressing this issue, Vick left the gambling issue unresolved.

To a lesser degree, Vick utilized the image restoration strategy of bolstering to reduce the offensiveness of his actions. Delivering his press conference with no notes was an effective method for delivering the apology as it provided an opportunity for Vick to speak for himself. This allowed Vick to speak freely, without appearing as someone unrepentant reading a script prepared by lawyers or handlers.

One image restoration strategy that might have improved Vick's discourse was the use of transcendence. Vick could have transcended the issue from the context of Michael Vick and to the broader issue of dogfighting in the South as a problem. Comments from other professional athletes like Washington Redskins running back Clinton Portis and New York Knicks point guard Stephon Marbury emphasized that dogfighting was not as bad as it was being portrayed in the media. Portis stated, "I don't know if he was fighting dogs or not, but it's his property. It's his dog. If that's what he wants to do, do it" (Maske, 2007, p. E1). When Portis was told dogfighting was a felony, he responded, "It can't be too bad of a crime" (Redskins RB Portis, 2007). Marbury added, "I think, you know, we don't say anything about people who shoot deer or shoot other animals. You know, from what I hear, dogfighting is a sport. It's just behind closed doors" (Stephon Marbury defends, 2007). Portis and entertainer Whoopi Goldberg discussed the prevalence of dogfighting in the South. Portis stated, "I know a lot of back roads that have the dog fighting if you want to go see it" (Redskins RB Portis, 2007). Whoopi Goldberg agreed with this sentiment when she stated on her first episode of *The View*, "one of the things I haven't heard anybody say is you know, from his background this is not an unusual thing for where he comes from, it's like cockfighting in Puerto Rico" (Goldberg, 2007). Although all three celebrities backed off their comments within days of their controversial remarks, their initial statements provide cause for concern that dogfighting is a larger problem than Michael Vick. If Vick had utilized transcendence by stating that dogfighting was a common practice in the culture he grew up in, then he could have provided the larger contextual problem of dogfighting in the South and that he was just a product of this environment.

Commentary

Within the Atlanta community, *Atlanta Journal-Constitution* columnist Mark Bradley (2007) was impressed with Vick's delivery, lack of using a prepared statement from a lawyer, and his insistence on taking full responsibility. Bradley pondered what life would be like when Vick is released from prison:

> Vick will go to jail and serve his NFL suspension, and then there'll be the rest of his life. It need not be a tale of woe. With the right amount of contrition (from him) and compassion (from us), it might even become a heartening story in three acts: The rise, the fall, the redemption. (Bradley, 2007, p. 6A)

This positive column ended with Bradley stating of Vick, "There's hope for this one yet" (p. 6A). Vick's use of mortification after pleading guilty repaired his image some and opened the opportunity for him to repair it more once out of prison. Even in the Atlanta community which lost the face and best player of its football team seemed receptive to his apology.

Nationally, ESPN commentators Tony Kornheiser and Michael Wilbon discussed the Vick news conference on the August 27, 2007 episode of *PTI* (Cohen, 2007). Tony Kornheiser opined,

> It's a lot different in tone from the guy who said that "everybody in the world loves Michael Vick" this is a different person. He apologized completely, irrevocably, that's a very good thing to do. He apologized for lying, he took full responsibility for this thing. So I think this is a good start, now you have to see deeds, I know he wants to get back to the NFL, and you have to see how he redeems himself as he said he would. But this was a good start, it appeared to be from the heart. You know, it never would have come to this, it didn't have to come to this, you know, but now it is at this point I think it's a good start and I think you do too.

Michael Wilbon echoed Kornheiser's comments:

> I do Tony. Good first step, no notes, not reading for a text prepared by a lawyer or by a handler. He went out there and just looked at people and said this. What impressed me in this first step is the humility cause we ain't seen that from Michael Vick and if there had been any humility he probably wouldn't have wound up in this place. I take exception with one thing, the notion that I made a mistake. You know a mistake when you make a left turn onto the wrong way of a one-way street and hit another car and hurt somebody, that's a mistake. He was involved in on-going criminal activity for six or seven years maybe longer than that, this is not just a mistake, there's a lot to pay for, but I think this was the right note to sound.

Much like Bradley's editorial, Kornheiser and Wilbon agreed that the apology appeared sincere and created an opportunity for Vick to repair his image and possibly return to the NFL.

Polling Data

A Gallup (2007) poll conducted August 23 to 26, 2007, asked various participants questions about Michael Vick. This polling occurred before Vick's August 27, 2007 statement so the responses represent the public perception of Vick leading up to the statement. The phone survey asked respondents if Vick should go to jail and if yes, should it be a long or short prison sentence. The majority of respondents stated that Vick's punishment should be a "short prison sentence" (51 percent), with "long prison sentence" next with 35 percent of responses, and 12 percent stated he should receive no prison time. With regard to football, 58 percent of respondents stated they do not believe Vick should be allowed back into the NFL, while 40 percent stated he should be reinstated after serving jail time. Furthermore, when participants were asked if they would want the football team they root for to sign Vick after his prison sentence, 75 percent of respondents stated they would not want Vick to play for their football team and only 22 percent of respondents said they would want him to play for their football team. These responses display the dismay people have for Vick's role in Bad Newz Kennels.

IMPLICATIONS

The primary implication provided by Vick's rhetorical situation is that when one is caught in criminal activity, he/she should take full responsibility for their actions and apologize unconditionally. After four months of denying the charges and claiming his innocence, Vick finally admitted guilt and expressed seemingly sincere remorse. If Vick had utilized mortification when he first spoke in April 2007 his reputation might not have taken such a downturn. Yet, even after lying to the American public, Commissioner Goodell, and Atlanta Falcons owner Blank, the response to his apology on August 27, 2007, was positive. Vick's use of mortification after staunch denials might provide other athletes who have denied wrongdoing (athletes accused of performance-enhancing drug use, for one) that mortification is still a viable rhetorical option. The American media and public were receptive to Vick's apology, which gave him the ability to rejoin the NFL with the Philadelphia Eagles after he was released from prison.

CONCLUSION

Since being released from prison, Vick has returned to NFL prominence. Vick returned to football seemingly changed from prison, paying closer attention to detail during practice and during film sessions. Vick had the best season of his career in 2010, setting "career highs in passer rating (100.2), completion percentage (62.6) and passing yards (3,018)" (McLane, 2011, p. C1). After the 2010 season, Vick was voted the comeback player of the year, which is voted on by 50 members of the media. Yet, a February 2012, a *Forbes* poll found that Vick was tied with Tiger Woods as the most disliked athlete in America (Murphy, 2012). Culturally, dogs are a part of many American families and are viewed as household members. For some people, Vick will never be forgiven for torturing and killing dogs in the name of gambling. However, Vick's apology on August 27, 2007, was the first, and possibly most important, step toward returning to the NFL, which without a complete and believable apology would never have been possible.

REFERENCES

Bernstein, V. (2004, August 5). Humbled, but not for long; A toned-down Michael Vick returns with grand expectations; NFL. *The New York Times*, p. 17.

Bradley, M. (2007, August 28). The Michael Vick case: Show of regret step in right direction. *The Atlanta Journal-Constitution*, p. 6A.

Cohen, J. (Executive Producer). (2007, July 18). *Pardon the Interruption* [Television broadcast]. Washington DC: Entertainment Sports Programming Network.

Cohen, J. (Executive Producer). (2007, August 27). *Pardon the Interruption* [Television broadcast]. Washington DC: Entertainment Sports Programming Network.

Falcons' Vick indicted by grand jury in dogfighting probe. (2007). Retrieved on June 8, 2009 from http://sports.espn.go.com/nfl/news/story?id=2940065.

Gallup Organization (2007, August 23-26). Majority of NFL fans say Vick should not be allowed to play again; Most fans favor a short prison sentence for Vick.

Goldberg, W. (2007, September 4) *The View*.

Knobler, M., & Wyche, S. (2007, April 28). Vick: Family members are to blame. *The Atlanta Journal-Constitution*, p. 2D.

Markon, J. (2007, July 31). Co-Defendant in Vick case pleads guilty. *The Washington Post*, p. E1.

Markon, J., & Maske, M. (2007, August 25). NFL suspends Falcons' Vick indefinitely; Dogfighting involvement admitted in documents; Atlanta hasn't ruled out releasing quarterback. *The Washington Post*, p. E1.

Maske, M. (2007, May 23). Goodell slams remarks by Portis; NFL won't pursue disciplinary action. *The Washington Post*, p. E1.

McLane, J. (2011, August 30). $100 million man. *The Philadelphia Inquirer*, p. C1.

Murphy, P. (2012, February 8). Michael Vic, Tiger Woods among US's most disliked athletes. *The Christian Science Monitor*.

Myers, G. (2001, April 22). Chargers' pick: Pass on Vick Falcons trade up to No. 1 position. *The New York Daily News*, p. 55.

Newberry, P. (2003, January 6). Vick puts Favre, Packers on ice: Atlanta surprises Lambeau faithful in wild-card win. *The Associated Press*.

O'Dell, L. (2007, August 28). A remorseful Michael Vick pleads guilty, calls dogfighting a 'terrible thing.' *The Associated Press.*

Redmon, J. (2007, August 27). Vick goes to court today for guilty plea; Future uncertain: Falcons quarterback, suspended by the NFL, likely to go to prison in dogfighting case; sentencing expected this year. *The Atlanta Journal Constitution*, p. 1A.

Redskins RB Portis: Vick can do what he wants. (2007, May 22). Accessed on July 21, 2008, http://sports.espn.go.com/nfl/news/story?id=2878099.

Roberts, S. (2007, August 19). Vick is trapped in his circle of friends. *The New York Times*, p. SP1.

Schmidt, M. S., & Battista, J. (2007, August 18). Two more plea deals put pressure on Vick. *The New York Times*, p. D1.

Schultz, J. (2007, January 19). Enough! Time for Falcons to punt Vick. *The Atlanta Journal Constitution*, p. 1H.

Stephon Marbury defends Michael Vick, calls dogfighting a sport. (2007, August 22). *The Associated Press.* Sugiura, K. (2004, December 24). The $130 million man; Blank aims to make Vick 'a Falcon for life.' *The Atlanta Journal Constitution*, p. 1A.

Sugiura, K. (2005, April 15). 'Mexico' jerseys sacked by NFL. *The Atlanta Journal Constitution*, p. 1E.

Text of Vick apology: 'I was not honest . . . I need to grow up.' (2007, August 27). *The Associated Press.*

Text of Vick's statement regarding dogfighting charges. (2007, July 26). *The Associated Press.*

The United States of America vs. Purnell A. Peace, Quanis L. Phillips, Tony Taylor, Michael Vick. 18 U.S.C. § 371 (2007).

Vejnoska, J. (2007, July 25). Poll: Ban Vick if he's guilty. *The Atlanta Journal-Constitution*, http://www.ajc.com/sports/content/sports/falcons/stories/2007/07/25/0726poll.html.

Wyche, S. (2006, November 28). Vick: The day after: 'I apologize sincerely'; Frustration led to gesture, star QB says. *The Atlanta Journal Constitution*, p. 1D.

Wyche, S. (2007a, January 18). Drug allegation for Vick; Falcons star probed in incident at Miami airport. *The Atlanta Journal Constitution*, p. 1D.

Wyche, S. (2007b, July 31). Banished Vick: 'It pains me'; In radio interview, QB hopes to be Falcon again. *The Atlanta Journal-Constitution*, p. 1C.

Wyche, S. (2007c, April 27). Dog-fight claims arise in a Vick property raid. *The Atlanta Journal-Constitution*, p. 7H.

Wyche, S. (2007d, May 16). Virginia to begin review in Vick case; Authorities to decide whether dogfighting charges warranted. *The Atlanta Journal-Constitution*, p. 1D.

Wyche, S. (2007e, May 22). Link to Vick in evidence seizure; Envelopes found addressed to him. *The Atlanta Journal-Constitution*, p. 1B.

Wyche, S. (2007f, June 8). Feds show up, search Vick's site; Warrant executed at Virginia property. *The Atlanta Journal-Constitution*, p. 1H.

Wyche, S., & Ledbetter, O. (2007, May 20). Controversy around Vick; Some questions and answers surrounding the dogfighting investigation at the Virginia property owned by Falcons quarterback Michael Vick. *The Atlanta Journal-Constitution*, p. 2E.

Chapter Ten

The Failed Comedy of the NBA's Gilbert Arenas: Image Restoration in Context

Theodore F. Sheckels, Randolph-Macon College

The exact details of what transpired in the Washington Wizards' locker room at the Verizon Center in Washington, DC, on December 21, 2009, emerged gradually. A few are still in question. Despite an early, widely repeated report in the *New York Post*, two National Basketball Association (NBA) players did not draw guns on each other (Abramson & Garcia, 2010a). Rather, one, former all-star guard Gilbert Arenas, placed four guns on a chair near another player's locker, along with a note telling the other, injured reserve Javaris Crittenton, to pick one. The event was an extension of an argument the two men had had on a team flight from Phoenix. Crittenton had threatened to shoot Arenas in his surgically repaired knee; Arenas was, jokingly, daring him to do so. Crittenton responded by throwing one of Arenas's guns across the locker room floor and, then, producing his own from a knapsack. Neither man pointed a gun at the other (what the *New York Post* had claimed), and the confrontation quickly ended. The two men were guilty of violating both the NBA collective bargaining agreement and District of Columbia law. The agreement forbade the possession of firearms in NBA facilities; the law forbade the possession of unlicensed firearms. Although both men were guilty, the attention focused on Arenas—because he was a star and because his violations seemed more egregious. He had four guns, not one; and he provoked Crittenton into displaying a weapon that might otherwise have remained undiscovered.

This study explores Gilbert Arenas's attempts to apologize for his offenses. It is complicated by the fact that Arenas did not speak once but rather many times. I will treat as one the many statements he made shortly after the event. Some of these were statements issued through his lawyer; some were statements made to reporters; some were his tweets. These early statements were quite contradictory in substance and tone. They culminated in his statement upon pleading guilty to a single charge of illegal possession of a gun on January 16, 2010. I will then treat the statements Arenas made at and after a late-January meeting with NBA commissioner David Stern and an op-ed piece Arenas wrote for publication in the *Washington Post* on February 2 as a second statement and his verbal comments and nonverbal appearance on the day of his sentencing (March 28) as a third.

Four research questions inform this study: Q1: Did Arenas's strategies of apology change over time? Q2: Did the effect of the strategies change over time? Q3: Did the media's emphasis in its portrayal of Arenas change over time? Q4: Did the media contextualization if the story change over time?

In addressing the first two questions, I will rely on the methodology developed by Benoit (1995), which is explored in detail elsewhere in this volume. That methodology, which has a critic designate the use of the strategies of denial, evading responsibility, reducing offensiveness, corrective action, and mortification, provides a lens through which one can discern a text's rhetoric. That methodology expands upon Ware and Linkugel's (1973) earlier listing of just four strategies. When a study deals with multiple texts, the methodology permits comparisons that can lead to useful conjectures about the efficacy of particular approaches if the effects of the texts vary. How to measure effects is problematic. In this case, I will consider three audiences' responses to Arenas's efforts at apologizing: that of the NBA, that of the Washington Wizards, and that of reporters and bylined sports commentators.

The third and fourth questions require a preface. Gilbert Arenas has a complex personality. A perennial fan favorite, he is a self-confessed "goofball" whose antics are legendary (Knott, 2009). Those antics can be portrayed positively by the media or negatively. Is he a clown, or is he a troubled young man whose jokes are often not very funny and reveal pathological needs? Arenas is also famous in the Washington media market at least for his generosity, throwing lavish parties for friends and—more important—contributing his time and his money to help young people, particularly those from similarly disadvantaged backgrounds. The media, then, often has a choice to make in its portrayals of Arenas among these very different personae: a crowd-pleasing jokester? A bullying prankster intent upon disempowering lesser players? A psychologically wounded young man who is "acting-out"? A generous, community-serving saint? There is evidence for all four; thus reporters can choose.

Washington, DC, is also a complex place to play basketball. The history of the Wizards provides a context in which to discuss Arenas's transgressions and apologies. So do the history and politics of the city. Implicit in these is the issue of race, which must be raised in discussing the NBA although the terms of that discussion are fraught with difficulty.

The Wizards were the Bullets. Arguably, they were the Bullets because the nickname alliterated with Baltimore, but, even after Abe Polin acquired the franchise and moved it to Washington, he retained the name. Sensitivity to the high incidence of gun crime in Washington and the assassination of Polin's good friend Israeli prime minister Yitzhak Rabin prompted Polin to search for a less offensive name.

Guns can, of course, be wielded by any race or ethnic group. However, since Washington, DC, is a heavily African-American city, the gun violence in it had a racial tinge. That picture only served to reinforce a history of racial division—and racism—in the city. After World War II, there was an influx of African Americans. That influx plus a generalized desire on the part of city residents for a single-family home and the other supposed benefits of suburban life led to white flight (Cohen, 2003). That flight was often accompanied by declining city property values so that many who fled did so with less than they felt was their due. The losses were, of course, blamed on African Americans, although they were the result of socioeconomic and historical factors coincident with race. Many if not all cities in the eastern half of the United States were affected by these dynamics, but Washington, DC was more dramatically affected than most. The urban rioting following the assassination of Dr. Martin Luther King, Jr., in April 1968 exacerbated the problem. In Washington, two commercial corridors were most affected: H Street NE in an African-American neighborhood and upper 14th Street NW in a racially mixed neighborhood (Columbia Heights). However, even the downtown commercial corridor of F Street NW was affected insofar as the suburban white population that had been patronizing that corridor occasionally began avoiding it completely.

Sports was not unaffected by these racial dynamics. Many suburbanites expressed fear at traveling to Griffith Stadium near the intersection of 7th Street and Florida Avenue NW because of the racial composition of the surrounding neighborhood and the absence of safe stadium parking. Both the Washington Senators (baseball) and Redskins (football) played there. When the Senators left for Minnesota and the expansion Senators (later, Texas Rangers) began playing at the new DC Stadium (renamed RFK Stadium in 1968), attendance problems partially explained by the merger of race and gun-related violence/crime persisted. The stadium had parking, but, at night, the lots were dark and adjoined impoverished African-American neighborhoods. The Redskins, who played in daylight (usually) at the same stadium, were less affected. When Polin moved the Bullets to Washington and when he introduced the hockey Capitals to the city, he housed both teams in the Capital Center, an arena he built in the Prince George's County suburbs, which were then still predominantly white. The absence of a suitable arena in the city was only part of the story, for Uline Arena (renamed Washington Coliseum) had hosted the American Basketball Association Washington Caps for their single season (before becoming the Virginia Squires) and perennially hosted the Icecapades, as well as the Beatles' first U.S. concert in February 1964. The arena was in a blighted area just north of Union Station (itself blighted then). Polin's eventual construction of a new arena (MCI Center; now Verizon Center) might then be seen as his eventual decision to revive the F Street NW corridor, something he would not dare attempt in the late 1960s.

Washington, DC, is, of course, a federal enclave. Although its residents still lack representation in Congress, they did eventually acquire limited home rule. Then, their government began addressing the city's problem with guns by enacting some of the strictest legislation in the nation, legislation that has become a national flashpoint. It inspired the lawsuit that led to the U.S. Supreme Court case of *United States v. Heller* (2008) that invalidated some provisions in the gun control laws as violations of the Constitution's Second Amendment. City Council revisions of those laws have not gone far enough in the eyes of gun interests in Congress, so, since Congress still has ultimate authority over the federal enclave, attempts have been made by legislators from places thousands of miles from the District to countermand the strict gun laws the residents' elected representatives have enacted. For example, the latest bill to grant the District representation in Congress was amended by pro-gun congressmen so that a vote for representation meant what DC's non-voting Congressional delegate and many others saw as a gutting of the city's gun control laws.

Race and guns then are part of the Washington, DC context in which the Arenas controversy must be viewed. They are also relevant to the NBA context, for the NBA is dominated by African-American players and, according to some commentators, the "thug" image (whether it be the product of white racism or a misperception of the "street" swagger of some players) is more on display in the NBA than in sports such as football, where the number of players is larger and the tattoos that signal "thug" or "street" to some viewers are hidden by bulky uniforms.

The various texts through which Arenas addressed the Verizon Center incident and this rich context prompt four hypotheses:

> H1: Arenas's apology or image restoration strategies will shift from the earlier cluster of texts to the later interview with Stern and op-ed piece and the still later verbal and non-verbal discourse on the day he receives his sentence.
> H2: As the strategies shift, their effectiveness will increase.

H3: As the strategies shift from less effective to more effective, the contexts provided by Washington, DC and the NBA will diminish in importance.

H4: As the strategies shift from less effective to more effective, the media image of Arenas will shift to one of the more positive versions.

ARENAS'S EARLIER APOLOGIES

Arenas's Statements

Arenas's first comments admit that he brought weapons to the Verizon Center from his home in Virginia. He reduces the offensiveness by telling reporters, as 2009 ended, that he did so for the understandable if not praiseworthy reason that he did not want guns at home after the birth of his third child (Abramson & Garcia, 2010a; Lee, 2010a).

On January 1, Arenas denies the story that is circulating. He tells reporters that the story is not the true one, but he does not say what the true story is (Lee, 2010a). On his Twitter account, he tries to reduce the offensiveness of the story by joking about the event, suggesting that the media story evoking the "OK Corral" and depicting him as a kind of "John Wayne" was ridiculous (Abramson & Garcia, 2010a; Lee, 2010a). Arenas, in a tweet, suggests that he knows the matter is serious, but claims he is "a goofball," suggesting his personality as an excuse for both the event and his less than serious response to it afterward (Abramson & Garcia, 2010a).

On January 2, Arenas admits to reporters that he had exercised "bad judgment" (Arenas, 2010a). In response to the Wizards' comments that the locker room confrontation was "dangerous" and his behavior "disappointing," he agrees, presenting that more as agreement with the late Abe Polin's position on gun violence than agreement with the Wizards' characterization of Arenas himself (Arenas, 2010a; Himmelsbach, 2010a). Besides giving this agreement a self-serving twist, he also tries to reduce the offensiveness of his actions by repeating his reason for bringing the guns to Verizon Center and noting that bringing the guns to the Center was better than throwing them in the trash, where anyone might grab them (Himmelsbach, 2010a). He also repeats that he is "a goofball" (Abramson, 2010a; Arenas, 2010a; Saunders defends, 2010a).

On January 3, Arenas tweets that the reports that are circulating are incorrect. In response to reports that the confrontation was over a gambling debt, Arenas evades the issue, noting how generous he is with money toward his teammates, thereby implying that fighting over money would be out of character for him. He seems upset that the false reports are making him look bad and attacks those who are making these reports (Abramson, 2010a). In comments to the press, he suggests that the incident was being blown out of proportion (Saunders defends, 2010a). He does not say by whom.

On January 4, Arenas releases a carefully phrased written statement that extends what seems to be his strategy of accepting responsibility while reducing the offensiveness of his actions. In this statement, he characterizes the incident as a "misguided joke" (Arenas, 2010b; Arenas sorry, 2010a; Beck, 2010a; The day, 2010a). He does, however, admit that both bringing guns to the Center and joking about the incident were wrong, and he apologizes for the effect the incident has had on the team, his teammates, the NBA, and Wizards fans and promises reform (Alexander, 2010a; Arenas sorry, 2010a; Beck, 2010a; Lee, 2010b). He comes close to enacting the strategies of mortification and corrective action. However, he insists he brought the guns in for a good reason. He also stressed that the guns were unloaded and that he never pointed even an unloaded gun at anyone (Abramson, 2010c; Beck, 2010a; Lee, 2010b; The day, 2010a). He even suggests that a misunderstanding of Washington, DC's gun laws played a role in his decision to transfer the guns from Great Falls, Virginia, to the locker room (Lee, 2010b; The day, 2010a). So, he continues trying to reduce the offensiveness of his actions.

On January 5, Arenas seems to reject this tightrope-walking strategy. Egged on by teammates (he will claim, thereby evading responsibility somewhat), he surrounds himself after pregame introductions in Philadelphia by his fellow players and uses his hand as a gun to shoot them (Abramson, 2010b, 2010c; Arthur, 2010a; Falgoust, 2010; Heisler, 2010; Lawrence, 2010a; Lee, 2010c; Pitts, 2010a; Rhoden, 2010). Some pretend to be hit; players are laughing. Throughout the game, Philadelphia fans taunt Arenas; NBA officials, out of embarrassment over the gun incident and its aftermath, try to restrain the crowd by confiscating the homemade anti-Arenas signs (Abramson, 2010b, 2010c). Later, through Twitter, Arenas both apologizes for this skit (in case it offended anyone), says he was just trying to lighten the atmosphere, requests an apology from those he says are slandering him, and calls NBA commissioner David Stern "mean." He says he would be remorseful if he had done anything wrong, but he says that he does not believe he really did anything wrong. To reporters, when asked about the NBA's potential response to the incident, he comments that he does not expect a severe reprimand, noting that he has looked at previous infractions of the NBA gun policy and what punishments the league meted out. He also tells reporters who he is—a comic, a jokester, a prankster—and expresses his anger at how fans are now beginning to see him as "bad" (Abramson, 2010b, 2010c; Lee, 2010c). Although he does apologize for the skit, most of his comments (and speech acts) on January 5 fall into the categories of evading responsibility and reducing offensiveness.

On January 6, Arenas had to deal with the fact that his previous statements, termed by many contradictory, had not succeeded (Steinberg, 2010a; Wise, 2010a). Those statements, coupled with the shooting skit in Philadelphia, had prompted the NBA to suspend him indefinitely. To reporters, Arenas indicates that he understands why the league has acted (Arthur, 2010a; Falgoust, 2010; Lawrence, 2010a). Arenas then calls Stern to personally apologize, and he (or someone close to him) shuts down his Twitter account (Abramson, 2010d; Lawrence, 2010a; Wise & Lee, 2010a). He seems to be remorseful—some might say finally, but he still, in a diminishing number of comments, tries to reduce the offensiveness of his conduct by citing both the fact the guns were unloaded and his claim that he brought them to the locker room to get them out of harm's way at home (Wise, 2010b).

Arenas said little between January 6 and when he pleaded guilty in DC Superior Court on January 16. His demeanor that day was reported as quiet, somber (Alexander, 2010b; Barakat, 2010; Quiet Arenas, 2010). His written statement took full responsibility for his crime; his words were, for the most part, limited to "Yes, sir" and "No, sir."

Effectiveness

Early, the NBA exercises restraint in responding, wanting to wait until law enforcement personnel had done their job (Abramson & Garcia, 2010a; Lee, 2010a). However, after Arenas's pregame skit in Philadelphia on January 5 (and, perhaps, Arenas's statement to reporters that he anticipated a relatively light penalty and Arenas's tweet terming Stern "mean"), the NBA suspends Arenas indefinitely. Later, Stern will say he suspended Arenas for his own self-protection: to prevent him from doing himself further damage (Beck, 2010b; Lee, 2010c). (Stern was guessing correctly, it would seem, for, the next game, Arenas and Wizards guard Nick Young had planned to enact a midcourt Old West style shootout [Wise & Lee, 2010a].) More than a week later, an NBA official is quoted saying that Arenas would not be welcomed back in the league until he takes full responsibility for his actions (Wise & Lee, 2010a). One would therefore conclude that Arenas's image restoration strategies had not been effective with the NBA audience.

The Wizards, from the beginning, express dismay. They term the event "dangerous" and express their disappointment at the behavior of Arenas and Crittenton (Arenas, 2010a; Himmelsbach, 2010a). Media sources suggest that the Wizards, even before the incident in Philadelphia, were considering the possibility of voiding Arenas's lucrative contract (Lee, 2010b). After the incident and after Stern's suspension of Arenas, the Wizards express their complete support for the commissioner's action (Abramson, 2010c). The rumor persists that the Wizards are considering voiding Arenas's contract (Arthur, 2010a; Basketball, 2010a; Lawrence, 2010a). The Wizards are also said to be upset with other players who are acting as if the matter is a joke (Arenas, 2010c). At this point, the team removes Arenas's huge banner from the façade of Verizon Center, discontinues the sale of all Arenas merchandise, and fines most of the other Wizards players who laughed at Arenas's Philadelphia skit (du Lac, 2010; Lee, 2010d; Wise & Lee, 2010a). The Wizards then ask team leader Antawn Jamison (who laughed but was not fined) to step to center court and apologize to the fans for the team's collective behavior (Lee, 2010d; Wise & Lee, 2010a). Even after Arenas's guilty plea on January 16, the team remains "disappointed" (Alexander, 2010a; Himmelsbach, 2010b). The team's official comment was characterized by the press as "cold-blooded" (Wilbon, 2010d) and "terse" (Abrams, 2010a), suggesting to these sports commentators that Arenas will never play again for the Wizards. One would therefore conclude that Arenas's strategies were just as ineffective with the Wizards as with the NBA.

Fans are initially rather indifferent to the accusation (Himmelsbach, 2010a). Media will then begin to talk to fans, broadcasting some fans' negative reactions. Mayor Adrian Fenty, on the other hand, does not criticize the star athlete harshly, and Fenty's election challenger, City Councilman Vincent Gray, reminds people of Arenas's generosity when Katrina refugees were being housed at the DC Armory (du Lac, 2010).

The media, however, senses a good story. As early as January 2, the *Washington Post*'s Tracee Hamilton (2010) suggests that Arenas's latest persona, one she terms "Gilbert the Kid," is not funny. She suggests that Arenas may be psychologically troubled. The New York press is harsher, criticizing Arenas severely (Slam dunk, 2010). On January 6, the *Post*'s Michael Lee (2010c) refers to Arenas as "[o]nce famous for being quirky and goofy," suggesting that his persona now is something other, and, on that same day, still another *Post* writer, Mike Wise (2010a), while recalling all of Arenas's charitable work, laments, "Gil, you've really blown it now." The tone of media coverage is undergoing a change. His teammates are disgusted, Wise says; the fans want Arenas gone. Out-of-town press was even harsher: the New York *Daily News*' Mitch Lawrence (2010a) wants Stern to send a message about guns in the NBA and ban Arenas from the league for life. If the Washington media were guardedly negative and the New York media hostile, the popular media—i.e., Letterman and Leno—thought the matter was one for jokes. Thus, an Arenas explanation list becomes a Letterman "Top Ten" (du Lac, 2010).

Post-Philadelphia, the Washington media will mention Arenas's charitable works in passing (Jenkins, 2010; Simmons, 2010). They will focus on his prankster side but will color those pranks darkly. They will suggest that some were cruel, some were criminal, and some were downright disgusting, with defecating in Andray Blatche's shoe an example of the last (Steinberg, 2010a; Wise & Lee, 2010). There seems to be an awareness in reports that

Arenas has multiple personae; however, the positive ones have clearly been replaced, although not obliterated, by the negative, as Sally Jenkins' (2010) January 10 column in the *Washington Post* suggests: Gilbert the jokester and Gilbert the saint have been largely replaced by his more troubled personae. The drift of the media coverage would also suggest that Arenas's initial image restoration strategies were ineffective.

After Arenas announced that he plans to plead guilty, media coverage relents. *USA Today*'s DeWayne Wickham (2010) notes that Arenas is showing remorse rather late in the game, but also notes that others in the NBA have done far worse than Arenas. The *Washington Post*'s Mike Wilbon (2010b) seconds this point and also observes that Arenas had long had enablers on the team and in the media who encouraged his antics. After Arenas's plea, Wilbon (2010d) recalls the likeable Gilbert of previous seasons, but concludes that the gap is too wide between Gilbert and management and Gilbert and fellow players for him to be forgiven and welcomed back. The shift in Arenas's strategies at the end of this period may then have effected a slight change in the media's response.

Evocations of Context

From very early in the media coverage, the existence of a "gun culture" in the NBA was mentioned (Abramson & Garcia, 2010a; Abramson & Garcia, 2010b; Slam dunk, 2010). As the days unfold, it will be mentioned more frequently. Quickly, the potential effect of this culture on young children is noted. Just as quickly, the Reverend Al Sharpton in New York and African-American sports commentator Michael Wilbon in Washington interject race into this discussion of culture. Wilbon—soon joined by others—lists other African-American men in professional sports who have been involved in incidents involving guns (Abramson, 2010d; Wilbon, 2010a). The discussion even makes it to the pages of the Toronto-based *National Post*, where reporter Bruce Arthur (2010a) mentions the public's impression that NBA players are "thugs," before backing away from the characterization by noting that the number is far lower than some people think. Arthur quotes *Forbes* magazine editor Michael Ozanian as saying the NBA is "full of thugs," and he notes how the imposition of a dress code and the hiring of former Bush public relations specialist Matthew Dowd demonstrates the NBA's awareness of the existence of this negative image and the need to address it. A day later, he offers a roll call of NBA athletes who have contributed to the "thug" image (Arthur, 2010b). In the New York press, the existence of a "gun culture" motivates one writer to call upon Stern to send a message to the players by banning Arenas forever (Lawrence, 2010a). Press coverage then broadens the context—guns are a problem, but so is gambling (Cribb, 2010; Rhoden, 2010).

From almost as early, Washington media note the irony of this gun law violation in the locker room of a team that had changed its name from Bullets to Wizards (Arenas sorry, 2010; Himmelsbach, 2010a; Slam Dunk, 2010a). Then, in a few days, the media fill in that story. They note that the name change was Abe Polin's idea, motivated by both the gun violence in Washington and the assassination of his personal friend, Israeli prime minister Yitzhak Rabin (Cribb, 2010; Du Lac, 2010; Wise, 2010a). The press then mentions the gun violence in the nation's capital as well as the existence of some of the country's strictest gun laws there. However, the press refrains from discussing the gun violence in racial terms, although it recognizes that the Arenas incident has evoked a racialized picture (Pitts, 2010). Nor does the press mention how contentious gun control legislation has proven in Washington, DC. A fuller Washington, DC context may well have been in residents' minds; however, the press neither evokes it nor emphasizes it. Based on the evidence of what the press says—not conjectures about how residents (especially long-term ones) might view the city's gun violence, one can conclude that a racially tinged NBA "gun culture" was indeed evoked by the Arenas story, thereby complicating Arenas's image restoration, but that a similar Washington, DC, "gun culture" was perhaps not as strongly evoked. That local culture and the legal controversies it had evoked might well be in the minds of Washington, DC area residents, however.

ARENAS'S INTERVIEW WITH STERN AND OP-ED PIECE

Arenas's Statements

On January 27, Commissioner Stern suspends Arenas for the rest of the season. Through his attorney, Arenas issues a remorseful statement, taking full responsibility for the locker room incident. He acknowledges that he violated the law and NBA rules and that his actions were detrimental to the league. He says he would not take issue with the suspension and, furthermore, hopes that his punishment will send a message to other players about their conduct on and off the court (Beck, 2010b; Lee, 2010d). Several days later, he will deliver a similar message to the Washington, DC, public.

Arenas (2010d) adopts a contrite tone on February 2. He declares that he has "done a number of things wrong recently," and he lists both his violations of the NBA collective bargaining agreement and DC law and his "making light of a serious situation" in their aftermath. He notes how he put his "teammates in a tough position and let down our fans and Mrs. Irene Polin, the widow of longtime Wizards owner Abe Polin." He especially notes how his offenses might have affected young people in the DC area. After engaging in mortification, he notes that a "message of nonviolence will be front and center as I try to rebuild my relationship with young people in the DC area"; and he notes that he has already written "a letter to students in DC schools that was also about owning up to my mistakes." He plans, he says, to do more to help students learn the lesson he has learned: "I plan to do that work by partnering with public officials and community groups to teach kids to avoid trouble and learn from their mistakes, to strive for success by working hard and persevering, and to try to make the right choices." Thus, Arenas adds promises of corrective action to mortification. The op-ed piece, then, reflects a very different set of strategies than the contradictory responses offered in the first half of January.

Effectiveness

The media covered the January 27 statement and, then, simply and rather briefly noted that Arenas had issued a print follow-up on February 2. (The brevity was probably because reporters typically do not cover op-ed pieces as news.) In response to the first, the NBA, through Stern, indicates that Arenas has expressed remorse and appeared contrite (Beck, 2010a; Lee, 2010c) while the Wizards released a statement supporting Stern's decision and repeating how Arenas's crime violated the spirit that had led Polin to rename the team. General Manager Ernie Grunfeld was reported to have said that the team was "exploring all our options" with regards to Arenas (Lee, 2010c).

In response to the second, the NBA and the Wizards were rather silent. Then, two weeks later, Wizards general manager Ernie Grunfeld announced that "He's under contract and he's going to be with us. He's part of the organization. If he wants to play, he's going to play here" (Lee, 2010e; Wizards plan, 2010). This statement ended rumors that the Wizards would seek to void Arenas's contract as well as rumors that the team would try to trade him away. The Wizards, who had cut all ties with Arenas, seemed to be welcoming him back. Grunfeld added sympathetic words: "Gilbert's a basketball player. That's what he likes to do, that's his life and obviously this is a tough situation for him. It's a tough situation for everybody and I think we all feel for him" (Lee, 2010d). One needs, of course, to be careful in making cause-effect claims; however, it is certainly striking that Arenas's different strategies in both his interview with Stern and his op-ed apology evoked initially neutral responses from the NBA and the Wizards and then a surprisingly positive response from the team.

If the Wizards' attitude was softening in the wake of Arenas's op-ed apology, that of the U.S. Attorney's Office was not. Assistant United States Attorney Christopher R. Kavanaugh was seeking jail time for Arenas because the player had initially offered inconsistent information to investigators and because he had, in Kavanaugh's opinion, exhibited insufficient remorse. Arenas's lawyer, Kenneth L. Wainstein, countered with a 127-page sentencing memo. That memo, whose contents were mentioned by print and broadcast media, outlined Arenas's generous contributions to the community and appended letters from community leaders supporting Arenas. Wainstein's submission did contain only one letter of support from the Wizards, that from the team's community relations director (Abrams, 2010b; Alexander 2010b). Through the coverage of this debate over what would be an appropriate sentence for Arenas, the media brought the more saintly image of the player back into the public's view. The media's attitude at this point might be best characterized as wavering. They are neutrally covering Wainstein's sentencing memo that portrays Arenas positively, but they are not averse to puncturing Arenas's piety by reporting that, when he met with Stern, in addition to his contrite words, Arenas expressed selfish concern over the possibility that the Wizards might void his contract (Lee, 2010c).

Evocations of Context

After Arenas's January 26 interview with Stern and the February 2 op-ed piece in the *Washington Post*, discussion of either the "gun culture" in the NBA or the level of gun violence in predominantly African-American Washington, DC ends. The Arenas matter proceeds onward as if it were just his story as opposed to an event with deeper implications in either the league or the city. One might argue that the story was no longer newsworthy; however, how commentaries evoking either context suddenly ceased is striking.[1]

SENTENCING

Arenas does not receive a jail sentence on March 26. The judge, known to be tough on gun criminals, sentences Arenas to thirty days in a halfway house and four hundred hours of community service. The judge cites a number of factors that argued in Arenas's favor: he had no history of violence; the guns were unloaded; the crime was illegal transportation of guns, not an armed confrontation; Arenas owned the guns legally in Virginia; Arenas took responsibility for the crime early on, pleading guilty to a felony in mid-January; and Arenas had a history of working with and for local charities (Duggan, 2010; Lawrence, 2010b).

Arenas's Statements

After the judge addresses him, characterizing his behavior negatively, Arenas apologizes and states, "Every day I wake up wishing it did not happen" (Lawrence, 2010b). Arenas characterizes his actions as "stupid, irresponsible," although he does cite his joking personality as an excuse for "taking it lightly" (Duggan, 2010). He says little else, but he does communicate non-verbally. He wears a dark blue suit; his voice is "low and occasionally catching" (Duggan, 2010). He exhibits mortification at his sentencing, although a tiny touch of reducing offensiveness is apparent in his reference to his comic personality.

Effectiveness

Washington, DC, Superior Court Judge Robert E. Morin undoubtedly had his mind made up before Arenas appeared before him that day. So, Morin's comments were probably inspired by what transpired before then. Morin told Arenas that "What you did was a stupid and immature act," and said that, "You should have taken this a lot more seriously. But I think you have demonstrated genuine remorse" (Duggan, 2010; Lawrence, 2010b). One might conclude that Arenas's image restoration strategies in the op-ed apology—combined with his attorney's sentencing memo—had proven effective. Arenas's statements and demeanor on March 26 did nothing to alter Morin's opinion.

The Brady Campaign to Prevent Gun Violence criticized Morin's lenient sentence (Lawrence, 2010b). Those interviewed by broadcast media and those who wrote letters to the editor or blog entries to the *Washington Post* seemed split into "too lenient" and forgiving camps. *Washington Post* coverage tried to remain objective, but the only Arenas personae that came through in the newspaper's coverage were the comical Arenas and the generous Arenas. The *Post*, for example, mentioned that Arenas had given Crittenton's mother $30,000 she needed for an operation (Duggan, 2010). One might argue that the interview with Stern, the op-ed piece, and the courtroom behavior had positively affected the media's presentation of Arenas by eliminating references to the player as either a nasty or psychologically troubled prankster that reporters had made.

Former teammate Larry Hughes said Arenas was not "a bad guy" and predicted that "people will forgive him." Wizards coach Flip Saunders said he wished that the team had been in town when Arenas was sentenced so that he and other members of the team could have been in the courtroom to support Arenas. Saunders said, "now he can move forward." The team, in its official statement, expressed its feeling that the sentencing provided closure and said "we now look forward to moving on" (Lee, 2010g). *Post* columnist Michael Wilbon (2010e) refused to interpret Saunders's or the team's comments as necessarily positive, but did remark that he thought the city would forgive Arenas. In the same comment, however, Wilbon took a swipe at Arenas's *ethos* by comparing the basketball player to the scandal-plagued former DC mayor Marion Barry. So, while Wilbon and some fans remained skeptical, the team and other fans had been swayed by Arenas's mortification and promises of corrective action.

Evocations of Context

Although Arenas's actions may still have evoked images of "thuggery" in the NBA or images of gun violence (perhaps African-American gun violence) in the District of Columbia in the minds of some observers, nothing in the media evoked either context at this point. The media treated the sentencing appearance in a decontextualized manner.

CONCLUSIONS

This study has offered rather clear answers to the questions posed at its onset. Arenas' strategies did indeed change over time and, as they shifted from a contradictory mishmash to expressing mortification and promising corrective action, they became more effective. Parallel to this increase in effectiveness was a positive shift in how the media portrayed Arenas. When Arenas was using multiple, inconsistent strategies, the media evoked both a negative NBA context and a negative Washington, DC, context—with at least the former presented in racial terms. When Arenas became contrite, the media ceased talking about either context and, by doing so, at least deemphasized that context as an interpretive framework for audiences.

All four hypotheses were confirmed: Arenas did change image restoration strategies (H1); as he did so the effectiveness seemed to increase (H2); the importance of context seemed to decrease (H3); and the media's presentation of Arenas's personality became more positive.

One cannot generalize from a single case study, but this one does at least prompt two hypotheses for further research. First, the study suggests that mortification and corrective action have more positive effects than other image restoration strategies; second, the study suggests that a negative interpretive framework may be evoked if effective image restoration strategies are not used. In other words, if effective strategies do not restrain the media by bringing closure to a matter, then there might well be a tendency to explore the matter's implications and do so in a negative manner. This case study finally evokes a question future researchers might want to pose: to what extent were the contradictions among Arenas's earlier responses the problem as opposed to the strategies he chose to use. Stated in more generalized language, is the coherence of a strategy the crucial variable, and not the specific strategy/strategies chosen? This case suggests that Arenas would have fared better if he had initially exhibited mortification and corrective action rather than denial, evading responsibility, and reducing offensiveness; however, there are suggestions in at least the press coverage that Arenas's early strategic inconsistencies (i.e., saying one thing but tweeting another) at least added to his apologies' lack of success.

NOTE

1. Newspaper articles were sought using Lexis-Nexis Academic, which indexes major U.S. and international newspapers. Descriptors "Arenas" and "gun/s" were used. Other U.S. papers, especially those in NBA cities, undoubtedly carried the story, but one would expect the coverage there to follow the pattern in Washington, New York, Los Angeles, and Toronto.

REFERENCES

Abrams, J. (2010a, January 19). A gun charge, a guilty plea, a contract at risk. *The New York Times*, p. B14.
Abrams, J. (2010b, March 24). Arenas sentencing Friday. *The New York Times*, p. B14.
Abramson, M. (2010a, January 4). Arenas looks to unload as DC officials await. *Daily News*, p. 57.
Abramson, M. (2010b, January 6). Arenas fires away, claims slander, rips Stern. *Daily News*, p. 55.
Abramson, M. (2010c, January 6). Arenas fires away, calls commissioner "mean." *Daily News*, p. 55.
Abramson, M. (2010d, January 8). Sharpton fires back at Arenas. *Daily News*, p. 82.
Abramson, M., & Garcia, J. (2010a, January 2). Nets' Harris: 60% of players own weapons. *Daily News*, p. 40.
Abramson, M., & Garcia, J. (2010a, January 2). Nets' Harris: 75% of players own weapons. *Daily News*, p. 40.
Alexander, K. L. (2010a, January 6). Panels begins review of Arenas case. *The Washington Post*, p. D9.
Alexander, K. L. (2010b, January 16). Arenas pleads guilty to felony count. *The Washington Post*, p. D1.
Alexander, K. L. (2010c, March 24). Prosecutors: Arenas led a cover-up, deserves jail. *The Washington Post*, p. D1.
Arenas, G. (2010a, February 2). Learning to be a better role model. *The Washington Post*, p. A17.
Arenas: Gun play was misguided effort at joke. (2010b, January 5). *Newsday*, p. A49.
Arenas: It was bad judgment. (2010c, January 3). *Newsday*, p. A71.
Arenas "not currently fit to take the court in an NBA game," Stern says. (2010d, January 7). *The Globe and Mail*, p. S1.
Arenas sorry for "misguided effort to play a joke." (2010, January 5). *The Toronto Sun*, p. S13.
Arthur, B. (2010a, January 6). Picking the wrong target. *National Post*, p. S1.
Arthur, B. (2010b, January 7). Sit down Arenas, the joke's on you. *National Post*, p. S1.
Barakat, M. (2010, January 16). Arenas pleads guilty. *Newsday*, p. A39.
Basketball: Guns-in-locker saga has big implications for NBA. (2010, January 9). *The New Zealand Herald*, p. S1.
Beck, H. (2010a, January 5). Arenas says unloaded guns were misguided joke. *The New York Times*, p. B16.

Beck, H. (2010b, January 28). Stern issues suspensions to deter use of guns. *The New York Times*, p. B13.

Cribb, R. (2010, January 10). Gun play. *The Toronto Star*, p. A1.

Cohen, L. (2003). *A consumers' republic: the politics of mass consumption in postwar America.* New York: Alfred A. Knopf.

The day in sports: Arenas says gun incident was "effort to play a joke." (2010, January 5). *Los Angeles Times*, p. C5.

Duggan, P. (2010, March 27). Arenas avoids jail sentence in gun incident. *The Washington Post*, p. A1.

Du Lac, J. F. (2010, January 8). Word on the street: Seriously stupid, Gil. *The Washington Post*, p. B1.

Falgoust, J. M. (2010, January 7). NBA suspends Arenas. *USA Today*, p. C1.

Hahn, A. (2010, January 17). NBA Insider: Adidas drops Arenas after his suspension. *Newsday*, p. A71.

Hamilton, T. (2010, January 3). Players, guns and money. *The Washington Post*, p. D1.

Heisler, M. (2010, January 7). Arenas takes shot at humor and misfires. *Los Angeles Times*, p. C1.

Himmelsbach, A. (2010a, January 3). "Bad judgment" cited by Arenas in gun case. *The New York Times*, p. SP7.

Himmelsbach, A. (2010b, January 16). Wizards' Arenas pleads guilty to one felony gun charge. *The New York Times*, p. D5.

Jenkins, S. (2010, January 10). Who is Gilbert Arenas? *The Washington Post,* p. D1.

Knott, T. (2009, September 29). Toss the hibachi in storage. *The Washington Times*, p. C2.

Lawrence, M. (2010a, January 7). Gives Arenas lifetime ban. *Daily News*, p. 58.

Lawrence, M. (2010b, March 27). Arenas gets off without jail time. *Daily News*, p. 58.

Lee, M. (2010a, January 2). Arenas comes under close scrutiny. *The Washington Post*, p. D1.

Lee, M. (2010b, January 5). Arenas meets with detectives. *The Washington Post*, p. D1.

Lee, M. (2010c, January 6). Personal foul. *The Washington Post*, p. D1.

Lee, M. (2010d, January 10). At Verizon Center, Zero presence. *The Washington Post*, p. D1.

Lee, M. (2010e, January 28). Arenas, Crittenton suspended for year. *The Washington Post*, p. D1.

Lee, M. (2010f, February 19). Grunfeld: Arenas likely will stay with franchise. *The Washington Post*, p. D3.

Lee, M. (2010g, March 27). Fellow Wizards relieved for Arenas. *The Washington Post*, p. D3.

NBA gunplay. (2010, January 31). *The Washington Post*, p. A16.

Pitts, L. (2010, January 10). Hey, Arenas. *Newsday*, p. A31.

Quiet Arenas pleads guilty to gun charge. (2010, January 16). *St. Petersburg Times*, p. C6.

Rhoden, W. C. (2010, January 8). The loose cannon in the locker room for the NBA. *The New York Times*, p. B11.

Saunders defends Arenas. (2010, January 4). *Newsday*, p. A37.

Simmons, D. (2010, January 8). Can we talk: Arenas rightly under the gun. *The Washington Times*, p. B5.

Slam dunk on guns. (2010, January 5). *Daily News*, p. 20.

Steinberg, D. (2010a, January 6). Arenas's official statement contrasts with thoughts he shares on Twitter. *The Washington Post*, p. D2.

Steinberg, D. (2010b, January 8). Now it's no laughing matter, but for years there were pranks. *The Washington Post*, p. D2.

Steinberg, D. (2010c, January 16). Breaking down Arenas's day in court. *The Washington Post*, p. D6.

Ware, B. L., & Linkugel, W. A. (1973). They spoke in defense of themselves: On the generic critique of the apologia. *Quarterly Journal of Speech, 59*, 273-283.

Wickham, D. (2010, January 12). Arenas guilty of bad judgment. *USA Today*, p. A9.

Wilbon, M. (2010a, January 6). Sharpton's savvy call to disarm. *The Washington Post*, p. D8.

Wilbon, M. (2010b, January 7). A star's career path takes a wrong turn. *The Washington Post*, p. D1.

Wilbon, M. (2010c, January 14). Let's not erase Arenas. *The Washington Post*, p. D1.

Wilbon, M. (2010d, January 16). In the end, it's time for a new beginning for all involved. *The Washington Post*, p. D1.

Wilbon, M. (2010e, March 28). Smile and take Arenas back. *The Washington Post*, p. D1.

Wise, M. (2010a, January 6). Dear Gilbert, you've really blown it. *The Washington Post*, p. D1.

Wise, M. (2010b, January 17). When it all changed, good and bad. *The Washington Post*, p. D1.

Wise, M., & Lee, M. (2010a, January 10). For Arenas, goodwill is gone. *The Washington Post*, p. A1.

Wise, M., & Lee, M. (2010b, January 15). A frayed marriage. *The Washington Post*, p. D1.

Wizards plan on keeping Arenas. (2010, February 19). *The Toronto Sun*, p. S4.

Chapter Eleven

Plaxico Burress Takes His Best Shot

Mark Glantz, St. Norbert College

Will Rogers famously said, "there's no trick to being a humorist when you have the whole government working for you" (Peter, 1979, p. 285). In contemporary American society, it seems that professional athletes have joined the humorists' workforce as well. When New York Giants wide receiver Plaxico Burress shot himself in the right thigh at a Manhattan nightclub, *The Daily Show*'s Jon Stewart both summarized and satirized the circumstances:

> Plaxico Burress, the star wide receiver of the New York Giants . . . went to a nightclub on Friday and while there, shot himself. Why is this a story? Well, because he shot himself in the *leg*—one of the two legs that he needs to be the star wide receiver for the New York Giants. Now, if he were Plaxico Burress the famed wheelchair-bound private detective, it doesn't even really make the papers. If *that* guy shoots himself in the leg, he's still out there solving crimes. (Stewart, 2008)

The visual component of this message featured a still image of Burress dressed as Sherlock Holmes, smoking a pipe, and seated in a wheelchair. Stewart's tone is one of total incredulity. This excerpt ridicules Burress and explains why there was so much outrage and intrigue surrounding the incident. Stewart's contemporaries, such as David Letterman and Stephen Colbert, also made jokes about Burress (Colbert, 2008; Letterman, 2008). From his alleged choice of attire at the nightclub (sweatpants), to the apparent silliness of his first name, Plaxico Burress and the hole in his leg were fodder for mockery.

Importantly, not everybody found humor in the situation. Many fans, already weary of Burress's off-the-field antics, were quick to dismiss the nine-year veteran as a moron and a rogue who was not worth the trouble he had caused. New York City mayor Michael Bloomberg also took the matter very seriously, publicly recommending that Burress be prosecuted to the fullest extent of the law for carrying and discharging an unlicensed handgun in the city of New York.

As an image repair case study, the Plaxico Burress self-shooting incident is interesting for several reasons. First, the act of which he was accused is inherently remarkable. Although it easy to argue that Burress's decision to bring a handgun into a nightclub could have ended with more disastrous results, the reality is that his crime was relatively victimless. Second, even before the shooting, Burress's image was never very reputable. This raises important questions about if, why, and how Burress should repair his image. Using Benoit's (1995) theory of image repair discourse, this chapter examines the unique charges against Plaxico Burress and evaluates the effectiveness of the image repair strategies he executed. The objective of this chapter is to evaluate the success or failure of Burress's image repair efforts in relation to his desire to return to the NFL after serving his prison sentence. Given scarce rhetorical resources, Burress seems to have done a reasonably effective job of using his public appearances to achieve redemption. His discourse consistently highlighted the punishment he received and detailed his misfortune. Consistent with Burke's (1968) concept of mortification and purification, these strategies can be an effective way to achieve image restoration.

PERSUASIVELY ATTACKING BURRESS

According to Ryan (1982), it is necessary to understand the accusations of wrongdoing (*kategoria*) in a particular case in order to understand the corresponding defense (*apologia*). Therefore, this section will examine the details of the offensive acts Burress allegedly committed. The primary charge against Burress was that he discharged an unlicensed handgun in a public place, consequently shooting himself in the leg. Two additional charges related to the shooting—that Burress tried to cover up the incident and that he spoiled a potential championship for the New York Giants—are also examined here because they were integral parts of the Burress saga.

Discharging an Unlicensed Firearm in a Public Place

On November 29, 2008, news wires lit up with reports that Plaxico Burress had accidentally shot himself in the leg at a Manhattan nightclub in the early hours of the morning (Giants' Burress injured, 2008). Even these early news stories were able to report that the gunshot injuries were "minor" and would cause Burress to miss little more than two weeks of football (Giants' Burress suffers, 2008). Therefore, the public never had the opportunity to fret about

Burress's well-being. Rather than exert any energy worrying if he would be okay, fans and anti-fans alike leapt right into wondering, "what in the hell was he doing?" and ultimately deciding, "he's an idiot" (Schmiedeberg, 2008). In short, public scrutiny of Burress was swift and harsh.

The characteristically sensational *New York Post* presented headlines such as "Giant Jerk Shoots himself—No More Reason to Placate Plax" (Vaccaro, 2008), and "Coddled Jock Can No Longer Pass the Buck" (Peyser, 2008). These sentiments clearly connect the shooting with Burress's prior public failings and fiascos. Burress was already widely regarded as a difficult and selfish personality because he was known to skip team meetings and complain publicly about his contract. He had also been in trouble earlier in 2008 for domestic disturbance events (Vacchiano, 2008). Although nobody could have *expected* Burress to shoot himself in the leg, the behavior did not strike many observers as being particularly out of character for the controversial wide receiver.

Ultimately, Burress was indicted on two counts of criminal possession of a weapon and a third count of reckless endangerment (Eligon, 2009a). He was sentenced to two years in prison for his crimes (Eligon, 2009b). This stern punishment may have been related to comments made by New York City mayor Michael Bloomberg, who declared of the Burress case: "It would be an outrage if we don't prosecute to the fullest extent of the law" (Lombardi, Gendar, & Lemire, 2008, para. 9). Clearly, Burress upset a lot of people, some of whom were very important. Although Burress was never known to be an ideal teammate, citizen, or role model, his nightclub shooting was nonetheless a major disruption to the established orders of society and professional sports.

Attempting to Cover Up the Shooting

Burress's reticence to share information about the shooting led to additional accusations. Burress, along with the New York Giants franchise and the hospital to which he was admitted after the shooting, were accused of trying to cover up the mishap. Mayor Bloomberg expressed explicit disapproval of the Giants' lack of cooperation with authorities, and a New York City Police Department spokesperson asserted that the Burress incident was enveloped by a "universe of silence" (Lee, 2008, para. 3). As for the hospital's failures, Baker (2008), reported that New York-Presbyterian Hospital broke the law by not informing the police that Burress was being treated for gunshot wounds at their facility. This so-called "universe of silence" led observers to speculate as to whether Burress conspired to keep the shooting a secret.

Failing to Meet His Obligations to the Giants

There are few NFL fans who would deny that Plaxico Burress played a large role in the New York Giants 2007-2008 championship season. By shooting himself in the leg, and missing much of the 2008-2009 season, Burress hurt the Giants' chances of returning to the Superbowl. At first, Giants fans and sports journalists argued that the team would still be Superbowl contenders without Burress (Lazarowitz & Yaniv, 2008). These claims were based at least in part on Burress's reputation as a malcontent and a distraction. Attitudes began to change, however, when the Giants started losing games in Burress's absence. They were eliminated in the first round of the playoffs. Experts lamented the absence of Burress's ability to make big plays and power to command mental and physical attention from opposing defenses (LaPointe, 2008; Robinson, 2008). This evidence suggests that Plaxico Burress may have cost the New York Giants the chance to repeat as NFL champions.

PERSUASIVELY DEFENDING BURRESS

Plaxico Burress's situation was unique from that of other athletes accused of wrongdoing. For instance, when Tiger Woods was attacked in the media for his rampant infidelity, he fell, or better yet, *plummeted*, from grace. Plaxico's image, however, was never very positive. He never even presented himself as someone who cared what people thought of him. Even if Burress could have restored his image to the condition it was in before the nightclub shooting, he still would not be anybody's darling. So what, then, was Burress's purpose for trying to repair his image? It seems almost out of character that he would make such an attempt in the first place. Whereas athletes such as Tiger Woods might try to ascend to a place of previous public adoration, Burress's purpose seems simpler and more modest. As his image repair efforts demonstrate, Burress's goal was to persuade audiences not that he is a good person, or that he is worthy of the public's trust, but that he had suffered substantially as a result of his accidental shooting and deserved the opportunity to play football again.

Having examined three overarching components of the accusations against Burress, this essay turns to an analysis of Burress's attempts to repair his image. Burress's communication addressed each of the accusations examined here, albeit in different ways. Considering his scarce rhetorical resources, his image repair attempts effectively positioned him for a return to the NFL.

Burress's primary attempt to repair his image came in the form of an August 26, 2009, interview with ESPN's Jeremy Schaap. Notably, this date is eight months after the initial shooting incident at the Latin Quarter night-club. At the time of the exclusive interview, Burress had already been in-dicted and sentenced. It is interesting that Burress chose a televised interview as the best place to express himself. Had he chosen to hold a press confer-ence, issue a written statement, or post an apologetic video on the Internet, he would have arguably had more control over his messages. Televised inter-views, on the other hand, require that Burress's words be given shape and meaning by the interviewer as well as the editing and production crews. That said, the piece does not aim to vilify Burress. In fact, Jeremy Schaap's questions are based loosely around the three accusations against which Bur-ress had to defend himself. Schaap asked questions that gave Burress the opportunity to invite viewers to empathize and understand his actions. In addition to Burress's own attempts to defend himself, this analysis will also consider available comments from third parties who publicly defended Bur-ress's actions and reputation.

Explaining Self-Inflicted Gunshot Wounds

Burress used several strategies to account for his self-inflicted gunshot wound. Some of these strategies, such as claiming the act was accidental, and admitting to the act, were relatively straightforward and unsurprising. Other strategies, such as transcendence, differentiation, and provocation, were de-signed to reframe the act.

Accident

Plaxico Burress never denied shooting himself in the leg. When it came time to present an account of the incident, he said what everyone expected him to say—the shooting was an accident. This is exactly what the media had been reporting for months. Burress explained that after he was let into the Latin Quarter nightclub, he was offered a place in the upstairs VIP room. However, he never actually made it to the VIP room:

> And I'm walking up the stairs and I miss a step. And so my gun, like, slides down my pants. So it's getting ready to hit the ground, and I don't want it to hit the ground so when it's sliding down my jeans, you know, I go to stop it from hitting the ground. And I don't think you could do it in a million times that through your pants you could try to stop it from hitting the ground and my finger, like, hit right on the trigger.

Moments later, he says his pants were wet with blood and he saw some red on his Chuck Taylor shoes. Burress's narrative clarifies that he was not playing with, nor flaunting his weapon the night he shot himself. The weapon was concealed, and only because of bad luck did the gun fire. Although Burress's contention that the shooting was an accident is one of the most foundational image repair strategies he employed during his ESPN interview, it is by no means the most interesting. Those who claim that an offensive act was committed by accident can still be judged as idiots and/or criminals. The discourse that is co-constructed by Burress and Schaap seems to recognize this point, thus explaining the presence of other rhetorical strategies.

Mortification

One of Burress's most frequent rhetorical strategies is mortification. Burress admitted to making egregious mistakes and expressed regret about his situation. When asked why he didn't have a holster for his gun, Burress simply said "bad judgment." Burress also took responsibility for his actions when he was asked how reckless a decision it was to take a loaded gun into a crowded nightclub. He said:

> I knew I had the gun on me. And I stepped out of the car and was like, maybe I should leave it in the car. And I second-guessed myself right there. Right then, that decision got me to where I'm at right now.

This excerpt communicates that Burress understands the consequences of his actions. He is able to calculate the exact moment at which he sealed his fate. This account also suggests that even before he shot himself in the leg, he was aware that he could have chosen not to bring his weapon into the club.

Arguably, Burress had little choice but to use the image repair strategies of claiming his act was an accident and confessing to grave errors in judgment. These strategies seem appropriate because they are entirely consistent with what the public already knew about the nightclub incident. However, neither of these image repair strategies is necessarily designed to reframe the Burress episode. The next strategy examined here, transcendence, is designed to change the way people understand Burress's experiences and circumstances.

Transcendence

In his interview with Schaap, Burress frequently attempted to play the victim and encourage audiences to empathize with his situation. This recurring strategy constitutes a form of transcendence because every time Burress spoke about his severe physical injuries, he essentially reminded audiences that what really mattered in this situation is that he is still alive. The value of human life should presumably take precedence over all other matters in this case. There are few places in the interview where transcendence is more evident than when Burress described his thoughts in the immediate aftermath of the shooting:

> The first thing that went through my mind was, I don't want to bleed to death, and I just want to see my family. Because when it happened, it was like everything I had did in my life flashed before my eyes . . . and I was like, I just want to see my family, because I didn't know if I was going to die [long pause] or not.

Burress told Schaap that he was genuinely concerned for his life. The American public knew fairly early on that Burress's situation was not very serious, but there was a brief period of time where even Burress did not know the extent of his injuries. By expressing his fears and claiming that his thoughts were of his family, Burress humanizes himself and reminds audiences that the situation was extremely difficult for him.

Although Burress had previously portrayed himself as unlucky, his transcendence strategy actually requires that he present himself as a lucky person for not suffering worse injuries. In fact, at one point Burress actually said, "pfeew, I was lucky." Burress also told Schaap that the MRI and the X-rays show that the bullet was "like two millimeters" from his femoral artery. Burress's attempt to find something positive in the ordeal and appeal to matters of higher importance is clearly designed to reduce the offensiveness of his act.

One of the most interesting and high-profile individuals to publicly defend Burress also relied heavily on transcendence. In his ESPN.com blog, multi-platinum hip-hop artist Lil Wayne expressed concern for Burress's well-being and chided the media for being crass and uncaring. He wrote:

> The whole Plaxico thing kind was crazy because immediately afterward everyone was talking about the legal implications and what are the Giants going to do with him now, and no one stopped and said, My God, this guy just shot himself. Is he okay? Was it stupid? Of course. I mean I accidentally shot myself when I was twelve and that's a scary lesson to learn. But before you go yelling at him and talking about his punishment for being so stupid, it's like, Guy, is your leg okay? I was amazed no one was asking that question. The guy just shot himself in the leg! (Lil Wayne, n.d.)

Wayne's transcendent appeal is far more direct and complete than Burress's. This, of course, is one of the advantages of letting surrogate speakers speak on an accused party's behalf. If Burress were this direct with his comments, he might be perceived as selfish and spiteful. However, an individual such as Wayne, who is more removed from the situation, can make these claims without fear of backlash. By reminding people that Burress's life was at stake in the shooting, Burress and Wayne attempt to stifle some of the rampant criticism. This strategy is immediately important to Burress's image repair strategy that if one statement from the Burress interview could be held up as representative of the form and content of Burress's rhetorical strategies it would be his earnest declaration, "I got to go to prison for almost killing my own self." As an image repair strategy, this variety of transcendence is designed to change how people understand Burress's situation. Another image repair strategy that Burress employed to meet roughly the same end is differentiation.

Differentiation

Burress further attempted to reduce the offensiveness of his act by distinguishing an accidental shooting from more heinous gun crimes. He told Schaap, "you know, I'm not a criminal. I'm not going around, like pulling my gun out and robbing people and stealing. I'm not a criminal. I'm protecting Plaxico Burress." Although this statement is a bit inaccurate (he is, by definition, a criminal), Burress did a reasonable job of distinguishing between those individuals who carry guns with intent to break the law and harm others, and himself—a man who only carried a gun to protect himself from people who might target NFL players. Continuing with differentiation, he also argued that his accident was not even as bad as it could have been. He said, "My situation could have been a lot worse. It could have went off, and you know, killed somebody, killed myself." Of course, the point Burress tried to make here is that he did not kill anybody. Of course, killing somebody would have been a much worse offense than simply shooting himself in the leg. By describing an act he *didn't* commit, Burress is clearly trying to make the act he *did* commit seem less harmful and abhorrent. Thus far, most of the messages examined here have addressed the shooting, but not necessarily Burress's reason for having a gun in the first place. To address this problem, Burress used provocation.

Provocation

Seen through the wrong lens, provocation seems like a ridiculous explanation for why anybody would shoot themselves in the leg. The public would have to assume that Burress's right thigh represented some sort of threat to Burress and that for the sake of his own safety and well-being, he had to put a bullet in that thigh. In reality, Burress's provocation defense explains that because NFL players are known targets of criminals, Burress needed to carry a weapon. Although the ESPN interview does not use Burress's own words, Schaap summarizes Burress's position on the matter with the following statement:

Burress said the message that NFL players are targets had been driven home in 2007 when Darin Williams of the Broncos and Sean Taylor of the Redskins were both shot to death. Even now, Burress wears a bracelet to honor Taylor, who had been a close friend. Three nights before Burress shot himself at the Latin Quarter, his teammate Steve Smith had been held up at gunpoint outside his home in New Jersey.

Burress later explained that he only brought his gun because before going to the Latin Quarter, he had to pick up his friend and teammate, Ahmad Bradshaw, in the same complex at which Smith was robbed. In summary, this argument asserts that because the world is a dangerous place for NFL players, Burress needed to carry a gun. Burress's responses during the ESPN interview describe his own experiences having his house broken into twice, and his belief that hiring bodyguards is an ineffective means of protection. His tone during this part of the interview is plaintive without being whiny, thus potentially earning the sympathy of some viewers.

Miami Dolphins wide receiver Joey Porter empathized publicly with Burress's fears, and with his perceived need to carry a firearm:

> It's nothing but safety. . . . After the first time you've been robbed or something like that, the first thing that goes in your mind for the next time, for the rest of your life is I'd rather be caught with [a gun] than without. (Kelly, 2008, para. 7)

According to Porter's account, NFL players feel provoked by a dangerous world to carry a weapon for self-defense. Like several of the strategies Burress used, provocation reframes Burress as a victim rather than an offender.

Attacking the Accuser

Burress attacked and blamed Mayor Michael Bloomberg for the harsh punishment he received. Burress claimed that as soon as Bloomberg spoke out against him his bail was increased: "So, three or four minutes before I'm supposed to stand before the judge, Bloomberg goes on TV. My bail went from ten thousand dollars to two hundred fifty thousand dollars in three minutes." Burress claimed that it became crystal clear at this point in his legal struggle that he would spend substantial time in prison.

Burress used the attacking the accuser strategy a bit differently than other accused parties have used it in the past. Burress did not try to reduce Bloomberg's credibility in hopes of raising doubts about the charges against him. Instead, Burress attacked Bloomberg in an effort to portray himself as the unfair target of Mayor Bloomberg's anti-crime crusade.

Thus far, all of Burress's messages have been understood in relation to the major offense of which he was accused. However, it is also important to understand how Burress defended himself against lesser charges related to the shooting incident. More specifically, the following sections examine how Burress addressed concerns that he may have tried to hide the shooting from the police and that he ruined the Giants' 2008-2009 season.

Attempting to Cover Up the Shooting

Although Burress used many different strategies to deflect criticism about his accidental shooting, his discussion of an alleged cover-up is relatively one-dimensional. Burress denied that he tried to cover up the incident and he denied any knowledge of a potential cover-up by the New York Giants organization.

Denial/Blame Shift

When asked why he registered under the name Harris Smith at the hospital, Burress said, "I had nothing to do with that" and "I did not do that." Schaap rightly perceived that Burress was not denying that he was signed in under a fake name, but that he was simply claiming it was not his idea—not his doing. When pressed harder, Burress managed to shift blame to another party. Quite masterfully, however, Burress manages to avoid pointing a finger at anybody in particular.

> They put me in there under somebody else's name because I'm a celebrity. That's what they do to protect you from the media, or whatever was going on outside. I had nothing to do with that. I signed my name out, discharged, signed my name when I got in. I didn't even know they put me in under somebody else's name.

Even a casual observer is left wondering who "they" are. With more probing, Burress eventually denied any wrongdoing on the part of the Giants organization. Therefore, responsibility for the cover up fell to New York Presbyterian Hospital. Although it had already been reported that a team-friendly doctor at the hospital helped keep the shooting incident under wraps (A Giant mess, 2008), Burress, perhaps out of loyalty, refused to explicitly vilify those who tried to help him.

Failing to Meet His Obligations to the Giants

In addition to being accused of covering up the shooting, Burress was accused of spoiling the Giants' 2008-2009 season. On this point, Burress resorted to mortification.

Mortification

It is important to understand the context provided in the rest of the interview to understand how Burress's confession of letting down his team might be perceived by viewers. The first sentence of the interview reminds audiences that Burress played an integral role in helping the Giants win Superbowl XLII. The second sentence of the transcript reminds audiences that soon after the Superbowl, Burress signed an enormous contract with the Giants. Later, Schaap noted that the Giants performed very poorly when Burress was removed from the lineup. Arguably then, audiences were primed to believe Burress's absence hurt the Giants' chances of winning football games.

When asked if he thought he "cost the Giants a return trip to the Superbowl," Burress released a heavy sigh and said:

> That's rough. I really think we had a good team. I was saying that I think we had a little dynasty over there. We knew we were going back. We knew it. Back to back. Two times in a row. And I felt like I took it away from them a little bit, so to speak.

Burress takes some blame for the Giants' failed season. His response is qualified with phrases such as "a little bit" and "so to speak" because claiming full responsibility for the Giants' failed season would mean overemphasizing individual efforts over the importance of team play. Still, the manner of his response speaks to missed opportunities (for both himself and the team), a deep feeling of regret, and an understanding of the value of winning in professional sports.

The ESPN interview addressed each of the charges against Burress, albeit in different ways. The following section of this chapter discusses reactions to the Burress interview and assesses the effectiveness of his image repair efforts.

DISCUSSION

As one might expect, the comments posted beneath the streaming video of the interview at the ESPN webpage were mixed. Even ESPN reporters could not come to agreement regarding Burress's image repair efforts. For instance, Cris Carter, a former wide receiver himself, criticized Burress for an apparent "lack of remorse" (Carter: Lack, 2009). Jeremy Schaap, on the other hand, was more empathetic about his interviewee, noting that Burress had "no malicious intent" and would be paying a "very, very, steep price" (Burress talks, 2009). This notion that Burress was adequately punished for his crime and that justice was served is absolutely crucial to the entirety of Burress's image repair efforts.

At first glance, Burress's apologia seems to take a kitchen sink approach. The disparate strategies he employed (accident, mortification, transcendence, differentiation, attacking the accuser, and denial) are not particularly well organized, and Burress seems to have had no clear agenda or talking points. However, what each of his strategies have in common, and what they manage to achieve when considered as a whole, is a consistent recitation of the breadth and depth of Burress's punishment.

Burress's combination of image repair strategies is predicated on the assumption that the public is more likely to forgive an offender, or at least view an offender with less derision, if the offender has been justly punished for their offense. Throughout the interview with Schaap, Burress described his physical injuries, spoke of how Mayor Bloomberg's outspokenness may have resulted in a harsher sentence, and wept openly upon being reminded that his prison sentence would cause him to miss the birth of his daughter. Burress took every opportunity to describe the suffering he has endured as a result of the accidental shooting.

Burress's tales of suffering are more than mere attempts to play the victim and cultivate sympathy. According to Burke (1968), in order for a polluted individual such as Burress to be redeemed in the eyes of the public, they must endure a symbolic death. By choosing mortification, Burress invited the scorn, disapproval, and all-encompassing guilt of a nation of sports fans. To execute this strategy, Burress had to permit sports fans to aim their disgust and vitriol in his direction. In order to be purified, he had to let the public revel in his suffering. This is perhaps the only strategy by which an individual as reviled as Burress could redeem themselves in the mind of sports fans. By demonstrating in the most dramatic of performances that he is paying his debt to society, Burress managed to repair his public image. He performed his suffering rather well in the ESPN interview, thus taking decent strides toward his ultimate redemption.

In early 2010, Burress was given a similar opportunity to demonstrate that he has been adequately punished. In a segment that aired during the pregame coverage of Superbowl XLIV, his former head coach Bill Cowher traveled to prison to interview Burress. The piece was not analyzed here because it revealed no new information about the Burress case, and did not include any new image repair strategies on Burress's part. Still, the story is overwhelmingly pro-Burress. Although it is hard to imagine a feel-good news story about a guy in prison, Cowher's interview with Burress approaches just that. Like the ESPN interview before it, the Cowher conversation focuses on Burress's perceived need to carry a handgun, his time in prison, and his separation from his family. For the first time in his career, Burress claims that he is concerned with how he is perceived by others: "being in [prison], all you do is have time to think about how do I want to perceived when I get out" (CBS Sports, 2010). He also vowed to be a better husband, father, and brother when released from prison. The interview ended when Cowher told Burress, "nobody is pulling for you more than I am" (CBS Sports, 2010). This endorsement from a well-respected former NFL coach probably proved valuable to Burress's goal of playing professional football again.

Even before shooting himself in a nightclub, Burress was never a media darling. Therefore, to once again earn a living as a productive professional athlete is probably the most he could have ever hoped to achieve with his image repair efforts. Ultimately, that is exactly what Burress accomplished. After his release from prison, he signed a one year, $3.017 million contract with the New York Jets. A major highlight of his comeback came on October 23, 2011, when he scored three touchdowns in a Jets victory over the San Diego Chargers.

In professional sports, success goes a long way toward earning the public's forgiveness. However, the Burress case suggests that forgiving and forgetting are two different things. His reputation as a numbskull and his status as a topic of humor persists. For instance, on November 27, 2011, a new Burress-inspired touchdown dance was created. When Buffalo Bills wide receiver Steve Johnson scored a touchdown against the New York Jets, he entered the endzone, used his fingers to signify handguns, and then pantomimed the act of shooting himself in the leg. Although Johnson was penalized on the field and later fined $10,000 for the act (Boone, 2011), the dance nonetheless served as a reminder that Burress may always be remembered for his mistake.

CONCLUSION

Plaxico Burress appears to have done a rather compelling job of using an apparent weakness (his time in prison) as an unlikely means of persuasion. By demonstrating in as many ways as possible that he was adequately punished for his mistake and that he paid his debt to society (with interest), Burress positioned himself for a return to the public eye. He may still be the butt of the joke, but he's the butt of the joke that made over $3 million as a professional athlete in 2011.

REFERENCES

A giant mess [electronic version]. (2008, December 5). *New York Daily News,* p. 46.

Baker, A. (2008, December 2). Police question why hospital did not report Burress's wound [electronic version]. *New York Times*, B12.

CBS Sports. (2010, January 31). Cowher interviews Plaxico Burress. Retrieved May 11, 2010 from http://urbanreup.com/index.php?option=com_seyret&Itemid=5&task=videodirectlink&id =848

Benoit, W. L. (1995). *Accounts, excuses, and apologies: A theory of image restoration discourse*. Albany: State University of New York Press.

Boone, R. (2011, December 1). Johnson fined $10G [electronic version]. *Newsday*, A78.

Burke, K. (1968). *Counterstatement*. Berkeley: University of California Press.

Burress talks about the night he shot himself in the leg. (2009, August 25). *ESPN.com*. Retrieved May 12, 2010.

Carter: Lack of remorse from Plaxico. (2009, August 25). *ESPN.com*. Retrieved May 12, 2010, from http://espn.go.com/video/clip?id=4421211.

Cimini, R. (2011, July 31). Plaxico Burress signs with Jets. *ESPNNewYork.com*. Retrieved December 1, 2011 from http://espn.go.com/new-york/nfl/story/_/id/6820679/plaxico-burress-new-york-jets-agree-one-year-deal-sources-say.

Colbert, S. (2008, December 2). The word: A man named Plaxico. *The Colbert Report*. Retrieved May 12, 2010, from http://www.colbertnation.com/the-colbert-report- videos/211989/december-02-2008/the-word—-a-man-named-plaxico

Eligon, J. (2009a, August 4). Ex-Giants star who shot himself is indicted on gun counts [Electronic Version]. *The New York Times*, A16.

Eligon, J. (2009b, August 21). Burress will receive 2-year prison sentence [electronic version]. *New York Times*, A23.

Florio, M. (2010, May 3). Plaxico lost recreation time for lying to prison guard. NBC Sports Pro Football Talk. Retrieved May 13, 2010 from http://profootballtalk.nbcsports.com/2010/05/03/plaxico-lost-recreation-privileges-for-lying-to-a-prison-guard/.

Giants' Burress injured by accidental gunshot—reports. (2008, November 29). *Agence France Presse*. Retrieved May 12, 2010, from Lexis Nexis Academic.

Giants' Burress suffers gunshot wound. (2008, November 29). *Canwest News Service*. Retrieved May 5, 2010 from Lexis Nexis Academic.

Kelly, O. (2008, December 9). Dolphins' Porter defends Burress' actions [electronic version]. *South Florida Sun-Sentinel.*

LaPointe, J. (2008, December 18). Light in mood and on his feet [electronic version]. *The New York Times*, B13.

Lazarowitz, E., & Yaniv, O. (2008, December 1). Fans eager to brush plax off [electronic version]. *New York Daily News*, 4.

Lee, T. (2008, December 4). Giants offer chronology of shooting's aftermath [electronic version]. *New York Times*, B18.

Letterman, D. (2008, December 19). A Plaxico Burress Christmas. *The Late Show with David Letterman*. Retrieved May 12, 2010 from http://www.cbs.com/late_night/late_show/video/?pid=ZZ4sradOIZmVR93uil6zjB6w26FgRrM_&play=true

Lil Wayne. (n.d.). My closer song? Closing time by Semisonic. *Lil Wayne's Blog*. Retrieved May 8, 2010 from http://sports.espn.go.com/espnmag/story?id=3762300

Lombardi, F., Gendar, A., & Lemire, J. (2008, December 2) Throw the Bloomin' book at Burress. Mayor sez it's an "outrage" if receiver isn't fully prosecuted [electronic version]. *New York Daily News*, 3.

Peter, L. J. (1979). *Ideas for our time*. New York: Collins.

Peyser, A. (2008, December 2). Coddled Jock can no longer pass the buck [electronic version]. *New York Post*, 4.

Robinson, J. (2008, December 11). Giants' passing game is feeling Burress' absence [electronic version]. *New York Times*, B16.

Ryan, G. (1982). Kategoria and apologia: On their rhetorical criticism as a speech set. *Quarterly Journal of Speech*, 68, 254-261.

Schmiedeberg, J. (2008, November 29). Update on Plaxico Burress story. *Big Blue View Blog* (comments). Retrieved May 5, 2010, from http://www.bigblueview.com/2008/11/29/675555/update-on-the-plaxico-burr.

Stewart, J. (2008, December 1). John Stewart touches kids—Plaxico Burress. *The Daily Show with Jon Stewart*. Retrieved May 12, 2010 from http://www.thedailyshow.com/watch/mon-december-1-2008/jon-stewart-touches-kids—-plaxico-burress.

Vaccaro, M. (2008, November 30). Giant jerk shoots himself—no more reason to placate Plax [Electronic Version]. *New York Post*, 4.

Vacchiano, R. (2008, September 30). More woes for plax [electronic version]. *New York Daily News*, 54.

Chapter Twelve

In the Dark at Texas Tech: News Coverage Involving the Image Repair Discourse of Mike Leach and Adam James

Kevin A. Stein, Southern Utah University,
Paul Turman, South Dakota Board of Regents, and
Matthew Barton, Southern Utah University

As the NCAA Division I-A bowl season was underway in late December 2009, college football was shocked by the administration's decision at Texas Tech University to suspend their successful coach due to allegations of mistreating one of his players. Head coach Mike Leach denied the allegations, and insinuated that the player was retaliating for his lack of playing time and Leach's unorthodox coaching practices that were used to push players to peak performance. Leach filed an injunction against the university in the hopes that he would be reinstated in time to coach his team at the Alamo Bowl on New Year's Day. A number of current and former players stepped forward to defend their coach, as well as various athletic boosters who threatened to withdraw future support to the university if steps were not taken to reinstate Leach. Just hours before the court hearing to determine whether Leach would coach his team in the Alamo Bowl, Texas Tech terminated its relationship with Leach citing his refusal to apologize for his actions and change his coaching strategies. Since that time, Leach has maintained his position that his actions were appropriate, and that the suspension and termination were the result of collusion among campus administration and trustees to terminate his contract without cause.

Leach's defense of his behavior to the media and his fans represents an important feature for the way that sport is produced and consumed within today's society. Consistent with what Ryan describes as the speech set of *kategoria* and *apologia* (attack and defense), this type of self-defense discourse suggests that the critical focus on the apology should also examine the attack preceding it. Many would agree that Leach's judgment may have been in question during this particular situation which would necessitate the need for him to defend, and possibly apologize for, his actions. Many felt that his actions during the aftermath of the event placed a significant blemish on his illustrious coaching career. However, we argue in this chapter that focusing exclusively on Leach's defense of his behavior ignores a third component which Stein (2009, 2006) refers to as *antapologia* (response to *apologia*). *Antapologia* is an important feature of the apologetic situation because the rhetor may choose to construct the initial image repair based on what he or she perceives to be the likely response by the offended person(s). When the discourse addresses the account of the act, it constitutes an instance of *antapologia*. Thus, the purpose of this chapter is to not only address the attack and defense, but also the theoretical implications of sport *antapologia* that result from fan reaction to coach image repair by using the Leach vs. Texas Tech incident as an illustration of *antapologia* rhetoric.

NATIONAL CONTEXT

At the heart of any coaching position is the need for a coach to develop player skills, manage player relations, and instill the various life lessons that come from sport participation. Additional complexity is added for those who coach team sports as team cohesion, roster management and playing time must also be managed to produce the right mixture of team dynamics that will result in success. However, beyond these management responsibilities coaches are faced with a difficult set of circumstances as they navigate the ongoing tensions associated with winning and serving an important instructional role for their players. Coaches at all levels are expected to win, and must make difficult decisions about player welfare (playing with injury), governing policies (violating caps on contact hours), and ethics (leaving recruits for another team). Such issues have emerged more frequently during the past decade as the dramatic increase in coach salaries has further exemplified this emphasis that winning and success are important drivers for collegiate teams. For instance, Mac Brown (head football coach at the University of Texas) received a $2 million salary increase after advancing his team to its second championship game in four years. At the time he became the highest paid coach in the country, with a annual salary of $5.1 million, due largely to the fact that the University of Texas was interested in discouraging other programs from recruiting him away. The average salary and total compensation for coaches from the Bowl Championship subdivision reached well above $1 million as far back as 2006 (Upton & Wieberg, 2006). This "arms race" in college athletics places campus administrations in a difficult position as university and college presidents are faced with managing individuals who make up to ten times their own yearly salary. For instance, in 2010 an assistant coach with the Kansas State University men's basketball team was awarded a $420,000 contract, which was $80,000 more than that institution's president. When coaches are rewarded primarily on a "win at all cost" mentality, it creates a context where coaches are likely to square off against campus administration when it comes to determining who controls the factors that impact team success.

THE LEACH TERMINATION

Prior to 2000, the Texas Tech football program had consistently been in the middle of the pack in the Big 12 Conference. Despite being the only team to record a winning season in each year since the Big 12 Conference was formed in 1996, the program was often obscured by in-state rivals such as Texas and Texas A&M. After going a decade without a bowl appearance, Texas Tech replaced its former coach, Spike Dykes, who led the team to an 82-67 record over a thirteen year span. Mike Leach was hired in spring 2000 to breathe new life into the program, and after taking the helm he led the team to ten straight winning seasons, nine consecutive bowl appearances, and five bowl victories. Leach quickly became the program's winningest coach, and received AP Big 12 Coach of Year honors in 2008 after he led his team to an 11-1 season and a BCS Bowl victory. After the 2008 season, Leach signed a three-year contract extension worth $2.5 million, guaranteeing his position with the team through the 2013 season.

After Leach led his team to an 8-4 season in 2009, they were scheduled to play in the Alamo Bowl on New Year's Day when he was suspended indefinitely just five days before the game pending an investigation of inappropriate treatment of one of his players. During the second to last game of the season, senior wide receiver Adam James suffered a concussion, and was unable to practice after examinations identified an abnormal heart rate. When James notified Leach that he would be unable to practice, he was ordered to report to a dark equipment shed where he was required to stand alone throughout the duration of the practice. Adding complexity to the situation was the fact that James's father was former NFL running back and current ESPN college football analyst Craig James, who approached university officials regarding the mistreatment of his son after being notified about the incident. Campus administration asked Leach to apologize in writing to the James family by a December 28 deadline or face suspension by university officials.

After Leach refused to apologize, Texas Tech released a statement noting that Leach would face indefinite suspension until further investigation. Leach's attorney filed a temporary restraining order shortly afterward to allow him to coach his team during the Alamo Bowl on January 1, and a court date was scheduled for December 30. Prior to hearing formal testimony, Leach received a termination letter and Texas Tech released a statement noting his "defiant act of insubordination" in the institution's attempts to resolve the complaint that had come forward from the James family. Shortly afterward, Leach released his own statement which indicated that:

> Over the past several months, there have been individuals in the Texas Tech administration, Board of Regents and booster groups who have dealt in lies, and continue to do so. These lies have led to my firing this morning. I steadfastly refuse to deal in any lies, and am disappointed that I have not been afforded the opportunity for the truth to be know. (Schad, 2009, para. 7)

After the termination, additional facts about the events surrounding James continued to surface. An athletic trainer for the football program reported that Leach had forced him to place James in the shed as punishment for his unwillingness to practice. Players reported numerous instances where Leach criticized James for being lazy, and that Leach viewed the concussion as an excuse to simply avoid strenuous practice workouts. Leach was reported to have told James that he would be removed from the team if he left the shed before the end of practice. Assistant Coach Lincoln Riley noted in a letter to the administration prior to the suspension that "Two practices before Adam James claimed he had a concussion; Coach Leach and I were forced to discipline him for poor effort," which was something that had become "a common theme about Adam's work ethic and attitude during his entire career" (Schad, 2009, para. 6). Despite these reports Craig James used his position on ESPN to continually frame Leach as an abusive coach with disregard for his players. These events set the stage for a give and take between Leach, the Texas Tech administration, and the James family that continued months after the termination.

ON THE ATTACK

Despite a long and valuable history of study regarding apologies that began with Ware and Linkugel's (1973) initial claim that accusations and apologies for behavior are so common that they needed to be studied as a separate genre, little work has been done to nail down important areas of study outside of examining the perceived effectiveness of the apology itself. For example, although Benoit's (1995) theoretical extension about image repair shaped the way scholars thought about the rhetorical situation, far too many rhetorical and public relations studies have defined this situation too narrowly by looking at the apology only without considering the overall flow of the discourse. Ironically, although there is a strong and interesting body of literature that has applied Benoit's work in studying various infractions in politics (Benoit & Wells, 1996), popular culture (Benoit, 1997) and corporate behavior (Benoit & Brinson, 1994), as Ryan (1982) argued, apologies should be studied not as if they occurred in a vacuum, rather as a two-part speech set. This composition would involve an examination of the initial attack (*kategoria*), and the subsequent apology for the perceived wrongdoing (*apologia*). Stein (2008; 2007) has extended Ryan's ideas by arguing that scholars' claims of effectiveness are questionable unless they examine the response to the apology (*antapologia*). Although Ryan's (1982) essay explained that *kategoria* was an important component of the speech set, the author failed to elaborate on the concept beyond arguing that attack centers on issues of policy and character. Obviously, when scholars are interested in questions of fit when they examine apologies, they run the risk of being incomplete unless they truly examine the precipitating attack.

In the spirit of Ryan's challenge to bring forth more work on the attack, Pfau, Kenski, Nitz, and Sorenson (1990) identified three broad options for attack: attacking first, counterattacking, and preventing attack (refutation). Jamieson (1992) listed two options: identification, which associates two ideas, and apposition, which involves contrast. There is some agreement among scholars that an attack consists of two basic elements (Pomerantz, 1978). First, a person or group must assign responsibility for an offensive act to another person or group. And second, the target of the attack must be perceived to be responsible for the act by the relevant audience. Subsequent research has led to a typology of strategies used as a primary method for analyzing persuasive attacks. For example, Benoit and Wells (1992) examined the persuasive attack in the 1992 presidential debates and Benoit and Dorries (1996) analyzed *Dateline NBC*'s persuasive attack on WalMart charging that the company's "Buy America" campaign was misleading consumers. Benoit and Harthcock (1999) followed by evaluating strategies utilizing internal evidence (textual) and external evidence (polls, newspaper commentary). Although illuminating to some extent, these studies are a reminder that more work still needs to be done. Much like studying an apology in isolation from the connected strains of discourse and making claims about why it succeeded/failed, studying the attack alone does not necessarily account for the success of the discourse. Moreover, in spite of the gigantic popularity of sports and the common falls from grace that athletes and coaches experience, few studies in *apologia* have attempted to look at the discourse as a whole (Kruse, 1977, 1981a, 1981b). Even those sports studies that have looked at issues like peer defense used to protect pro tennis icon Billie Jean King who had an extramarital lesbian affair with her secretary or the infamous Winter Olympic figure skating attack involving Tonya Harding and Nancy Kerrigan (Benoit & Hanczor, 1994), have fallen short in being able to adequately account for effectiveness.

The present study attempts to create a conversation that can drive *apologia* scholarship further by showing the importance of broadening the parameters of the rhetorical situation of an apology through examination of the three-part speech set. The Mike Leach/Adam James controversy is a useful case for understanding these theoretical extensions. There are five reasons why this case is of particular value. First, too much scholarship treats all apologetic situations as similar, but as will be shown in this case, each situation is unique and needs to be studied in this light. For instance, the discourse shows that although he had leveled allegations against Leach, James had no explanation for his behavior. Leach's comments are equally puzzling because the financial consequences were so steep, yet he briefly denied any wrongdoing and then went on the attack. Second, *apologia* studies need to be examined more carefully because they don't always give a complete picture of the situation, and more importantly, there is no clear sense of the way the relevant audience actually reacted to the message making the study of *antapologia* so important (Husselbee & Stein, 2010). Third, by looking at the precipitating exigence that structured the discourse, scholars can understand the constraints the speaker perceived as important. Fourth, future studies can begin to canonize the reasons people respond the way they do, providing a more complete understanding of the rhetorical situation, thus making conclusions drawn about adequacy much more solid. Last, although we recognize the important contribution *apologia* studies have made, too much time has been spent only on the apology without considering the way that *kategoria* and *antapologia* impact the ultimate lesson(s) each study provides (Stein, Turman, and Barton, 2009).

With these ideas in mind, two different sets of questions drive this investigation. First, what type of discursive strategies did ESPN.com and the *Lubbock Avalanche-Journal* reporters use (either directly or indirectly through citation) to attack Mike Leach and Adam James? Understanding these strategies provides key insight into the content of the actual apology (or lack thereof). Second, what discursive strategies were used by newspapers (direct-ly or indirectly) to respond to the explanations offered by Mike Leach and Adam James?

METHOD

In order to systematically examine the newspaper discourse attacking Mike Leach and Adam James, as well as the newspaper responses to the accounts of the incident, we utilized two distinct theoretical frameworks. First, we used Benoit's typology of *kategoria* to analyze the attacks levied against Leach and James. Second, we utilized Stein's (2005) typology of *antapologia* strategies to analyze the newspaper discourse in response to Leach, and James's accounts of their behavior.

Benoit's typology was originally developed in his examination of attack and defense during the 1992 presidential debates between George Bush, Bill Clinton, and Ross Perot. He further developed the theory in subsequent stud-ies on *Dateline NBC*'s attack on WalMart and attack advertisements against the tobacco industry (Benoit and Wells, 1996). In each of these three studies, Benoit argued that there are four rhetorical strategies for increasing perceived responsibility for an act: 1) argue that the accused committed the crime before, 2) argue that the accused planned the act, 3) claim that the accused knew the likely consequences of the act, and 4) show that the accused bene-fited from the act. He also argued that there are six strategies for increasing the offensiveness of a particular act: 1) emphasize the extent of the damage, 2) illustrate the persistence of negative effects, 3) show the effects on the audience, 4) argue that there is an inconsistency on the part of the offender, 5) claim the victims are innocent or helpless, and 6) show an obligation to protect the victims.

Stein's typology of *antapologia* (response to *apologia*) was developed in his analysis of the Soviet Union's response to U.S. image repair during the 1960 U-2 incident. It has since been applied in other prominent *apologia* contexts, such as the 2006 World Cup headbutting incident, the Hurricane Katrina disaster, Tiger Woods's infidelity, and Mel Gibson's anti-Semitic tirade. According to Stein, there are two primary functions of antapologic discourse. One function is to strengthen the initial attack and the other to weaken the *apologia* offered by the accused. Strategies for strengthening the initial attack include pointing out concessions made in the *apologia* and refining the attack to make it stronger. Strategies for weakening the *apologia* include arguing the *apologia* is untrue, the accused has contradicted him/herself, the *apologia* does not take adequate responsibility, the *apologia* reflects character flaws of the accused, harm will come from the *apologia* itself, there is motive behind the *apologia*, and the *apologia* mirrors earlier speeches. Additionally, there may occasionally be a response to accusations made in the apology itself. Our intent is to use these two theoretical frameworks as a starting point for the analysis, with the expectations that additional categories might emerge inductively due to the unique features of this particular context.

The texts used in the analysis include all ESPN.com articles published between December 28, 2009, and January 12, 2010, addressing Mike Leach's firing by the Texas Tech University. We also utilized all of the Leach articles published by *Lubbock Avalanche-Journal* during this time frame. We felt that these two publications would provide an interesting contrast between the national news coverage and the local coverage of the event.

NEWSPAPER COVERAGE OF MIKE LEACH'S DISMISSAL FROM TEXAS TECH

In our analysis of the newspaper coverage following Mike Leach's firing from Texas Tech University, we focused our attention primarily on the attack (*kategoria*) preceding Leach's image repair and the *antapologia* discourse in response to Leach's statements. We noticed early on in our examination of the texts that even when Leach defended himself, he would typically utilize strategies of denial ("I didn't do anything wrong") and attacking his various accusers. Although most research tends to examine *kategoria* and *apologia* separately, we see this as a specific area in which these two parts of the speech set are intertwined. Therefore we chose to systematically break down the specific attack strategies utilized in the image repair category of attacking the accuser. Our analysis also examined the plethora of attacks offered by other individuals such as Texas Tech administrators, players, coaches, Adam James's father, Craig James, and various attorneys representing the different sides. Conspicuously absent from these exchanges is Adam James himself, whose voice was represented by various surrogates, particularly his family and his attorney. In addition to our analysis of the attack, we also discovered a limited amount of *antapologia* discourse, which comments on the public statements made by Leach during his interviews with the *New York Times* and ESPN.

Attacks Leveled from Multiple Directions

A wide variety of attack strategies were utilized during the Mike Leach controversy. Although newspapers would sometimes refer to Leach's general level of responsibility for his termination, primary strategies used to increase overall responsibility for the act were the accused committed the act before and the accused planned the act. Strategies for increasing the offensiveness of the act included inconsistency on the part of the accused and extent of damage. A new category emerged inductively through the analysis where those involved chose to denigrate the character of the accused in order to elevate the offensiveness of a given behavior.

Committed the act before

One specific strategy that was used to elevate Leach's responsibility for his termination was to argue that he had engaged in harmful behaviors before. In using the strategy, the attacker hopes that multiple offenses will be less forgivable than an isolated case. For example, Texas Tech's official statement argued: "In a defiant act of insubordination, Coach Leach continually refused to cooperate in a meaningful way to help resolve the complaint. He also refused to obey a suspension order and instead sued Texas Tech University" (Leach fired, 2009). While Texas Tech utilizes the term "continually" in order to articulate a pattern of behavior, the university focused on other acts of insubordination that were separate from his alleged treatment of James. However, others criticized Leach for a specific pattern of behavior related to his treatment of players. For example, offensive lineman Brandon Carter said, "I don't want to say anything bad about the fans, but this is not the first situation that something like this has happened. This is just the first time someone stepped forward. I don't want fans thinking that Adam James did this because he was upset but it was just kind of the last straw, and sooner or later something was going to come out. This is the first situation that someone spoke up about" (Caplan, 2010). Both statements function to paint Leach as a coach who is perpetually abusive toward his players and consistently defiant toward his immediate supervisors.

Accused planned the act

This strategy is used to show that an individual accused of wrongdoing had an awareness that he was engaged in a harmful behavior. Several individuals during the Mike Leach fallout were attacked using this strategy. One was Leach himself, who was attacked for intending to inflict punishment on James. Newspapers reported the following statements by Texas Tech administrators: "His statements make it clear that the coach's actions against the player were meant to demean, humiliate and punish the player rather than to serve the team's best interest" (Carver, 2009a). A writer for ESPN also reported: "A source briefed on the situation said that on the first day in question, Leach asked trainers on the field, 'Well, what can he [James] do?' and the coach was told James could not have strenuous activity and should

avoid sunlight and so Leach instructed, 'Well, then put him over there'"
(Schad, 2009). Both statements attack Leach for having deliberately decided
to relegate Leach to the "dark closet."

Others involved in the situation were also attacked in this way. Mike
Leach returned fire at Adam James by arguing he intended to manipulate the
situation. An ESPN reporter cited Leach as saying, "Adam James voluntarily
placed himself in the electrical closet and apparently took pictures with his
phone camera" ("Suit alleges," 2010). Obviously, the semantic differences
between being confined to a closet and "voluntarily" placing oneself there
are great. The attack portrays James as a person willing to intentionally
fabricate a bizarre scenario in order to solicit a negative outcome for Leach.
Texas Tech administrators were also attacked for having planned to fire
Leach. The *Lubbock Avalanche-Journal* cited Dallas attorney Stephen Fox:
"Perhaps most detrimental to the university's hopes of fighting a Leach lawsuit are e-mail communications between boosters and Tech Chancellor Kent
Hance during last year's contract negotiations. Leach can use the e-mails that
discuss the cost of firing him to try to prove to a jury that the school had it
out for him from the beginning" (Carver, 2009b). Leach also attacked Texas
Tech administrators, arguing they intended to defame him: "Fired Texas
Tech coach Mike Leach Friday accused his former bosses of making slander-
ous and libelous statements intended to damage his reputation and hurt him
financially. Court documents filed Friday said statements from university
administrators were made intentionally to harm Leach and expose him to
financial harm" ("Tech intended," 2010). The key element of the strategy,
regardless of who levels the attack, is to argue motive or intent behind a
harmful behavior. In this particular situation, the specific behaviors under
scrutiny vary, but not the manner in which responsibility is elevated by
claiming the accused knew what he was doing.

Inconsistency on the part of the accused

Once a certain level of responsibility is established, other strategies are used
to elevate the overall offensiveness of a given behavior. One strategy for
increasing offensiveness is to claim that someone engaged in an inconsistent
behavior or made inconsistent statements. This strategy was most frequently
used during attacks on Texas Tech University. For example, Leach attacked
various members of the organization: "Over the past several months there
have been individuals in the Texas Tech administration, Board of regents,
and booster groups who have dealt in lies and continue to do so. These lies
have led to my firing. I steadfastly refuse to deal in any lies and am disappointed that I have not been afforded the opportunity for the truth to be
known" ("Leach fired," 2009). The inconsistency highlighted in this statement is an inconsistency with what Leach perceived to be the "truth" in the

rhetoric offered by Texas Tech administrators. Newspapers also covered other Leach statements expressing an inconsistency: "In Friday's filing, Leach's attorneys claim Texas Tech officials have given conflicting statements about the basis for Leach's dismissal, casting doubt on their reasons for firing him." While the former statement addressed a conflict between truth and fiction, the latter statement addressed an inconsistency between explanations for Leach's termination. In this case, the truth is unknown, at least to Leach and those covering the dispute. Adam James's parents also utilized this attack strategy when they discussed Leach's treatment of their son. The *Lubbock Avalanche-Journal* wrote: "Mr. and Mrs. James took the step with great regret and after consideration and prayer to convey to the Texas Tech administration that their son had been subjected to actions and treatment not consistent with common sense rules for safety and health" (Schad, 2009). Here, James's parents make the claim that Leach's behavior toward their son was inconsistent with what normal people would deem safe and healthy. The strategy of arguing an inconsistency elevated the overall offensiveness of the accusations by providing contrast to those behaviors that would be more appropriate in the context. By illuminating the inconsistency the harmful behavior becomes much more glaring, especially when in the national spotlight.

Extent of damage

This attack strategy elevates the offensiveness of a harmful behavior by illustrating the specific damage that resulted from it. Obviously, if a behavior is not perceived by the relevant audiences as damaging, there will be no subsequent harm to the accused individual's image. In this particular case, the newspaper coverage functioned to explicitly describe Mike Leach's behavior toward Adam James. For example, an ESPN article quoted athletic trainer Steve Pincock: "A source close to the family told me that James sustained a concussion on December 16, was examined on December 17 and told not to practice because of the concussion and an elevated heart rate. The source said Leach called a trainer and directed him to move James 'to the darkest place, to clean out the equipment and to make sure that he could not sit or lean. He was confined for three hours.'" An *Avalanche-Journal* article was even more descriptive of the circumstances: "'Leach further said something to the effect that he wanted me to tell James that I lock his f------ p----a—in a place so dark that the only way he knows he has a d--- is to reach down and touch it,' which I repeated to James. "'Leach further told me to have him stand in the dark during the entire practice'" (Williams, 2010b). These statements all elevate the offensiveness of Leach's behavior by portraying it as very extreme rather than just another way of rehabilitating an injured player.

Denigrating the character of the accused

This particular attack strategy is not represented in Benoit's typology of attack, but is especially prominent in this context. In fact, one might expect a new category that emerges inductively to be less represented than some of the more established categories. However, in this case, character attacks were by far the most frequently utilized type of attack. Additionally, these attacks came from nearly every direction and almost no one was immune from having their name dragged through the mud. For example, Mike Leach was portrayed in news coverage as a bit of an odd duck. One reporter cited a Tech player as saying Leach was "different" (Leach anticipates, 2009). Another reporter argued: "Leach's idiosyncrasies extended well beyond the spread offense that rewrote the NCAA record book. His disheveled appearance made it clear he held collared shirts and ironed slacks in the same regard as holding penalties. Leach's news conferences held an air of unpredictability. You might hear about his summer trip to Europe. You might hear about his love of pirates, which became fodder for his recent cameo on the TV series *Friday Night Lights* (Maisel, 2009). Other news articles seemed to describe Leach as a bit abrasive:

> Following a 52-30 home loss to Texas A&M in October, Leach said his team was listening to "their fat little girlfriends" instead of focusing on the Aggies. On the Monday after the game, Leach said he was willing to go to "fairly amazing lengths" to get his players to focus. "I don't know if I will be success-ful this week or not, but I am going to try and there will be some people inconvenienced. And, if it happens to be their fat little girlfriends, too bad." (Durrett, 2009)

Obviously, these excerpts show little restraint on Leach's part and the news-papers were more than willing to print his more outlandish statements. The last major character attack involved Leach's coaching prowess. Adam James's father, Craig James, was quoted as saying: "You coaches are crazy and you're screwing my kid. . . . You don't know what you're doing. Adam James is the best player at the wide receiver position. If you've got the [blank] to call me back, and I don't think you do, call me back" ("Suit alleges," 2010).Whether objective or not, Craig James felt that any coach who did not choose to play his son was not competent enough to hold his position.

Some character attacks were directed at Adam James, most claiming he was lazy and arrogant. For example, athletic trainer Steve Pincock said that "Adam showed up to practice in street clothes, no team gear, and dark sun-glasses. Adam walked about 40 to 50 yards, very slowly with a non-caring attitude" (Schlabach, 2009). An ESPN report offered a similar perspective: "In a letter last week to Texas Tech administrators Riley [acting offensive coordinator] called James 'unusually lazy and entitled.' . . . Riley wrote that James is the type of person who makes 'excuses or blames people for things that go wrong in life'" (Riley offers, 2009). Riley would also claim later that he was worried about the effect that James would have on the other receivers because of his "weak and conceited attitude" (Leach anticipates, 2009). Mike Leach himself described Adam James as "really, a guy that we could never get to work hard and wanted to fall back on his father any time he wasn't playing" (Williams, 2010a). These excerpts illustrate the way in which Adam James was criticized for his poor attitude toward the football team and its coaching staff. Adam James's father was also denigrated heavily for being too involved in his son's football career. For example, ESPN posted the following statement by Mike Leach: "When you call coaches, when you call me, you call his position coaches, both of them, you call other administrators on campus or you come to practices and want to have constant discussions on your son and their playing time. . . . Craig James required more time than all of the other parents combined" (Williams, 2010a). Leach also claimed that James "used his position at ESPN to try to coerce me into allowing Adam to play more . . . I'm deferring to the judgment of 12 people as we look at the film on who should play and who should play when and then we make our decision based on that. I don't feel like it's fair to the other players and I don't think it's the right way to do business to allow influence and position to dictate when you play a young man" (Schlabach, 2009). In both examples, Leach attacks Craig James's character by claiming that he overstepped his bounds. Leach implies that this is likely due to a sense of entitlement James developed being an announcer for ESPN.

Antapologia Discourse in Reply to Leach's Public Statements

Although much more limited in this context than in others previously studied, some newspaper discourse was designed to specifically address public statements made by Mike Leach. These strategies include arguing the *apologia* is incomplete, the *apologia* is untrue, there is motive behind the *apologia*, and a new type of strategy of no response or refusing to respond.

Apologia is incomplete

This strategy involves arguments that the *apologia* statements are somehow inadequate or in some way fail to meet the specific exigencies required of the rhetorical context. For example, newspapers would claim Leach's attacks on his accusers were not nearly specific enough: "In the statement, Leach did not explain how he felt the school was lying. He said his reputation had been damaged but that 'there will be time to answer questions about this issue in the future, but the serious legal nature of this situation prevents me from going into further detail at this time'" (Leach fired, 2009). The newspaper articulated a position that Leach should have indicated which parts of the Texas Tech case against him were lies.

Apologia is untrue

In the above example, newspapers simply claimed ambiguity or a lack of completeness. In this strategy, the response to the *apologia* will include claims that specific elements of the account or patently false. For example, Craig James responded to Leach's argument that he meddled in his son's football career: "Coach Leach has made damaging and untrue comments about my actions, about my son, and about a business relationship—which does not exist—between me and the leadership of the university" (Schlabach, 2009). In this example, Craig James states very explicitly that the attacks leveled against him by Mike Leach are completely untrue.

Arguing motive behind the *apologia*

Another common *antapologia* strategy is to claim that there is motive behind the *apologia*. This strategy is used to weaken the *apologia* by showing a lack of sincerity or authenticity. Obviously, an apology that has too much "intent" behind it is less likely to be a genuine attempt to articulate a truthful accounting of events. A good example of this strategy can be seen in Craig James's explanation of why Leach offered the coercion for playing time argument. He argued, "He's simply trying to shift attention from his own actions and from the findings of a University investigation which we believe was fair and thorough. As we have said over and over, our concern was about the safety and well being of our son and of all the other fine young men on the team. Any parent who found their son in this situation would step forward" (Schlabach, 2009). Here, James attempted to represent Mike Leach's statements as more of a strategy for shifting attention away from his program rather than a reflection on the real discourse that took place between Craig James and Mike Leach about James's playing time.

Strategy of no response

A new *antapologia* strategy that emerged as a result of this analysis is a strategy of no response or a statement implying no response will occur. Although we had reservations about creating a category of discourse where little to no discourse actually takes place, there is some precedent for this type of category as Benoit (1995) argued that he nearly included a category of "silence" in his typology of *apologia* strategies because the act of not responding can actually communicate a great deal. In this situation, several individuals employed this strategy when asked to respond to specific statements made by Leach. One example of this was reported in the *Lubbock Avalanche-Journal*: "Tech spokesperson Sally Post said Friday that Chancellor Kent Hance would release a statement responding to the Leach interviews. Later in the day, she said there would be no statement" (Williams, 2010a). Craig James also utilized this strategy in the following newspaper quote:

> "Any parent would have done what we did, regardless of the consequences and I would do it again," James, a former SMU star and now a sports analyst at ESPN, told reporters. "And however that impacts anything that I do in my life is inconsequential. I did what was best—what we had to do for our son." However, he declined to comment on what Leach's attorney and legions of supporters of the fired coach allege—that he lobbied Leach and even the administrator to get more playing time. "Obviously, that's a matter that Texas Tech and the coach are dealing with right now, and it would be inappropriate for me to say anything else about it." (Rangel, 2010)

In each example, it is clearly stated that a response will not be forthcoming, usually because of some circumstance unique to the situation.

IMPLICATIONS

By applying the typologies of attack and *antapologia* to the events surrounding Mike Leach's firing from Texas Tech University, we are able to draw a number of implications regarding the effectiveness of this type of discourse, the utility of examining multiple components of the newly extended *apologia* speech set, and the relative non-linearity of most image repair contexts.

First, one particular attack strategy seems especially effective due to its internal consistency and plausibility. This strategy is the denigration of character in order to elevate the offensiveness of a given behavior. One reason why this strategy was effective was because it was probably difficult to verify the credibility of either side's depiction of the events. Once the situation digressed to a contest of unverifiable facts, a logical next step was for those involved to destroy the character of the other individuals offering their version of the "facts." Additionally, we learn from Attribution Theory that people will often attribute the negative behaviors of others to internal causes, such as personality or a lack of ethics. This is fairly consistent with the choices made by the people involved in the Mike Leach debacle to attack character. However, it remains uncertain whether those utilizing the strategy are simply using the strategy to divert attention from the real issues at hand or if they are actually trying to provide legitimate explanations for the harmful behavior by citing character as a critical factor. Another attack strategy

that was likely effective was Leach's argument that the Texas Tech administrators had planned the firing long before the James controversy emerged. In
this case, Leach's arguments were verified with a series of e-mails between
various booster clubs and Tech chancellor Kent Hance. The correspondence
discusses the fallout that might result from Leach's termination.

Most of the attack strategies used by all involved were relatively ineffective. First, the attack by Texas Tech University indicating that Mike Leach
had planned to lock James in a closet was nonsensical. Leach's coaching
staff confirmed that the location where James was actually placed during his
injury was the size of a two-car garage and that no injured players were ever
allowed to simply do nothing during their rehabilitation. Additionally, Leach
had two opportunities to gain favor from the audiences with which he was
trying to repair his image. Audiences could either believe Leach did nothing
outside of his normal coaching routine or they may believe he did, but that
James's attitude warranted a more extreme response from the coach. Second,
it was ineffective for either side to argue an inconsistency in terms of conflicting statements and outright lies. It becomes difficult for most people
following the story to track the statements made by all involved and to
compare them for consistency. Third, Leach's argument that the administrators' actions had caused devastating harm to the entire Red Raider nation is a
bit illogical. The media covering the situation, particularly ESPN.com, were
quick to compare Mike Leach's alleged actions to other prominent coaching
scandals in collegiate sports. In most cases, the incidents being compared to
the Leach situation had already moved outside of the public consciousness.
Therefore, audiences probably felt like the Leach story would eventually die
as well.

The *antapologia* strategies used to respond to Mike Leach's statements
were probably also fairly ineffectual, particularly Craig James's strategy of
claiming he would not respond to Leach's accusation that he meddled in his
son's football career. At the point that this statement was made, James had
already responded to Leach's attack. James also argued that Leach intended
to shift responsibility from his poor coaching to James's overzealous relationship with the football coaching staff. These statements are not likely to
resonate with relevant audiences because of the difficulty in ascertaining
motive as well as the fact that there was an inherent connection between
Adam James's lack of playing time and his alleged mistreatment by Leach.
Audiences may recognize that the reason, at least in Leach's mind, was not
simply the injury, but the poor attitude of Adam James and the constant
pestering of his "little league dad" ("Tech suspends," 2009). In fact, several
polls published at the time of the incident indicate that the general public
sided more with Mike Leach than Adam James. For example, a poll published by the local newspaper in San Angelo, Texas, reported that 81 percent
of individuals felt that Mike Leach's firing was not justified, whereas only 15

percent felt that it was justified ("Was the firing," 2010). Another poll, this one not native to Texas, reported that 72 percent felt Mike Leach did not deserve to be fired ("Did Texas Tech," 2009). A *Times Union* poll asked fans if ESPN should continue to employ Craig James. To this question, 89 percent suggested that ESPN should not continue to employ James. These poll results are fairly consistent with our assessment that the strategies, particularly those attacking Leach or responding to his statements, were not all that effective. In the end, they did little change the public's generally favorable view of the coach.

As a whole, *antapologia* discourse was much less prominent in the Mike Leach context than it has been in other image repair events already studied. The main reason for this is probably Leach's heavy focus on attacking his accusers as his primary image repair strategy, particularly with the use of character attacks. This lessened the opportunities for a discourse which pragmatically responds to *apologia* strategies. When Mike Leach, Craig James, Tech players, and university administrators responded to each other, they usually did so in the form of counterattacks rather than to comment on the effectiveness of the *apologia*, which is customary with most *antapologia* discourse.

This study adds to our understanding of *kategoria*, *apologia*, and *antapologia* as a three-part speech set, though in many ways it probably complicates the relationship between the three as well. For example, the Mike Leach context illuminates some interesting dilemmas associated with studying several components of the speech set simultaneously. First, there is usually one individual or organization at the forefront of public scrutiny. We can easily follow who exactly made the big mistake, who is criticizing them, and what statements they make in their defense. In the context in focus, there are attacks leveled against a range of individuals and it can be difficult to monitor the attacks issued by all involved. Once we do, we look at the subsequent defenses offered in this context and we see the *apologia* strategy of attacking the accuser emerge as the most utilized. This blurs the line between attack and *apologia* because both stages involve heavy amounts of attack discourse. Clearly, the stages of an apologetic situation do not unfold in a linear fashion. Future research should examine these various stages in order to identify how the three parts of the speech set mutually influence each other. The attack provides clues about the rhetorical exigencies constraining a person accused of wrongdoing and the *antapologia* provides clues about how well the individual dealt with those various constraints. In Mike Leach's case, he responded to criticism by going on the attack. We suggest that an analysis of his strategy is utterly incomplete when we ignore the discourse preceding it and the discourse that followed it.

REFERENCES

Benoit, W. L. (1995) *Accounts, excuses and apologies: A theory of image restoration strategies*. Albany: State University of New York Press.
Benoit, W. L. (1997). Hugh Grant's image restoration discourse: An actor apologizes. *Communication Quarterly*, 45, 251-268.
Benoit, W. L., & Brinson, S. L. (1994). AT&T: "Apologies are not enough." *Communication Quarterly*, 42, 75-88.
Benoit, W. L., & Hanczor, R. S. (1994). The Tonya Harding controversy: An analysis of image restoration strategies. *Communication Quarterly*, 42, 416-433.
Benoit, W. L., & Dorries, B. (1996). *Dateline NBC*'s persuasive attack on Wal-Mart. *Communication Quarterly*, 44, 463-477.
Benoit, W. L., & Harthcock, A. (1999). Attacking the tobacco industry: A rhetorical analysis of advertisements by the campaign for tobacco-free kids. *Southern Communication Journal*, 65, 66-81.
Benoit, W. L., & Wells, W. T. (1996). *Candidates in conflict: Persuasive attack and defense in the 1992 presidential debates*. Tuscaloosa: University of Alabama Press.
Carlin, J. (2010, January 3). AD: Hiring process will be fairly fast. ESPN.com.
Carver, L. G. (2009a, December 30). Tech fires Leach; stiff legal fight vowed. *Lubbock Avalanche-Journal* [online].
Carver, L. G. (2009b, December 31). Pending Leach legal battle likely to be settled out of court. *Lubbock Avalanche-Journal* [online].
Carver, L. G. (2010, January 9). Leach lawsuit claims fraud, defamation. *Lubbock Avalanche-Journal* [online].
Durrett, R. (2009, December 30). Leach's players were prepared for this. ESPN.com.
Leach fired short of Tech's bowl game (2009, December 30). ESPN.com.
Heider, F. (1958). *The psychology of interpersonal relations*. New York: Wiley.
Husselbee, P. H., & Stein, K. A. (2010). Tiger Woods' apology and newspapers' responses: A study of journalistic *antapologia*. Paper presented at the AEJMC conference, Denver, Colorado.
Jamieson, K. H. (1992). *Dirty politics: Deception, distraction, and democracy*. New York: Oxford University Press.
Kruse, N. W. (1977). Motivational factors in non-denial *apologia*.*Central States Speech Journal*, 28, 13-23.
Kruse, N. W. (1981a). *Apologia* in team sport. *Quarterly Journal of Speech*, 67, 270-283.
Kruse, N. W. (1981b). The scope of apologetic discourse: Establishing generic parameters. *Southern Speech Communication Journal*, 46, 278-291.
Leach anticipates firing soon (2009, December 29). ESPN.com.
Leach fired short of Tech's bowl game (2009, December 30). ESPN.com.
Maisel, I. (2009, December 30). No winners in Leach firing. ESPN.com.
Mcgowan, M. (2010, January 10). Hance denies having problem with Leach prior to James incident. *Lubbock Avalanche-Journal* [online].
Pfau, M., Kenski, H. C., Nitz, M., & Sorenson, J. (1990). Efficacy of inoculation strategies in promoting resistance to political attack messages: Application to direct mail. *Communication Monographs*, 57, 25-43.
Pomerantz, (1978). Attributions of responsibility: Blamings. *Sociology*, 12, 115-121.
Rangel, E. (2010, January 15). James says family has no regrets. *Lubbock Avalanche-Journal* [online].
Riley offers support to James (2009, December 31). ESPN.com.
Ryan, H. R. (1982). *Kategoria* and *apologia*: On their rhetorical criticism as a speech set. *Quarterly Journal of Speech*, 68, 256-261.
Schad, J. (2009, December 28). Leach suspended after player complaint. ESPN.com.
Schad, J. (December 30, 2009). Leach anticipates firing soon. ESPN. Retrieved on May 25, 2010 from: http://sports.espn.go.com/ncf/bowls09/news/story?id=4779341

Schad, J. (December 31, 2009). Leach fired short of Tech's bowl game. ESPN. Retreived on May 24, 2010 from: http://sports.espn.go.com/ncf/bowls09/news/story?id=4781981

Schlabach, M. (2009, December 31). Trainer says James was monitored. ESPN.com.

Stein, K. A. (2008). *Apologia, Antapologia* and the 1960 Soviet U-2 Spy Plane incident. *Communication Studies*, 59, 19-34.

Stein, K. A., Turman, P. D., & Barton, M. H. (2008). Understanding the voice of the fan: *Apologia, Antapologia*, and the 2006 World Cup Controversy. In L. W. Hugenberg, P. M. Haridakis, & A. C. Earnhardt (Eds). *Sports Mania: Essays on Fandom and the Media in the 21st Century* (pp. 86-102). Jefferson, NC: McFarland.

Suit alleges phone calls by James' father (2010, January 15). ESPN.com.

Tech intended to soil reputation (2010, January 8). ESPN.com.

Tech suspends Leach after complaint (2009, December 29). *Lubbock Avalanche-Journal* [online].

Upton, J., & Wieberg, S. (November 16, 2006). Contracts for college coaches cover more than salaries. *USA Today*. Retrieved on May 25, 2010 from: http://www.usatoday.com/sports/college/football/2006-11-16-coaches-salaries-cover_x.htm

Ware, B. L., & Linkugel, W. A. (1973). They spoke in defense of themselves: On the generic criticism of *apologia*. *Quarterly Journal of Speech*, 59, 273-283.

Williams, D. (2010a, January 2). Leach takes aim at Jameses, Texas Tech in ESPN interview. *Lubbock Avalanche-Journal* [online].

Williams, D. (2010b, January 3). Doctor, trainer say Leach mistreated James. *Lubbock Avalanche-Journal* [online].

Chapter Thirteen

How Bobby Knight Changed His "Bad Boy" Image to Become a Media Darling

Ric Jensen, Ashland University

BOBBY KNIGHT'S TUMULTUOUS CAREER

In more than twenty-nine seasons as the head men's basketball coach at the University of Indiana, Robert Montgomery "Bobby" Knight won 902 games (more than any other Division I coach), eleven Big Ten Conference championships, and three national championships. However, his tenure at Indiana University was tainted by his repeated behavioral problems on and off the court. Some of the major incidents include the following events:

- In 1979, Knight was involved in an altercation with a policeman in Puerto Rico while he was coaching the USA team in the Pan American Games (Rhoden, 2009).
- During the 1991 Final Four, Knight dumped a Louisiana State University fan into a garbage can, saying the man had cursed him. The university offered a statement saying it regretted the coach's actions (Rhoden, 2009).
- In 1985, Knight tossed a chair across the court during a game against Purdue to protest a referee's call (Wieberg, 2006).
- During a 1988 interview with reporter Connie Chung of CBS News, Knight compared getting blown out of a basketball game to being raped, saying, "If it's inevitable, you may as well sit back and enjoy it" (Balko, 2004).
- In 1997, Knight grabbed Hoosier guard Neil Reed by the throat during practice. Knight denied choking Reed until CNN broadcast a video showing the coach with his hand around Reed's neck.

- In 2000, IU freshman Ken Harvey saw the coach on campus and shouted "Hey, what's up, Knight?" Harvey alleged that Knight yanked his arm and yelled at him. That incident led IU President Myles Brand to fire Knight in 2000 for "a pattern of uncivil, defiant and unacceptable behavior" (Hamel and Evans, 2008). However, Knight was so popular that the student body protested and Brand had to seek police protection (Tyrrell, 2009). Players, assistant coaches, and fans rushed to Knight's defense (Strauss, Hutchens and Walton, 2009).

In 2001, Knight left Indiana to become the head coach at Texas Tech University. Knight was hired because of his reputation to coach competitive teams, to graduate student-athletes without getting into trouble with the National Collegiate Athletic Association (NCAA), to sell tickets and increase athletic fundraising (Sweany, 2001). However, anger management problems followed the coach as he moved to Lubbock, including the following incidents:

- A Texas Tech student leading on-campus tours cautioned visitors about what they should do if they encountered Knight on the way. She said, "Don't take his picture; just remain calm" (Sweany, 2001).
- In 2004, Texas Tech University chancellor David Smith approached Knight at a salad bar in Lubbock and told the coach he had been doing a very good job. Knight responded by snapping back at Smith and later confronted him in the parking lot. Apparently, Knight took Smith's comments as inferring that he had only been doing a good job coaching "lately" (Vecsey, 2004).
- During a 2006 game, Knight appeared to have slapped sophomore Michael Prince on the chin during a timeout. Some people reacted by suggesting that Knight hit the player; the coach defended his actions by saying he was just trying to get the player's attention so he could teach him and Prince later referred to being slapped as a teaching moment (Evans, 2006). Knight was not disciplined for this incident but it was widely discussed in the media.

In spite of these incidents, Knight enjoyed widespread support when he took the Texas Tech job. For example, most of the Texas Tech students surveyed about how the coach was portrayed in the ESPN reality television show *Knight School* (where a Texas Tech student tries out for the team) said that they had a positive image of the coach (Bichard et al., 2008).

THE GENERAL CHANGES CAREERS AND JOINS THE MEDIA

While at Texas Tech, Knight became the first college basketball coach in the nation to "NASCAR-ize" his wardrobe in 2004 when he wore the patch of a corporate sponsor on one of his sweaters during a game in Dallas. The game was sponsored by O'Reilly Auto Parts, who purchased the rights to sponsor the coach for two seasons. Said Ron Byerly, the vice president of marketing for O'Reilly, "Coach Knight made (the space on his sweater) available to us and we jumped at the opportunity. It's really one of the last places you can put a logo" (Rovell, 2004). Since that time, Knight has pitched such diverse products as Volkswagen, the Guitar Hero video game, and Pizza Hut.

In 2005, ESPN announced that Knight would star in a reality television series titled *Knight School* in which the coach would decide which student would earn a spot on the Texas Tech basketball team. In some ways, Knight's personality (often being volatile, demanding, and profane) was thought to be a big plus in making the series entertaining and highly watched (Sandomir, 2005).

In 2008, Knight was hired by ESPN as a color commentator and analyst for its college basketball games. Although several media critics thought it was ironic that Knight joined forces with journalists he was routinely at odds with, Charles Barkley (a college basketball star who now analyzes games for TNT) suggested Knight's hiring might work. He said Knight "Can't just do x's and o's. . . . That ain't no fun for the fans. I think he has a sense of humor and it's just a matter of whether he's going to open up. The biggest key for Coach Knight is will he let his personality show" (Deitsch, 2008). As Sandomir (2008) commented, "People (were) betting when he'd explode on the air." By 2010, Knight was being praised for his ability to comment on the game as a teacher who could explain to viewers the strategies and techniques used in games in an entertaining way (Saunders, 2010).

A BACKGROUND INTO IMAGE RESTORATION STRATEGY

William Benoit developed some of the most landmark theories about image restoration in 1995. According to Benoit (1995), people who view their reputation as being threatened can take any one of several actions, including some or all of the following:

• Denying that an undesirable act occurred or shifting the blame.
• Evading responsibility for the act (e.g., the victim was provoked, acted with good intentions, or claiming an accident occurred).

- Reducing the offensiveness of the act by using such strategies as bolstering (enhancing public approval for the guilty party), minimizing the consequences of the act, transcendence (placing the act in a broader and more
  favorable context), attacking the accuser, and compensating those who
  were harmed.
- Correcting the action by fixing the problem and promising not to repeat
  the problem.
- Employing a strategy of mortification, in which one admits responsibility
  for the wrongful act, expresses regret, and asks for forgiveness.

Once an image crisis has occurred that may damage one's reputation, how
should public relations managers respond? Coombs (2007) suggests the first
step is to respond quickly, accurately, and consistently. There is an urgent
need for organizations to get their message in front of the media first because
an information vacuum may arise if you fail to effectively communicate in a
timely manner. Coombs suggests the second step should be to make sure
your organization is expressing concern and sympathy for any victims of the
crisis. To repair the crisis, Coombs suggests that organizations should determine if factors exist that might intensify the crisis, including the extent to
which the organization has a history of similar crises or has a negative poor
reputation. In these cases, more public relations work may need to be done to
reassure victims that the organization is truly trying to change its behavior.

Apologia is a concept related to image restoration in which individuals
attempt to disassociate or distance themselves from a problem they helped
create. Hearit (2001) describes the steps of *apologia* as denial, counterattack,
differentiation, apology and legal remedies. One specific type of *apologia* is
the rhetoric of atonement; it is used once a person has caused harm that
cannot be denied, justified, or transcended. Stages of atonement rhetoric
include confessing the act, committing to a change of heart where this behavior will not recur, realizing that some good may come out of this bad action,
and public statements wherein the guilty party expresses genuine remorse or
sorrow for those who may have been harmed.

In order to determine the extent that a potential crisis might affect an
organization's image and which response strategies might be most appropriate, Wilson, Stavros, and Westberg (2010) suggest that incidents should be
grouped into a typology. Using this framework, public relations managers
can discern between accidents (unintentional events occurring inside the organization), transgressions (intentional actions that occur inside the company), and faux pas (unintentional events that occur outside the organization).
Each of these occurrences may require a different image restoration strategy.

Which image restoration strategy might be most effective? A 2009 study
by Dardis and Haigh suggests that rhetorical strategies to reduce the offensiveness of the act consistently outperformed other techniques, such as deny-

ing or evading responsibility. In other words, it's essential that an organization publicly acknowledge it is sorry such actions occurred and that it cares about the welfare of those who may have been hurt. After the Philip Morris tobacco company found that its image had been severely damaged by allegations the firm had not honestly communicated the adverse health effects of smoking, the company developed an image restoration campaign using bolstering and mortification strategies that highlighted its good deeds and how its employees were working to make a difference and later a public relations program to reinforce the health risks of smoking (Sczczypka et al., 2007).

HOW IMAGE REPAIR STRATEGY HAS BEEN APPLIED TO SPORTS

The appropriate role for public relations professionals to play in situations where athletes have risked damaging their reputations is still evolving. In many instances, the extent to which amateur and professional athletes have utilized image repair strategy has been analyzed in case studies.

While National Football League player Terrell Owens was in the process of negotiating a new contract with the Philadelphia Eagles, he became sullen with the press, belligerent with his coaches, and vocally critical of his quarterback. After he was deactivated by the Eagles, Owens and his agent attempted to repair his damaged reputation with a press conference. However, Brazeal (2008) writes that Owens's strategy was unsuccessful because he refused to fully acknowledge his blame in the conflict.

Major League Baseball had to repair its image after congressional hearings investigated the alleged use of steroids and human growth hormone by some of the game's most respected players. According to Haigh (2008), Barry Bonds, Rafael Palmeiro and Gary Sheffield applied some aspects of Benoit's image restoration strategy, but for the most part they did not apologize for their actions. As a result, their image repair efforts were not successful.

Two recent public relations crises affected professional car racing. In one case, NASCAR stock car driver Tony Stewart attacked a photographer following a 2002 race. Because there was no possibility of denying what Stewart had done or justifying his actions, Stewart and NASCAR treated the incident as a transgression or a sin that needed to be atoned for by the driver. Stewart took great pains to admit that he had anger management issues, was seeking treatment, and hoped to change his behavior (Jermone, 2008). In the other case, Formula One drivers running in the Grand Prix event at the Indianapolis Motor Speedway in 2005 were besieged by problems with tires that wore rapidly and disintegrated. As this crisis grew, the company that provided the tires (Michelin), the sport's governing body, and the corporation that runs the races (Formula One Management) each developed public relations strategies to restore their image. Pfahl and Bates (2008) suggest that each of these distinct stakeholder groups developed their own PR strategy, rather than working together to protect the brand of Formula One racing. As a result, each of the organizations shifted the blame and the messages which were communicated were fractured because of infighting between the groups.

Duke University's response to allegations of rape by members of its lacrosse team provides a landmark cases in how a university tried to manage a crisis. In 2006, members of the all-white Duke lacrosse team were accused of beating, strangling, and raping an African-American female exotic dancer they had hired. Three days after the incident was reported, police went to the scene of the party and searched for DNA evidence. Before the players went to trial, local district attorney Mike Nifong stated "I feel pretty confident a rape occurred." Ultimately, two Duke players were indicted and the university responded to the scandal by canceling the team's season. Throughout this controversy, Duke president Richard Brodhead took personal leadership and became the university's main spokesman who would respond to the crisis. He sent a letter to the entire Duke community to announce that external committees were being established to examine the actions of the lacrosse team, and how the university administration responded. Broadhead formed a working group between members of the university, towns in the region, and key stakeholders that was charged with developing recommendations about how to resolve this situation and to keep it from recurring. In analyzing how this crisis was managed, Fortunato (2008) suggests that Duke's emphasis on persuasive advocacy and getting its message out in front of the media and on building relationships throughout the community were elements in making this effort succeed.

The multitude of ways in which athletes can damage their image when holding out for a new contract were discussed in an article by Bishop (2009). Bishop chronicled how the holdout of Cleveland Browns tight end Kellen Winslow, Jr., was covered by the mass media. At various times in the negotiations, Winslow was portrayed as being greedy and selfish, a petulant child, an outsider who didn't care about the needs of the team, and as having temper tantrums. Each of these had the potential to damage the positive image a professional athlete had worked so hard to create over many years.

In Australia, several ethical and moral scandals occurred during the early 2000s involving professional rugby and Australian Rules Football (ARF) players, ranging from driving while intoxicated to gambling to on- and off-the-field violence. Wilson, Stavros, and Westberg (2008) examined these incidents with the goal of determining how such public relations fiascos may affect sponsors. They suggest that the most important way to offset such crises is to anticipate that these incidents may occur. If a crisis does hit, organizations must communicate with sponsors and other key stakeholders, be transparent with the media, and accept responsibility for bad behavior. Another study examined the public relations strategies that were used to help ARF teams repair damaged reputations following a scandal associated with the salary cap. Bruce and Tini (2008) describe how one team used a diversionary public relations strategy to manage an image crisis by admitting the organization acted wrongly while asking that the players and the fans be treated as innocent victims. By shifting responsibility toward team management, and away from players and fans, the club was able to lessen damage to its reputation.

In Denmark, researchers investigated an incident when the coach of one of the elite women's handball teams in that nation took her team off the court in the middle of a match to protest poor officiating. The coach, Anja Andersen, was criticized for actions that represented a serious threat to the reputation of the club. Soon afterward, the coach apologized to the public on television but in doing so, she did not ask for forgiveness from all the parties who were involved. Frandsen and Johansen (2007) suggest that the coach's apology was not fully effective because it did not meet all the standards required in an *apologia* setting.

As a preventive measure, it may be possible to identify the extent to which a potential sports celebrity spokesperson may be likely to get into trouble and cause a public relations nightmare. Freberg (2008) suggests there may be certain traits that could identify a high-risk sports celebrity, including a lack of empathy and a history of not having shown remorse. Perhaps sports teams and sponsors could use this type of screening to avoid damaging reputations that later have to be restored. Summers and Morgan (2008) suggest that organizations must honestly and transparently acknowledge mistakes before trying to repair relationships with fans and other publics. This is especially critical if the organization has a high profile and if the crisis is directly related to the sport and not an off-the-field issue.

APPLYING IMAGE RESTORATION THEORY TO BOBBY KNIGHT

This chapter will examine three distinct events that mark the career of Bobby Knight: a) How he reacted after he was disciplined and later fired by Indiana University; b) How he reacted after he hit Texas Tech player Michael Prince on the chin and later had an vocal disagreement with the chancellor; and c) How he has transitioned from coaching to become a commentator for ESPN and a corporate pitchman.

In 1997, Knight allegedly choked player Neil Reed during practice. CNN broadcasted a report about these allegations in 2000. Knight initially denied the charge, but on March 14, 2000, CNN broadcast a tape of a Hoosiers practice from 1997 that showed the coach with his hand around Reed's neck (Rhoden, 2009). Knight later claimed in his autobiography that the video actually exonerates him and demonstrates he did not choke Reed (Anderson, 2002). On May 15, IU president Myles Brand stated he would have "no tolerance" for any more transgressions by the coach as a condition for keeping his job. A few days before the IU Board of Trustees met to consider if he should be fired, Knight issued a written apology in which he admitted to having problems with his temper and promised to mend his ways. In response, Knight was ordered to pay a $30,000 fine, issue a general apology for his actions, and to personally apologize to a secretary he had a thrown a vase at (Tresniowski, 2000). On September 8, 2000, IU freshman Ken Harvey saw the coach on campus and shouted, "Hey, what's up, Knight?" Harvey claimed that Knight yanked his arm and yelled at him. Knight admitted putting his hand on the student's arm and lecturing him on civility, but denied that he was rough or raised his voice. That incident led IU president Myles Brand to fire Knight during a widely televised television news conference on September 10, 2000, for a pattern of uncivil, defiant, hostile, and unacceptable behavior that included making inflammatory comments about IU officials, as well as gross insubordination and acting disrespectfully to alumni (Hamel and Evans, 2008). Brand seemed to be especially troubled by the fact that Knight did not honor his pledge to more fully live within the university's rules after he apologized. Brand said, "These actions . . . make clear that coach Knight has no desire to, contrary to what he personally promised me, to live within the zero-tolerance guidelines we set out" (Strauss, Hutchens and Walton, 2009).

However, Knight was so popular that many students protested later that day, some threatening Harvey by printing posters that said "Wanted: Dead" next to his photo, and Brand had to seek police protection (Tresniowski, 2000). That evening, Knight spoke at the IU Assembly Hall and promised "To tell my side of this thing" (Tresniowski, 2000). On September 11, Knight called a news conference (without telling Brand beforehand) in which he diagrammed the encounter on a chalkboard and denied handling the student roughly or cursing at him. On September 12, Knight appeared on ESPN where he accused Indiana University officials of distorting the truth. Dane Fife, one of his loyal players, agreed that Knight had been victimized by IU, saying, "I think he's probably glad to leave the university they way they've treated him. University officials have lied to him and deceived him" (Strauss, Hutchens, and Walton, 2009). Upon leaving IU, Silverthorne (2006) suggests that Knight was unrepentant in his behavior and unwilling to change his behavior.

The trials Bobby Knight endured because of his temper followed him to Texas Tech. In 2004, Texas Tech university chancellor David Smith approached Knight at a salad bar in Lubbock and told the coach he had been doing a very good job. Knight responded by snapping back at Smith and later confronted him in the parking lot. Apparently, Knight took Smith's comments as inferring that he had only been doing a good job coaching "lately" (Vecsey, 2004). After the incident, Texas Tech initially responded by choosing to suspend the coach. However, after Knight provided his side of the story to the school's Board of Regents claiming that he didn't instigate the confrontation, the coach was reprimanded. During a 2006 home game, Knight appeared to slap sophomore Michael Prince on the chin during a timeout. Knight explained that Prince's head was down when the coach tried to speak with him to offer encouragement. "I flipped his chin up and told him to look me right in the eye so he could do the job we want," Knight said. "If that's an issue then I'm living in the wrong country" (Katz, 2006). Prince later referred to being slapped as a teaching moment in which Knight reassured him to not be afraid of making mistakes (Evans, 2006). Knight was not disciplined for this incident.

After the public relations fiascos that Knight became embroiled in at Texas Tech, one might logically assume that the coach would be treated as some type of pariah that the mass media would scorn or avoid. In fact, the opposite occurred. Sports giant ESPN and the fans who watch it couldn't get enough of seeing Bobby Knight on the air and wondering how the volatile coach might react or what he might say next. While coaching at Texas Tech, Knight began hosting a reality TV show on ESPN titled *Knight School* that first aired in 2005. In 2008, he joined ESPN as a color analyst and commentator. In general, Knight's work as a commentator has been praised for being honest, refreshing and insightful—some of the same character traits that may have gotten him into trouble at IU and Texas Tech (Deitsch, 2008; Sandomir, 2005). Shortly before working for ESPN, Knight had begun a new career as a pitchman for several companies while coaching at Texas Tech, going so far as to wear an auto parts company logo on his sweater during games (Rovell, 2004; Sweany, 2001; Saunders, 2010). This demonstrated that despite his many temper tantrums, there was something about Bobby Knight's personality that made him appealing to corporations and advertisers.

CONCLUSION

In sum, the lesson of public relations travails of Bobby Knight seems to be that it can be very difficult for someone to change their behavior over the long term if they firmly believe that the people they have to deal with are constantly out to get them. In Bobby Knight's case, it appears as though he was always wary that his bosses, alumni, and most especially the media were conspiring to get him in trouble. George Vecsey offered this interesting insight into Knight's persona in 2004. "Knight has reached the point that poor, addled Billy Martin reached in his later years. Even when he was trying to behave himself, Martin was the target of every marshmallow salesman who wanted to engage him. For Knight, there is a perceived insult at every salad bar." Richard Sandomir (2008) quoted Knight as saying, "I have probably lost my temper a lot less than most people who've been in my profession. I didn't create these images."

In a similar way, the Bobby Knight story also has to be viewed through the lens of how the coach felt he could be obliged to satisfy some people (his coaching staff, his players) while at the same time ignoring any need to be responsible to the media and those who hired him. Chris Suellentrop wrote that Knight doesn't seem to realize that he's not just a coach; instead, he represents the face of the university to many constituencies. He wrote, "Knight idolizes men like Vince Lombardi and Ted Williams, who carried themselves with masculine authority and inner arrogance, but it's Knight's outer arrogance that gets him in trouble. A college coach, especially one as successful as Knight, is more than a mentor to the players on the team. He's the face of the university and a role model for every student." Similarly, a large part of the problem may stem from the fact that Knight believes he is accountable only to the players and coaches who work with him—not to the public or certainly not to the media. In 2006, Joe Drape quoted Knight as saying, "You don't find any kid who's ever played for me or any coach who's coached with me saying (negative things). They are who I'm answerable to. I've done what I thought I had to do, and haven't worried what other people think" (Drape, 2006).

In other words, I don't doubt that Knight tried to sincerely apologize for some of his bad actions. He admitted to having anger management issues and at times gave lip service to the idea he would reform his behavior. However, in some cases (especially his apology after choking Indiana player Neil Reed during practice), the apologies seem insincere and appear as though they were meant only to help the coach save his job.

Knight's image problems also show that there are inherent dangers when leaders demand behavior from others that they are not willing to abide by themselves. Columnist Mark Starr commented in 2008, "To the extent that Knight's tale rises to the level of tragedy, it is because he was incapable of meeting the high standards he demanded of others. And he refused to take responsibility for his failures of temperament, casting blame scattershot and pointing fingers at pretty much everyone but himself. It was so sad, even pathetic, to see a man of such talent and breadth cast himself as the eternal victim—of idiot bureaucrats, of incompetent refs, and of unscrupulous reporters." In a similar vein, Alex Tresniowski wrote in 2000 that "Knight refused to do the very thing that may have saved his IU job had he done it earlier—examine his own behavior in the same unforgiving light in which he chose to view the conduct of others. Finally, it seems, Knight's demise was inevitable because he couldn't admit he had a problem."

Ultimately, in situations like these, an organization has to consider the liabilities of hiring a leader who may be incapable of following the standards of good behavior. Columnist Brian Sweany wrote in 2001 about the potential public relations backlash that Texas Tech might encounter if Knight's volatile temper erupted again, writing, "The university has far more to lose than Knight does. Its credibility is at stake and writers all across the country are just waiting to make Lubbock the punch line in the latest round of Bobby Knight jokes."

Finally, a cautionary tale must be made about how Bobby Knight has applied the principle of apologizing for his misdeeds. Knight's mode of operation often seems to consist of first denying that a problem exists, then apologizing for wrongdoing if and when the facts are presented, and later acting without remorse and reengaging in the same ill-thought-out actions that got him in trouble in the first place.

Although this may add to some of the charm of Coach Knight as a spontaneous and intriguing personality because you never know what Bobby Knight may do, it may likely cause grief for those who have to supervise the coach, work with him, or who have a stake in the various publics who might be adversely affected.

REFERENCES

Alper, J. (2009, March 30). Bobby Knight: Guitar Hero. *NBC New York*. Retrieved May 15, 2010 at http://www.nbcnewyork.com/news/sports/Bobby-Knight-Guitar-Hero.html.

Anderson, D. (2002, March 10). Bob Knight delivers his rebuttal to Indiana in his autobiography. *The New York Times*. Retrieved May 15, 2010 at http://www.nytimes.com/2002/03/10/sports/sports-times-bob-knight-delivers-his-rebuttal-indiana-his-autobiography.html?fta=y

Balko, R. (2004, June 17). Ambushed athletes make great news. *FoxNews*. Retrieved May 15, 2010 at http://www.foxnews.com/story/0,2933,122891,00.html

Benoit, W. (1995). *Accounts, excuses, apologies: A typology of image restoration strategies.* Albany: State University of New York Press.

Bichard, S., McElroy, M., Durham, A., Goode, L., Wooten, A., Tichenor, J., Winegar, S., McCallister, C., and Amerson, K. (2008). The difference between day and Knight: Reality television and the framing of Bobby Knight. *Southwestern Communication Journal*, 69-83.

Bishop, R. (2009). It hurts the team even more: Differences in coverage by sports journalists of white and African-American athletes who engage in contract holdouts. *The Journal of Sports Media*, 4 (1): 55-84.

Brazeal, L. (2008). The image repair strategies of Terrell Owens. *Public Relations Review*, 34: 145-150.

Bruce, T., and Tini, T. (2008). Unique crisis response strategies in sports public relations: Rugby League and the case for diversion. *Public Relations Review*, 34: 108-115.

Coombs, W. (2007). *Crisis Management and Communications*. Gainesville, FL: Institute for Public Relations.

Dardis, F., and Haigh, M. (2009). Prescribing versus describing: Testing image restoration strategies in a crisis situation. *Corporate Communications: An International Journal*, 14 (1): 101-118.

Deitsch, R. (2008, March 3). Long disdainful of the press, Bob Knight joins ESPN. *Sports Illustrated*. Retrieved May 15, 2010 at http://sportsillustrated.cnn.com/2008/writers/richard_deitsch/02/28/knight.espn/index.html.

Drape, J. (2006, December 28). Closing in on history, Knight remains unchanged. *The New York Times*. Retrieved May 15, 2010, at http://www.nytimes.com/2006/12/28/sports/ncaabasketball/28knight.html

Evans, T. (2006, November 16). Knight raises chin and holds his head high. *The New York Times*. Retrieved May 15, 2010, at http://www.nytimes.com/2006/11/15/sports/ncaabasketball/15knight.html

Fortunato, J. (2008). Restoring a reputation: The Duke University lacrosse scandal. *Public Relations Review*, 34: 116-123.

Frandsen, F., and Johansen, W. (2007). The apology of a sports icon: Crisis communication and apologetic ethics. *Hermes*, 38: 85-103.

Freberg, K. 2008. Perceptions of sport celebrities among college students: Are high-risk sport celebrity endorsers more negative perceived than low-risk sport celebrity endorsers? In K. Yamamura (Ed.), *Proceedings of the 11th Annual International Public Relations Conference* Coral Gables, Fl: Institute of Public Relations, 190-206.

Haigh, M. (2008). The cream, the clear, BALCO, and baseball. *The Journal of Sports Media*, 3 (2): 1-24.

Hearit, R. (2001). Corporate apologia: When an organization speaks in defense of itself. In R. Hearit (Ed.), *Handbook of Public Relations*. Thousand Oaks, Calif: Sage Publications, Inc.

Jerome, A. (2008). Toward prescription: Testing the rhetoric of atonement's applicability in the athletic arena. *Public Relations Review*, 34: 124-134.

Katz, A. (2006, November 14). Knight: I didn't do anything wrong, would do it again. *ESPN*. Retrieved May 15, 2010 at http://sports.espn.go.com/ncb/news/story?id=2661787

Pfahl, M., and Bates, B. (2008). This is not a race, this is a farce: Formula One and the Indianapolis Speedway tire crisis. *Public Relations Review*, 34: 135-144.

Rhoden, W. (2009, December 21). There's more than one way to lack integrity. *The New York Times*. Retrieved May 15, 2010, at http://www.nytimes.com/2009/12/21/sports/ncaabasketball/21rhoden.html.

Rovell, D. (2004, January 8). Exposure for coaches finally adds up. *ESPN*. Retrieved May 15, 2010, at http://espn.go.com/sportsbusiness/s/2004/0108/1703483.html.

Sandomir, R. (2005, August 9). Coming soon: Bob Knight the reality star. *The New York Times*. Retrieved May 15, 2010, at http://www.nytimes.com/2005/08/09/sports/ncaabasketball/09sandomir.html.

Sandomir, R. (2008, March 29). In ESPN's studio, Knight remains in command. *The New York Times*. Retrieved May 14, 2010, at http://www.nytimes.com/2008/03/29/sports/ncaabasketball/29sandomir.html.

Saunders, D. (2010, March 15). Bob Knight impresses as basketball analyst. *The Denver Post*. Retrieved May 15, 2010, at http://www.denverpost.com/colleges/ci_14676150.

Sczczypka, G., Wakefield, M., Emery, S., Terry-McElrath, Y., Flay, B.Starr, M., and Chaloupka, F. (2007). Working to make an image: An analysis of three Philip Morris corporate image media campaigns. *Tobacco Control*, 16: 344-350.

Silverthorne, S. (2006, August 14). On managing with Bobby Knight and Coach K. Harvard Business School Cases. Retrieved May 15, 2010, at http://hbswk.hbs.edu/item/5464.html.

Starr, M. (2008, February 21). A Knight's story: Forget about a return engagement in Bloomington. Indiana U. has had all the embarrassments it can stand. *Newsweek*. Retrieved May 15, 2010, at http://www.newsweek.com/id/114373.

Strauss, J., Hutchens, T., and Walton, R. (2009, September 16). Brand's defining moment: Firing Bobby Knight. *The Indianapolis Star*. Retrieved May 15, 2010, at http://www.indy.com/posts/brand-s-defining-moment-firing-bob-knight.

Suellentrop, C. (2002, March 15). Bob Knight: It's ok if you hate him because he hates himself, too. *Slate.* Retrieved May 15, 2010 at http://www.slate.com/id/2063218.

Summers, J., and Morgan, M. (2008). More than just the media: Considering the role of public relations in the creation of sporting celebrity and the management of fan expectations. *Public Relations Review*, 34: 176-182.

Sweany, B. (2001, June 1). The cash machine: Texas Tech hired Bobby Knight for one reason, to make money. *Texas Monthly.* Retrieved May 15, 2010, at http://www.texasmonthly.com/2001-06-01/sports.php.

Thamel, P., and Evans, T. (2008, February 5). Bob Knight resigns as coach of Texas Tech, *The New York Times*. Retrieved May 15, 2010, at http://www.nytimes.com/2008/02/05/sports/ncaabasketball/05knight.html.

Tresniowski, A. (2000, September 25). Flaming out: Consumed by his own anger, Indiana coach Bobby Knight gets himself fired. *People.* Retrieved May 15, 2010, at http://www.people.com/people/archive/article/0,,20132393,00.html.

Tyrell, R. (2009, December 17). The politically correct and altercationists anonymous. *The American Spectator*. Retrieved May 15, 2010, at http://spectator.org/archives/2009/12/17/the-politically-correct-and-al.

Vecsey, G. (2004, February 4). At salad bar with Knight, praise only the cherry tomatoes. *The New York Times*. Retrieved May 15, 2010, at http://www.nytimes.com/2004/02/08/sports/sports-of-the-times-at-salad-bar-with-knight-praise-only-the-cherry-tomatoes.html.

Wieberg, S. (2006, November 28). Knight still standing on his principles. *USA Today.* Retrieved May 15, 2010, at http://www.usatoday.com/sports/soac/2006-11-27-knight_x.htm.

Wilson, B., Stavros, C., and Westberg, K. (2008). Player transgressions and the management of the sport sponsor relationship. *Public Relations Review*, 34: 99-107.

Wilson, B., Stavros, C., and Westberg, K. (2010). A sport crisis typology: establishing a pathway for future research. *International Journal of Sports Marketing and Sponsorship*, 7(1): 21-31.

IV

On-Field Actions

Chapter Fourteen

Belated Remorse: Serena Williams's Image Repair Rhetoric at the 2009 U.S. Open

LeAnn M. Brazeal

INTRODUCTION

Whether or not you follow tennis, it's hard to miss Serena Williams. Serena, along with older sister Venus, has dominated women's tennis for well over a decade. The sisters' powerful style of play has profoundly changed the women's game, and their success continues to provide a strong working-class counterpoint to the country club set of the tennis elite (Parrotta, 2010; Price, 2009). She is unquestionably the best player of her generation, and some might argue the best women's player ever (Tebbutt, 2009). Her various outside interests—fashion, television, business, celebrity—have garnered her fans outside the tennis world and made her "one of the most recognized female athletes ever," mentioned in the same breath as Tiger Woods (Waldstein, 2009). Image is an important part of Williams's life and career, and maintaining favor among fans is certainly an important part of that legacy. As one of the most successful and famous athletes in the world, Williams's public image and efforts to repair it are worthy of study.

Williams faced a tough public relations challenge in the aftermath of an on-court meltdown at the 2009 U.S. Open. After a questionable call at a critical point in her semifinal match, she lashed out at the line judge with threats, profanity, and an aggressive posture. As a result, Williams drew her second code violation of the match, which handed the win to her opponent. Criticism of her on-court behavior began almost immediately, and Williams was forced to defend her actions. This essay examines the image repair rhetoric of Serena Williams, using Benoit's (1995) typology of image repair strategies described earlier in this volume. After providing context for Williams's image repair efforts, I will examine four separate efforts to address the incident, discuss the effectiveness of Williams's rhetoric, and draw implications for sports image repair.

SERENA WILLIAMS'S OUTBURST AT THE 2009 U.S. OPEN

In September 2009, Williams was sitting on top of the world—almost. Despite winning the Australian Open and Wimbledon, two of tennis's four Grand Slam tournaments, she was ranked second in the world behind Russian Dinara Safina. Safina, considered a relatively weak number one player, did not have a single major title to her credit. Instead, she ascended to her place atop the rankings on the strength of two Slam final appearances and three non-Slam titles (Ackert, 2009; Haber, 2009). This hole in Safina's resume did not go unnoticed by Williams, who was vocal in her criticism as the U.S. Open approached (Ackert, 2009). As the defending champion, Williams was determined to add to her trophy collection and prove she was the best female tennis player in the world.

Williams cruised through the early rounds into the quarterfinals, where she defeated Daniela Hantuchova, 6-2, 6-0 (Smith, 2009). But in the semifinals on Saturday, September 12, Williams ran into a formidable opponent in former U.S. Open champion Kim Clijsters of Belgium. Clijsters was playing well, in spite of having just returned to the Women's Tennis Association after a 27-month hiatus. Williams struggled throughout the match, earning a warning from the umpire for smashing her racket after losing the first set (Rey, 2009). Down 5-6 in the second set, Williams was called for a foot fault on second serve that gave Clijsters double match point. Williams turned and unleashed an angry invective at the line judge who had made the call, cursing and brandishing the ball. "You'd better be f----ing right!" Williams is credited with saying. "You don't f----ing know me! I swear to God I'm going to take this ball and shove it in your f---ing throat!" (Price, 2009). The line judge, a small Japanese woman whose name was withheld from the press, appeared intimidated by the larger and more powerful Williams. The tirade continued, and Williams continued to move toward the judge, poking the racket at her for emphasis. It was difficult for anyone outside the immediate vicinity of the judge, including the viewers at home, to decipher exactly what had been said due to the whistling and booing from the crowd. Once Williams had finished and turned to go back to the baseline, the chair umpire called over the line judge for a report. Williams shouted toward the chair umpire as he was speaking to the line judge, and once the line judge had returned to her post, Williams pointed her racket and started again toward the line judge in a threatening manner. The line judge returned to the chair umpire. Tournament referee Brian Earley was called in, and after speaking with the line judge and over Williams's protests, Earley explained to Williams that she would receive a second code violation for unsportsmanlike conduct. This would award Clijsters a point—and the match (Rey, 2009). Resigned to the outcome, Williams approached a confused Clijsters to offer congratulations and a handshake, and then left the court amid a chorus of boos ("Clijsters stuns," 2009; "Serena loses temper," 2009).

Williams's meltdown was instant news. Clips of the confrontation were replayed on network and cable media outlets ranging from ESPN to CNN. Discussion lit up the blogosphere, and there were plenty of people attempting to learn the art of lip-reading in order to transcribe Williams' exact words. Pundits as varied as ESPN's Stephen A. Smith, television psychologist Dr. Phil, and the women of ABC's morning talkfest *The View* weighed in on Williams's rant. By Sunday night, one day after the match, video of the incident had made the "trending topics" list on YouTube with over a half-million clicks ("Officials reviewing," 2009).

Few took Williams's side in the confrontation, and most of her supporters could understand Williams's frustration but not justify her reaction. There was some question as to whether or not the call was correct, and many commentators argued that such minor infractions are simply not called at such a crucial point in the match ("Serena loses," 2009; Tebbutt, 2009). Some believed that her reaction stood out because of the genteel nature of tennis (Siegel, 2009), while others maintained that it was her gender (Bondy, 2009; Killion, 2009) or race. Regardless, high-profile figures in the sport called for contrition (Ford, 2009b; Bondy, 2009).

Ultimately, Williams publicly addressed the incident four times in three days. In order to evaluate the effectiveness of Williams's image repair rhetoric, transcripts and video (when available) of all four public statements were analyzed using Benoit's typology. Of particular interest are the following research questions:

> RQ1: Were Serena Williams's image repair strategies effective?
> RQ2: What role, if any, did the timing of Williams's apology play in the effectiveness of her image repair rhetoric?

In the analysis that follows, each of these questions will be addressed.

ANALYSIS OF WILLIAMS'S IMAGE REPAIR EFFORTS

Williams addressed the incident at the post-match press conference, in two written statements, and at a post-match press conference after her doubles final. All of Williams's attempts at image repair were widely reported throughout the print and television media. This section will examine each of these efforts in turn.

Post-Match Press Conference: Singles Semifinal

Williams's first opportunity to address the incident came almost immediately following the match, in her post-match press conference on September 12 (Williams, 2009a). She appeared remarkably calm in spite of having just had a major confrontation with a line judge and losing the match on the resulting penalty. She seemed resigned to the loss, but unhappy with the call. Williams was understandably reluctant to discuss the incident in detail or repeat what she had said. During the press conference, Williams employed denial, corrective action, and bolstering in order to repair her image. She did not, however, express remorse, instead hinting that she was provoked.

The reporters barely waited until Williams was seated to begin asking for specifics on what she had said to the line judge. She could not deny the incident in a traditional manner, because it had taken place in front of television cameras and a gallery full of witnesses. Instead, Williams employed denial by steadfastly refusing to confirm any specific details of the incident. Rather than claiming the incident did not happen, she denied having any information about the substance of the incident. This strategy did not fool anyone, but it did allow her to avoid repeating what she had said.

Williams enacted this form of denial in two ways. First, she evaded all direct questions about what she had said to the line judge. She did so awkwardly at first, and it appeared that such questions initially took her off guard. For example, the very first question of the press conference asked her what she said, and she replied, "Well, I said something, [and] I guess they gave me a point penalty. Unfortunately, it was on match point." Williams realized answering the question directly would have done even more damage, so she refused to offer up those details to the press.

In addition, Williams also enacted an indirect form of denial by answering questions with questions. When Williams failed to answer the first question directly, the reporters asked again: "What did you say [to the line judge]?" Williams's response was, "What did I say? You didn't hear? Oh." She then shrugged her shoulders, and it was clear that she would not volunteer the information. Similarly, when a reporter asked, "Do you think that the lineswoman had any reason to feel threatened?" Williams answered, "She says she felt threatened? She said this to you?" By answering questions with questions, Williams avoided answering the questions outright and maintained control over the press conference.

Williams stuck with these two strategies for the remainder of the press conference, employing them nearly every time reporters tried to get a direct answer. Later in the press conference, however, Williams was asked, "Did you say something to the linesperson that could be construed as a threat?" She replied, "No, I didn't threaten," which is a traditional denial—and also untrue—but quickly backtracked with, "I didn't say—I don't remember anymore, to be honest." It is clear that Williams recognized that what she said to the line judge was damaging, and knew it would be even more damaging for her to discuss specifics.

After settling into the press conference, Williams seemed to find her rhetorical footing. She focused her answers on the match and eventually gave a stronger answer to the ever-present question about what was said to the line judge. Her new answer hints at corrective action: "I don't think that [it's] necessary for me to speak about that. I've let it go, and I'm trying to better— to, you know, to get—to move on." Again, she refused to confirm specifics, but this time combined the denial strategy with corrective action. Although this instance of corrective action was not as smooth as it might have been, Williams offered a better one later on:

> [I]'m young and I feel like in life everyone has to have experience that they take and that they learn from, and I think that's great that I have an opportunity to still be physically fit, to go several more years and learn from the past. I like to learn from the past, live in the present, and not make the same mistakes in the future.

Interestingly, after Williams alleged she could not remember what was said, she suggested that she might learn from the incident. This theme of personal growth was present in several of her image repair efforts, but it is important to note that Williams's offers of corrective action did not extend to the line judge—she did not offer to meet her, tender a personal apology, and so on. This self-centered approach to corrective action was not as effective as it might have been.

Along with various strategies of denial and corrective action, Williams also engaged in bolstering. Specifically, Williams discussed her passion for all that she does, and how that affects her emotions: "[I] am just a really intense person, and I give 200% in everything I do, whether I'm playing tennis or I am doing something else. I just go for it." We expect athletes to play hard and care about winning, and it seems reasonable that emotional players will get upset during frustrating moments. Since we desire these qualities in our athletes, Williams is turning her weakness into a strength.

Further into the press conference, one of the reporters remarked that she seemed to have let go of her anger very quickly, and Williams jumped at the opportunity to be positive: "I try to be really professional. I think Kim played a wonderful match, and I think I played good, too. . . . If I get hit, I say I got hit, you know. I play by the rules." Williams showed here that she understands, to some degree, the character traits expected of elite tennis players—professionalism, grace, and honesty—and that she does try to exhibit them.

Williams failed to employ one key strategy: mortification. Despite many opportunities, Williams simply would not apologize for her tirade against the line judge. When asked if she regretted losing her temper, she replied, "I haven't really thought about it to have any regrets." Instead, she seemed to feel that her reaction was justified because the line judge made what Williams felt (and what others also suggested) was a bad call at a critical point. Adding fuel to the fire was the fact that she had been called for foot faults several times during the tournament. She explained how this frustrated her: "I haven't been called for a foot fault all year until I got to New York, so maybe when I come to this tournament I have to step two feet back." Williams did not rely on provocation as a primary strategy, but it does help to explain her lack of mortification. However, the public did not see these foot fault calls as justification for her behavior, and they expected an apology. One reporter tried in vain to offer her an opportunity to apologize:

Q: Do you think the lineswoman deserves an apology?
A: An apology for?
Q: From you.
A: From me?
Q: For the yelling and what you said.
A: Well, how many people yell at linespeople? So I think, you know, if you look at—I don't know. All the people that, you know, kind of yell at linespeople, I think it's—kind of comes sometimes. Players, athletes get frustrated. I don't know how many times I've seen that happen.

From her statements here, it seems that Williams truly felt the lineswoman had made a bad call and deserved to be abused in that manner. Williams also justified her behavior with minimization (players yell at linespeople all the time) and provocation (players get frustrated). She did not address how this justified the profanity and threatening nature of her outburst at the lineswoman, which the public would undoubtedly want to know.

Williams's lack of remorse did not sit well with the public. Though many fans took to the Internet in her defense, Williams did not find the winds of public opinion shifting in her direction after the press conference. Martina Navratilova, though sympathetic, told ESPN she felt Williams had missed an important opportunity to make good in the press conference (Ford, 2009a). Another former U.S. Open champion, Virginia Wade, expressed dismay that

Williams did not take responsibility. Even the *New York Times* weighed in, with an editorial chastising Williams for what the editorial staff called "glib self-forgiveness" and for behaving "as if what had happened on the court affected only her" ("Zen and the art," 2009). Clearly, Williams's efforts to deny, offer corrective action, and bolster her image were not enough.

Written Statements

After much criticism of Williams's initial post-match press conference, she released a written statement through her public relations agency on Sunday, September 13 (Williams, 2009b). That same day, Williams was also fined $10,500 for the two semifinal violations. The following day, she released a second "clarifying" statement just prior to her doubles final with sister Venus (Williams, 2009c). These statements were made available to the press and were posted online. They were widely reported on in the press, and neither was longer than 130 words (Williams, 2009b; Williams 2009c).

In the first statement, Williams continued some of the themes from the press conference. Her primary strategy was bolstering, where she again pointed out that she was showing emotions typical of elite athletes: "Now that I have had time to gain my composure, I can see that . . . in the heat of battle I let my passion and emotion get the better of me and as a result handled the situation poorly." Though this is something of an admission of wrongdoing, it is couched in terms that make her aggression seem more acceptable. She also made it clear that she felt provoked: "I don't agree with the unfair line call." She also hinted vaguely at corrective action: "I look forward to continuing the journey, both professionally and personally, with you all as I move forward and grow from this experience." As in her press conference, Williams did not apologize to anyone, including the line judge, but did thank her fans for understanding that "I am human."

Once again, Williams took criticism for the fact that she did not actually apologize in this initial statement (Rhoden, 2009), and she issued a second statement the following day before her doubles final. In the statement, she finally offered a mortification strategy: "I want to amend my press statement of yesterday, and want to make it clear as possible—I want to sincerely apologize FIRST [*sic*] to the lines woman, Kim Clijsters, the USTA and mostly tennis fans everywhere for my inappropriate outburst." Though the apology was the lead-off sentence of the statement, she also bolstered, with statements such as, "I'm a woman of great pride, faith and integrity, and I admit when I'm wrong." Finally, she ended with another nod toward corrective action with, "[W]e all learn from experiences both good and bad. I will learn and grow from this, and be a better person as a result." Though

Williams clearly employed mortification in this statement, it was met with some skepticism in light of the fact that it took two days for her to apologize (Gagne, 2009; Williams, 2009c).

Post-Match Press Conference: Doubles Final

Despite talk of banning Williams from the tournament ("Officials review-ing," 2009), she was able to continue play in the doubles competition with her sister, Venus. The pair made the doubles final and won in straight sets over reigning champions Liezel Huber and Cara Black (Brown, 2009). The post-match press conference (Williams & Williams, 2009) focused as much on the ongoing drama as on the sisters' victory. As a result, Williams ended up defending both her initial actions and her public statements about them. Williams employed mortification (alone and in combination with other strat-egies), bolstering, corrective action, and provocation. She also reiterated her earlier denial.

Early in the press conference, Williams focused on mortification—but also had to defend the timing and method of her apology. In fact, the very first question of the press conference concerned the 48-hour wait for an actual apology. Williams replied by reciting excerpts from her second written statement: "I wanted to apologize first to the lineswoman, to the USTA, and my fans most of all, and to Kim Clijsters who ended up having such a wonderful tournament. . . . I just really wanted to apologize sincerely." This, of course, was a complete turnaround from her press conference two days earlier, where she refused to acknowledge an apology was necessary.

The reporters did not allow Williams's belated attempts at remorse go unquestioned. First, they raised the issue of her first statement not including an actual apology. Williams attempted to explain why two statements were necessary, if the second statement was not meant to offer the overlooked apology: "I definitely think an apology was warranted. You know, I just felt like the [first statement] was an apology as well. This one, I wanted to make sure that I also congratulated Kim . . . and also to just everyone else [*sic*]." While Williams praised Clijsters and thanked her fans repeatedly, the lines-woman was barely mentioned. Thus, the reporters also raised the issue of a face-to-face apology. When pressed on whether she had attempted to speak directly with the lineswoman, Williams defended her new found remorse with defeasibility: "I have not at all, because I have no information on her. That was definitely something that I really wanted to do." Williams later said that if given the chance, "I would like to give her a big ole hug and let her know that I'm just—just [*sic*] put it all behind us like I have and move on from it." Here, rather than emphasizing the remorse she feels for her actions, Williams emphasized her desire to move on.

Though mortification was probably Williams's most important strategy choice, the strategy she employed most often was bolstering. Early on, she noted that she is "a very prideful person and I'm a very intense person and a very emotional person." Though these qualities were certainly channeled in the wrong direction a few days earlier, Williams highlights them because these same qualities also allow her to be the fiery athlete her fans love. Williams also emphasized her independence and authenticity, which fans also appreciate, by explaining, "I think it's important to be yourself. It's important to express who you are. I'm never gonna . . . not get angry . . . because this is how I am." Here, as in her first press conference, she reminded the audience that these are the qualities they admire.

Interestingly, Williams also revealed that the experience had been humbling for her: "I think any experience can be really humbling, especially this one, per se. I really think that it definitely is [humbling]. I think that if it wasn't, then I would not be able to learn from the past." Williams also bolstered her image by emphasizing her sincerity, explaining, "Most of all, I'm a very sincere person. I wanted to offer my sincere apologies to anyone that I may have offended." Humility and sincerity are character traits critical to a successful apology, and these bolstering statements supported her efforts at mortification.

Another prominent strategy Williams used in her second press conference was corrective action. She did not address making amends with the line judge, but did suggest that she would try to handle such situations differently in the future: "I think the whole point of learning from your mistakes is not to do the same thing. I definitely would, I think, have a more professional way of voicing my opinion." She also quipped, "I want to get another bad line call so I can get more practice and see how I do." Though corrective action was not a new strategy for Williams, this instance marked the first time she mentioned changing a specific behavior.

One last strategy Williams employed was provocation. Though it was not her main emphasis, it still played an important role in her explanations. One of the reporters asked about her written statement's characterization of the foot fault call as "unfair." She responded, "I don't think my foot touched the line in that call." However, this time she was more charitable to the line judge, adding, "Looking back on it, I think the lady did the best she could. She was just doing her job. . . . She was doing her best." This differed from her earlier claims of provocation in that she was sympathetic toward the person who had provoked her anger.

It is also worth noting that Williams continued to claim that she could not remember what she had said to the line judge. However, this final press conference seemed to lay the issue to rest, as much as possible under the circumstances.

DISCUSSION

Serena Williams faced a threat to her image that was largely of her own making. One of the interesting features of Williams's defensive discourse is that it was spread out over a period of time, with slightly different image repair strategies emphasized in each rhetorical effort. Eventually, Williams offered a fairly good defense; however, her "incremental" approach to mortification continued to inflict damage well after the precipitating event. Here, I will evaluate Williams's image repair efforts and discuss implications for sports image repair.

In her first opportunity to address her situation, the post-match press conference, Williams did not choose effective strategies. From the very first question, she was on the defensive, enacting denial by refusing to confirm the specifics of what had been said to the lineswoman, and by answering questions with questions. It was probably wise for Williams to avoid repeating what had been said, as the repetition can inform audience members who may not have heard the first time (Benoit, 1999). However, answering questions with questions is a double-edged sword—while it allows the speaker to maintain control of the conversation and postpone answering an uncomfortable question, it also makes the speaker appear evasive (Litton-Hawes, 1977). Williams certainly appeared evasive, and answered as though she knew full well what she had said was wrong. This creative form of denial was not an effective image repair strategy.

Additionally, Williams refused to employ the one strategy that would likely have defused the controversy right away—mortification. Even when offered opportunities, she snubbed any suggestion that an apology was needed. Instead, she employed strategies of provocation and minimization. In doing so, Williams showed a stunning lack of awareness of how this situation would be perceived by the public. While it may be true that other tennis players throw rackets and yell at linespeople out of frustration, Williams's threatening outburst was in a different league entirely. Despite Williams's assertion, this is not at all common in tennis.

In addition, Williams's refusal to show remorse for her outburst undermined her other strategic efforts, such as bolstering and corrective action. Her gracious treatment of her opponent and claims of professionalism stood at odds with her behavior toward, and failure to apologize to, the line judge. Had Williams chosen to acknowledge guilt and ask for forgiveness, the two critical elements of an effective mortification strategy (Benoit, 1995), she might have been able to repair her image more quickly and successfully.

Williams's next image repair attempt, a brief written statement, merely reinforced the prevailing view that Williams did not accept responsibility and was not sorry. Though she admitted to "handling the situation poorly," she did not use the words "I'm sorry" or "I apologize," and again claimed she was provoked by an "unfair line call." The statement referenced her fans and supporters, but said nothing about the lineswoman. As a result, a second written statement was necessary. Though this statement finally included an apology to the lineswoman, her opponent, and many other people she "may have offended," her apology was much too brief and seemed disingenuous given how long (and how many public statements) it took for her to apologize.

Williams was forced to defend her actions and her previous failed attempts to repair her image in her second post-match press conference. It was in this press conference that Williams was most effective, primarily because she apologized in person and confessed that she did feel one was warranted. She explained that this situation had humbled her, which bolstered her image and made her a more sympathetic figure. Her use of mortification also supported her other strategies, such as bolstering and corrective action. While she still maintained that the foot-fault call was unfair, she softened her criticism by acknowledging that the lineswoman was only doing her job. On the whole, Williams appeared less arrogant and more remorseful in this final attempt to repair her image. However, in spite of this being Williams's best image repair effort to date, the late timing of the apology diminished its impact. Furthermore, because she did not apologize personally to the lineswoman, nor did she "give her a big ole hug," Williams's sincerity can certainly be questioned. If Williams had been truly remorseful, she could have sought out the linesperson and apologized to her directly.

Williams's image repair rhetoric was largely ineffective, due in large part to her refusal to engage in mortification. Instead of immediately acknowledging that her behavior was inappropriate, she initially attempted to justify her outburst by implying she had been provoked. Her lack of remorse also undermined the success of her other image repair strategies, and her belated efforts to apologize made her appear a bit insincere. Williams's rhetoric would have been more effective had she employed mortification at the earliest opportunity. Though this incident will not ruin her career, it will always be a part of her public image.

Several implications can be drawn from Serena Williams's ineffective image repair discourse. First of all, the timing of an apology is critical to its success. Hearit (2006) argues that a failure to apologize right away signals resistance to reconciliation and communicates a lack of concern. Not only did it take two days for Williams to apologize, it also took two written statements and two press conferences before she used the actual words "I'm sorry." Indeed, audiences may have difficulty accepting other image repair strategies until the person who committed the wrongful act offers a sincere apology. Unlike corporations, individuals do not typically risk legal liability by offering an apology, and have much to gain by apologizing (Benoit, 1997; Coombs, 2000).

By waiting, Williams also put herself in the very difficult position of answering for two transgressions—her outburst and her failure to apologize—rather than one. This type of "compounded" threat to one's image is difficult to untangle, and risks creating a cycle of criticism and response that further damages the athlete's image. Such compounding is avoidable if the athlete is capable of immediately recognizing the gravity of the transgression and is willing to ask for advice in dealing with the press. Athletes who are high self-monitors will likely have an easier time with this than low self-monitors (Leone, 2006). As a result, PR professionals should know their clients well and be prepared to step in as needed to avoid prolonging the crisis.

Second, athletes must understand the culture of their particular sport and be willing to embrace its values (Brazeal, 2008). Each sport has its own culture, which has as its foundation certain bedrock values that are prized by fans, athletes, coaches, former players, and others who are involved in the sport. In team sports, these values tend to revolve around the willingness to sacrifice one's self for the good of the team (Kruse, 1981). In individual sports such as golf and tennis, personal integrity, honor, and etiquette are important values. When an athlete has run afoul of these values, it is important to rhetorically reengage them in order to fully reconcile the athlete to the sporting community (Brazeal, 2008). In Williams's case, she might have acknowledged the importance of respect for the officials or admitted that her use of profanity was particularly inappropriate. Making a threat against an official is a grave transgression in any sport (Siegel, 2009), regardless of the race or gender of the athlete (Rhoden, 2009), and Williams needed to reaffirm her commitment to the values of her sport in order to fully overcome the damage done to her image.

Finally, athletes should be firm in their stand against rehashing their failings for the press. Hearit (2006) argues for disclosure of key facts that may influence how the transgressor's actions would be viewed. In corporate apologia, where a wrong may have been committed against a group of people, or where the facts may not be fully known by the victims, this is often quite appropriate. However, there are also instances where a wrongful act was committed against an individual or small group of people, and the details need not be exposed to the general public. In these cases, knowing the nature of the wrongdoing is quite enough. Arguably, the Williams outburst could fall into this category. It was not necessary for the public to know exactly what was said—it was clear to anyone watching that Williams was in the wrong. Instead of offering non-answers and answering questions with questions, which made her appear evasive, Williams should have taken a clear stand: "It's not necessary for me to repeat that. I was wrong, and I'm sorry." Combined with a mortification strategy, a straightforward refusal to answer could dismiss the issue quickly.

In the end, despite Williams's less-than-effective image repair efforts, the Grand Slam Committee, comprised of representatives from all four Grand Slam events, fined Williams $82,500—the largest fine in Grand Slam history—and placed her on probation. Any further incidents at Slam events over the next two seasons would result in a ban from the next year's U.S. Open and raise the fine for the 2009 incident to $175,000 (Clarey, 2009). An important mitigating factor was Williams's record of never before having argued with an official, and there is hope in the tennis community that Williams has learned a valuable lesson from this episode. By the end of 2009, Williams had regained the world's number one ranking, and was celebrating her latest award, the Laureus World Sportswoman of the year.

REFERENCES

Ackert, K. (2009, September 2). Safina manages to win despite Serena's and her own misgivings. *New York Daily News*, p. 52.

Benoit, W. L. (1997). Hugh Grant's image restoration discourse: An actor apologizes. *Communication Quarterly, 45(3),* 251-267.

Benoit, W. L. (1999). Acclaiming, attacking, and defending in Presidential nominating acceptance addresses, 1960-1996. *Quarterly Journal of Speech, 85,* 247-267.

Bondy, F. (2009, September 14). A raging success: Serena's outburst is good for tennis. *New York Daily News,* p. 69.

Coombs, W.T. (2000). Designing post-crisis messages: Lessons for crisis response strategies. *Review of Business, 21(3),* 37-41.

Clarey, C. (2009, December 1). Probation and fine for Serena Williams' tirade. *The New York Times,* p. B16.

Clijsters stuns Serena at U.S. Open. (2009, September 12). Retrieved from http://www.cbsnews.com/stories/2009/09/12/sportsline/main5306343.shtml

Ford, B. D. (2009a, September 14). Serena's breakdown leads to questions. Retrieved from http://sports.espn.go.com/sports/tennis/usopen09/columns/story?columnist=ford_bonnie_d&id=4470853.

Ford, B. D. (2009a, September 15). Serena: 'I want to sincerely apologize.' Retrieved fromhttp://sports.espn.go.com/sports/tennis/usopen09/news/story?id=4472638.

Ford, B. D. (2009b, November 30). Judgment passed on Serena long ago? Retrieved fromhttp://sports.espn.go.com/sports/tennis/columns/story?columnist=ford_bonnie_d&id=4672434.

Gagne, M. (2009, September 14). Serena Williams issues apology for her 'inappropriate outburst' at U.S. Open. Retrieved from http://www.nydailynews.com/sports/more_sports/2009/09/14/2009-09-14_serena_apology.html

Haber, B. (2009, September 2). Serena isn't No. 1, but it isn't unjust. *USA Today*, p. 3C.

Killion, A. (2009). Serena's outburst common among athletes—but not women. Retrieved from http://sportsillustrated.cnn.com/2009/writers/ann_killion/09/15/serena/index.html

Kruse, N.W. (1981). The apologia in team sport. *Quarterly Journal of Speech, 67(3),* 270-283.

Leone, C. (2006). Self-monitoring: Individual differences in orientation to the social world. *Journal of Personality,* 74(3), 633-657.

Officials reviewing Serena's actions. (2009, September 14). Retrieved from http://sports.espn.go.com/sports/tennis/usopen09/news/story?id=4469987.

Perrotta, T. (2010, May 11). Williamses still at tennis' summit. Retrieved from http://espn.go. com/sports/tennis/blog/_/name/tennis/id/5180686/williamses-still-at-tennis-summit.

Rey, J. (2009, September 13). Clijsters' comeback continues after Williams loses cool. Retrieved from http://2009.usopen.org/en_US/news/match_reports/2009-09-13/200909131252819557531.html.

Rhoden, W.C. (2009, September 16). One standard: Over the line is over the line. *The New York Times*, p. B11.

Serena loses temper, then match. (2009, September 13). Retrieved from http://sportsillustrated. cnn.com/2009/tennis/09/13/us.open.serea.clijsters/index.html.

Serena fined 10K for tirade, still being reviewed. (2009, September 14). http://sports.espn.go.com/sports/tennis/usopen09/news/story?id=4469987.

Siegel, R. (2009, September 14). Serena Williams' meltdown may prove costly. *All Things Considered*. [Radio News Program]. Retrieved from Lexis Nexis.

Smith, T. (2009, September 7). Last Williams standing displays no sign of fall. *New York Daily News*, p. 45.

Tebbutt, T. (2009, September 14). Serena Williams/Anatomy of a meltdown. *The Globe and Mail (Canada)*, p. S1.

Waldstein, D. (2009, September 15). Serena Williams adds a doubles title and an apology. *The New York Times*, p. B11.

Williams, S. (2009a). An interview with Serena Williams. Retrieved from http://2009.usopen. org/en_US/news/interviews/2009-09-12/200909121252748398140.html.

Williams, S. (2009b). Serena releases a formal statement, acknowledges that she is 'human." Retrieved from http://www.onthebaseline.com/2009/09/13/serena-williams-releases-a-formal-statement-acknowledges-that-she-is-human/print/.

Williams, S. (2009c). Serena Williams apologizes again—Part II. Retrieved from http://www.tennis-x.com/xblog/2009-09-14/2344.php.

Williams, S. and Williams, V. An interview with Serena and Venus Williams. Retrieved from http://2009.usopen.org/en_US/news/interviews/2009-09-14/200909141252985074812.html.

Zen and the art of the sports cliché. (2009, September 15). *The New York Times*, p. A32.

Chapter Fifteen

Unsports(wo)manlike Conduct: An Image Repair Analysis of Elizabeth Lambert, the University of New Mexico, and the NCAA

Jordan L. Compton, Ohio University

If one passed Elizabeth Lambert on the street, the 5'8" twenty-one year old would not strike fear into the passersby. A quick glance at her athletic profile describes a typical college student who enjoys camping and surfing, is majoring in university studies with a focus on occupational therapy, and her favorite food is tacos ("Player Bio," 2010). However, this women's soccer player for the University of New Mexico Lobos quickly turned into a household name with her violent, aggressive play in a semifinals match in the Mountain West Conference Tournament against Brigham Young University (BYU). The 1-0 match, eventually won by Brigham Young, featured a hard-fought, physical game. It was not the result of the game that made the headlines, however. It was the aggressive play of Elizabeth Lambert, who was seen "committing a series of excessively rough plays, including kicking, tackles, a forearm shiver to the back and yanking BYU forward Kassidy Shumway to the ground by her hair" ("New Mexico player," 2009). This physical play from Lambert created a media firestorm and she soon became an Internet celebrity. Relative (2009) notes, "Lambert's behavior on the soccer field was tantamount to a martial arts/rugby blend, wholly oblivious to soccer's no purposeful bodily contact rules." The following study seeks to examine Elizabeth Lambert's story in greater detail. Her actions within the game will be chronicled as well as the reaction of the media and the general public. Her image repair strategies will also be examined on top of the strategies used by her coach and the Mountain West Conference/NCAA and I will offer analysis of the strategies used.

On November 5, 2009, Elizabeth Lambert lost the game, but gained a spot in the history of sport. This little-known college athlete soon became a household name and a YouTube sensation. Women's soccer is rarely covered on major sports networks, especially at the collegiate level. Longman states, "It is probably no exaggeration to say that most games produce more goals than news accounts" (2009a, p. B15). That night, however, ESPN's *Sports-Center* showed a clip from the game that lasted a minute and a half. The first part of the video shows the only goal being scored in the entire match on a header by BYU's Carlee Payne ("New Mexico suspends," 2009). The next minute and fifteen seconds is dedicated to highlighting the behavior of Lambert. First, she is seen punching an opposing player in the small of her back. Next, it focuses on Lambert's rough play as she is going after ball, insinuating that she is going above and beyond her normal duties as a defender. The most appalling behavior is highlighted next, with Lambert "pulling the ponytail of one BYU defender so hard and quick she hit the ground" (Relative, 2009). Finally, she is seen taking swings at an opponent as they are both going after the ball. Many of the aggressive plays by Lambert are common within the game of soccer. New Mexico head coach Kit Vela relates:

> We could take any game from any school in the country, and take everything . . . the tackles, the arms in the back . . . and you'd find much of the same thing, some worse, some not as bad. Soccer is a contact sport, and there's a lot of stuff that happens. (Brennan, 2009, p. 3C)

The opposing coach, Jennifer Rockwood, seemed to echo Vela's sentiments.

> Soccer at the Division I level is very physical. Some games are more physical than others, and like I tell my players, we just need not to react when those things happen and make sure we do the best that we can. (Trujillo, 2009)

However, the most heinous of behaviors (hair pulling and throwing punches) are what caught the attention of the media and therefore caught the attention of the public.

Media Reaction

Following the report on ESPN's *SportsCenter*, Lambert's acts were seen on multiple news stations and sports shows ("Elizabeth Lambert," 2009). With 24-hour sports networks it appears as though the public is often hearing more about unsportsmanlike behaviors than witnessing the positive attributes that athletics brings to our society (Walsh, 2010). Fans are curious when it comes to athletes, yet they are quick to judge when it comes to their actions and personal lives (Summers and Johnson Morgan, 2008). *Good Morning America* (ABC), *The Today Show* (NBC), *The Early Show* (CBS), and ESPN's *First Take, Around the Horn,* and *Pardon the Interruption* all featured segments on the video as well as offering analysis of her actions. Even *The Late Show* with David Letterman provided a voiceover of the video, putting their spin on the situation (Longman, 2009a, p. B15). Beyond the television, sports writers and radio hosts also spent several minutes discussing a sport that rarely receives attention, women's soccer.

While the majority of the reaction was negative, some argued that the coverage could be seen as a learning tool. Dan Doyle, founder of the Institute for International Sport, notes that many players will learn more from their mistakes, missteps, and losses than from their positive behaviors and their wins (Nelson, 2009, p. C8). Likewise, those viewing those actions can learn more from witnessing the damage it has inflicted on Lambert, her team, and her sport. Julie Foudy, a women's soccer analyst for ESPN, appeared on the network numerous times to offer her perspective. Foudy mentions that most of the actions by Lambert were a part of the game. Including the hair pulling. However, she cautions, "if you're going to pull someone's ponytail and about snap her head off with it, that's going over the line" (Longman, 2009a, p. B15). While the rough play was not seen as going over the line, it was the punches and the viciousness of the hair pulling that drew attention to Lambert's actions.

Internet Reaction

Beyond the reach of the 24-hour news channels rests the Internet. The video sharing-website, YouTube, created an easy way for viewers to watch the video as many times as they wanted. From an athlete's perspective this means an extra set of eyes are on the action at all times. The referees and umpires during sporting events cannot view every aspect of the game. Therefore, Lambert got away with her behavior on the field because it was only the video cameras that caught her actions. The cameras, however, do not lie. Sullivan warns, "Athletes had better watch out. The Internet sees all. It also can replay all, over and over again. So even if you think you've escaped an official's whistle, you still might get caught for your dirty play" (2009, p. S02). In the case of Elizabeth Lambert, the Internet did see all, playing the video millions of times. In just two weeks after the game, the video was played over ten million times (Clayton, 2009). Shockingly, that was only one copy of the video. There are multiple copies of the video on YouTube alone as well as on blogs, message boards, and other news sites. "Video of the incident has spurred a national debate about sportsmanship, gender roles, double standards regarding aggressiveness and news media coverage and the sexualized portrayal of female athletes" (Longman, 2009a, p. B15). These themes will be further discussed in the remainder of the study.

Beyond the videos, Lambert also received e-mail messages, telephone messages, and even had her parents' home phone number published. One response went as far as telling Lambert that she "should be taken to a state prison, raped, and left for dead in a ditch" (Longman, 2009b). The messages and attention did not end there. Facebook groups were also created. Interestingly, there were groups created against Lambert, yet there were also groups that showed appreciation for Lambert's physical play. One group that was against Lambert was called "Ban Elizabeth Lambert from college soccer" with many comments likening her play to physical assault rather than an athletic endeavor. A group supporting Lambert called "Go Elizabeth Lambert," states, "If the offense doesn't fear you, you're not doing your job" (Longman, 2009a). While Lambert found sympathy in the eyes of some, it was clear that her actions in the game against BYU left her viewed as unfavorable in the eyes of many. The following section addresses her tarnished image.

Tarnished Image

Clearly, the actions of Elizabeth Lambert caused a great deal of controversy. While the aggressive play shown by Lambert is generally accepted in the activity, she took it too far when she threw punches toward her opponents and viciously pulled the hair of Kassidy Shumway. This caused a media firestorm and damaged her image. In response to her actions, the New Mexico head coach, Kit Vela, announced through a press release the following morning that "Effective immediately, Lambert is prohibited from participating in all team practices, competition and conditioning activities" ("New Mexico Women's," 2009). Noticeably missing from this statement is a timeline saying how long Lambert would be suspended from team activities. An actual punishment was never formally announced. As this was their final game of the season, Lambert did not miss any playing time.

Beyond the shame brought on her, Lambert also brought unwanted attention on her team, her school, and her sport. Her coach, Kit Vela, came under some scrutiny for not catching her actions on the field and not taking her out of the game. She is also under the microscope as to whether Lambert's punishment will carry over next year into her senior season. Additionally, the Mountain West Conference and the NCAA also are at fault. They are responsible for the referees who officiated the game. During the entire match, "Lambert was the only player to be penalized in the game, getting a yellow card in the 77th minute for colliding with a BYU player who was driving toward the Lobos' net" ("New Mexico suspends," 2009). In a match with so much physical action, the lack of penalties on both teams is questionable.

The following sections will address the image repair strategies used by all individuals involved and will offer analysis as Lambert, the University of New Mexico, and the Mountain West Conference/NCAA attempt to remove the black eye sustained by the sport of women's soccer.

Research Questions

1. What are the image repair strategies used by Elizabeth Lambert, the University of New Mexico, and the Mountain West Conference/ NCAA?
2. Do the strategies used by these three entities differ in their functions?
3. Does Lambert's gender and type of sport played affect the way this incident was covered?

METHODOLOGY

In an effort to diminish her actions, Elizabeth Lambert issued a written response in the press release announcing her suspension the morning after her game ("New Mexico Women's," 2009). Additionally, she held an interview nearly two weeks after the game with the *New York Times* (Longman, 2009b). Both of these statements will be analyzed to discover the image repair strategies used by Lambert.

Kit Vela prepared a written response that was included with the press release announcing the suspension ("New Mexico Women's," 2009). She also made additional statements to reporters later in the week (Brennan, 2009). The Mountain West Conference also issued a press release the same morning as the University of New Mexico's endorsing their swift reaction ("Statement from the Mountain West," 2009). In order to analyze the effectiveness of their image repair strategies, Benoit's (1995) image repair typology will be used for assessment. A detailed description of the image repair strategies can be found at the beginning of this volume. Analysis of the statements may differ based on the individual doing the analysis, so excerpts of the statement will be used to support the claim.

ANALYSIS OF IMAGE REPAIR EFFORTS

Lambert

In her prepared statement and her interview with the *New York Times*, Elizabeth Lambert engaged in multiple image repair strategies. The three strategies employed most often were mortification, bolstering, and corrective action. The following analysis will focus on these three strategies as well as mentioning the other image repair strategies used by Lambert.

Mortification

With Lambert's aggressive actions caught on camera and viewed by millions, the first step was to simply apologize. Her first statement in the press release began with the apology: "I am deeply and wholeheartedly regretful for my actions" ("New Mexico Women's," 2009). With the apology out of the way at the beginning that allows Lambert to focus on other aspects of her statement. However, that was not the end of her apologies. She went on to apologize to her teammates, the university, and to her opponents from BYU: "I am sorry to my coaches and teammates for any and all damages I have brought upon them. I am especially sorry to BYU and the BYU women's soccer players that were personally affected by my actions" ("New Mexico Women's," 2009). This apology focuses on the people who were directly affected by her actions in an attempt to alleviate any negative feelings toward her conduct on the field.

Lambert continued her remorseful responses when she held an interview with the *New York Times* two weeks after her match: "I still deeply regret it and will always regret it and will carry it through the rest of my life not to retaliate" (Longman, 2009b). This statement is a mix of mortification and provocation. The word "retaliate" evokes a sense of wrongdoing on the part of her opponents, an issue that will be addressed later in this study. Lambert's mortification strategy is arguably the most effective as there is no doubt that she is guilty of her actions on the field of play. This strategy develops a good first step in the image repair process.

Bolstering

Like any athlete, Lambert is also cognizant of elaborating on her good qualities that would be easy to dismiss after witnessing her performance. In her statement she lets the public know that "This is in no way indicative of my character or the soccer player that I am" ("New Mexico Women's," 2009). Here, Lambert subtly indicates that she has a different persona on and off the field. While she does not mention it, she is an all-conference academic player (Longman, 2009b). By highlighting her performance in the classroom, she could have put another aspect of her collegiate career in the public's mind. She continues, "I look at it [the video] and I'm like, 'That is not me.' I have so much regret. I can't believe I did that" (Longman, 2009b). Lambert continues the notion that she is not the same person on and off the field. When she watches the video, she does not recognize herself or her actions. While she stresses her good traits, Lambert misses an opportunity to focus on her positive characteristics by failing to mention that she is an all-conference academic player.

Corrective action

The person we witnessed on the field of play is not the person that Elizabeth Lambert knows. As a way to try to understand why she acted the way that she did, Lambert employs the use of corrective action to try to fix her emotional flare-ups: "I'm working on my mental game to never let that happen again" (Longman, 2009b). In order to do this, Lambert is seeing a clinical psychologist to help her understand why she acted out. Also, she has taken it upon herself to speak with youth players in the area to let them know what she did was wrong and that is not the way they should react during their games (Clayton, 2009). This is an appropriate step in winning back the public by showing that she is responsible for her actions. Relative (2009) states, "The manner in which they're called accountable and held responsible, the measures by which they are disciplined, are also seen by those same young people via television, Internet, and radio." In addition to what she mentions in her interview, Lambert also led her teammates in a volunteer project for, ironically, Locks of Love.

> This is a great cause and it's something that me and my whole family have taken part in before. I have hair that will grow back, so why not donate it to kids who don't have any. I did it when I was a junior in high school and I have no problem helping out again. A custom-made hairpiece will help boost the self-esteem level of a child in need. ("Lobo Women's Soccer," 2010)

While this action came months after her initial statement, it can still be considered as an act of image repair. This is indicative that every move Lambert makes will be scrutinized during her senior year. By organizing her team to take part in this charity, Lambert is able to assume a leadership position once again with her teammates while sending a positive message to the public.

Other strategies

Lambert used other strategies in her image repair attempts. While the three most prevalent have already been discussed, her additional strategies deserve attention. One of the more intriguing strategies Lambert used to reduce offensiveness was minimization. A large portion of the media coverage and the comments left on the Internet focused on her gender. In an aim to point this out, Lambert attempts to minimize the situation by opening the door to the gender equality discussion:

> . I definitely feel because I am a female it did bring about a lot more attention than if a male were to do it. It's more expected for men to go out there and be rough. The female, we're still looked at as, oh, we kick the ball around and score a goal. But it's not. We train very hard to reach the highest level we can get to. The physical aspect has maybe increased over the years. I'm not saying it's for the bad or it's been too overly aggressive. It's a game. Sports are physical. (Longman, 2009b)

The gender issue has been a focus of the debate surrounding her controversy. This issue will be elaborated on in the discussion section.

With only one penalty being called in the entire game, some of the attention must be focused on the referees. Lambert drew attention to this issue by attempting to shift the blame, stating that if the referee had called more penalties, "It would have been a very different game" (Longman, 2009b). Had more attention been paid to the extracurricular activities going on away from the ball, the players would have been more aware of their actions.

Finally, the majority of the negative attention has been focused on Lambert. However, upon further viewing of the video it is clear that the BYU players were not innocent bystanders. Before Lambert threw a punch to her opponent's back, video shows that Lambert caught an elbow to the chest. Also, before Lambert pulled her opponent's hair we see her opponent grab Lambert's crotch. She was also called names by her opponents and the fans and received her fair share of cheap shots (Longman, 2009b). This opens the door for Lambert to be able to use provocation as a defense. However, this never appears within her quotes. It only comes up within the article of her interview. Next, the response from the university will be assessed.

The University of New Mexico

Head coach Kit Vela and other administrators at the University of New Mexico were placed in a tough situation with this incident. They wanted to appear to be tough and authoritative when handing down their punishment as well as appearing to be on the side of their student-athlete. Coach Vela was also under scrutiny as Lambert performed these actions under her watch. Coach Vela and the administration used two primary strategies: bolstering and defeasibility.

Bolstering

Part of the job of being a university coach is to discipline your players when they get out of line. Another part of the job description is caring for your players and guiding them to be the best at what they do. In the Elizabeth Lambert case, Coach Vela had to toe the line of watching out for herself and standing behind her player. In the press release announcing Lambert's suspension, Vela makes it known that the Lambert she knows is not the Lambert we saw in the video. "Liz is a quality student-athlete" ("New Mexico Women's," 2009). Vela expresses that Lambert has many redeeming qualities. The administration also stressed that Lambert did not normally play at this level of aggression. They stated that Lambert had only received two yellow-card warnings in the more than 2,500 minutes that she had played on the women's soccer team (Longman, 2009b). This is a staggering statistic and helps illustrate that the student-athlete is not known for her violent play.

Defeasibility

After the video was released, many questions arose about the accountability of the athletes. Why was Lambert allowed to stay on the field with her actions? Vela used a defensibility strategy to answer these questions. Meaning she did not know what was happening on the field. "I wish I had seen it. If I had seen the hair pull, I would have pulled her off the field and we wouldn't be sitting here today. . . . But nobody saw the hair pull in the run of play" (Brennan, 2009). Vela was not the only person that missed the play. The referee, assistant referees, assistant coaches, and players on the bench also did not see the play or they failed to speak up. "We didn't see it. The refs didn't see it. Believe me, I wish I had" (Brennan, 2009). With these words Vela assumes that had something been done to penalize the player immediately after the play was over the entire situation would be downplayed, with a possibility of it not being reported at all.

Mountain West/NCAA

In the aftermath of the game, there was not an official response from the NCAA. The Mountain West conference issued a press release in conjunction with the University of New Mexico. Their press release stated that they agreed with the punishment handed down by the university and they would continue to internally review it and would make no further comments on the situation ("Statement from the Mountain West," 2009). The Mountain West's response in regard to the punishment handed down to Lambert was appropriate, but to refuse to comment on the play and the referees who were working the game, who should have put a stop to the rough play when it started, shows a complete lack of authority from the conference. After all, this was a conference tournament game, one of the highest profile matches all season.

DISCUSSION

Athletic image repair is an issue that the sports world has been and will continue to tackle for years to come. Elizabeth Lambert's image repair strategy offers a unique insight as we witness a college athlete attempt to come to terms with seemingly irreparable damages. It also allows us to witness how a university has to walk the narrow line between upholding a certain standard as well as supporting their student athlete. In the case of Lambert, it was clear that the main strategy used by her and by the university was bolstering. Athletes have a tendency to promote their better qualities whenever possible and we see this translate to this case as well. The unique aspect in the Lambert case is it is clear that the acts she committed on the playing field were violent. Yet her strategy and the strategy of the university remained focused on showing the world that what they viewed was not the true Elizabeth Lambert.

The similarities between the image repair strategies end at bolstering. Through Lambert's other approaches of mortification, corrective action, and minimization she paints the picture of an individual who is trying to make up for her wrongdoings. She is attempting to get back into the good graces of her coaches, teammates, university and fans and every step she takes gets her that much closer to achieving her goal of playing for the Lobos in her senior season. The simple fact that she was an organizer in getting her teammates to participate in Locks for Love shows that what she is doing so far is working, if only in the eyes of her coaches and teammates.

The most puzzling strategy mentioned is provocation. As already mentioned, Lambert was never quoted as saying her opponents provoked her. After looking at the video of the game, it was clear that Lambert was retaliating due to actions that were taken against her. It is interesting that she does not use this technique as she is clearly being attacked, a fact that did not go unnoticed by most viewers of the video. If anything, this case proves the old saying that it is typically the person who retaliates who gets caught.

Lambert's use of minimization also provides greater opportunity to discuss the gender bias in sport. There is often a sense that the women's game does not require as much athletic skill as the men's game and therefore should not be as aggressive. Bruce Arena, former coach of the United States men's team relates, "Let's be fair, there have been worse incidents in games than that . . . I think maybe people are alarmed to see a woman do that, but men do a hell of a lot worse things" (Longman, 2009a). It is a clear reminder that there is a different standard between male and female athletes. When a linebacker makes a big hit on a quarterback, a fight breaks out in hockey, or there is a collision on a play at home plate, the athletes are cheered for their rough, aggressive play. When a female takes it too far in a soccer game, it becomes national news. One of the big concerns over Lambert's story coming from advocates of women's sports is it could give opponents of Title IX ammunition to repeal the legislation that allows for greater female participation in sports (Longman, 2010, p. 1L).

One of the more bizarre aspects of this story is the lack of officiating during the game. Generally we see too much of the officials in college sports, but in this case, they were clearly missing. The referees assigned for this game have been criticized for their lack of supervision. However, there was no suspension handed down by the conference or the NCAA for their failure to step in and stop the aggressive play by both sides. Many of the aggressive plays occurred off the ball where it would be harder to see the act, but there were other aggressive plays that occurred on the ball as well. When Lambert pulled Shumway's hair, it should have been an automatic red card. Receiving a red card is the toughest penalty that can be handed out by the referee, which means the player is automatically disqualified from the game. The one foul that was called on Lambert, a trip, was the least offensive play she made on the field (Mick, 2009, p. L5). Had the referee stepped in on the first foul committed we probably would not recognize the name of Elizabeth Lambert.

Finally, unlike many of the other athlete image repair scenarios, this was an offense that happened on the field of play. Unlike other athletes who get in trouble with marriage disputes, partying, reckless behavior, and the inappropriate tweet, Lambert's actions came on the field of play, during the game. This fact seems to make her behavior that much more offensive. In Lambert's statement she even mentioned that she is regretful that she hurt the beauty of the game. Not only did this tarnish her image, her team's image, and her university's image, but also she harmed the image of the game of women's soccer.

CONCLUSION

After the video of her violent actions during her game, it was imperative that Elizabeth Lambert apologize and offer corrective action for her misdeeds. By stepping up and taking responsibility for her actions she helps to minimize the impact her actions created against her, her team, and her sport. Lambert was suspended for the first two games of the 2010 season before being reinstated. It is safe to assume that through her apology and steps to become a better role model in the soccer community, Elizabeth Lambert was back on the soccer field for her senior season, attempting to draw attention for her sports(wo)manship.

REFERENCES

Benoit, W. L. (1995). *Accounts, excuses, and apologies: A theory of image restoration strategies.* Albany: State University of New York Press.

Brennan, C. (2009, November 12). Coach sees both side of foul play. *USA Today.* p. 3C.

Clayton, A. (2009, November 18). Ponytail-yanking New Mexico soccer player Elizabeth Lambert breaks silence to express regret. *New York Daily News.* Retrieved from http://www.nydailynews.com/fdcp?1273517590548.

Elizabeth Lambert hair pull video back in news: Soccer player speaks out. (2009, November 19). Retrieved from http://www.cbsnews.com/8301-504083_162-5709718-504083.html.

Lobo women's soccer teams up with locks of love. (2010, April 16). Retrieved from http://www.golobos.com/sports/w-soccer/spec-rel/041610aab.html.

Longman, J. (2009a, November 11). For all the wrong reasons, women's soccer is noticed. *The New York Times,* p. B15.

Longman, J. (2009b, November 18). Those soccer plays, in context. *The New York Times.* Retrieved from http://www.nytimes.com/2009/11/18/sports/soccer/18soccer.html.

Longman, J. (2010, March 21). Women's sports push back at stereotypes. *The New York Times,* p. 1L.

Mick, H. (2009, November 12). People don't expect female athletes to act that way. *Globe & Mail (Toronto, Canada).* p. L5.

Nelson, K. (2009, November 20). Sportsmanship takes center stage award ceremony Saturday at Chase Park Plaza celebrates good behavior on and off field. *St. Louis Post-Dispatch.* P. C8

New Mexico suspends Lambert for hair pulling. (2009, November 6). Retrieved from http://soccernet.espn.go.com/news/story?id=695183&sec=ncaa&cc=5901

New Mexico player banned, apologizes. (2009, November 6). Retrieved from http://sports.espn.go.com/ncaa/news/story?id=4629837.

New Mexico women's soccer player suspended indefinitely. (2009, November 6). Retrieved from http://www.golobos.com/sports/w-soccer/spec-rel/110609aaa.html.

Player bio: Elizabeth Lambert-NEW MEXICO OFFICIAL ATHLETIC SITE. (2010). Retrieved May 4, 2010 from http://www.golobos.com/sports/w-soccer/mtt/lambert_elizabeth00.html.

Relative, S. (2009, November 6). Elizabeth Lambert dirty video leads to New Mexico soccer suspension. *Associated Content.* Retrieved from http://www.associatedcontent.com.

Statement from the Mountain West Conference regarding incidents in the New Mexico-BUY women's soccer match on Thursday, November 5. (2009, November 6). Retrieved May 4, 2010 from http://www.themwc.com/sports/w-soccer/spec-rel/110609aab.html

Sullivan, T. (2009, November 8). Nowhere to hide on internet. *The Record (Bergen County, NJ).* p. S02.

Summers, J. & Johnson Morgan, M. (2008). More than just the media: Considering the role of public relation in the creation of sporting celebrity and the management of fan expectations. Public Relations Review, 34, 176-182.

Trujillo, M. (2009, November 6). Women's soccer player suspended indefinitely. *New Mexico Daily Lobo.* Retrieved from http://www.dailylobo.com/index.php/article/2009/11/womens_soccer_player_suspended_indefinitely.

Walsh, S. (2010, March 11). Poor sportsmanship more visible. *The Times-Tribune* (Scranton, PA).

V

The Organizational Turn

Chapter Sixteen

No Pepper: Apologia and Image Repair in the 2002 Labor Negotiations Between Major League Baseball and the Players Association

Kevin R. Meyer and Craig W. Cutbirth, Illinois State University

This chapter examines the explanatory power of apologia and image repair theories when applied to the 2002 labor negotiations between Major League Baseball (MLB) and the Major League Baseball Players Association (MLBPA). The message of central concern involves the discourse used by MLB to announce the 2002 labor agreement between the two sides. The results of this analysis indicate that both apologia and image repair theories fail to fully explain the discourse MLB and the MLBPA utilize in their messages to the public at-large, fans, and media. The authors suggest areas for subsequent development of image repair theory.

Keywords: apologia, image repair, labor negotiations, Major League Baseball

For as long as the sport of professional baseball has existed, so too, it seems, have disputes between the ball club owners and the players. The last two labor disputes in baseball have been particularly nasty. Barzilla (2002) explains that:

Labor battles in all of the professional sports have been brutal, but they have always been worst in baseball. Labor battles caused the cancellation of the 1994 World Series and threatened to alienate baseball fans on a permanent basis. Unfortunately, there is always the possibility of another war between the owners and the players. (p. 182)

During the 2002 season, the owners of the thirty Major League Baseball (MLB) teams and the Major League Baseball Players Association (MLBPA) battled over several crucial issues. As the two sides hardened their respective positions, each was subjected to intense criticism from fans and the news media alike. The discourse employed by MLB on behalf of the team owners concerning the announcement of the 2002 labor agreement thus seems a clear example of what has come to be called image repair. It therefore affords an excellent opportunity to examine the current theoretical explanations of this recurring form of communication.

The purposes of this chapter are served by examining the following elements. First, we briefly discuss the "standard" approaches to the rhetorical act of self-defense; specifically, Ware and Linkugel's (1973) discussion of apologia and Benoit's (1995) typology of image restoration/repair. Second, we review the details of baseball's 2002 labor dispute and the August 30, 2002, press conference announcing a peaceful resolution for the country's national sport. Third, we examine the press conference as a species of rhetoric designed to repair the damage to baseball's reputation. Fourth, we discuss the adequacy of apologia and image repair theories in explaining the owners' discourse. Finally, we submit several suggestions for the future evolution of apologia and image repair theory.

THEORETICAL APPROACHES TO THE RHETORIC OF SELF-DEFENSE

Apologia

The rhetoric of self-defense has been studied extensively for a number of years. Ware and Linkugel (1973) originally labeled speeches of self-defense as examples of apologia. They argue that apologic discourses constitute a unique form of public address, and identify four factors of self-defense found therein: denial, bolstering, differentiation, and transcendence. Denial and bolstering are psychologically reformative, while differentiation and transcendence are psychologically transformative (Ware & Linkugel, 1973). Ware and Linkugel also describe the four major rhetorical postures in apologia: absolution, vindication, explanation, and justification. Each posture involves a combination of reformative and transformative factors (Ware &

Linkugel, 1973). Reformative factors do not attempt to alter the understanding or feelings of the audience regarding the charge leveled against the apologist. Rather, they attempt to remove the link between the alleged transgression and the image of the rhetor. Transformative factors, on the other hand, work to alter the audience's perception of the charge so that it loses its potency as a means of undermining the rhetor's image.

Kruse (1981) examined apologia in team sport. She explains that team sport has psychological and social significance, is an important cultural phenomenon, has important emotional dimensions for spectators, offers more than just entertainment and escape, fulfills a collective fantasy, offers fans something to believe in, and provides an extended family wherein individual players function as the fans' surrogates. Kruse observes that sport apologists appeal to the team sport ethic that the team is greater than any individual player. Players who perceive themselves to be individuals rather than members of the team risk negative evaluation "by fans and the general public alike" (p. 277); players must defend their moral worth and cannot threaten team harmony. Fans believe that players who oppose societal norms and ethics lack good character, thus disrupting "the fabric of sport's shared reality for the fans" (p. 278). She notes that players use various strategies, including bolstering, verbal acts of contrition, regret and remorse to acknowledge a temporary lack of faith and take the first step on the way to mending. These statements tend to be brief and general, rarely elaborating on the particular circumstances of the wrongdoing; what happened and what took place is less important than assurances that everything is fine now (Kruse, 1981). In the end, Kruse contends that team sport is a social construct wherein fans judge players on the field, but any transgression poses a symbolic threat to the game; players must demonstrate their moral value and assure fans that balance has been restored. While much has been written on apologia, not much, with the exception of her study, addresses team sport; no studies examine sports organizations or entire leagues.

While there are no studies that connect organizational apologia to team sport, Rowland and Jerome (2004) offer insight into organizational apologia as a category. They explain that the ultimate purpose of apologia is getting the individual or organization out of crisis and returning public attitudes to the state they were in prior to the crisis. According to Rowland and Jerome, the organization will act and speak in order to enhance and protect their credibility and image. Apologia thus serves the dual functions of image restoration and maintenance for organizations.

Image Repair

Another line of research that has proven heuristic is that of image repair. Benoit and his colleagues place a variety of case studies into the categories of the image repair typology. Research using Benoit's typology, however, is reminiscent of Black's (1978) criticism of the neo-Aristotelian paradigm. Black complained that neo-Aristotelian analysts were so caught up in the assumptions of their method that they became essentially "blind" to alternative ways of looking at rhetorical practice. There is always a temptation to look for the typology and nothing else, so that the typology winds up imprisoning our thinking. Black indicted the neo-Aristotelian paradigm on the basis that it tended, in large part, to allow the typology to drive analysis and thought. We find a parallel between Black's conclusions and current analyses of image repair.

THE 2002 BASEBALL LABOR DISPUTE

When the collective bargaining agreement between owners and players expired on November 7, 2001, labor negotiations concerning a new agreement began in earnest ("Peace on turf," 2002). No off-season agreement was reached. Thus, the 2002 baseball season began without a labor contract in place (Thomaselli, 2002). This placed the sport in a precarious situation. Labor negotiations in baseball have had a history of causing turmoil. Chase (2002) explains that, "in baseball history, negotiations have most often led to games being canceled" (p. 25). Going into the 2002 negotiations, there had been eight consecutive work stoppages since 1972; five were player strikes and three were lockouts by the owners (Schmuck, 2002). This history added increased pressure on the relevant parties in their attempts to preserve labor peace. Baseball holds a sacred place in the hearts and minds of its fans, having historical and cultural ramifications. Past failures in labor negotiations created a negative image of the 2002 events and served as a source of negative fan and general public perceptions of owners and players alike. However, several relevant events must be understood to appreciate the 2002 labor negotiations.

1994 Strike

The 1994 strike dealt a serious blow to baseball. When the season ended on August 12, 1994, it resulted in the first cancellation of a World Series since 1904 and the loss of 920 games, and signaled the onset of what proved to be a 232-day labor stoppage (Jenkins, 2002; Thomaselli, 2002). The next season, "baseball returned to a harsh landscape" (Verducci, 1995); for the mood of the fans had changed. Many fans approached the 1995 season with a cynical, angry, and chilly attitude toward both owners and players (Verducci, 1995). Opening-day attendance figures reflected the fans' perception that baseball had betrayed them (Verducci, 1995). Many fans felt that "the very people entrusted with being the caretakers of the game—the owners and players—have neglected it" (Verducci, 1995, p. 18). In the end, the damage from the 1994 strike was enormous. Advertisers estimate that the 1994 strike ended up costing baseball 20 percent of its fan base (Elliott, 2002). Thus, when just a few years later another round of labor talks appeared to be leading to a second strike within a decade, fans were understandably distraught.

Competitive Balance

As the new century began, baseball faced serious economic problems. Small-market teams were unable to compete effectively with teams from larger economic bases. The competitive balance of the sport, and the continued existence of some franchises, was called into question. In the 2002 labor negotiations, revenue sharing between wealthy teams and less affluent teams, as well as a proposed luxury tax on free-spending clubs designed to check rising player salaries were sticky issues that divided the owners and players (Jenkins, 2002; O'Brien & Siemaszko, 2002). The owners hoped these measures would improve competitive balance, but the players worried the ultimate effect would be to cut their pay (Schmuck, 2002).

Player salaries escalated dramatically between 1994 and 2002. Player salaries grew faster than revenues, and were at or near record levels (Barzilla, 2002; Chass, 2002). In 2000, a "blue ribbon task force" appointed by MLB commissioner Bud Selig to study the economic problems in baseball concluded that between 1995 and 2000 only three ball clubs made a profit (Barzilla, 2002). Since MLB has an anti-trust exemption, there is no way of knowing if these figures are correct (Barzilla, 2002). Complete control of this information by the owners led to skepticism from players and fans. Because the owners have always refused to open their financial books to the MLBPA, the players have concluded that the owners are stretching the truth (Barzilla, 2002). The owners' insistence on keeping financial records secret also damaged their position with fans. Thus, the release of MLB's financial figures was greeted with a lukewarm response, since players and fans could not be certain that the numbers were telling the whole story.

The owners believed that due to salary inflation and the need to share revenue to achieve competitive balance, the elimination or contraction of two teams was necessary. On November 6, 2001, MLB owners voted to eliminate two of the thirty teams ("Peace on turf," 2002; Thomaselli, 2001). The possibility of contraction strongly influenced and even skewed labor negotiations going into the 2002 season. Rather than simply dealing with issues of revenue sharing and salary caps, contraction brought a whole new dimension to the talks that had not been present in previous labor disputes (Thomaselli, 2001). The contraction proposal, in essence, would have automatically reduced the number of major league jobs available to players. Thus, the MLBPA was opposed to the plan. Fans of the two ball clubs that were on the chopping block, Minnesota and Montreal, were also upset about the idea.

No Lockout

The off-season prior to the 2002 baseball season was filled with speculation over whether the games would even be played. Selig promised not to lock out players (Thomaselli, 2001, 2002) or attempt to change the terms and conditions of labor rules during the course of the 2002 season ("Peace on turf," 2002). This message served to create a positive image of the owners that portrayed them as willing to work with the players. Selig explained the pledge as a means of protecting the season's integrity and allaying fears of a work stoppage (Thomaselli, 2002). Thus, MLB's pledge demonstrated to the fans and media that the owners were working toward a peaceful resolution of the labor dispute. However, since Selig's promise meant that new work rules could be imposed after the 2002 season, the players were left with an in-season strike as the only option to counter the owners (Thomaselli, 2002). In essence, Selig's pledge dictated that the players would be seen as the bad guys if an in-season strike ensued.

All-Star Game

In the midst of the 2002 labor negotiations, baseball came to its midway celebration of the game. Prior to the 2002 All-Star Game in Milwaukee, fans and players were generally giving Selig a chance (Couch, 2002). The general mood was one of excitement and peaceful, albeit momentary, coexistence between MLB and the players. When the National League and American League teams ran out of available pitchers in the extra-inning affair, Selig had to make the difficult decision to end the game in a tie. Fans were outraged by the idea that the game was so meaningless that it could be allowed to end without a winner (Couch, 2002). The fallout from the All-Star Game tie was tremendous, and Selig bore the brunt of the criticism for the fiasco.

Corporate Sponsorship and Fan Reaction

As the hurt of the 1994 strike gradually subsided, corporate sponsorship of baseball began to improve, increasing nearly threefold between 1998 and 2002 (Elliott, 2002). But, the smooth sailing came to an end when the collective bargaining agreement expired in 2001. In fact, advertising interest declined from November 2001 through the August 2002 labor agreement (Friedman & Thomaselli, 2002). Ironically, while sponsorship of baseball had never been healthier, the delay in signing a new labor agreement was jeopardizing the continuing commitment of corporate sponsorship (Thomaselli, 2002). A 2002 strike would likely have been the last straw for corporate sponsors. A strike would have hurt corporate sponsorships and revenue generation (Friedman & Thomaselli, 2002). If a strike had occured, relationships with advertisers would have been seriously and irrevocably changed (Elliott, 2002).

An additional danger was that a 2002 strike could have created greater fan anger than the 1994 strike did, and threaten advertising interest and television ratings (Friedman & Thomaselli, 2002). For MLB, the fans and advertisers were inherently connected audiences. Marketing agencies believed that the 2002 labor strife would seriously damage or sever the already frayed ties between baseball and fans (Elliott, 2002). Thus, corporate sponsors were keenly sensitive to any loss of fan support by MLB. The difference this time was that rather than reacting after the fact, as fans did in 1994, the fans in 2002 reacted proactively:

> Unlike 1994, fans haven't waited until after play was shut down to vent their wrath. Since the union's executive board voted unanimously to set an August 30 strike date, fans have taken to flashing dollar signs and chastising players from the stands and around the ballparks. (Jenkins, 2002, p. A1)

Thus, the primary audience of baseball, its fans, reacted negatively in anticipation of what they believed was to be yet another work stoppage. The damage from a strike in 2002 to the game's standing with fans, who were slow to return from the 1994 strike, might have been incalculable (Jenkins, 2002). Consequently, MLB and the MLBPA were playing with fire during the 2002 labor negotiations; one wrong move and baseball might never be the same.

The stakes were raised as labor negotiations extended well into the 2002 season without resolution. On August 16, 2002, the executive board of the MLBPA voted unanimously to set a 3:00 p.m. August 30 strike date ("Peace on turf," 2002). The decision of the MLBPA to set a strike date was the most powerful act of defiance by the players' union during the labor negotiations. Selig reacted quickly, becoming officially involved in the negotiation talks on August 28 (O'Brien & Siemaszko, 2002). He warned that midnight on August 29 was crucial because, "if we don't have a deal by then, we're on very dangerous ground," adding that he remained optimistic a strike could still be averted (O'Brien & Siemaszko, 2002). Thus, his efforts served to position MLB as the reasonable party in these labor negotiations.

THE 2002 PRESS CONFERENCE AND SUBSEQUENT DISCOURSE

Press Conference

On August 30, 2002, at 1:00 p.m. Eastern time, in New York City, a press conference was held to announce an oral agreement on a new, four-year labor contract between the owners and the MLBPA ("Peace on turf," 2002; Schmuck, 2002). During the press conference, Selig made several statements designed to present a unified front between MLB and the MLBPA, both of which shared a mutual interest in the health of the game. The idea was that if the owners and players could present the agreement as a sign of peace and solidarity between the two sides, then the fans would remain loyal to the game. Don Fehr, the players' union chief negotiator and executive director of the MLBPA, and two player representatives, Tom Glavine and B. J. Surhoff, appeared alongside Selig at the press conference. Selig (2002) heralded the new collective bargaining agreement as an "historic" achievement. He explained that:

> This is a historic agreement because it represents the first time in baseball history that we have reached a collective bargaining agreement without the loss of a single game. We also believe that this agreement will make significant contributions to restoring competitive balance. (p. 2)

Later in the press conference, Selig made a point of reiterating that no games were lost and that the agreement was historic. By emphasizing that no games were lost in 2002, he was clearly separating this labor dispute from the previous situation in 1994, in hopes that the public would forgive baseball for the anxiety the labor negotiations had caused the fans. This served as a keynote to the basic approach to image repair used in this situation. MLB attempted to retain its fan base and portray a positive image of baseball by demonstrating that 2002 was a different situation than those experienced by baseball fans in past. In essence, Selig's comments during the press conference indicated that baseball had solved its problems and was moving forward with changes that both sides had agreed to abide by. Selig (2002) beamed, "I think the thing that makes me the happiest is we can now, once again, turn our complete attention to the field" (p. 2). This statement represented another attempt to shift the focus of the fans back to the games and away from the labor turmoil. Selig (2002) praised the people involved in the talks, on both sides, for having their hearts in the right place and successfully bringing the talks to a "happy conclusion" (p. 3). The word choice of a "happy conclusion" seemed intended to allay fears of a 2002 strike or any future strike. Additionally, his discourse demonstrated MLB's desire to preserve the rest of the baseball season for the fans to enjoy. When responding to questions from reporters, Selig made a deliberate attempt to show solidarity between the owners and players, by remarking that the agreement was not an issue of which side won. Instead, he noted that the two parties came together to make a meaningful deal, in the best interests of the game.

Selig (2002) explained at the August 30 press conference that "this agreement, clearly in my judgment, is in the best interests of the game for a myriad of reasons" (p. 3). He concluded that "this has been a long, very difficult and winding road, spanning over three-plus decades" (p. 3). Selig's discourse was consistent with the overall sentiment of fans for the baseball season to continue without interruption. In the end, the press conference was designed to encourage fans to continue to attend games and support the institution of baseball. Additionally, MLB's discourse was designed to encourage corporate sponsors to continue to invest in the game.

Press reaction to the news conference indicated a general acceptance of the apologia, thus demonstrating the effectiveness of the image repair effort. Etkin (2003) concurred that the "agreement was historic, not only because it avoided another work stoppage but because it came in a sport criticized for being hidebound and stodgy" (p. 4H). However, some journalists did offer criticism of the discourse. For instance, Schmuck (2002) noted that Selig's claim that the agreement was historic was not quite true. Schmuck explained that the 1969 labor agreement was reached without the interruption of a single game. By and large, however, the public accepted the 2002 labor agreement as a move in the right direction. Considering the alternative of a strike in 2002, the reaction to the new labor agreement was positive.

Subsequent Discourse

There were several effects of MLB's discourse on its image during the 2002 labor agreement that are noteworthy. There is reason to believe, albeit incomplete reasons since the full effects of the 2002 labor dispute may not be known for several years, that the discourse was successful. Baseball has been free of subsequent labor disputes, fan interest seems stable, and corporate investment seems good, while issues such as salary increases and competitive balance continue to prove problematic. At the very least, baseball's discourse was successful in delaying, but not fully repairing baseball's image.

Following the press conference, MLB has continued to work on repairing its image. First, Selig's discourse continued to demonstrate a desire to bring all interested parties and audiences together. Second, in order to avoid a repeat of the disastrous 2002 All-Star Game, MLB enacted several rule changes for future games. Beginning with the 2003 All-Star Game, the winning league was awarded home field advantage during the World Series and roster sizes were expanded (Etkin, 2003). Selig observed that "we need to reenergize the game. The game is too good just for it to be floundering" (Etkin, 2003). The ultimate effects of the labor dispute may not be known for several years. Baseball is not yet far enough removed from the events of 2002 to properly evaluate the effectiveness of the apologia and image repair employed during the labor dispute. The 2002 collective bargaining agreement resulted in a progressive luxury tax, a new revenue-sharing plan, increased minimum player salaries, and a postponement of contraction plans until 2007 (Schmuck, 2002). These changes, however, did not fully accomplish all of the goals the owners had during negotiations.

THE PRESS CONFERENCE AS IMAGE REPAIR

Current knowledge and use of apologia and image repair theories can be improved substantially by considering the 2002 labor negotiations between MLB and the MLBPA. Existing theories of apologia and image repair fail to sufficiently address all of the questions surrounding the labor negotiations. We need a closer examination of the interplay between image repair strategies and the context in which these strategies occur. Ryan's (1982) speech set analysis posits that one has to understand kategoria, which is the charge or attack, in order to understand the defense or apologia. Understanding the attack is essential in assessing the effectiveness of image repair techniques. We agree, but suggest that the kategoria is but a subset of the larger context in which the image repair effort is found. Understanding the entire context becomes a necessary prerequisite to understanding the choices made by the entity undertaking the image repair effort. Because MLB and the MLBPA acted to prevent a potentially devastating labor stoppage, many of the accusations leveled against both groups lost potency. This is a critical realization as it may have widespread explanatory power for this particular rhetorical situation.

As we examine this press conference we find examples of the other apologic factors identified by Ware and Linkugel (1973). Denial, bolstering, and transcendence each appear in the statement by Selig. However, none of these three is used in such a manner as to warrant its designation as the second factor emphasized in the discourse. Ware and Linkugel's analysis requires a combination of reformative and transformative factors to create one of their postures of self-defense. Since differentiation is transformative in nature Ware and Linkugel tell us to look for a reformative factor, bolstering or denial, to pair with differentiation to discover the self-defense posture utilized in this example. While it is possible to do this, we believe that in the situation we are studying the choice of denial or bolstering as the secondary element is an arbitrary decision of the critic rather than an objective reflection of the discourse's content.

The press conference studied in this analysis relies heavily on the technique of differentiation. MLB and the MLBPA laud their success in preventing a strike, and repeatedly point out that the current situation is thus very much unlike the 1994 dispute. This is the centerpiece of their message and forms the foundation for their projection of a better future ahead for the game and its fans. The fact that this discourse is dominated by differentiation challenges existing beliefs about the effectiveness of image repair techniques. The thrust of image repair research would lead us to anticipate the use of mortification and corrective action. However, the circumstances surrounding this incident clearly indicate the utility of other choices. Since the strike was averted there is little to mortify and correct. MLB and the MLBPA were damaged by the extended negotiations, but the damage was grounded in the anticipation of another strike. The negotiations successfully avoided a work stoppage. It underscores our belief that the analyst must view discourse within its context. This is the only way to fully understand and appreciate the strategic choices made in constructing an image repair message.

Clearly, the dominant strategic choice of MLB in announcing settlement of the labor dispute was to emphasize that 2002 was not 1994; hence our identification of differentiation as the image repair technique of choice. If we probe more deeply into the context of the press conference, we gain important insight into the way this technique likely functioned when received and processed by baseball fans. Consistent with Ryan's (1982) assertion that the charge must be understood to appreciate the defense, we note that MLB faced an incomplete indictment in 2002. The dispute bore a striking resemblance to previous bitter labor disagreements in baseball. The anticipation of another work stoppage fueled fan dissatisfaction with the owners and players alike. Yet, the settlement demonstrated that the expected work stoppage would not occur. This realization deepens our understanding of both apologia and image repair.

Avoiding a 2002 baseball strike functioned as a graphic, undeniable *denial* of the expectation that a strike was inevitable. The parties were able to reform their images by denying that the season would be interrupted once again. Differentiation functioned to separate 2002 from 1994, thus transforming the audience's perception of the 2002 labor negotiations. This single factor can be seen to operate on both the reformative and transformative planes for baseball fans.

In terms of image repair theory, we can again understand the differentiation used by Selig as functioning in several distinct yet related manners. We recall the discussion of effectiveness advanced by Benoit and Drew (1997) and consider their research finding that the mortification technique and the plans for corrective action technique were evaluated most positively by the sample population in their study. By successfully averting the strike, MLB and the MLBPA embodied corrective action rather than merely announcing a plan for it. A plan for corrective action can be effective only to the degree the audience believes that it will indeed be implemented and that the plan will bring about the desired corrections. The successful resolution of this dispute clearly demonstrated that the past history of bitter disagreement between the owners and players was not an inherent feature of baseball's labor negotiations. Work stoppages could be avoided, and indeed were avoided in the present circumstance.

CONCLUSIONS: THE FUTURE OF IMAGE REPAIR

The 2002 labor agreement between MLB and the MLBPA can be viewed as an example of sports apologia and image repair. While the research on apologia and image repair research has been widespread, these approaches fail to answer all the questions raised in the 2002 baseball labor negotiations. Both apologia and image repair theories should be revised in order to address the questions raised in the 2002 labor dispute. For instance, image repair theory could consider how recurring patterns of image threats to sports figures sullies the image of the sport as a whole. Moreover, baseball has a greater number and variety of audiences for its discourse than do individuals or corporations who have been previously studied with image repair theory. In addition, the presence of dual rhetors in the 2002 labor dispute is uniquely different from previous case studies. Since MLB and the MLBPA acted as independent rhetors until the August 30 press conference, where they acted in unison, there is little in the way of prior image repair theory that offers a means of analyzing such an example.

Although Benoit (1995) suggests that apologia theory can be applied to sports figures, he does not recommend applying apologia to an entire sports league. Yet, a need exists to analyze the discourse of those who represent an entire sports league. Benoit's image repair theory tends to be overly linear in that it focuses almost exclusively on the apologist; the theory should also include the response of the public to image repair messages. The present artifact is unique from extant case studies of image repair theory, since MLB sought to repair its image in the hearts and minds of its fans. Whereas sports apologia offers a method of understanding how fans forgive individual players, the situation in question occurred on a far larger scale. Specifically, MLB and the MLBPA represented an entire team sport and league. The issue was not the popularity of an individual player or salary, but the reputation of the entire sport. The distinction here is one of existing theories addressing the discourse of particular individuals versus the need to find a theoretical lens to evaluate the discourse of an entire industry, or in this particular artifact, an entire sports league. While the public may forgive, and even forget, the actions of an individual player, they are less forgiving of the entire sport.

Existing theories address discourse by individuals and corporations, but not the discourse of an entire industry. Organizational apologia focuses on corporations, as opposed to entire industries. While organizational apologia tends to examine case studies involving faceless corporations (e.g., companies with no recognizable figurehead or personality), the sport of baseball in an entirely different entity. The sport of baseball does have recognizable faces and names that the public associates with the sport. Thus, the image of the individuals involved in the 2002 labor negotiations (e.g., Selig, Fehr, Glavine, and Surhoff) is intrinsically intertwined with the image of the sport itself. The distinction is one of focusing on the means of image repair and apologia as "standard" theories do, versus a new focus on the effects of the discourse. For the fans, regardless of the continuation of the 2002 season, the underlying sense of distrust and cynicism was the residue that colored their perceptions of the entire sport.

MLB was aware of an atmosphere of negative public reactions during the years prior to 2002 to suspect actions of large corporations. Given the general intolerance of the public for the reprehensible acts of corporations in other industries, MLB had every reason to expect that public reaction would be critical to any discourse concerning a possible labor stoppage. Therefore, MLB engaged in what was essentially preemptive apologia during the press conference; MLB and the MLBPA were not apologizing for a strike, shortened season, or cancellation of games. In fact, none of those feared events actually occurred. Instead, the sport of baseball was apologizing for causing any worry that the season might be interrupted. The wrongdoing that the August 30 press conference sought to address never really happened. The discourse of the press conference urged fans to return their focus to the games on the field and not worry anymore about the particulars of the labor dispute. In this case, the apologia did not seek to redress any act, but, rather, the threat of an act. Baseball was attempting to repair its image in order to prevent fans from becoming disillusioned with the sport. MLB apologized for the stress and threat of wrongdoing without the actual event having occurred. This situation is inherently different because image repair theory does not explain an apology over an anticipated event, or the avoidance of wrongdoing. Consequently, the present artifact helps to explain certain aspects about existing theories that, thus far, have not been addressed.

Future research should concentrate more heavily on seeking an understanding of the audience's reception of the discourse by the apologist. Furthermore, research should address the discourse of those who represent an entire recognizable industry as opposed to faceless corporations and individ-

ual persons. The continued comparison of apologia and image repair perspectives is beneficial in understanding why image repair techniques do or
do not work. Instead of categorizing the discourse and naming the techniques, we should focus more attention on how the techniques function to
repair the image. This was a strength of the original Ware and Linkugel
(1973) formulation. Their analysis of transformative and reformative factors
was insightful and allowed for the framework to lead to a discussion of the
effectiveness of apologia. Image repair theory, while broader and perhaps
more insightful than the original apologic formulation, can still benefit from
the detailed study of effective image repair situations.

REFERENCES

Barzilla, S. (2002). *Checks and imbalances: Competitive disparity in Major League Baseball.*
    Jefferson, NC: McFarland.
Benoit, W. L. (1995). *Accounts, excuses, and apologies: A theory of image restoration strate-
    gies.* Albany: State University of New York Press.
Benoit, W. L. & Drew, S. (1997). Appropriateness and effectiveness of image repair strategies.
    Communication Reports, 10, 153-164. doi: 10.1080/08934219709367671.
Black, E. (1965). *Rhetorical criticism: A study in method.* New York: MacMillan.
Chass, M. (2002, September 6). Scoring the big money. *New York Times Upfront, 135,* pp. 24-
    25.
Couch, G. (2002, July 10). Bittersweet break for Selig. *Chicago Sun-Times,* p. 122.
Elliott, S. (2002, August 29). Marketers and agencies make contingency plans for a baseball
    strike and worry about fan loyalty. *The New York Times,* p. C8.
Etkin, J. (2003, July 14). Stars and strife: Bud Selig's popularity ranks right up there with
    baseball and its annual exhibition extravaganza, but the commissioner still believes he's got
    game. *Rocky Mountain News,* p. 4H.
Friedman, W., & Thomaselli, R. (2002, July 29). Could MLB strike strand Fox, others. *Adver-
    tising Age, 73,* 19.
Jenkins, C. (2002, August 30). Extra innings, baseball talks 2002: Baseball negotiations go past
    strike deadline. *The San Diego Union-Tribune,* p. A1.
Kruse, N. W. (1981). Apologia in team sport. *Quarterly Journal of Speech, 67,* 270-283.
    doi:10.1080/00335638109383572.
O'Brien, E., & Siemaszko, C. (2002, August 29). Baseball's last pitch try: Commish joins labor
    talks as clock runs down. *Daily News* (New York), p. 3.
Peace on turf: Trace the route to an agreement. (2002, August 31). *Star Tribune* (Minneapolis,
    MN), p. 8C.
Rowland, R. C., & Jerome, A. M. (2004). On organizational apologia: A reconceptualization.
    Communication Theory, 14, 191-211. doi: 10.1111/j.1468-2885.2004.tb00311.x
Ryan, H. R. (1982). "Kategoria" and "apologia": On their rhetorical criticism as a speech set.
    Quarterly Journal of Speech, 68, 254-261. doi: 10.1080/00335638209383611
Schmuck, P. (2002, August 31). New deal leaves strike calling to umpires: Owners, players
    beat deadline by a matter of hours. *The Baltimore Sun,* p. D1.
Selig, A. H. (Guest). (2004, April 4). Steroids: President's challenge meets with opposition.
    This week [Television broadcast]. New York: American Broadcasting Companies News
    Transcripts.
Selig, A. H. (Press conference). (2002, August 30). Press conference: Baseball players, man-
    agement reach agreement. *CNN breaking news* [Television broadcast]. Atlanta: Cable News
    Network.

Thomaselli, R. (2001, November 12). Labor pains MLB comeback. *Advertising Age, 72,* pp. 3, 54.

Thomaselli, R. (2002, April 1). Pro baseball begins an uncertain season. *Advertising Age, 73,* 4.

Verducci, T. (1995, May 8). Anybody home. *Sports Illustrated, 82,* 18-23.

Ware, B. L., & Linkugel, W. A. (1973). They spoke in defense of themselves: On the generic criticism of apologia. *The Quarterly Journal of Speech, 59,* 273-283. doi: 10.1080/00335637309383176.

Chapter Seventeen

Giving Them the Ol' Misdirection: The NCAA and the Student-Athlete

Mike Milford, Auburn University

The core symbol for the NCAA is the student-athlete, which functions as a synecdoche, a symbolic form that is a concentrated representative of an organization's ideological essence. For the NCAA the student-athlete came to represent the core of the organization's mission to promote academics and amateurism (NCAA Executive Committee, 2004, p. 3). However, over the past twenty years the NCAA has come under increased scrutiny for its alleged exploitation of student-athletes. Critics asserted that the NCAA used student-athletes as unpaid labor because the structure of the NCAA was designed to prevent student-athletes access to their coffers. As the NCAA shifted from a simple governmental body to a massive media giant, it picked up significant amounts of money along the way, for example the recent $10 billion deal with CBS and the Turner cable networks to broadcast the men's basketball tournament (Sandomir and Thamel, 2010, para. 12). This was a monumental deal, worth nearly $771 million a year, especially for a nonprofit organization like the NCAA, but only the tip of the financial iceberg when one considered the millions paid out for other sports like football. The significant financial activity of the nonprofit NCAA seemed inconsistent with their ideology of education and amateurism, which led to accusations of hypocrisy and greed. Kenneth Burke (1954) frames this problem as "cultural lag," in which the orientation of an organization "survive[s] from conditions for which it was fit into conditions for which it is unfit" (p. 179). In this case, the idealistic, educationally branded NCAA had trouble explaining the bulge in its nonprofit wallet.

The cultural lag of the idealized student-athlete framed by the NCAA proved problematic for the NCAA, a problem common in synecdochic relationships: if the student-athlete is right, the NCAA is right, but if the student-athlete is wrong, the NCAA is wrong (Peterson, 1960, p. 234). Any insinuation made against the identity of the student-athlete became an indictment of the NCAA as well, and as the cultural lag widened, the criticisms increased. The root of the condemnation of the NCAA was the perceived incompatibility between their policies and their actions. Put simply: Which came first, the student or the athlete? Hatching an answer exposes the implications of the use of synecdoche as an organization's core image. Because of the significant ideological power of the synecdoche, any mismanagement sends ripples across the whole association. By examining the NCAA's framing of the student-athlete synecdoche, the attacks on the synecdoche, and the NCAA's response, the implications of the fixed image are made clear. Organizations that fail to maintain their synecdoches fall victim to cultural lag, exposing ideological inconsistencies that can undermine the organization's image in the public sphere.

THE SYNECDOCHE AS IDEOLOGICAL IMAGE

Kenneth Burke identifies the synecdoche as one of his four master tropes. Burke (1969) argues that a synecdochic relationship is present in any "act of representation" when "some part of the social body . . . is held to be 'representative' of the society as a whole" (pp. 508-509). The synecdoche's function is representation, "part for the whole, whole for the part, container for the contained, sign for the thing signified, material for the thing made . . . cause for effect, effect for cause, genus for species, species for genus, etc." (pp. 507-508; 1973, pp. 25-26). For example, Lewis and Onuf (1998) explore the creation of Thomas Jefferson as a synecdoche for America, finding that Jefferson often acts as the embodiment of the nation's ideological essence. It is the act of ideological representation that makes Jefferson a synecdoche. Because of its representative nature the synecdoche "plays an important role in the creation of public images," just as the student-athlete does in the public image of the NCAA (Brummett, 1981, p. 144). The power of the synecdoche is its ability to sum up an organization's "essence," centering the audience's attention on a particular ideological principle (Foss and Domenici, 2001, p. 242). In choosing the synecdoche, the organization is using a carefully structured symbolic form that becomes a vessel for its substance, directing the focus of the audience toward elements of the organization's choosing (Madsen, 1995, p. 416). The synecdoche is thus a "master trope" for organizations to promote a "settled ideology" (Moore, 1993, p. 259). And as long as they are maintained, they can become "'God' terms . . . for the group as a whole" (Sproule, 1988, p. 469).

The unique symbolic structure of the synecdoche allows for ideological transference via a "*relationship* or *connectedness*" that "extends in either direction," from the organization to the synecdoche and back (Burke, 1969, p. 509). Both sides, the part and the whole, become a "sign, symbol, or symptom of the other," sharing substance (Foss and Domenici, 2001, p. 243). In this fashion the synecdoche is less an image of the organization and more a concentrated summary. However, organizations that use the synecdoche must be aware that it has an open door at each end. This characteristic, when coupled with the cultural lag endemic in any symbolic construction, creates a unique set of problems for organizations that use the synecdoche as their master symbol. Any disparity between the ideologies in the synecdoche and the activity of the organization undermines the ideological framework of the group. It is in this way that the NCAA found the representative of the student-athlete an open door for attacks on its ideological principles.

The implications of the ideological relationship between a synecdoche and an organization can be seen clearly in the case of the NCAA. The NCAA used the synecdoche of the student-athlete to promote its ideological tenets of amateurism and education. The problem was that the NCAA found itself in circumstances that were an ill fit with the ideals contained in the synecdochic vessel. The discrepancy between the promoted ideology and the enacted ideology was highlighted, giving critics the ammunition they needed to use the student-athlete synecdoche against the NCAA, that instead of the *student*-athlete, the NCAA is instead focused on the student-*athlete*. The differences in the depictions and enactments of amateurism and education in the symbol of the student-athlete demonstrate how the synecdoche is a two-way interaction. I will begin by outlining the NCAA's synecdoche of the student-athlete, and then demonstrate how criticism of that image affects the ideological foundations of the organization.

THE NCAA AND THE *STUDENT*-ATHLETE

The NCAA purposefully constructed the student-athlete to convey the core tenets of their ideology: education and amateurism. As the NCAA defined the student-athlete, the latter was purposefully subordinate to the former, emphasizing a concern for education over athletics (NCAA, 2008, p. 61). Their stated purpose was the integration of "intercollegiate athletics into higher education so that the educational experience of the student-athlete is paramount" (NCAA Executive Committee, 2004, p. 3). In the NCAA's institutional rhetoric, there was no chicken/egg debate: the student had primacy. Intercollegiate athletics were relegated to a *"supporting role . . . in the higher education mission"* (NCAA Executive Committee, 2004, p. 3, NCAA's emphasis). Athletics were seen as a byproduct of the undergraduate education, and the preferred measurement of student-athletes was by "Academic success" rather than competitions won (p. 3; Division I academic reform, 2008). The construct of student-athlete was clearly built on an ideological foundation of education.

However, being a student was not enough; one must also have embraced amateurism in the interest of taintless competition. The NCAA's purpose in emphasizing amateurism was to refine the competition between student-athletes, giving the NCAA the purest form of sport. In fact, the *2008-2009 NCAA Division I Manual* listed the requirements of student-athlete status as first, being a student, and second, reporting to an "intercollegiate squad . . . under the jurisdiction of the athletic department," clearly and succinctly defined in one single page of legalese (p. 61). The third requirement was the athlete's amateur status, a qualification they take seriously enough to define in five full pages, covering sections 12.1.1 to 12.1.3 (pp. 61-66).

The integration of amateurism and education created a sense of idealism in the NCAA's student-athlete, and by virtue of the dual nature of the synecdoche, promoted the NCAA as an organization of idealized motivations as well (Nakamura & Adande, 1995, p. C07). Amateurism was the key to maintaining purity of motive in sport and the NCAA worked diligently to protect it.[1] They were quick to dismiss anything that would "essentially ruin the integrity of the college game," such as paying players in revenue-earning sports like football and basketball (Whiteside, 2004, p. 3C). The notion of amateurism also contributed to the "educational mission of intercollegiate sports," putting the latter in a place of primacy (Bandow, 2001, p. A17). As a result the NCAA's rhetoric surrounding the student-athlete synecdoche was designed not only to protect the ideology of education and amateurism but promote it as well. Former NCAA executive director Cedric Dempsey asserted that the organization's goal was to be "part of higher education and part of the education of the student-athletes," emphasizing the *student* in the synecdoche, simultaneously reasserting the NCAA's impeccable motives (Carey & Mihoces, 1998, p. 2C). The NCAA served a *"priesthood function,"* seeking to protect the given orientation of the student-athlete (Burke, 1954, p. 179, Burke's emphasis). The synecdoche of the rhetorically stylized student-athlete allowed the NCAA to "beam" a truncated ideology of education and athletic purity to their audience with each viewing of the student-athlete at play (Sproule, 1988, p. 474). Clearly the NCAA's synecdoche was designed to underscore the student aspect of the student-athlete in an effort to emphasize the ideology of education and amateurism. Unfortunately, the NCAA's actions often seemed at odds with this proposed ideology, creating a cultural lag between the images presented and the ideology enacted. The lag provided critics with the opportunity to use the student-athlete synecdoche to critique the NCAA's motives, arguing that the organization was more concerned with athletes than students.

THE NCAA AND THE STUDENT-*ATHLETE*

The cultural lag between the idealistic student-athlete of the NCAA's official policy and the student-athlete of the NCAA's current actions was startling to some. The NCAA, a nonprofit organization, was charged with using student-athletes in revenue-generating sports like football and basketball to create a media empire generating funds in the billions of dollars while graduation rates slumped. For critics, this was an example of a NCAA that wasn't living up to the ideological underpinnings of the student-athlete synecdoche they worked so hard to create. For example, in 1995, former NCAA chair Cedric Dempsey argued that the NCAA's actions called the very "definition of the student-athlete" into debate, citing hypocritical discrepancies between the two (Weiberg, 1995, p. 9C). Another former executive director, Walter Byers, agreed: "When you say the amateur principles of 1956 should control the commercial realities of 1995, it is an illogical and defenseless position" (Romano, 1995, p. 1C). Byers sneered that the student-athlete had gone from "big men on campus" to "big men in the campus ledgers" over the past forty years (p. 1C).

Byers's last comment shed light on the issue most commonly argued by critics: money, the most obvious symptom in the cultural lag of the NCAA's synecdoche. Critics pointed to the millions earned by coaches and universities, as well as the billions earned by the organization itself, as the best example of the dichotomy between the NCAA and the student-athlete ("Harsh NCAA rules," 1996, p. 14A). They charged that while the NCAA has shifted to a position of big business, they have maintained the traditional notion of the student-athlete out of greed (Bloom, 2003, p. A21). The massive television contracts made the traditional notion of the amateur student-athlete extinct, a "myth" of a bygone era (Loverro, 1999, p. B1). They called on the NCAA to "drop the pretense" of the student and accept the athlete's primacy in their new policies (Knott, 1990, p. D1; 1999, p. B1). In the hands of critics, the two-way street of the synecdoche was turned against the organization. Instead of being infused with ideological principles like education and amateurism, it was packed with hypocrisy and greed.

Cultural lag allowed critics to challenge the foundation of amateurism that the NCAA demanded from its student-athletes in the spirit of pure competition. Critics asked how a *nonprofit* organization could generate such income, much of it tax-free. Since the NCAA's stated goals are educational, it is not required to pay entertainment tax on any monies earned from TV deals, in critics' eyes a perfect example of the NCAA's hypocritical policies ("Brawn, not brains," 1996, p. 22; Fry, 2000, p. 1C). When coupled with the "no pay for play" rule, which strongly disciplined any athlete suspected to taking unsanctioned monies for athletic performance, the critics were able to frame the NCAA as hypocritical on an ideological level ("Harsh NCAA rules," 1996, p. 14A; Loverro, 1999, p. B1). Critics seized upon these inconsistencies and argued that in this operational climate the student-athlete became an "indentured servant" and an "unpaid employee" working not for an education but for NCAA greed (Elder, 2000, p. A16; Knott, 1999, p. B1). The lone reward for their services, the academic scholarship provided by the university and *not* the NCAA, turned out to be a "meager reward when compared to the profits an athlete might be generating for a school" (Romano, 1995, p. 1C). The massive financial windfalls of the NCAA coupled with their archaic politics turned intercollegiate sports into a "labor pool" for their "minor league system" designed to feed professional teams (Knott, 1999, p. B1; Romano, 1995, p. 1C).[2] Thus, amateurism was rendered by the NCAA's actions "a nostalgic term applied as an economic principle to control the marketplace for the colleges" and "In light of the hypercommercialization of today's college athletics, dramatic changes [were] necessary" (Mizell, 1995, p. 1C). The ideal of amateurism was turned against the NCAA in order to expose its suspicious economic activities.

The educational emphasis of the NCAA also came under fire. The NCAA was charged with paying "lip service to academics" in order to maintain their traditional image (Knott, 1999, p. B1). For example, Romano (1995) sarcastically remarked that the NCAA cared little about athletes who "participate in healthy activities that build character and enhance the educational experience" (p. 1C). Romero and others questioned why the athletes' academic and personal lives were put on hold for multibillion-dollar TV deals negotiated by the NCAA, with 9:30 pm kickoff times that are more in the broadcaster's interest than the student-athletes'. As the athlete became more significant the student suffered. The NCAA, in order to maintain its synecdoche, still required some semblance of a "student" identity. This led to a culture of "academic light," in which student-athletes were given a substandard education so that they could focus on their primary job as "the athlete-entertainer" (Streeter, 2001, p. D1). Many universities, critics argued, found their "principal challenge . . . to make it appear that their least gifted student-athletes [were] actually students," resulting in a group of athletes only "pretending" to be scholars (Bandow, 2001, p. A17). The notion that the intercollegiate athlete was also a student, much less *importantly* a student, was met with charges of "hypocrisy" on a practical level ("Brawn, not brains," 1996, p. 22).

The cultural lag between the ideology promoted by the NCAA and the enacted policies provided fertile ground for invective. After the synecdoche of the student-athlete was reinterpreted as a vessel for greed, the truncated ideological image was one of hypocrisy (Barr, 2000, p. D02; Hooper, 1998, p. 1C; Naylor, 1990, p. B1; Saraceno, 2007, p. 8C). For example, Knott (1999) caustically remarked, "The N in NCAA stands for Nauseating" (p. B1). One union chief went so far as to accuse the NCAA of running a "sweatshop" (Ferguson, 2002, p. E11). With the student-athlete synecdoche in the hands of its attackers, the NCAA was not an organization concerned with education and competition, but instead purposefully lied to limit the opportunities of student-athletes to retain profits (Bloom, 2003, p. A21; Fry, 2000, p. 1C). The synecdoche proved to be a tricky trope for an organization like the NCAA, as its nature of "connectedness" allowed for the same image to be used to embody competing ideologies that could be turned against the parent organization (Burke, 1969, p. 509). Thus ideologically and practically the student-athlete synecdoche was turned against the NCAA.

THE NCAA'S "MISDIRECTION"

The NCAA was faced with answering two challenges. First, that the NCAA cared more about its athletes than its students, and second that the financial policies undermined its message of amateurism. The NCAA answered its critics most visibly in a series of public service announcements (PSAs) designed to highlight the NCAA's commitment to the student over the athlete, and a membership report designed to provide a semblance of financial transparency. However, a close examination of the PSAs and the NCAA's accompanying rhetoric reveal a strategy of misdirection. In their failure to address the critics' main contention the NCAA's campaign to redefine the student-athlete in the public sphere fell flat. A brief analysis of recent PSAs, as well as rhetoric on the NCAA's website, demonstrates that the gap between the core ideology and the enacted ideology of the NCAA is too wide to be spanned by the fixed image of the student-athlete synecdoche without a significant overhaul.

The NCAA aired a series of PSAs in times of significant viewership, such as the Bowl Championship Series in football in the fall and the March Madness basketball tournament in the spring. The goal was to reinforce the image of the athlete as a student seeking employment outside of professional sports. A brief summary of the ads from 2008 showed this to be the case. The first ad, titled "Basketball," showed a group of people in a darkened arena playing a game of basketball in slow motion. However, instead of wearing basketball uniforms the athletes were wearing uniforms from different vocations: a firefighter, nurse, judge, police officer, and other more generic business-style clothing. All the while the NCAA's slogan came through via a voiceover: "There are 380,000 NCAA student-athletes, and most of us will go pro in something other than sports."[3] The intent was clear. The ad attempted to redefine the athlete by showing people engaged in athletic activities dressed as everyday citizens. It functioned to *misdirect* the attention, the NCAA's own word for their strategy, redefining the student-athlete from a potential pro to one with multiple vocational avenues.[4]

The second PSA did much the same thing. In "Cards" the PSA opened with two young kids exiting a convenience store with a pack of trading cards. The cards had two pictures on them: one showing the student-athlete as an athlete, and the other showing the same person engaged in a traditional vocation. For example, the first was a hockey player/stock trader. The kids, instead of celebrating the athletic achievements, showed their enthusiasm for the occupational aspects of the student-athlete. One kid was excited about getting the card of a "three-time architect of the year," while the other was excited because the student-athlete on his card "dominates the lab." A similar theme followed in the "Field Hockey" PSA. Here a group of people in white lab coats watched a women's field hockey practice. The coach called over one of the players and commented, "The med school scouts are out early today." The suggestion was that the student-athlete was scouted for her intellectual acumen and not her athletic ability. The final spot, "Shoe," retained the NCAA's theme of the student-athlete succeeding in the workplace. The PSA depicted a marketing meeting between a prospective "someone," played by an athletic-looking African American male, and representatives from a shoe company. The marketing director was excited about designing the shoe for the "three time All-American," a descriptor usually saved for athletic achievement, but here used as a misdirection when the shoe is revealed to be a wingtip oxford. The marketers praised the "mad smarts, and slick leadership skills" of the student-athlete, and pointed out the student-athlete's GPA embossed on the heel. This, like the other three PSAs, ended with the NCAA's tagline reminding the audience that the majority of student-athletes will be going pro in something other than sports.

The PSAs were designed to combat the presumption that the student-athletes participate in intercollegiate athletics as a sort of "minor league" for professional sports leagues like the NFL or the NBA. The problem with the PSAs is that their misdirection was misdirected. As was previously noted, the challenges to the NCAA's synecdoche were less concerned with the student-athletes' future than their present. Judging from the PSAs it is clear that the NCAA believed its biggest hurdle lay in the assumption that NCAA athletes are all future professional athletes. Yet, the previous summary of the arguments against the NCAA showed that the critics were focused on the disparity between the significant financial gain of the NCAA and the treatment of the student-athlete. The clash is centered on the number of zeros on the non-profit organization's balance sheet, for it is there that the ideological disparity lies. The PSAs, then, were designed to combat an argument that is peripheral at best.

The NCAA's response to the challenge of financial chicanery was more problematic. Further research on the NCAA's site revealed just how misdirected their argumentative position was. The NCAA's *Membership Report*, supposedly designed to provide accountability for their finances, did more to expose the cultural lag of their ideology than any critic. The membership report contained a flash video presentation designed to provide accountability for the NCAA's expenditures separated into sections with titles like "Where Does the Money Come From?" and "Where Does the Money Go?"[5] The first section on the NCAA's income was clearly outlined and easy to access. The NCAA reported an income of $636 million in 2008, 86 percent of which came from TV revenue, a $148 million increase over the last five years. The "Year in Review" section was full of perspicuous pie charts and graphs showing how much money came from where, which sports generated what, and so on. The income section was clear and easy to understand, even for someone who is not a financial whiz.

The problems started in the "Where the Money Goes" section, which was a multimedia presentation. It began with a voiceover admitting, "It can be difficult at times to determine from the membership report how these figures support student athletes" while pictures of student athletes in various activities pass by. Gone were the charts and graphs and percentages. They were replaced by equivocations and evasions asserting that money was distributed "through multiple channels to create a robust support system for student athletes across the country." No actual figures are mentioned, simply promises that students benefited in the form of "tuition assistance, uniforms and equipment, facility support, healthcare, insurance, and educational programs." The voice then explained how the money funded the 88 championships that the NCAA offers. From there the voice stated, "At the individual level, this funding can have a more profound effect," and it is here that the NCAA's response to their synecdoche's dangerous position took a most disappointing turn.

In this section, in lieu of clear rational explanation and argument, the NCAA turned to short, supposedly hypothetical, vignettes overflowing with pathos, essentially abandoning even a pretense of the logos that dominated the rest of the report. The first short story was overly simplistic and somewhat offensive. It began with a picture of an African-American male on a bus as the voiceover stated, "Imagine a student-athlete born in Mississippi who travels to a championship in Minnesota in February. That look of shock upon exiting the team bus is not because he forgot to pack his coat, but because he never had owned a winter coat." At this point there was a sequence of animated still photos showing the athlete descending the bus steps with an awkwardly enthusiastic smile that turns to a cartoonish grimace as he wrings his hands in the cold. The voice continued, "The Association makes funds available so clothing can be purchased in these situations. And while the coat might not be his style, it does prevent him from getting sick right before final exams." At this point the picture shows the student wearing a garishly outdated coat from the 1990s with a sheepish grin. The vignette clearly shows how out of touch the NCAA is with their detractors. Instead of financial accountability, the audience gets a *Sesame Street* story about the "Boy Who Forgot His Coat."

The second vignette was worse as it completely eschewed any sense of rational argument and instead relied solely on emotional appeals. It began, "Here's another example. Imagine a student whose mentor in life was her grandfather. Her love of swimming developed early on thanks to his encouragement and training." Pictures accompany the voice showing a European-American female swimming competitively. The voice continued, "Now in college on a swimming scholarship [student shown grinning in a classroom] she keeps in touch with her number one fan on her progress." At this point, the empathetic voice took on a healthy dose of pathos, "But as she prepared for the championship her grandfather passed away. The Association makes funds available for emergency travel so she was able to attend the funeral and go on to win the championship in his honor." The final picture in the slide show was of the swimmer victorious. The presentation was summed up by the same tagline from the PSAs, that most athletes will go pro in something other than sports.

Any rhetorical critic could easily recognize that the vignettes were designed to circumvent rational argument by recasting the financial picture of the student athlete with humorous stories about forgotten coats and pathetic appeals centered on lost family members. The fact was that the NCAA was quite forthcoming with its earnings, but its expenditures remained hidden by poorly constructed rhetorical misdirection. The danger of the synecdoche as the central image is that it is indeed ideological, and that core ideology must be protected. However, instead of protection through redefinition or recasting the student-athlete in light of the NCAA's financial situation, the Association instead remained rigid in its characterization. As a result, the synecdoche of the student-athlete became a Maginot Line facing a blitzkrieg of attackers: woefully outdated and unprepared. The fixed synecdoche proved to be less of a stabilizing anchor and more of a damning millstone.

CONCLUSION

Clearly the lesson to be learned here is one of maintenance. The synecdoche, as one of Burke's master tropes, is a powerful rhetorical device, and like most powerful devices, demands constant vigilance. Without maintenance on either the organization's image or ideology the synecdoche quickly ceases to be an avenue of ideological promotion. Instead, when exposed by cultural lag, the synecdoche works against the organization, the rhetorical equivalent of the bully's classic ploy, "Why are you hitting yourself?," beating the offender with its own fists. The NCAA, then, serves as a cautionary tale to organizations that utilize tropes with significant ideological composition: Maintain. A shift in the operating policies of the organization should be mirrored by a shift in the image it uses to promote itself. In failing to do so the organization exposes its soft ideological underbelly to attack.

This is evident in the PSAs and the membership report. They fail rhetorically because they rely on a fixed synecdoche. When exposed by cultural lag, an organization is wise to adapt to the changing circumstances. However, when an organization like the NCAA uses a synecdoche as its primary image it is crucial that they maintain the image with their current practices because of the ideological nature of the synecdoche. Failure to do so is not simply a failed advertising campaign but an act that seriously undermines the ideological underpinning of the organization. The NCAA's strategy was faulty, but they seem to be making efforts to improve. During the 2010 NCAA men's basketball tournament they aired a new PSA titled "Where Does the Money Go?" focusing on revenues from TV rights.[6] The explanation is clearer, as they argued that the funds go primarily to supporting championship events and providing financial aid, but the information is still thin, especially compared to the charges the NCAA faces from critics. Overall the NCAA's rhetoric still failed to answer the attacks on faux-amateurism and financial hoarding. Their PSAs come off as non-sequiturs. It is the insistent reliance on the fixed ideological image that has created more problems for the NCAA than it has solved.

NOTES

1. The emphasis on amateurism was at one time the most important reform in the NCAA's rulebook. In the early twentieth century it was common for teams to field players who only stepped on campus for that week's game. Watterson (2006) comments that it wasn't uncommon for players to be paid to play together for one university one week and against each other the next.

2. In fact, Nebraska state senator Ernie Chambers argued for paying athletes on the grounds that offering them a scholarship invalidated any sense of amateurism that might have existed in the first place: "Whenever you get something of value for performing athletically, you're a professional. They call it a scholarship, fees, books, tuition and so forth" (Whiteside, 2004, p. 3C).

3. The NCAA PSAs are available on the NCAA channel on Youtube. These four were retrieved on April 24, 2008, from www.youtube.com.

4. The NCAA has posted a behind-the-scenes video for the PSA, also available online. In it the director shares that the point of the 2008 campaign was a "misdirection," meaning that the viewer might not know the purpose of the commercial until the end. This was retrieved on April 24, 2008, from www.youtube.com.

5. The NCAA Membership Report is available at http://web1.ncaa.org/web_video/membership_report/2008/index1.html, retrieved March 26, 2009. All references are contained in the report.

6. The PSA is available on You Tube on the NCAA's channel. It is labeled "NCAA TV Spot." Retrieved April 20, 2010.

REFERENCES

Bandow, D. (2001, April 4). Loot for the NCAA. *Washington Times*, p. A17. Retrieved November 6, 2008, from Lexis-Nexis database.

Barr, J. (2000, June 28). NCAA considers changes in rules on amateurism. *Washington Post*, p. D02. Retrieved November 6, 2008, from Lexis-Nexis database.

Division I academic reform. (2008, September). *NCAA: Behind the Blue Disk*. Indianapolis. Retrieved November 6, 2008, from www.ncaa.org.

Bloom, J. (2003, August 1). Show us the money. *New York Times*, p. A21. Retrieved November 6, 2008, from Lexis-Nexis database.

"Brawn, not brains." (1996, March 30). *The Economist*, p. 22. Retrieved November 6, 2008, from Lexis-Nexis database.

Brummett, B. (1981). Gastronomic reference, synecdoche, and political images. *Quarterly Journal of Speech, 67*, 138-145.

Burke, K. (1954). *Permanence and Change*, 3rd ed. Berkeley: University of California Press.

Burke, K. (1969). *Grammar of Motives*. Berkeley: University of California Press.

Burke, K. (1973). *Philosophy of Literary Form*, 2nd ed. Berkeley: University of California Press.

Carey, J., and Mihoces, G. (1998, June 30). Dempsey: NCAA much more than a regulatory body. *USA Today*, p. 2C. Retrieved November 6, 2008, from Lexis-Nexis database.

Elder, L. (2000, May 2). Exploiting student-athletes. *Washington Times*, p. A16. Retrieved November 6, 2008, from Lexis-Nexis database.

Ferguson, R. (2002, January 18). NCAA a "sweatshop", steelworkers chief says. *Toronto Star*, p. E11. Retrieved November 6, 2008, from Lexis-Nexis database.

Foss, K. A., and Domenici, K. L. (2001). Haunting Argentina: Synecdoche in the protests of the Mothers of the Plaza de Mayo. *Quarterly Journal of Speech, 87*, 237-258.

Fry, D. (2000, March 4). Porter incident reveals larger NCAA problems. *St. Petersburg Times*, p. 1C. Retrieved November 6, 2008, from Lexis-Nexis database.

Harsh NCAA rules can make life tough for athletes. (1996, June 17). *USA Today*, p. 14A. Retrieved November 6, 2008, from Lexis-Nexis database.

Hooper, E. (1998, May 22). Is the NCAA due for an overhaul? *St. Petersburg Times*, p. 1C. Retrieved November 6, 2008, from Lexis-Nexis database.

Knott, T. (1990, January 10). NCAA's outdated reforms doomed to fail. *Washington Times*, p. D1. Retrieved November 6, 2008, from Lexis-Nexis database.

Knott, T. (1999, March 24). NCAA: dispenser of lies. *Washington Times*, p. B1. Retrieved November 6, 2008, from Lexis-Nexis database.

Lewis, T., and Onuf, P. S. (1998). American synecdoche: Thomas Jefferson as image, icon, character, and self. *The American Historical Review, 103*, 125-136.

Loverro, T. (1999, November 26). NCAA will have to pay athletes someday soon. *Washington Times*, p. B1. Retrieved November 6, 2008, from Lexis-Nexis database.

Madsen, A. (1995). The synecdochic and metonymic processes and the political image construct. *Alta Conference on Argumentation, 1995 Argumentation and Values*, 413-430.

Mizell, H. (1995). Byers offers idea in era of college dollar. *St. Petersburg Times*, p. 1C. Retrieved November 6, 2008, from Lexis-Nexis database.

Moore, M. P. (1993). Constructing irreconcilable conflict: the function of synecdoche in the spotted owl controversy. *Communication Monographs, 60*, 258-274.

Nakamura, D., and Adande, J. A. (1995, March 31). Final Four notebook; New revenue could aid student-athletes. *Washington Post*, p. C07. Retrieved November 6, 2008, from Lexis-Nexis database.

Naylor, J. (1990, January 31). Senator's resolution urges payments for college athletes. *Washington Times*, p. B1. Retrieved November 6, 2008, from Lexis-Nexis database.

NCAA. (2008). *2008-2009 NCAA Division I Manual*. Indianapolis, IN: NCAA Services. Retrieved November 6, 2008, from www.ncaapublications.com.

NCAA Executive Committee. (2004, April). *NCAA Strategic Plan*. Retrieved November 6, 2008, from www.ncaa.org.

Peterson, M. D. (1960). *The Jefferson Image in the American Mind*. New York: Oxford University Press.

Romano, J. (1995, March 30). Higher earning. *St. Petersburg Times*, p. 1C. Retrieved November 6, 2008, from Lexis-Nexis database.

Sandomir, R., & Thamel, P. (2010, April 22). TV deal pushes NCAA closer to 68-team tournament. *New York Times*. Retrieved April 23, 2010, from http://www.nytimes.com.

Saraceno, J. (2007, January 5). Saying the system exploits collegians stretches the point. *USA Today*, p. 8C. Retrieved November 6, 2008, from Lexis-Nexis database.

Sproule, M. J. (1988). The new managerial rhetoric and the old criticism. *Quarterly Journal of Speech, 74*, 468-486.

Streeter, K. (2008, June 1). NCAA exempt from taxes, not hypocrisy. *Los Angeles Times*, p. D1. Retrieved November 6, 2008, from Lexis-Nexis database.

Watterson, J. S. (2006). *College Football: History, Spectacle, Controversy*. Baltimore: Johns Hopkins University Press.

Weiberg, S. (1995, January 9). Dempsey seeks fresh look at student-athlete benefits. *USA Today*, p. 9C. Retrieved November 6, 2008, from Lexis-Nexis database.

Whiteside, K. (2004, September 1). College athletes want cut of action. *USA Today*, p. 3C. Retrieved November 6, 2008, from Lexis-Nexis database.

Chapter Eighteen

A Death, a Family Feud, and a Merger: The Image Repair of Teresa Earnhardt and Dale Earnhardt, Inc.

Angela M. Jerome, Western Kentucky University

On February 18, 2001, legendary NASCAR driver Dale Earnhardt died in a crash on the last lap of the Daytona 500.[1] In the aftermath, his wife of eighteen years, Teresa, was left to single-handedly run Dale Earnhardt, Inc. (DEI), the multi-million dollar business the two founded together in 1980 (www.daleearnhardtinc.com, 2010).[2] From day one, Teresa played a central role at DEI, handling a great deal of its day-to-day business endeavors, contract negotiations, and licensing and merchandising agreements. She and Taylor, their daughter who was a minor at the time of Earnhardt Sr.'s death, were also with him at almost every race. When he died, Teresa was left to lead their company to success while navigating the difficulties of five women who are helping the sport as it heads into a new decade. Earnhardt had three adult children from two previous marriages: Kerry, Kelley, and Dale Jr. Kerry (with wife #1) was raised by his mother and stepfather, but Kelley and Dale Jr. (with wife #2) moved in with Dale Sr. and Teresa at the ages of eight and six, respectively.

For a few years, all seemed to be running fairly smoothly. Though many would argue that DEI was not as strong as it had been before Earnhardt Sr.'s death, with two wildly popular drivers in the sports top series, Earnhardt Jr. and Michael Waltrip, the company arguably was recovering from its patriarch's death as well as could be expected. Waltrip, who joined the team at the beginning of 2001, won the race in which his boss perished; Earnhardt Jr. finished second (Dixon, 2007). Later that year, Earnhardt Jr. finished first and Waltrip finished second in the Pepsi 400 at Daytona International Speedway (nascar.com, 2010). Waltrip continued to win races in 2002 and 2003, but did not win another while at DEI, and a quick look at the data shows that his number of top-five and top-ten finishes as well as his championship points rankings steadily decreased (nascar.com, 2010). Trouble may have been foreshadowed by Waltrip's choice to leave DEI and start his own race team at the end of 2005. On his decision to leave Waltrip stated, "I almost think it would be a challenge for DEI to run three teams given the ability that they have right now. . . . They might think that they can and they might well do it. But it didn't look like it would favor me if that's what they decided to do" (James, 2005, n.p.). He was referring to DEI's decision to expand to a three-car team with former Busch Series champion Martin Truex Jr. at the helm of the third car.

Even with Waltrip's departure, the company was still left with the ever-popular Earnhardt Jr. and his highly lucrative Budweiser sponsorship. In 2001, Earnhardt won three races, including the race directly following the 9/11 terrorist attacks, the October race at Talladega (the last place Earnhardt Sr. had won a race), and he finished eighth in championship points (nascar.com, 2010). In 2002, he won two races and finished eleventh in points (nascar.com, 2010). In 2003, he won two races and finished third in points (nascar.com, 2010). In 2004, he won six races and finished fifth in points (nascar.com, 2010).

These successes, however, were tempered with some perceived failures. During the 2005 season, the same season Waltrip announced he was leaving DEI, Teresa split up Earnhardt Jr.'s team (no clear reason has ever been given for this change); he failed to make the "Chase" for the points championship, finishing nineteenth in points and winning only one race (Dixon, 2007; nascar.com, 2010). In 2006, he rebounded with a fifth-place finish in series points, but won only one race (nascar.com, 2010). Further, Earnhardt Jr. was the only driver at DEI to win in NASCAR's top series between 2003 and June 2007, when Martin Truex Jr. scored a win at Dover International Speedway (nascar.com, 2010).

DEI went into 2007 with three drivers: Earnhardt Jr., Truex Jr., and Paul Menard; it would end 2007 with only two. In May 2007, Earnhardt Jr. announced he would be leaving the company at the end of the season largely because his stepmother refused to give him majority ownership of DEI. It was later announced that he would join Jeff Gordon, Jimmie Johnson, and Casey Mears as a driver for Hendrick Motorsports, one of the most competitive teams in the series.

As a result of this ownership battle, Teresa Earnhardt's image and the image of DEI quickly began a downward spiral. To date, neither has fully recovered. In the remainder of this chapter, I review extant literature relevant to the three key constraints of this case: the vilification of stepmothers, the effect of the micropolitics of nonresponse on an image repair campaign, and the importance of winning on an athlete's/athletic organization's ability to repair a tarnished image. Then, I outline the three key constraints as they relate to this particular case. Next, I analyze the events of the case and demonstrate how/why the constraints played out in the case the way they did. I also demonstrate how recent actions taken by both Teresa Earnhardt and DEI indicate they understand the importance of overcoming these constraints if they are to be successful in the future.

LITERATURE REVIEW

As with the other chapters in this publication, the image repair strategies outlined by Benoit (1995) will be used to discuss the rhetoric used by Teresa Earnhardt and DEI to bring about image repair in this case. However, it is necessary to outline literature concerning the key situational constraints surrounding this case before an analysis may proceed.

Vilification of Stepmothers

Ceglian and Gardner (2000) begin their poignant article concerning attachment styles and the "wicked stepmother" spiral by stating,

> Mothers are loving, caring and nurturing of their children, but stepmothers are by nature cruel, vicious and jealous creatures. This view of loving mothers and cruel stepmothers has surfaced in different countries and cultures throughout history, handed down from generation to generation through such fairytales as *Snow White, Cinderella, and Hansel and Gretel* (Schullman, 1972), and in folklore where "evil" is most frequently represented by bears, wolves, giants, ogres, witches, and stepmothers (Sutton-Smith, 1971). This presents a cultural contradiction for stepmothers when they are expected to be distant or even hostile, yet acting in a role of a mother are expected to be loving and nurturing at the same time. (p. 112)

The myth of the "wicked stepmother" is not just an American phenomenon. It has been traced back to ninth-century China and has cut across a variety of cultures, including Spanish, Irish, Italian, and Greek (Cherlin, 1999; Noy, 1991; Wald, 1981). Regardless of cultural variants, these stories always develop around some key events: the biological mother dies, the widowed father remarries, the new wife has biological children who compete with his biological children for family resources, the stepmother champions her own children at the expense of his; however, his biological children somehow overcome oppression through some event which allows "good" to win out over "evil" (Ceglian & Gardner, 2000, p. 112). A study by Coleman and Ganong (1987) actually found that regardless of behavior, stepparents are perceived as evil, and Duberman (1975, p. 50) asserts "a stepmother must be exceptional before she is considered acceptable. No matter how skillful and patient she is, all her actions are suspect" (Ceglian & Gardner, 2000, p. 113). Weaver (1999) notes that mediated messages also feed into perceptions of stepmothers as less affectionate and loving than biological parents. Though Earnhardt Jr.'s mother was still very much alive, Teresa did become his custodial stepmother when he was six years old, and she did give birth to Earnhardt Sr.'s youngest child, factors which undoubtedly made it very easy for the media and the public to place Teresa in the role of evil stepmother barring evidence to the contrary.

Micropolitics of nonresponse

While Teresa Earnhardt and executives from DEI did make public statements in response to the bevy of image issues they faced during the time in ques-tion, they were few and far between compared to the rhetoric offered by Earnhardt Jr. and his representatives, the media, other NASCAR insiders, and fans. Further, rarely did anyone directly defend Teresa's image or offer counterarguments to those made by her opponents/accusers.

Using Foucault's concept of micropolitics of power to inform their study of image repair, Jerome, Moffitt, and Knudsen (2006) argued that Martha Stewart's lengthy period of nonreponse following allegations of insider trad-ing caused her significant rhetorical trouble. After the allegations surfaced in the media, it was months before Stewart, usually a frequent fixture in the mainstream media, or her associates provided much of a response. All the while her former employees, the media, and even her family members were vocally painting a negative picture of Stewart in the press.

When she finally spoke, it was through her attorneys. Her legal team called for the media to criticize the government's actions in Stewart's case. While their issues with the government's handling of the case may have been valid, they were once again giving power over to the media. Even when Stewart spoke, she did little more than reiterate the strategies used by her legal team. Jerome, Moffitt, and Knudsen (2006) contend,

> Even with all these responses offered by Stewart and her spokespersons, her lack of response to the actual events and omission of information that the public wanted functioned as a kind of nonresponse to the actual crisis. This silence by omission continued to damage her image as the issue progressed. (p. 95)

In most cases, the media simply continued to print/air their own version of the truth, a truth which made Stewart seem guilty. Jerome, Moffitt, and Knudsen (2006, p. 99) go on to argue, "Because Stewart did not deny or accept responsibility for the charges against her for months, publics had reason to believe her silence was a way to buy time in order to effectively hide the truth."

Foucault's concept of micropolitics of power is informative here because the selection of a nonresponse strategy relegated Stewart to a micro level of power, giving over power to the accuser. Jerome, Moffitt, and Knudsen (2006) argue, "If, however, an accused answers an allegation immediately, with a strong voice and clear position, the accused may move to the macro level of empowerment with control over her/his voice" (p. 102). Using the Firestone and Ford tread separation crisis as an exemple, Jerome and Rowland (2009) note the importance of offering credible data in strategically developed counterarguments to the image repair process.

The importance of winning

Discussing the use of apologia in team sport, Kruse (1981) asserts, "sport exists for the fans as a kind of secular religion" where "sporting contests are mythoreligious rites" which have unique ethical and rhetorical intricacies (Kruse, 1981, p. 283). One of those unique intricacies is the importance of winning. Kruse argues that fans are often willing to judge "acts that would indicate bad character" as "neither evil nor wicked" if those committing the act are winners (Kruse, 1981, p. 278). She goes on to note that fans are even sometimes willing to tolerate or even encourage morally reprehensible acts when they are done for the sake of winning (Kruse, 1981). Not surprisingly, she contends that winning is so important that it "controls all of the sport world's ethical precepts" and that "any conduct that might contribute to a team's loss violates those precepts and renders the agent vulnerable to criticism and rejection" (Kruse, 1981, p. 283). Jerome (2008) indicates that Tony Stewart's status as a top NASCAR driver may have been an integral factor in the forgiveness he was given by his team, sponsors, fellow drivers, NASCAR executives, and fans for punching *Indianapolis Star* photographer Gary Mook after Stewart posted a disappointing finish in the 2002 Brickyard 400 at Indianapolis Motor Speedway. Just as winning was an important component of the Stewart response, it would have undoubtedly been a helpful component to the image repair of both DEI and Teresa Earnhardt if it was achieved.

METHOD

To complete this study, the author collected texts from a number of sources. First, the Lexis-Nexis database was used to collect information concerning Teresa Earnhardt's image and the image of DEI during and after the battle over ownership of DEI. "Teresa Earnhardt" was the main search term used to retrieve this information. The majority of data was generated from news articles published from December 14, 2006, when Teresa Earnhardt made the first statement that publicly acknowledged problems between DEI and Earnhardt Jr., and the end of May 2007, the time period in which Dale Jr. announced and discussed his departure from DEI. To gain more information about the opinion of Teresa Earnhardt and DEI held by fans, journalists, and other NASCAR members, as well as information about DEI's mergers, Google searches were also done using search phrases such as "opinion of Teresa Earnhardt," "Earnhardt merger with Ginn," and "Earnhardt merger with Ganassi." Nascar.com and Google searches were also performed to gather data on driver statistics, race results, point standings, and driver changes.

Data for this project were also collected during several trips to DEI during February and May 2009 in conjunction with data for another project. During these trips, the author attended the February 2009 Dale Earnhardt Sr. Memorial Ceremony, the May 2009 Dale Earnhardt Day (which included a behind the scenes tour of DEI, the unveiling of the Earnhardt Sr. and Elvis Legend Series museum exhibits, a lunch and a dinner in the DEI trophy room with members of the DEI executive staff and family, speeches by Teresa Earnhardt and Jeff Steiner, executive vice president and general manager of DEI, and appearances by Taylor, Kerry, and Jeffrey Earnhardt, Kerry's son).

All materials collected were analyzed for critical incidents and responses. Then, the author drew connections between situational constraints, rhetorical strategy selection, and function, drawing conclusions concerning the impact of rhetorical strategy selection on the public image of Teresa Earnhardt and DEI.

KEY SITUATIONAL CONSTRAINTS

It is no secret that NASCAR is a male-dominated sport. Few women had risen to high-ranking positions in NASCAR prior to 2001. Nine years later, there are still few women in "power" positions within NASCAR. In 2003 Lesa France Kennedy, granddaughter of Bill France Sr., the founding father of NASCAR, became president of International Speedway Corporation. In 2009 she became its chief executive officer and was named by *Forbes* as "The Most Powerful Woman in Sports" (Van Riper, 2009). Within the confines of NASCAR, Teresa Earnhardt is arguably second only to Kennedy in terms of position and rank. Though many women are listed as car owners in conjunction with the teams operated by their sons and husbands, few are seen as having leadership roles in the industry. Teresa is the chief executive officer and president of DEI.

However, FOX Sports seems to have forgotten that fact. In 2010, FOX Sports selected Kennedy, Kelley Earnhardt (co-owner of JR Motorsports, which fields two Nationwide Series teams in conjunction with Hendrick Motorsports), DeLana Harvick (co-owner of Kevin Harvick, Inc., which fields Nationwide and Truck Series teams), Danica Patrick (who began driving a limited schedule for JR Motorsports in 2010), and Gillian Zucker (president of Auto Club Speedway in Fontana, CA) as the "five women who are helping the sport as it heads into a new decade" (White, 2010).

Interestingly, two of these women, Kelley Earnhardt and Danica Patrick, may never have made the list had it not been for DEI and Teresa Earnhardt. There would likely be no JR Motorsports without DEI. In 1994 Teresa and Earnhardt Sr. formed Chance, Inc. so that each Earnhardt's three oldest children could drive in a full season in NASCAR's late model series (www. daleearnhardtinc.com, 2010). JR Motorsports, with Kelley Earnhardt at the helm, was founded in 1999 as the management company for Earnhardt Jr., but he drove for DEI. It was not until five years *after* Earnhardt Sr.'s death that JR Motorsports began fielding Nationwide Series cars (jrmotorsports.com, 2010). Some may argue that JR Motorsports started fielding cars in 2006 because it foreshadowed the split with DEI, and that may be true, but JR Motorsports' entrance into the Nationwide Series undoubtedly could not have been made without the support of DEI and its owner, and Kelley undoubtedly learned to manage the NASCAR business alongside her stepmother. Yet, Teresa did not make the list.

From this, it is easy to see that being named one of the powerful women in NASCAR is clearly based on more than just rank and position; it is also based on image. If it were not, Teresa Earnhardt would clearly be close to the top of the list. Teresa's contributions to NASCAR have been overshadowed by the fact that many believe her to be an "evil stepmother," one whose greed is single-handedly destroying what was one of the most powerful companies in the industry. As will be demonstrated below, Teresa was easily cast in this role, and her unwillingness to address issues in a public forum led her to fall victim to the negative effects of the micropolitics of non-response. Though Teresa was a constant fixture at the track when Earnhardt Sr. was alive, she rarely gave interviews and led a fairly private life. She has not attended a race since his death, and still only gives rare interviews and public appearances.

Finally, there comes the issue of winning. Winning is an important component in sports of any kind. To be a top team in NASCAR, the team has to win races and points championships. In 2009, for example, Hendrick Motorsports driver Jimmie Johnson won his fourth Sprint Cup Series points championship (all four were won driving for Hendrick), amassing seven wins, 16 top five finishes, and 24 top ten finishes in the 36-race season (nascar.com, 2010). Mark Martin and Jeff Gordon, Johnson's Hendrick Motorsports teammates, finished second and third in points, respectively (nascar.com, 2010).

Gordon is a three-time Sprint Cup champion, driving to all three championships for Hendrick Motorsports (nascar.com, 2010). Two of the remaining
drivers in the 2009 points championship race drove for Stewart-Hass Racing,
which gets its engines from Hendrick Motorsports (nascar.com, 2010). The
only other team with two drivers in the chase was perennial powerhouse
Roush Fenway Racing (nascar.com, 2010).

DEI has never won a points championship in the Sprint Cup series, either
before Earnhardt Sr.'s death or since. However, as race teams go, DEI was
fairly young at the time of his death. Though it was founded in 1980, it was
not until 1996, when DEI fielded a truck for driver Ron Hornaday in the
inaugural season of the Craftsman Truck Series, that DEI fielded a car/truck
in one of NASCAR's top three series. Until that point it had existed only for
the management of Earnhardt Sr.'s career and other business holdings. Hornaday went on to win the Craftsman Truck Series Championship in 1996 and
1998 (daleearnhardtinc.com, 2010). DEI also won the 1998 and 1999 Busch
Series Championships with Earnhardt Jr. at the wheel (daleearnhardtinc.com,
2010). Truex Jr. also drove DEI cars to Busch Series Championships in 2004
and 2005 (daleearnhardtinc.com, 2010). DEI fielded its first Winston Cup car
in 1998, with Steve Park at the helm; two years later Park scored the first
Winston Cup victory for DEI, winning the August 2000 race at Watkins Glen
International Speedway (steve-park.com, 2010). Six months later Earnhardt
perished.

No one knows what DEI would have become if Earnhardt Sr. had lived,
but all signs pointed to DEI becoming a force to be reckoned with in the
sport's top series. However, DEI and Earnhardt-Ganassi, a merger forged by
DEI and Ganassi Racing prior to the 2009 season, have had limited success
and, as will be detailed later, the success it has had is largely attributed to
Chip Ganassi, not Teresa Earnhardt. Truex Jr. did make the chase for the
Sprint Cup Championship driving for DEI in 2007, and won one race, but
finished a disappointing eleventh in points (nascar.com, 2010). Juan Pablo
Montoya made the chase driving for Earnhardt-Ganassi in 2009, finishing
eighth in points, but he did not win a race all season (nascar.com, 2010).

Interestingly, Earnhardt Jr.'s move to Hendrick Motorsports has failed to
bring him much more competitive success than he had at DEI. In 2008, he
finished twelfth in series points, winning only one race (nascar.com). In
2009, as his teammates took the first three spots in the championship point
standings, and amassed thirteen combined wins, he finished twenty-fifth in
points and did not win a race (nascar.com , 2010).

ANALYSIS

The following analysis develops in four sections. First, the need for image repair will be established. Second, the rhetorical creation of Teresa as an "evil stepmother" will be outlined. Third, DEI's response to Earnhardt's leaving will be laid out. Last, the company's current situation will be explained.

A crisis in the making

Less than a month after the 2006 season ended, Teresa Earnhardt, the usually media-shy matriarch of DEI, gave the first public indication that there might be a problem between her and Earnhardt Jr. On December 14, 2006, Teresa was quoted in the *Wall Street Journal* as saying the following in regard to Earnhardt Jr.'s future with DEI: "Right now the ball's in his court to decide on whether he wants to be a Nascar driver or whether he wants to be a public personality" (Thompson, 2006, n.p.). Though the interview primarily discussed the hiring of Max Seigel as DEI's president of global operations, it squarely put discussions about Earnhardt Jr.'s future with the company and the future of the company itself in the media. Not surprisingly, his contract was up for renegotiation. For almost a month, Earnhardt Jr., who had been named 2006's fourth most popular active U.S. athlete, said nothing (Thompson, 2006).

Then, in early January 2007, Earnhardt Jr. began discussing the comment and his relationship with Teresa in the media. Speaking of the contract negotiations, he acknowledged that the two parties had "hit a few roadblocks" and noted, "I particularly would love to own DEI" (James, 2007a, p. 8C; Perez, 2007a, p. 12C). The only way for that to happen was for Teresa to willingly give it to him. An analysis of his statements makes it clear that, intentional or not, his statements and popularity led to the repeated telling of the "evil stepmother" narrative that, coupled with a relatively non-responsive Teresa Earnhardt and a relatively unsuccessful DEI, put both the CEO and her company on a collision course with image trouble.

In what seemed like a direct response to his stepmother's challenge, Dale Jr. asserted, "Right now, I want to drive for my father's company and drive the No. 8 Bud car. That's what I do. That's what I'm known for and how I want things to be" (Livingstone, 2007, p. 7C). On the comment, he stated that he was surprised at her statement and that he "didn't really appreciate" it (Perez, 2007a, p. 12C). He also said, "It should be every owner's dream to have a driver that's so easy to market. . . . I don't know, maybe she might have been having a bad day or something" (McNulty, 2007a, p. S10). He did note that he was unsure whether or not her comment was taken out of context and that neither he nor Kelley had talked to Teresa personally about the comment (Perez, 2007a). On his relationship with Teresa, he noted,

> Mine and Teresa's relationship has always been very black and white, very strict and in your face. . . . It is what it is. . . . It ain't a bed of roses. . . . The relationship we have today is the same relationship we had when I was 6 years old when I moved into that house with dad and her. It's always been the same. It hasn't gotten worse over the last couple of years or last couple of months. . . . The way I felt about her then is the way I feel about her now. (Perez, 2007a, p. 12C)

He did seem to temper his position by saying, "It's not as people would assume. I think everybody's always had this idea that we were very negative to each other" (Smith, 2007).

He also noted that such an absence of contact was not unusual, that they were cordial, but that they did not talk a great deal because Teresa's efforts were focused on managing the legacy of Dale Earnhardt Sr. rather than on the racing side of the business (Livingstone, 2007, n.p.). On that front, Earnhardt Jr. stated,

> When you go into her office and there are stacks of paper, most of it is dealing with my father and whatever they're doing with his name and what not. . . . So, we don't talk a lot. We don't have a lot of sit-downs about racing and the team and ownership and stuff because that's not at the top of her list. (Smith, 2007, n. p.)

He went on to explain,

> Five or six years ago—when Dad was alive—we didn't really discuss anything business-wise. . . . I talked to Dad about the race teams and racing and talked to Teresa about personal stuff, like "Hey, I'm going to buy a boat. What does that entail?" She knew about stuff like that. Now, she's the owner and I've got to talk to her about race teams and race cars and what I expect out of her efforts and the company. (Smith, 2007, n.p.)

He failed to note at this time, however, that DEI had a director of motorsports who handled the competitive side of the business.

Earnhardt Jr. also thanked all of the people that had been standing up for him, including members of the press (McNulty, 2007a). He went so far as to say that the media, as well as others in his life, could be credited with helping him see what he was actually worth. For example, he said, "When you guys write about the position I have and the leverage I have, it sort of helps me understand what my sister . . . has been trying to explain to me the last five or six years" (Romano, 2007a, p. 1C). Romano (2007a) reported that Earnhardt wanted ownership for not only himself, but also his sister Kelley, who was his manager and chief negotiator, and his half-siblings Kerry and Taylor. Earnhardt Jr. was quick to note that the negotiations would not be stifled because of money, noting that he had "plenty" (James, 2007b). Earnhardt, however, never explained how ownership would be divided amongst the siblings, but he wanted controlling interest which was at least 51 percent (Blount, 2007). The only public response about the issue the researcher could find from any of his siblings at this point in the case came from Kerry, who simply stated, "Dale Jr. is running good and had a good chance at the points championship last year and just fell a little short. . . . It's been a successful operating business and you'd like to see it continue" (James, 2007b, p. 1C).

It is clear from these statements that Earnhardt Jr. perceived Teresa's original statement as an attack on his commitment to the company, the sport, and winning. His responses were an obvious counterattack. However, as much as he tried to temper his statements, it would quickly become clear that the majority of the media and the public believed stepmother and stepson had always had a strained relationship and that she was the one to blame for the rift. Further, his explanation for why they rarely talked indicated that Teresa was more interested in focusing on her husband's legacy than winning. His expression of interest in owning the team and his acknowledgment of the leverage he had was a clear signal that he felt he would win the public's support and, thus, would not be bullied into accepting his stepmother's terms. It seems, in fact, that he was using the media and his popularity to bully her into accepting his terms.

In response to all of this, neither Teresa nor DEI had a great deal to say. In an interview with *USA Today*, Teresa noted that her family was "a typical family with just normal relations" (James 2007b, p. 1C). DEI director of motorsports Richie Gilmore revealed that Teresa had hired "outside" negotiators to handle the case because she felt "it'll happen faster, maybe if she takes the personal side out of it" (James, 2007a, p. 8C). Gilmore also said of her earlier criticisms of Earnhardt Jr., "I think it was taken out of context. . . . Our main focus every time we talk to Teresa, she wants Junior back. That's what's best for the company, that's what's best for Junior and that's what's best for DEI" (James, 2007a, p. 8C). These statements left doubt and unanswered questions on a number of fronts. Was the original comment taken out of context? Did she care about her stepson? What, if anything, was she willing to sacrifice to keep Earnhardt Jr. at DEI? Was she truly dedicated to winning?

The ascendant son and the evil stepmother

The media's role in this crisis is particularly interesting. After Earnhardt Jr.'s statements, countless media headlines cited the step-family relationship, often using contentious words. For example, "Earnhardt, stepmother have issues to address," "Dale Jr., stepmom face future . . . ," "Earnhardt family feud; Junior riled at stepmama . . ." (James, 2007a, p. 8c; Livingstone, 2007, p. 7C; McNulty, 2007a, p. S10). Sportswriter Brant James (2007b) called it a "Greek tragedy with a Carolina drawl" with a "fallen hero king, the queen who would hold the empire together" and "the ascendant stepson . . ." (p. 1C). James (2007b) went on to note that the stepson "victorious in battle, has won the hearts of the people and yearns for his father's throne" (p. 1C).

The media also repeatedly argued that Earnhardt Jr. was the future of the company, and that, without him, DEI could not and would not be competitive or successful. Whether or not that was the truth, one thing is for sure, Earnhardt Jr. was a multi-million dollar asset. In 2006, his salary and endorsements were estimated at $26 million by *Sports Illustrated*, a figure that was calculated without including profits from his merchandising deals (James, 2007b). He also afforded Budweiser, his sponsor, $183.1 million in "total value exposure" in 2006. In comparison, that was $40 million more than 2006 Sprint Cup champion Jimmie Johnson brought in for Lowe's (James, 2007b). James (2007c, p. 12C) foreshadowed what was to come when he contended, "She can't win in a public relations battle with her stepson and she needs to hope for a tie in negotiations." On February 8, Seigel again reiterated that keeping Earnhardt Jr. at DEI was a top priority, noting "I feel if there's a will there's a way. . . . If people are truly committed to a common goal, then you just figure it out" (Perez, 2007b, p. 6C). Seigel also acknowledged that he realized that Teresa's choice to stay out of the spotlight "leaves a lot of room for interpretation" (Perez, 2007b, p. 6C). The next day, surprisingly, Teresa released a statement saying she was not available for comment and that DEI would not release updates about the negotiation (Bernstein, 2007). Interestingly, Earnhardt Jr. also quit publicly commenting on the issue.

The fact that the contract had not been figured out more quickly and that neither side had much else to say publicly, however, left the media and NASCAR insiders to pontificate about the situation. Unfortunately for Teresa and DEI, a large majority of people reiterated and supported Earnhardt Jr.'s apparent position. Many argued that they could not understand why Teresa would even want to fight him. Romano (2007a, p. 1C) argued, "Frankly, it doesn't make sense for her to fight. Particularly because she has never seemed to revel in the role of car owner. She rarely shows up at the track and steadfastly avoids the media spotlight." He concluded his article by contending, "If she wants the best for her company, she may have to let it go"

(Romano, 2007a, p. 1C). NASCAR insiders also got in on the commentary. Famed driver Jeff Gordon stated, "They better figure out a way to come to terms because Dale could write his own ticket" (Bernstein, 2007, p. 10). Gordon asserted that Earnhardt Jr.'s sponsors and fans would follow him and that "He's in the best seat that you could possibly be in this sport, and I don't know if Teresa is really recognizing that" (Bernstein, 2007, p. 10). When asked what would become of DEI without Earnhardt Jr., Tony Stewart answered, "A museum" (Vega, 2007, p. C7), a sentiment that was echoed by James (2007c) when he asserted that without Earnhardt Jr. all Teresa would have left would be her late husband's image and souvenir sales. More detrimental to the deal, perhaps, were the many car owners who were publicly illustrating their interest in having Earnhardt Jr. on their teams, including Richard Childress (Ryan, 2007a).

It is important to note that Earnhardt Jr. did release statements in which he praised Teresa. He even directly defended her against the allegations of driver Kevin Harvick who called her a "deadbeat" owner. In her defense he noted, "Teresa, with everything that's happened, not just to the company but to the family over the last five years, she's had a full plate. . . . That's probably been the sole reason she hasn't been as visible at the racetrack. She's taking care of things that are most important when it comes to family" (Bernstein, 2007, p. 10). Regardless of Earnhardt Jr.'s support on this front, he would soon deliver Teresa Earnhardt and DEI a fatal blow.

Earnhardt Jr.'s final lap at DEI

On May 10, Dale Earnhardt Jr. announced that he would no longer drive for DEI, noting, "It is time for me to compete on a consistent basis and contend for championships. . . . What team I'll drive for next season, I don't know. We'll see who wants to hire me" (Clarke, 2007a, p. E01). He went on to say that he felt that his father would have blessed his decision (Clarke, 2007a). Specifically, he asserted, "It is time for me to continue his legacy, and [do it] the only way I can. . . . By taking the lessons that he taught me: be a man, race hard and contend for championships" (Clarke, 2007a, p. E01). Earnhardt Jr. also contended that his father's vision "and he said it himself, was for me to have a huge role in the company. . . . And I feel like me and Kelley came to the understanding that that was not in the cards" (Romano, 2007b, p. 1C). Earnhardt Jr. noted that the two sides "worked hard to find common ground, but were never close" (McNulty, 2007b). He also stated that he would continue to support DEI in any way he could (Ryan, 2007b).

The only public statement made by Teresa herself came only after Earnhardt Jr. announced he was leaving DEI. She stated,

While we are very disappointed that Dale Jr. has chosen to leave the family business, we remain excited about our company's future. Our aggressive expansion and diversification plans have not changed. This company has continued to thrive since Dale left it in 2001, and it will thrive following today's announcement. Dale and I built this company to be a championship contender, and those principles still apply. Dale Earnhardt Inc. will win, and we have other extremely talented drivers and hundreds of employees that are dedicated to the programs we founded. This company has a great legacy and a bright future, built on loyalty, integrity and commitment. (Dixon, 2007, p. 3C)

Seigel stated that DEI had an aggressive expansion plan in place, and that their job was to "develop all the assets at DEI so we have four Dale Juniors." (Ryan, 2007c, p. 11C).[3] DEI's technical director, Steve Hmiel, noted that the company would survive and that no employees he had talked to wanted to leave DEI, even though DEI employees were worried about job security. In response to that, he stated, "We're going to race. We're going to race forever. That's what (owner Teresa Earnhardt) wants to do. She's proved that time and time again through really bad situations for herself personally" (James, 2007, p. 1C).

These three responses focus on two main image repair strategies: bolstering and minimization. They focused on the solid history and goals of the company and worked to calm the fears of all those who likely felt that Earnhardt Jr.'s departure would mean the end of DEI. However, they gave no specifics on what the company was going to do to fill the gap left by Earnhardt Jr. or how the company was going to regain its winning status.

While Earnhardt Jr. said that he felt DEI would still be successful, others remained skeptical (Ryan, 2007c). The event was compared to the Red Sox losing Babe Ruth to the Yankees (Crandall, 2009). Former NASCAR champion Darrell Waltrip argued that the team was going to basically have to rebuild (Ryan, 2007c). Earnhardt Jr.'s cousin and crew chief at DEI, Tony Eury Jr., was quick to note his wiliness to leave DEI with Earnhardt Jr. (James, 2007e). Sportswriter John Romano (2007b, p. 1C) argued, "I think Teresa Earnhardt may have just discovered a new path to inconsequential. She took a team worth tens of millions and reduced its value and potential in exchange for having the last word in a family spat." More important, perhaps, is what the public thought. An espn.com poll with more than 50,000 participants showed that 80 percent of those responding blamed Teresa for Earnhardt Jr.'s departure from DEI, and 90 percent of respondents felt he was "not out of line for seeking controlling interest in DEI" (Romano, 2007b, p. 1C). Driver Greg Biffle, one of the leading candidates to take Earnhardt Jr.'s place at DEI, was skeptical about the situation there, noting, "There's something there that Junior is not happy with, and obviously, he thinks it's competition" (James, 2007e, p. 6c).

Few people defended Teresa Earnhardt, but some, like sportswriter Dean McNulty, did. In a very poignant piece, he argued that some of the claims made by Earnhardt Jr. and his supporters had little to no evidence to back them up. One potentially fallacious claim, he argued, was the widely circulated assertion that Earnhardt Sr. wanted DEI to go to his children. McNulty (2007c, p. S9) asked, "If that were true, and we are constantly being told it is, then to who did he say this?" Then he noted, "According to court records . . . Earnhardt's will was clear that in the event of his death, DEI would continue to be run and owned by Teresa—his wife and business partner for 19 years" (McNulty, 2007c, p. S9). He also asked, "would that be all of his children? Or did he mean that only Dale Jr. and Kelley . . . would get the company, leaving Kerry . . . and Taylor . . . on the outside looking in?" (2007c, p. S9). He also reminded readers that Teresa ran DEI while Dale was busy driving and asked if she was now expected to just give that up. These and other arguments were logical, but they were not winning public opinion.

Hope (or lack thereof) for the future

The company was still left with two drivers, Paul Menard and Martin Truex Jr. Both were young, and though Truex had won a Busch Series Championship, neither were very successful in Sprint Cup races nor were they among the series' favorite drivers. Though there had been talks of a possible merger between DEI and Robert Yates Racing, by May 18, those were halted, and DEI merged its engine-building program with Richard Childress Racing (James, 2007e, f). In a statement on the merger, Teresa said, "Richard and I both have committed substantial resources to this new company and we share the No. 1 priority to win championships" (James, 2007f, p. 1C). Though the teams worked together to build engines, they remained separate. The merger was particularly interesting because many thought Earnhardt Jr. would end up at Childress in a bid to continue his father's legacy. Earnhardt eventually announced that he would drive for Hendrick Motorsports.

The next controversy occured when Earnhardt Jr. decided to move to Hendrick Motorsports and wanted to take his car number (#8) with him. He had become famous driving the #8 Budweiser Chevrolet. NASCAR race teams own their car numbers. When Earnhardt Jr. began driving for DEI, the company bought the #8 from Stavola Brothers racing because Earnhardt Jr. wanted to drive using the number his grandfather Ralph Earnhardt made famous ("Teresa Earnhardt," 2009). If Earnhardt Jr. wanted the number, he and/or Hendrick would have to buy it from DEI. They tried to buy the number, but there were complications with that as well. One of Teresa's terms was that DEI be given the number back when Earnhardt Jr. was done using it. But that was not the key sticking point. She also wanted a percentage of the licensing revenue. Earnhardt Jr. and Hendrick walked away and bought #88 from Robert Yates Racing ("Teresa Earnhardt," 2009). While this may seem trivial to the average person, in the world of NASCAR it was a huge deal. Hendrick actually created an entire ad campaign focusing on his change in number. One television commercial featured "fans" having to change objects they had emblazoned with the #8 and changing them to #88, including tattoos. Once again, the "evil stepmother" is portrayed as having punished Earnhardt Jr. and his fans. To make matters worse, Budweiser switched to Evernham Racing and a sponsorship of the #9 car driven by the consistently popular driver Kasey Kahne.

Hope for the future (or lack thereof)

In July 2007, DEI announced that it would immediately absorb Ginn Racing in an effort to aid DEI in its vision of becoming a four-car team (Ryan, 2007d). In 2008, DEI fielded four cars. It retained Amirola and Mark Martin, drivers it had inherited in the merger with Ginn Racing, to split the driving for the #8 team which would now carry the U.S. Army sponsorship (Caraveillo, 2007; Newton, 2007). DEI also retained Truex Jr., Menard, and Regan Smith as the full-time drivers of its three other cars (Newton, 2008). The teams had no wins and Truex Jr., its highest ranked driver, finished only fifteenth in series points (nascar.com, 2010).

In November 2008, DEI merged with Chip Ganassi Racing to form a team that is now known as Earnhardt-Ganassi Racing. At the time of the merger, DEI had only secured full sponsorship for Truex's car for the 2009 season, and the Army had taken its sponsorship to Stewart-Haas Racing (Crandall, 2009; Lavarty, 2009). On the merger, Teresa stated, "Having a partner like Chip who is heavily involved on the competition side of the business is an ideal situation for DEI. . . . I think this is a case where we are stronger together than we are apart" (Laverty, 2008, n.p.). She also stated, "He has a long history of managing championship teams in the IndyCar and Rolex Grand-Am Series and I share his passion and goals of winning races and ultimately championships in the NASCAR Sprint Cup Series" (Crandall, 2009, n.p.). This statement clearly indicates that she understands the importance of winning, particularly in the face of such daunting image problems.

Earnhardt-Ganassi fielded three teams in 2009. The drivers were Truex Jr., Amirola, and Juan Pablo Montoya, who had been with Ganassi prior to the merger (nascar.com, 2010). By April 2009, Earnhardt-Ganassi no longer had enough funds to run Amirola's team full-time as it had not found sponsorships since the Army's departure ("Teresa Earnhardt," 2009). It was the first time in ten years a car bearing #8 would not be on the track. Though Montoya showed signs of success, and was even a title contender, Teresa, who Ganassi had said would appear at the track when she thought there was a chance they could win, was never seen (Crandall, 2009). The only time she had been seen at a race track was in July 2009 when she watched her daughter Taylor drive Earnhardt Sr.'s famed #3 in the Goodwill Festival of Speed.

Regardless of how much or how little involvement Teresa actually has at Earnhardt-Ganassi, media articles concerning Montoya's success overwhelmingly praised Ganassi for the organization's resurgence, with barely a mention of Teresa other than as an co-owner of the team (Crandall, 2009). Crandall (2009, n.p.) quipped, "The only things that DEI is holding these days are show cars, merchandise, memorabilia, and fan appreciation days." Crandall (2009) points out, however, that the truth is certainly open to interpretation, noting Teresa could be the brains behind the whole operation, just one who prefers to lead in private.

At the end of 2009, Truex Jr. left Earnhardt-Ganassi for Michael Waltrip Racing and was replaced by Jamie McMurray (nascar.com, 2010). McMurray, like Montoya, has had marked success; he won the Daytona 500, the first race of the 2010 season (nascar.com, 2010). But neither McMurray nor Montoya are among the series' most popular drivers, and Earnhardt-Ganassi is not among the top teams.

There are some glimmers of hope for DEI. As noted in the method section, I attended several events in Mooresville, NC, during February and May 2009 as part of a project on the legend of Dale Earnhardt. During that time, I made several observations. Kerry, the spitting image of his father physically, remains with DEI as a team liaison, and Jeffrey, carrying his grandfather's sly smile, has had a successful career as a driver for DEI in the Busch East Series. It appears that the family is beginning to understand the need to interact with the public more. All family members in attendance at these events interacted with fans, and Kerry visited my table and several others during the luncheon I attended. Kerry also stayed at the Walk of Fame Induction signing autographs and talking with fans seemingly until the last one was gone. Teresa gave a brief speech at the Dale Earnhardt Day celebration, and ate lunch amongst fans, but was not as interactive as Kerry, Jeffrey, and Taylor seemed to be. During neither trip did I find any photographs of Earnhardt Jr. or his sister Kelley at DEI. The only remnants of their time with the company seems to be a few cars driven by Earnhardt Jr. that were important to the history of DEI displayed in museum showrooms. The organization's website and public statements were virtually free of any mention of Kelley or Dale Earnhardt Jr. after his departure as well, save a few references to important events in the organization's history.

Interestingly, after returning from my trip in May 2009, I received an e-mail survey from DEI. Many of the questions revolved around image issues, some particularly about perceptions of Teresa. Since that time, the company seems to be making some gallant attempts at repairing its image. In October 2009, Earnhardt Sr. was voted in as an inaugural member of the NASCAR

Hall of Fame. After the announcement ceremony, Teresa gave a public interview, and on what would have been Earnhardt Sr.'s fifty-ninth birthday,
April 29, 2009, DEI, Richard Childress Racing, JR Motorsports, and Wrangler announced a joint venture relating to the induction. As a tribute to
Earnhardt Sr.'s induction into the Hall of Fame, Earnhardt Jr. will be driving
a replica of his father's famed #3 Wrangler Chevrolet in the July Nationwide
Series race at Daytona International Speedway. On the joint venture, Earnhardt Jr. said, "Me and Teresa always had a lot of respect for each other. . . .
Dad had a way of bringing everybody together. Everybody worked together
for the good of my father" (Newton, 2010, n.p.). *Bleacher Report* correspon-
dent Sandra MacWatters (2010, n.p.) reported, "There were smiles, laughter,
and absolutely no evidence there had ever been hard feelings between Dale
Jr. and Teresa Earnhardt." Inevitably, people quickly wondered if the joint
venture was an indication of a future reunification between Earnhardt Jr. and
DEI (MacWatters, 2010).

DISCUSSION

No one can say what would have happened to DEI if Earnhardt Sr. had not
died; no one can say what would have happened to DEI had Earnhardt Jr.
stayed with the company. What is not up for debate is that Teresa and DEI
did themselves no rhetorical favors during this image crisis. This case offers
some clear lessons for scholars of image repair. One could argue that Teresa
Earnhardt and DEI faced a no-win situation. Earnhardt Sr. is a legend; his
fans became the fans of his namesake. Teresa and DEI either had to give in to
Earnhardt Jr. or suffer a tarnished image. Justifying her position on the ownership battle certainly would not have been easy, but I argue that it was not
impossible.

The evil stepmother narrative was consistently rehashed in the media, yet
Teresa never took any significant step toward defending herself. There were,
as noted above, several logical arguments Teresa could have used to counter
arguments made by her accusers. Yet, she stayed relatively silent, giving all
of her power to her opponents, relegating herself to the micro level of power.
By doing so, she let others set the tone of this series of events. If she had
made arguments similar to those waged by McNulty (2007) she likely could
have justified her position to the public.

Given what we know about the importance of winning in the world of
sport, it is no surprise that DEI had to merge its racing operations with other
organizations after a few bad seasons. However, these bad seasons came not
only after Earnhardt Jr. left the company, but also in the midst of a global
economic crisis. There is no way to know if DEI could have maintained

independent racing operations even if Earnhardt Jr. had stayed, become a series champion, won several races, and drawn other popular drivers to DEI. Racing is a wildly expensive sport; several other top NASCAR teams have engaged in mergers to cut costs and increase outcomes in recent years. Earnhardt Jr.'s elusive success since leaving DEI indicates that he may not be capable of reaching the heights necessary to lead a successful team, a fact that has likely led many to conclude that he could not have saved DEI from a merger.

Recent events indicate that both Teresa Earnhardt and DEI are beginning to see their rhetorical errors and are taking steps to right them. DEI's commitment to have Kerry and Jeffrey Earnhardt as features of DEI's future is clear, and the recent joint venture waged by DEI, JR Motorsports, Richard Childress Racing, and Wrangler seems to indicate that family relationships are being repaired and that Teresa may not be an evil stepmother after all. However, the world of sport places winning at the forefront of importance. If DEI is to regain its status as one of the premier organizations in NASCAR, its competitive prowess must be restored to a level that meets or exceeds the level it had reached during Earnhardt Sr.'s life. Further, if Teresa is to be seen as a pivotal part of that resurgence, she will have to become more visible.

NOTES

1. NASCAR sanctions three series: the Sprint Cup Series (formerly known as Winston Cup/Nextel Cup Series), the Nationwide Series (formerly known as the Busch Series), and the Camping World Truck Series (formerly known as the Craftsman Truck Series). The Sprint Cup Series is the sport's highest ranking series, followed by the Nationwide Series and the Camping World Truck Series, respectively.

2. Dale Earnhardt never drove for his own company in NASCAR's Top Series. He drove in all seven of his championships for Richard Childress Racing.

3. NASCAR had recently established a rule that any one team can only own four cars. At that time, the strongest teams either had four or more cars or had plans to expand to that number.

REFERENCES

Bernstein, V. (2007, February 11). Simmering family feud clouds future of team and its namesake. *The New York Times*. Retrieved October 20, 2009 from the Lexis-Nexis database.

Caraviello, D. (2007, July 25). Dale Earnhardt, Inc., Ginn Racing complete merger: 15 car to receive 14's owner points, 13 car eliminated. *Nascar.com*. Retrieved April 4, 2010.

Ceglian, C. P., & Gardner, S. (2000). Attachment style and the "wicked stepmother" spiral. *Journal of Divorce & Remarriage, 34*, 111-129.

Cherlin, A. (1999) *Public and Private Families* (2nd ed.). Boston: McGraw-Hill College.

Clarke, L. (2007a, May 11). Leaving the team his legendary father built, Earnhardt will become a free agent at the end of season. *The Washington Post*, p. E01. Retrieved October 20, 2009, from the Lexis-Nexis database.

Clarke, L. (2007b, May 27). Split decisions; Where Earnhardt Jr. will land after DEI is the talk of auto racing. *The Washington Post*, p. E01. Retrieved October 20, 2009, from the Lexis-Nexis database.

Crandall, K. (2009, October 5). Will Teresa Earnhardt win the Sprint Cup Series Championship by default? Bleacherreport.com. Retrieved April 4, 2010.

Dixon, K. (2007, May 11). What move means for Junior, DEI. *St. Petersburg Times*, p. 3C. Retrieved October 20, 2009, from the Lexis-Nexis database.

Dorrell, L. (2009, February 16). Teresa Earnhardt: Give credit where credit is due. *Insiderracingnews.com*. Retrieved April 4, 2010.

Duberman, L. (1973). Stepkin relationships. *Journal of Marriage & the Family, 35,* 283-292.

James, B. (2005, July 17). Waltrip leaves teammate, legacy behind at DEI: The only Nextel Cup teammate Dale Earnhardt Jr. has had was picked by Earnhardt's father. *Tampabay.com.* Retrieved April 4, 2010.

James, B. (2007a, January 9). Earnhardt Stepmother have issues to address.*St. Petersburg Times*, p. 8C. Retrieved October 20, 2009, from the Lexis-Nexis database.

James, B. (2007b, January 20). Earnhardt family tiff rivets NASCAR. *St. Petersburg Times*, p. 1C. Retrieved October 20, 2009, from the Lexis-Nexis database.

James, B. (2007c, January 9). 8 that really matters. *St. Petersburg Times*, p. 12C. Retrieved October 20, 2009, from the Lexis-Nexis database.

James, B. (2007d, May 12). As Earnhardt chills out, fallout heats up. *St. Petersburg Times*, p. 1C. Retrieved October 20, 2009, from the Lexis-Nexis database.

James, B. (2007e, May 12). Earnhardt's ripple effect. *St. Petersburg Times*, p. 6C. Retrieved October 20, 2009, from the Lexis-Nexis database.

James, B. (2007f, May 19). New DEI-Childress alliance a wrinkle in Earnhardt move. *St. Petersburg Times*, p. 8C. Retrieved October 20, 2009, from the Lexis-Nexis database.

Jerome, A. M. (2008). Toward prescription: Testing the rhetoric of atonement's usefulness and applicability in the athletic arena. *Public Relations Review, 34,* p. 124-134.

Jerome, A. M., Moffitt, M. A., & Knudsen, J. W. (2006). Understanding how Martha Stewart harmed her image restoration through a micropolitics of power. In J. L. Courtright & P. M. Smudde (Eds.), *Power and public relations*. Cresskill, NJ: Hampton Press.

Kruse, N. W. (1981). Apologia in team sport. *The Quarterly Journal of Speech, 67,* 270-83.

Laverty, G. (2008, November 12). Dale Earnhardt, Inc., Chip Ganassi to merge Nascar operations. *Bloomberg.com.* Retrieved October 20, 2009, from the Lexis-Nexis database.

Livingstone, S. (2007, January 8). Dale Jr., stepmom face future; Deal nearing end; Earnhardt says he wants to stay. *USA TODAY,* p. 7C. Retrieved October 20, 2009, from the Lexis-Nexis database.

MacWatters, S. (2010, April 30). Dale Earnhardt Jr.: Could a return to DEI be in his future. *Bleacherreport.com.* Retrieve May 14, 2010.

McNulty, D. (2007a, January 9). Earnhardt family feud; Junior riles at stepmama over her questioning commitment. *The Toronto Sun,* p. S10. Retrieved October 20, 2009, from the Lexis-Nexis database.

McNulty, D. (2007b, May 11). In the driver's seat; Earnhardt Jr. quits company dad found after stepmom refuses to turn over power. *The Toronto Sun,* p. S14. Retrieved October 20, 2009, from the Lexis-Nexis database.

McNulty, D. (2007c, May 15). In defence of Teresa; Earnhardt's widow has been vilified. *The Toronto Sun,* p. S9. Retrieved October 20, 2009, from the Lexis-Nexis database.

Newton, D. (2007, September 12). Martin will join Amirola in No. 8 car for 2008 season. *Espn.com.* Retrieved April 4, 2010.

Newton, D. (2010, April 29). Earnhardts one big happy family?*Espn.com.* Retrieved May 14, 2010.

Noy, D. (1991). Wicked stepmothers in Roman Society and imagination.*Journal of Family History, 16 (4),* 345-361.

Perez, A. J. (2007a, January 9). Earnhardt Jr. speaks of rift with stepmom. *USA TODAY*, p. 12C. Retrieved October 20, 2009, from the Lexis-Nexis database.

Perez, A. J. (2007b, February 12). Retaining Dale Jr. is team's 'top priority.' *USA TODAY*, p. 6C. Retrieved October 20, 2009, from the Lexis-Nexis database.

Ryan, N. (2007a, February 14). Switching gears; A year of change in Nextel Cup includes six major stories to watch. *USA TODAY*, p. 3C. Retrieved October 20, 2009, from the Lexis-Nexis database.

Ryan, N. (2007b, May 11). Green flag drops on race to land Earnhardt; Hugely popular drivers says he's leaving DEI. *USA TODAY*, p. 1C. Retrieved October 20, 2009, from the Lexis-Nexis database.

Ryan, N. (2007c, May 11). DEI will be A-OK, sides say. *USA TODAY*, p. 11C. Retrieved October 20, 2009, from the Lexis-Nexis database.

Ryan, N. (2007d, February 14). Mergers take over right-of-way; DEI-Ginn union is part of trend to run at profit. *USA TODAY*, p. 8C. Retrieved October 20, 2009, from the Lexis-Nexis database.

Romano, J. (2007a, February 9). Junior will soon find out he's the real boss. *St. Petersburg Times*, p. 1C. Retrieved October 20, 2009, from the Lexis-Nexis database.

Romano, J. (2007b, May 11). At least one bond will never be broken. *St. Petersburg Times*, p. 1C. Retrieved October 20, 2009, from the Lexis-Nexis database.

Smith, G. (2007, January 8). Dale Jr. faces facts over driving future, determination. *USA TODAY.com*. Retrieved May 14, 2010.

Teresa Earnhardt and the end of the No. 8: Number had no value without Little E, which stepmom found out to late (2009, April 13).*Nbcsports.com*. Retrieved April 4, 2010.

Thompson, A. (2006, December 14). New executive brings diversity to Nascar team. *The Wall Street Journal.* Retrieved October 20, 2009, from the Lexis-Nexis database.

Van Riper, T. (2009, October 14). The most powerful women in sports.*Forbes.com*. Retrieved May 14, 2010.

Vega, Michael (2007, February 18). Earnhardt can't steer clear of fame. *The Boston Globe,* p. C7. Retrieved October 20, 2009, from the Lexis-Nexis database.

Wald, E. (1981). The remarried family: Challenge and promise. New York, NY: Family Service Association of America.

Weaver, S. (1999). A mothering but not a mother role: A grounded theory study of the nonresidential stepmother. Unpublished doctoral dissertation, University of Missouri, Columbia.

Chapter Nineteen

The Puck Stops Here: The NHL's Image Repair Strategies During the 2004-2005 Lockout

James R. DiSanza, Nancy J. Legge, H. R. Allen, and
James T. Wilde, Idaho State University

Given the amount of media coverage that professional sports receive in North America, a labor stoppage almost never comes as a surprise to fans. And so it was no surprise to anyone when on September 16, 2004, Gary Bettman, commissioner of the National Hockey League (NHL), initiated a labor lock-out that would last 310 days and make the NHL the first professional sports league to lose an entire season to a labor dispute. The NHL, which claimed losses of 273 million dollars in 2002-2003, initiated the lockout looking for some form of "cost certainty," preferably in the form of a salary cap, before it would agree to return. In so doing, the league angered fans and sponsors, damaged businesses surrounding NHL arenas, hurt employees who were laid off, endangered its TV contracts with ABC and ESPN, and risked dropping the NHL into permanent sporting obscurity in the United States (Farber, 2004). Already a distant fourth (and falling) of the so-called "big four" pro-fessional team sports in the United States, the lockout threatened to destroy the league outright, or at least drop it behind other up-and-coming sports such as NASCAR.

The crisis that precipitated the lockout was created by the league's own mismanagement through the 1990s, and the recalcitrance of the NHL Players Association (NHLPA), run by Bob Goodenow. Like any organization, image and credibility are vital to sports leagues, which must offset their enormous costs with billions of dollars in revenue from paying fans, television rights fees, sponsorships, and merchandise licensing. The NHL found itself in an image crisis of its own making—precipitated as it was by greed and misman-agement—one that surpassed almost anything experienced by the other three major professional team-sports leagues in the United States. Not even Major League Baseball's (MLB) 1994-1995 strike, which forced the cancellation of the World Series, or its later steroid crisis, threatened the economic viability of professional baseball to the degree that professional hockey was threat-ened in 2004.

Knowing all of these risks, the NHL nevertheless proceeded on its course and received the cost certainty it wanted from the union, a salary cap tied to annual league revenue. The league deployed an adroit combination of consis-tent image restoration strategies, improvements to the game, and new mar-keting strategies to emerge from the lockout in a stronger position than it had been in since the early 1990s. This case study illustrates that the right combi-nation of image restoration strategies and business practices—combined with a bit of luck—can restore an organization from even the worst self-inflicted crisis.

This chapter will proceed in three phases: First, we will examine the lockout itself, focusing on the factors that precipitated it, the image repair strategies used throughout the lockout, and the product improvements the NHL planned once the lockout ended. Second, we will examine the early post-lockout period (July 2005-June 2007), which brought, at best, mixed reactions to the NHL's return. Finally, in part three we will look at the later post-lockout period (July 2007-June 2010), where the NHL's business suc-cess legitimized its image restoration strategies.

THE LOCKOUT: PRECIPITATING FACTORS, IMAGE REPAIR TACTICS, AND PRODUCT IMPROVEMENTS

This section is divided into three parts, the first of which focuses on the economic factors that led to the 2004-2005 lockout. The second part exam-ines the image repair tactics the league used during the lockout and their effect. The third examines the changes to its product and marketing that the NHL made during the lockout.

Bettman and the thirty NHL team owners (or ownership groups) were well prepared for the work stoppage believing that it could take up to two years for the new collective bargaining agreement to be negotiated with the NHLPA, one that included cost certainty. To understand why they were willing to sit out for two years—to risk permanently alienating fans, spon-sors, and television executives—one has to understand the increasingly des-perate economic circumstances the league and the NHLPA created for them-selves through the 1990s.

Precipitating Factors: Cost Structure and Declining Popularity

The central point of dispute between the NHL and the NHLPA was the NHL's desire for "cost certainty"—some method to limit or cap player salaries so that they would not exceed a certain percentage (e.g., 50 percent) of the league's gross revenues. The desire for cost certainty is a natural one for any business owner. Cost certainty allows for better planning and more predictable profits and losses. Cost certainty, especially through a salary cap, was seen as a way to finally control the escalating player salaries that the league claimed were consistently outstripping individual team revenue.

Through the late 1980s and early 1990s, NHL economics were on a firm footing. League-wide average attendance was solid, at about 14,000 per game, and the average player salary was only $467,000. During the 1993-1994 season, the NHL had high hopes that its two marketable superstars, Wayne Gretzky and Mario Lemieux, its first decent national TV contract with Fox ($31 million over five years), and the thrilling victory of the New York Rangers over the Vancouver Canucks for their first Stanley Cup in fifty-four years, would win over new fans (Maney, 2005). In June 1994, *Sports Illustrated* ran a cover story with the headline: "Hot Not: While the NBA's image has cooled, the NHL has ignited surprising new interest in hockey"(Swift, 1994).

Much of that progress came to a halt during the lockout-shortened 1994-1995 season. This was Gary Bettman's first attempt to achieve cost certainty. Bettman had just come to the NHL from the NBA, where he was the number two man on commissioner David Stern's team, and was frequently credited with negotiating the NBA's collective bargaining agreement, which included a soft salary cap. He was brought in to do the same for the NHL, but this first lockout failed after 103 days when Bettman capitulated, at the behest of powerful large market owners in New York and Toronto, with little more than a rookie salary cap and a lot of lost "buzz" from the previous season. Ten years later, Bettman would avoid the same mistake by gaining far more complete commitment from the owners. Meanwhile, back in 1994, without a salary cap, player costs started to escalate out of control.

In any sports league that is organized like the MLB or NHL, team owners and their general managers compete against one another for a limited supply of top-quality athletic talent. As the law of supply and demand suggests, any market that has limited resources will lead to increasing prices. The need for teams to win in order to attract fans and revenue pushes general managers to ever higher offers to talented free-agent players, who can negotiate with any and all teams for their services. Unchecked, player salaries can quickly meet or exceed revenues, especially for small market teams that have a smaller fan base and smaller profits from their regional sports network (RSNs), such as the New England Sports Network (NESN) or any of the regional Fox sports networks. These broadcast rights are different from national broadcast rights sold to ESPN or NBC, which are negotiated by the league. Individual teams negotiate the broadcast rights with their local RSN and keep all of that money, but rights to the Rangers in New York City are obviously more lucrative than the rights to the Sabres in Buffalo, New York. The big four major sports leagues in North America use one of two methods to check the imbalance between large-market and small-market teams in order to assure reasonable profits and competitive balance: the luxury tax and the salary cap.

Major League Baseball uses a luxury tax system, whereby teams whose aggregate payroll (e.g., the New York Yankees) exceeds a certain figure (determined annually) are taxed on the excess of that amount. This tax is paid to the league which is redistributed to smaller market teams so that they may compete for talent on a relatively level playing field. The other method is a salary cap, whereby player salaries are limited to a certain percentage of league revenues. The National Basketball Association and the National Football League employ the salary cap as a way to assure adequate team revenue and cross-league competitiveness.

After the failed (from the NHL's point of view) lockout of 1994, the league had neither a luxury tax nor salary cap and player costs began to escalate. Before 1994, average player salaries were 57 percent of league revenue but by 2004, the payroll of the Detroit Red Wings had grown seven times, the Colorado Avalanche by 7.5 times, the Dallas Stars by 6.5 times, and Philadelphia, St. Louis and Toronto by six times. Overall player salaries had grown to 75 percent of total league revenue (Maney, 2005). Player costs ran 65 percent of revenue in football, 63 percent in baseball, and 55 percent in basketball (Farber, 2004).

According to *Forbes* magazine, the NHL went into the red in 2002, losing $8.2 million on revenue of $2.1 billion. In 2003, losses had widened to $123 million and revenue was flat at $2.1 billion (Maney, 2005). The losses were compounded by the high value of the American dollar compared to its Canadian counterpart. Through the late 1990s, the Canadian dollar was losing value compared to the American dollar, culminating in an all time low exchange value of $.61 cents on January 21, 2002 (Belson, 2009). This exchange rate severely damaged otherwise healthy Canadian teams because they took in their money in Canadian dollars, but paid out all player salaries in U.S. dollars.

Increasing player salaries also created a predictable competitiveness gap, shifting the advantage to wealthy teams like the Detroit Red Wings, and away from smaller but storied franchises in Calgary and Edmonton, and U.S. expansion teams such as Tampa Bay.

In 1992-93, the gap between the highest payroll team (Pittsburgh Penguins, $15.2 million) and the lowest (San Jose and Tampa Bay, each $6.9 million) was about double, Hockey Zone Plus figures show. In 2003-2004, the gap between the highest (Detroit, $77.8 million) and lowest (Florida, $26.4 million) was triple. (Maney, 2005)

In order to stay competitive, smaller teams felt pressure to pay out more for top-tier free agent players, which further escalated salaries and damaged the financial position of small-market teams, especially small-market Canadian teams.

Finally, as profits flatlined and more and more gross revenue was eaten up by salaries, team valuations began to decline. The most significant financial crisis for a team owner in any sport is declining franchise value. Most sports team owners do not make money on the annual profits, which are miniscule by the standards of most business operations. This is especially true of leagues without the mega-broadcast rights deals that are common for the National Football League, whose deals are worth a total of $20 billion through 2013. For an NHL team, the annual rights fees provided by the league's national broadcasting contract are many times lower than the fees provided by the NFL or MLB, and as a consequence, NHL team owners may lose money year after year—this fact changing only if the team makes a deep playoff run. Instead, the real money-making strategy involves selling the team for more than it cost to purchase. According to *Forbes* magazine, twenty-one NHL teams experienced valuation declines between 2000 and 2003. Table 19.1 below reports the Forbes valuations for nine selected teams.

Table 19.1.   Selected Forbes NHL Team Values, 2000-2003 (millions of dollars)

Team	Pre-Lockout				Post-Lockout	
	2000	2001	2002	2003	2008	2009
Toronto Maple Leafs	203	216	241	263	448	470
Dallas Stars	182	207	254	270	273	246
New York Rangers	263	277	263	272	411	416
Philadelphia Flyers	240	250	262	252	275	273
Detroit Red Wings	218	225	266	245	303	337
Boston Bruins	217	230	243	223	263	271
Colorado Avalanche	198	243	250	229	231	205
Montreal Canadiens	191	182	187	170	334	339

Data from *Forbes* magazine

As you can see in Table 19.1, the Toronto Maple Leafs, Dallas Stars, and New York Rangers are examples of teams whose value generally increased throughout the period depicted, but the other teams on this list saw valuations decline, especially in the two-year period prior to the lockout. The league believed that team valuations would continue to fall unless they could rein in costs, and player salaries were by far the most significant cost for NHL teams. Unlike the 1993-1994 lockout, the prospect of declining team valuations got the owners' attention and they lined up solidly behind Bettman. This time, there would be no deal without a salary cap.

In addition to its many financial problems, a variety of problems with the game itself contributed to a less exciting product on the ice and lower television ratings. Declining ratings would eventually lead to lower broadcast rights fees.

At the end of 1993, the NHL signed its most significant broadcast television deal ever with Fox Network, which brought in $31 million a year over five years. An additional non-exclusive deal for weeknight games on ESPN added another $14 million to the Fox figure. Fox intended to make the NHL a significant component of its growing sports presence, which also included a successful bid for NFL rights. Fox brought a number of innovations to sports broadcasting, including the "Fox Box," the inset box that continuously tracked the game clock and the score, and for hockey, the Fox Trax glow puck, a special puck that had a microchip in it that projected a glow around the puck for easier visibility. Although reviled by experienced fans, the glow puck was designed to make it easier for hockey neophytes to follow the sport.

Although Nielsen ratings during the 1994 lockout-shortened season were a solid (for hockey) 2.0, by the end of the contract they had declined to an average of 1.4. Fox and the NHL parted ways in 1999 when the league signed an exclusive broadcast rights deal with ESPN, which brought in $120 million a year for five years (total: $600 million). ESPN broadcast several games a week, including extensive coverage of the Stanley Cup playoffs. The deal also brought ABC in to broadcast five weeks worth of regional games on Saturday afternoons and games three to seven of the Stanley Cup finals. Most observers felt the ESPN/ABC offer was wildly inflated given the ratings drop that Fox had experienced and some believed the lucrative offer stemmed from Disney's (who owned ABC and ESPN) desire for supremacy over the entire American sports market at the expense of News Corp., which owned Fox. According to sportswriters Klein and Reif (1995), in their book entitled *The Death of Hockey*:

> But the real reason for the cash windfall had nothing to do with any belief in the NHL's ability to bounce back from its problems and everything to do with the television war being fought between Disney Corporation (owner of ABC and ESPN) and Rupert Murdoch's News Corp. (owner of Fox and Fox

Cable). . . . Furthermore, NewsCorp., whose sports-television empire already controlled much of the airwaves in Britain, Australia, East Asia, and South America, was using Fox Cable to mount a nationwide challenge to Disney's coveted and profitable ESPN. The battle, therefore, was not really over the right to telecast NHL games, but was rather a sideshow in the much greater donnybrook between two gigantic multinational media empires for supremacy in the world's most lucrative sports market, the United States. (p. 160)

The ratings for the new rights package on ESPN and ABC were less than successful. In 1999, ESPN's ratings were 0.6, and by the time of the lockout, they dropped to 0.5 (Maney, 2005). On ABC, regular season ratings started out lower than they had been on Fox (1.4 rating) in 1999-2000 and dropped to 1.1 by the last year of the contract, 2003-2004 (Stepneski, 2009). Game three of the Stanley Cup finals in the year before the lockout (2003) received a 1.4 rating, the second lowest for any prime-time show in the history of the major networks (Farber, 2004). In short, NHL ratings had become a laughing stock in the sports television industry.

How could ratings have fallen so steeply? Most observers note that while the NHL was busy mismanaging its fiscal house, it also allowed its product, the game on the ice, to become slow and boring. The 1990s became known as the "dead-puck" era, a time when the game slowed to a crawl, scoring declined, and the number of ties began to rival professional soccer.

The dead-puck era was created by a number of factors, starting with a new emphasis on stifling defensive systems such as the Left Wing Lock, practiced expertly by the Detroit Red Wings, and the Neutral Zone Trap, employed to perfection by the New Jersey Devils. These systems slowed teams down in the neutral zone (the area of ice between the blue lines), creating turnovers, and making it nearly impossible for teams to generate an organized attack.

Second, defensive hockey was further strengthened by the slow erosion of enforcement of the rules against interference, hooking (with the stick), and holding. This new game of interference was sometimes referred to as the "clutch-and-grab" game, and it limited the ability of talented forwards to sustain offensive pressure. Hall of Fame player Brett Hull referred to the hockey played through the 1990s as "rodeo on ice" (Klein & Reif, 1995).

Finally, goaltending equipment had gotten lighter and larger, and where goaltenders of the past were loners who worked on their game alone, today's goaltenders receive coaching in every nuance of movement and technique. These two innovations allowed modern goaltenders to cover more area than ever before, shrinking the open scoring spaces.

The three changes described above, defensive systems, clutch-and-grab, and improved goaltending, tilted the balance of the game in favor of defense, damaging the balance necessary for exciting play. Even NHL players had become tired of the game: "I talk to a lot of friends around the league and they say watching the National Hockey League isn't as much fun anymore," said then Phoenix Coyotes forward Jeremy Roenick. "It's boring hockey. That stupid trap system—whoever invented it should be shot. It's the stupidest friggin' hockey ever" (Klein & Reif, 1995, p. 33). Table 19.2 below lists the average save percentage ("Average save percentage," 2008), and goals scored ("NHL average goals,") starting in 1991.

Table 19.2. NHL Save Percentage and Average Goals Per Game (Regular Season)

Year	Save Percentage	Average Goals per Game	Year	Save Percentage	Average Goals per Game
1991-92	.888	6.96	2001-02	.908	5.24
1992-93	.896	7.25	2002-03	.909	5.31
1993-94	.908	6.18	2003-04	.911	5.14
1994-95	.892	5.97	2004-05	Lockout	Year
1995-96	.907	6.29	2005-06	.901	6.17
1996-97	.905	5.83	2006-07	.905	5.89
1997-98	.922	5.28	2007-08	.909	5.57
1998-99	.914	5.27	2008-09	.908	5.83
1999-00	.904	5.49	2009-10	.911	5.68
2000-01	.903	5.51			

Notice that prior to the lockout, goaltenders' save percentages have gone steadily upward and goals per game dropped from a high of nearly seven per game in 1991-1992 to a low of 5.14 in 2003-2004, just prior to the lockout.

The increasingly boring NHL received ever-smaller television ratings, which produced a predictable result: when ABC discussed renewing its broadcast rights with the NHL for the (soon-to-be canceled) 2004-2005 season, the network said they would not televise the Stanley Cup finals in prime time. Fortunately for the NHL, the lockout meant they did not need to accept or discuss this embarrassing offer.

Immediately after the lockout, NHL's TV rights deals hit bottom. The league signed a broadcast rights deal with NBC that included no upfront fees, merely an agreement that any profit that NBC received after covering costs would be split evenly with the NHL. The league also signed a cable package with the little-known Outdoor Life Network (OLN) for $70 million a year, the hitch being that OLN was in 20 million fewer homes than ESPN2, thus limiting the league's exposure.

The lockout, which began on September 16, 2004, and lasted for 310 days, ended with a complete victory for Gary Bettman and the NHL. Early on, the players union assumed that the league would eventually cave in and sign a deal sans the salary cap. By January 2005, with Bettman and the owners standing strong, the union offered a one-time salary rollback of 24 percent, an offer that was rejected by the league. By spring, Bob Goodenow, the PA's head, had become isolated from most daily negotiations, which were taken over by his second, Ted Saskin, and a group of players interested in resolving the dispute. As this group gained ascendance, the Players Association began to accept that a salary cap was inevitable (Podell, 2005). When the storm finally subsided, a new collective bargaining agreement was reached that included the following provisions.

- A hard salary cap set at 54 percent of league revenues (which included all player salaries, signing bonuses, and performance bonuses)
- 15 to 20 percent of player revenue would be placed in escrow and if the league failed to meet revenue projections, part of that money would be returned to the team
- A 24 percent across the board salary rollback on all player salaries
- Entry-level salaries were capped at $850,000 a year for three years
- A revenue-sharing plan was established wherein the top ten money makers would share a percentage of their revenues with the bottom ten teams
- The salary cap limit for the 2005-2006 season was set at $39 million based on anticipated league-wide revenue of $1.8 billion (Garrioch, 2005)

Five days after the players ratified the collective bargaining agreement, Bob Goodenow, the head of the NHLPA, resigned his position. The NHL had not only gotten everything it wanted in the CBA, but they had also rid themselves of Goodenow, a persistent thorn in Bettman's side. Gary Bettman's image with the owners could not have been higher. His image with fans and sponsors, however, needed help.

The NHL's Image Repair During the Lockout

The NHL engaged in a variety of image restoration tactics (Benoit, 1995) throughout the lockout and in the time period immediately following the lockout. The tactics the NHL used were consistent with one another and consistent with actions the league took after the lockout. By themselves, the tactics were not going to repair an image so tattered in the eyes of the fans. However, these tactics were also consistent with and supported by the actions the league took to fix its product and marketing. The NHL focused its image restoration on four tactics: mortification, transcendence, shifting the blame, and bolstering.

Mortification

Bettman made an explicit apology to fans and the people whose livelihoods depended on the NHL in mid-September 2004. In a press conference announcing the expiration of the CBA and the beginning of the lockout, Bettman apologized "to our millions of fans and the thousands of people whose livelihoods depend on our game." He went on to say, "It is truly unfortunate that we have to go through this. I assure you that no one is more unhappy about this situation than I am" ("NHL owners vote," 2004).

In our extensive examination of more than eighty news articles written prior to and during the lockout, this is the only example of mortification from the NHL that we could find. On the face of it, this may seem unusual. You might think that the commissioner of the first major sports league to lose an entire season to a lockout—a management-initiated action—would regularly apologize to its loyal fans. However, extensive mortification would have contradicted the next two image repair tactics, transcendence and shifting the blame.

Transcendence

Using transcendence, a person directs attention to other, allegedly higher values, to justify one's actions (Benoit, 1995). The NHL engaged in extensive transcendence during the lockout. The NHL justified the lockout as absolutely necessary and "the right thing to do" by appealing to two higher values: 1) the need for the league and all thirty franchises to operate on a solid economic footing, and 2) the need for a better competitive balance among the teams. In essence, the NHL stood behind its decision to lock out the players as absolutely necessary and right in order not only to save the game but to improve it once it did return.

Most of the transcendence tactics appealed to the need for a sound financial base for the league and its owners. In February 2004, Bill Daly, the NHL's deputy commissioner, said, "The conclusion that we have reached is that it's important at this stage that we do the right thing and not just make a deal to make sure we don't miss time. . . . Far more harm can come to this league by just doing a deal to do a deal" ("Counsel presents," 2004). Gary Bettman also engaged in transcendence throughout the lockout. A sampling of these appeals include:

> We have no interest in operating under the current system or anything that looks like the current system. (June 2004) (Burnside, 2004)
> The NHL has lost $1.8 billion over the 10 years of the existing collective bargaining agreement. We're out of time, we're out of gas, it's time to make it right. (September 2004) ("NHL owners vote," 2004)

It's about doing the right thing to ensure that the game and the franchises
are healthy. (October 2004) ("Doors locked," 2004)

The NHL supported its claims of financial losses with an independent audit
of its books conducted by former Securities and Exchange Commission
chairman Arthur Levitt, who said that the league had lost $273 million in the
previous season. Levitt said, "The results are as catastrophic as I've seen in
any enterprise this size. . . . They are on a treadmill to obscurity, that's the
way the league is going. So, something's got to change." Levitt said that if he
were a banker he would not underwrite any of the league's teams, "nor would
I invest a dollar of my own personal money in what appears, to me, a
business that's heading south" (Brehm, 2004). The NHLPA, who had itself
done an audit of four teams' books, claimed the Levitt report omitted millions of dollars in hockey-related revenue and that losses were not as serious
as reported. This response did little to diminish Levitt's credibility or his
strongly worded conclusions.

In early December, the NHLPA, in an attempt to end the lockout without
a salary cap, offered a one-time salary giveback of 24 percent. The NHL
refused this gambit and Bettman again brought the issue back to long-term
economic stability for the league and its franchises: "One aspect of the proposal [from the NHLPA] is very significant . . . that element is a recognition
by the union of our economic condition, but it is a one-time element [the
giveback] . . . . We have said consistently that the focus must be on the
overall systemic issues and the long-term needs and health of our game"
("Bettman intends," 2004). In this comment, Bettman brushes away the giveback because it does not offer any cost certainty. He also co-opts the PA's
offer by saying it supports his position on the need for a systemic solution to
systemic problems. (The NHL, however, did manage to keep the giveback on
the table during the negotiation and it was included in the final CBA agreement.)

A few days later, Bettman reiterated the need for "cost certainty" when he
said, "We only know of really one approach to meaningfully address and fix
our problems. And unless somebody can miraculously come up with another
approach, which I am highly skeptical of but always [eager] to listen, we're
committed to fixing this the right way" ("Bettman rejects proposal," 2004).

On other occasions, the league based its justification for the lockout on
the fans and the need for better competitive balance for both small-market
and large-market teams. When speaking at a press conference in September,
just before the lockout was announced, Bettman said that the teams in the top
one-third of the salary range were three times more likely to make the
playoffs than teams in the bottom third: "That is a status quo with which we
simply cannot continue to live. Our game and our fans deserve better. . . . We

need a system that will eliminate the disparities in payrolls, so that a team's ability to compete depends on its team building skills, not on its ability to pay" ("NHL owners vote," 2004). On different occasions Bettman said,

> We owe it to our fans, we owe it to the game to fix it. (September 2003) (Karl, 2003) We need to make the right deal to make this league and our franchises healthy. We owe it to the game. We owe it to our fans. We owe it to our franchises in the markets we play in. (October 2004) ("Bettman: NHL won't," 2004)

When all hope of an abbreviated season had faded in February 2005, Gary Bettman issued a letter to fans with the following statement:

> Our intention throughout the collective bargaining process has been, and continues to be, the creation of an enduring partnership with our players that will allow you to enjoy a world-class product, at affordable prices, and enter each season confident that your favorite team can compete for the most cherished trophy in pro sports, the Stanley Cup. Our resolve to deliver on that promise will not change. ("Gary Bettman's Letter to Fans," 2005)

Even at the end of the lockout, Bettman evoked transcendence, including the importance of both economic viability and competitive balance, to justify the lost year. "Today, our Board of Governors gave its unanimous approval to a Collective Bargaining Agreement that signals a new era for our league—an era of economic stability for our franchises, an era of heightened competitive balance for our players, and era of unparalleled excitement and entertainment for our fans" ("Collective bargaining agreement," 2005).

Transcendence was the NHL's primary image repair tactic deployed throughout the lockout. Using this, the league argued that the lockout was just and necessary for the survival of the league and betterment of the game. The reliance on transcendence tactics helps explain the minimal use of mortification. The labor stoppage was regrettable, claimed the NHL, but entirely justified based on the league's commitment to the higher values of financial viability and competitive balance. Regular apologies would have undercut this stance. In essence, the league's use of transcendence suggested it had little to apologize for. In place of mortification, the league also shifted the blame for the extended lockout to the players' union.

Shifting the blame

The NHL repeatedly shifted the blame for the lockout to the players. With rare exceptions, Bill Daly, the NHL's deputy commissioner, issued most of the comments blaming the NHLPA for the lockout. This allowed Bettman to stay above the fray, on the high ground of transcendence, while Daly handled the "dirtier" work of passing out blame.

For example, Daly said that "The National Hockey League made significant efforts over the past 5½ years to avoid having to miss any games this season" ("Doors locked," 2004), implying that the Players Association had not been doing its part to avoid the lockout. Daly blamed the union in harsh terms on a number of other occasions. "We want to move the process along. They're looking to stall. . . . It's clear that they're engaged in a charade. They want to fill the time between now and Sept. 15, force a lockout and take their chances. That's unfortunate for the sport, unfortunate for the players, and certainly unfortunate for our fans" ("NHL exec accuses," 2004).

The shifting the blame strategy is interesting in one aspect: it's a clear example of how the punctuation of action can be used to absolve oneself of blame and assign that blame to another. Watzlawick, Beavin and Jackson (1967) were among the first to notice that to outsiders a series of exchanged messages can be viewed as an uninterrupted sequence. However, the participants always introduce punctuation to that stream of communication by deciding what move started the interaction. This punctuation is often designed to assign blame. Looked at one way, the NHL was entirely responsible for the lockout because it was precipitated by owners and general managers throwing enormous amounts of money into questionable free agent contracts. Every new mega-contract set a higher baseline for the next similarly skilled free agent. But, the NHL chose to ignore this early phase of the problem, and started their discussions of the lockout with the various solutions they had proposed since 2000, all of which included cost certainty, and the PA's refusal to negotiate this issue. By this punctuation, the NHL absolved itself of responsibility because it started the negotiation by proposing solutions, all of which the PA ignored or rejected. The NHLPA never effectively responded to the blame shifting. They sometimes talked about the importance of the free market in determining player salaries, but such abstractions rarely count for much with the fans.

The few polls on the issue of the NHL lockout that were done suggest that there was some positive effect for the shifting the blame tactic. Gauging the effectiveness of an image tactic is always difficult outside of a controlled environment. In this case, measuring effectiveness is even more difficult given the lack of polling on the subject. We could not find any U.S.-based polls on the subject of the NHL lockout, perhaps a reflection of how far the league's popularity had fallen. This was not the case in Canada, however, where hockey surpasses national pasttime status and approaches a national obsession. A poll conducted by Canadian polling company Ipsos-Reid, done in mid-September 2004, showed that 52 percent of Canadians blamed the players for the impasse, while only 21 percent blamed the owners ("NHL owners vote," 2004). An online poll by TNS Canadian Facts, a market information firm, reported that only 11 percent blamed the owners exclusively for the lockout, while 31 percent blamed the players exclusively. The rest (58 percent) blamed both parties ("Players blamed," 2004). These poll results do suggest that the NHL's attempts to shift the blame were persuasive to Canadian audiences. It's also important to note that in most sports labor disputes over the past twenty years, fans have tended to place a higher burden of blame on the players than the owners. At the very least, the NHL's blame shifting tactic did not harm this bias among fans.

Research on image repair suggests that organizations should not shift the blame to stakeholders within the organization because the target of blame is part of the organization claiming innocence (Benoit & Brinson, 1994). However, professional athletes are not thought of as "employees" of their teams in any commonly shared sense of that term. Employees rarely make more money than their superiors, yet the highest paid professional athletes regularly make more money than any member of the organization, save the owner. The typical employee isn't able to advertise their efforts to other potential employers and generate other job offers just by showing up to work every day. And most employees do not have agents who market them to would-be employers. A better analogy than "employee" for the professional athlete is highly paid contractor. Because contractors have a more tenuous relationship to the organization, it is probably easier and more acceptable to shift blame to this group than it would to a group of employees. In addition to shifting the blame to the players, the NHL absolved itself of blame through bolstering.

Bolstering

The NHL repeatedly engaged in bolstering by indicating that it was always willing to negotiate. Again, Bill Daly did most of the bolstering for the league. In February 2004, Daly said, "We have made the players' association aware that we are ready to meet at any time . . . the more dialogue, the more exchange of information, the better understanding one side has of the other's position . . . the more that goes on, the better" ("Counsel presents," 2004).

In August, Daly said, "We told the players' association that we would make ourselves available every day between now and the end of the collective bargaining agreement to try to get this resolved" ("Labor talks shift," 2004). In September, Daly said of the NHLPA, "they're not serious about the process at this point, and until they get serious about the process, there's really not a whole lot to talk about" ("NHL allowance," 2004). Finally, also in September, Daly issued his strongest statement to date when he talked about six proposals the NHL made several months earlier, only one of which involved a hard salary cap:

> It's been 15 months and we're now three weeks away from the expiration of the collective bargaining agreement and we have absolutely nothing from them. . . . Meanwhile, we've made six proposals to them which they rejected after asking questions for almost six hours. Each of which would've solved our

problems, maintained an average player's salary of $1.3 million, guaranteed the players more than 50 percent of our revenues and we still would've seen multimillion dollar contracts in the sport. ("NHL exec accuses," 2004)

This bolstering tactic was shrewd. The league says that they've advanced a number of proposals, only some of which involved a hard salary cap. The claims of $1.3 million in average salaries and half of league revenues might have sounded fair to the average hockey fan. This effort at bolstering also paints the NHLPA as uncooperative and unreasonable, further reinforcing Daly's continued efforts to shift the blame, described above.

Through a focus on transcendence, shifting the blame, and bolstering, the NHL justified the need for the lockout, both in terms of economics and the fans, claimed that it was willing to negotiate, and shifted the blame for the lockout to the NHLPA. Although the polling data suggest the attempt to shift the blame was successful, most of the rest of the image repair tactics fell flat. Fans and sportswriters were angry about the loss of the game, and although a majority may have blamed the players more than the NHL, there was plenty of criticism to go around, and for the league, Bettman was the focal point of that criticism.

Steve Wilstein (2005), an AP writer, opined at the midpoint of the lockout that it was time for Bettman to go:

> NHL commissioner Gary Bettman spoke like an accountant and looked like a mortician—or maybe it was the other way around—as he directed the final services Wednesday in New York. . . . This was a day that could have been avoided if there had been an ounce of trust among the players toward the owners and their supposedly bloody red accounting books. It was a day that could have been avoided if the players didn't believe the owners were out to bust the union, not just win a better deal. . . . The NHL under Bettman, was run almost like a giant Ponzi scheme, nothing holding it up but hopes and promises and the vague idea that a TV deal would one day bail it out.

Although the NHL may have been able to get some people to blame the players more than itself for the lockout, that's a far cry from successfully repairing its image.

To summarize, although the NHL engaged in apology, it focused most of its comments on transcendence, shifting the blame, and bolstering. The combined focus of these tactics was to justify the need for the lockout by appealing to financial solvency and competitive balance, while presenting itself as willing, and the Players Association as unwilling, to talk.

The NHL's Product Improvements and New Marketing Strategy

The NHL took advantage of the lockout to plan a series of changes to its product, the game on the ice, as well as its television and marketing strategies. These changes amounted to a complete recasting of the game and how it would be presented to the fans after the lockout. We will begin by discussing changes to the game.

The NHL had long been aware of the complaints about "dead-puck hockey," but piecemeal attempts at solutions had consistently failed. The NHL used the time created by the lockout to plan a thorough and comprehensive set of changes.

In February 2004, the general managers from each team conducted a review of the rules and proposed six potential rule changes that were to be tested during the next American Hockey League season, the top minor league circuit in North America. In July 2004, the league's general managers and nine current players met in Detroit to further discuss potential changes to the rules. Most significantly, in December 2004, during the darkest days of the lockout, Detroit Red Wings forward Brendan Shanahan planned a two day conference dubbed "The Shanahan Summit" that discussed problems with the game and eventually submitted a series of suggestions designed to improve flow, tempo, and scoring. The summit members had no official endorsement from the NHL, but its final list of recommendations did carry endorsements from a variety of NHL players, coaches, and general managers.

The efforts of the NHL and the Shanahan Summit coalesced in July 2005, just after the new CBA was ratified, when the NHL Board of Governors approved a host of rule changes all designed to reduce the defensive tools that a team could employ and to create a corresponding benefit to the offensive part of the game ("NHL enacts rule change," 2005). Highlights of these changes include:

- Two-line, "stretch" passes (across the blue and red line) were allowed
- Zero tolerance on interference, hooking, and holding-obstruction
- The dimensions of goaltender equipment were reduced by approximately 11 percent
- If teams were tied after the five minute overtime, games would be decided by shootout ("A look at the NHL's new rules," 2005).

The two-line stretch pass was designed to reduce the ability of teams to choke off offense with the use of stifling defensive systems like the neutral zone trap. The zero tolerance policy was designed to eliminate clutch-and-grab hockey, freeing skilled offensive players to generate scoring opportunities. Reducing the size of goaltender equipment was designed to increase scoring, and thereby the excitement of the game. Shootouts eliminated the problem of tie games. Finally, a new competition committee was established to oversee the implementation of these rules and make other recommendations as needed, and Brendan Shanahan was among the first players appointed to the committee.

In addition to improving the product on the ice, the NHL also used the lockout to improve its TV broadcasts. The league hired John Shannon, the former producer of Toronto Maple Leafs TV, as senior vice president of broadcasting. His task was to revamp the league's TV product to show the improved game in the best possible light. Shannon's program included more uniform camera positions in the league's thirty venues, an instructional program for cameramen (many of whom were not familiar with hockey), and the creation of a centralized film library of player features for use by national and regional broadcasters. The league adopted other innovations, like the placement of a broadcaster between the team benches. This person was empowered to interview players and coaches during the game and overhear and report on some of the players' tactical discussions and chatter (Mickle, 2006b).

Shannon gave the broadcasters an extra two minutes during intermissions and allowed the free use of seventy two-minute player profile segments it had created. These features were part of the league's broader effort to market its star players. The profiles cost about $5,000 to make and would have been difficult for most regional sports networks to produce (Mickle, 2006b). The league also established more uniform and open access requirements for TV sports journalists among its thirty franchises, a long-held practice in the media-friendly NFL, but not common in the NHL, where individual team policies ruled.

Finally, the NHL used the lockout to completely revamp its marketing efforts. The NHL had long been criticized by fans for myopic and failed efforts to win over casual sports fans at the expense of the game's traditions and the die-hard fan. The height of this criticism came during the Fox years in the 1990s when the Fox Trax glow puck was used to make the game easier for newcomers. Sportswriters and long-time hockey fans Jeff Klein and Karl-Eric Reif (1995) found the Fox puck to be the perfect metaphor for a sport willing to dumb itself down to attract the casual fan:

> What can be said that hasn't already been said about the little blue electronic nimbus that rolls around the boards flickering like a flashlight with loose batteries and criss-crosses the ice leaving a stain of disappearing ink leaking behind it? It's distracting, it's hypnotic, it's infuriating—most of all it's insulting, because what it really says is this: Screw all the fans in the cities where they know and love hockey. Some drawling hick somewhere complained he *cain't foller that l'il ol' puck thang on the TV*, so the game is dumbed down about as far as it can go, short of having a representative from the NHL or Fox

actually standing in the living room, continuously indicating where the puck is by using his finger to point to it on the screen. Will the NHL not be satisfied until the game has been reduced to such bland uncomplicated pabulum that even the inbred hillbillies from *Deliverance* will be grinning and grunting in toothless enthusiasm? (p. 96)

The NHL's post-lockout marketing strategy appears to have been designed based on the criticisms of Klein and Reif. Instead of winning the casual fan over with TV gimmicks, the NHL would allow the better, faster, higher-scoring game to speak for itself. Post-lockout marketing would be aimed at avid fans in two ways: 1) Provide them with deeper, digitally driven access to the game and its stars. 2) Transform the die-hard fans' attraction to their home-town team (hockey fans are among the most tribal of the big four team sports in North America) to league-centered offerings (Sullivan, 2008). The NHL then hoped that the passionate fan base would become brand ambassadors who would share their passion with others.

It is often said that the NHL's fan base is younger and more digitally competent than fans in the other major sports. To take advantage of this, the NHL launched a variety of digital initiatives. First, the league's premier web site, NHL.com, was relaunched after the lockout with a cleaner design and the ability to deliver high-quality video of game highlights and interviews. The new site focused on dynamic content, including galleries, polls, and streaming video (Leggio, 2009). The league also launched NHL Network Online which includes game highlights, but goes further to connect fans with players through its Web-only studio show called "The Hockey Show," which focuses on the players in non-hockey settings, talking about their hobbies, families, and so on. In 2008, the league initiated Game Center Live, which allows fans to watch live games online via streaming video. This subscription site also allows live chats with other fans and exclusive camera angles not available to TV viewers. The site can be personalized so that fans can make one of the screens into a live chat or show team statistics. There is also a real-time statistics and action tracker (Leggio, 2009). Most recently, the league linked up with Verizon Wireless to enable hockey fans to listen to local radio game broadcasts via mobile phones.

To further satiate its most committed fans, the league launched the U.S. version of the NHL Network in 2007, which had been available in Canada since 2001. The NHL was the third of the four major team sports leagues in North America to launch a channel devoted entirely to its sport. The NHL Network has carriage agreements with Cablevision, Charter, Comcast, Cox Communications, DirectTV, Dish Network, and Time Warner Cable.

To summarize, in the decade between 1994 and 2004, the NHL had thoroughly mismanaged both its finances and its product. The lockout was planned and carried out by Bettman to solve the first problem. His image repair tactics throughout the lockout were remarkably consistent: some mortification, but an emphasis on transcendence, shifting the blame, and bolstering. The transcendence strategies justified the lockout by appealing to financial health for all teams, and improved competitive balance for the fans.

The league also used the labor dispute to fix the game, improve its look on television, and reorient its marketing toward digital platforms more acceptable to its young, technically savvy fan base. The NHL's image restoration tactics and its product and marketing changes were all tightly woven together, increasing the likelihood of a successful return from the lockout.

EARLY POST-LOCKOUT PERIOD: CRITICISMS AND NHL IMAGE REPAIR MESSAGES

We somewhat arbitrarily define the early post-lockout period as lasting from July 2005, when the new collective bargaining agreement was signed, to June 2007, when the second season after the lockout was completed. During this period, the effects of the new CBA, the new rules, and the new broadcast and cable partners were assessed intently by fans and the media. These changes, especially those brought about by the new CBA and the rule changes, were collectively and frequently referred to as "the New NHL." The use of this moniker diminished significantly at the end of the 2006-2007 season.

During the fall of 2005, the game returned to the ice and the reaction was decidedly mixed. Thrilled that the game itself was back, fan attendance actually increased from the year prior to the lockout and the new rule changes were generally, although not wholeheartedly, accepted. But criticism of Gary Bettman and the NHL's business were arguably more intense than during the lockout, and these attacks were focused on the league's anemic post-lockout Nielsen ratings and the new cable TV deal with the little-known OLN network.

The league did get two lucky breaks that suggested good things might be coming. The first was the emergence of a great number of young, dynamic superstars, led by Pittsburgh's Sidney Crosby and Washington's Alexander Ovechkin. Not since the early 1990s, the days of Wayne Gretzky and Mario Lemieux, had such a dynamic pair of stars skated in NHL arenas. The league quickly realized the marketing potential of these two, especially North American born Crosby (Ovechkin was born and raised in Russia), and he quickly became the projected face of the league. By the late post-lockout period, the Crosby/Ovechkin rivalry became epic and was heavily promoted by the league and its TV partners.

The second lucky break was the decline of the American dollar compared to its rising Canadian counterpart. By the late post-lockout period, the Canadian dollar had risen from a low of 61 cents to approximately 96 cents in 2010, and the six Canadian franchises were responsible for 30 percent of league revenues (Bellson, 2009). The strengthened Canadian dollar meant that the serious fiscal imbalance between Canadian and U.S. teams had rectified itself, regardless of the new CBA.

Mixed Responses After the Lockout

The most significant and positive post-lockout response came from the fans, who returned to the arenas in record numbers during the 2005-2006 season. Twenty-five of the thirty teams experienced increased attendance, led by the Pittsburgh Penguins, who drew 33 percent more fans to aging Mellon Arena than the during 2003-2004 season (Anderson, 2006). By the end of the 2005-2006 season, the first year after the lockout, attendance was up 2.4 percent, to average 16,955 per game, which represented 91.7 percent of capacity, and overall league revenue checked in at $2.1 billion, which is where it was before the lockout. The league had projected just $1.7 billion in revenue in the first post-lockout year (Allen, 2006). The higher attendance numbers were bought, in part, at the cost of strongly discounted ticket prices. For example, the Buffalo Sabres, a franchise in one of the league's strongest hockey markets, lowered season ticket prices to $1,160 from $1,600, and dropped per-game ticket prices from $68 to as low as $49 for a center-ice seat (Egan, 2006).

The increase in attendance is probably not, however, a reflection of the NHL's image repair strategies or changes to the game. Economic analysis of attendance after labor stoppages in the NBA, MLB, and NFL, including the 2004-2005 NHL lockout, concluded that although sports fans threaten to stay away, they don't follow through on this promise (Berri, Schmidt, & Brook, 2007). And so it was with the NHL, whose numbers indicated that ticket-buying fans had indeed returned to the game. Attendance numbers did weaken in the second post-lockout year when several softspots appeared, including Chicago and Los Angeles. Also that year, the Colorado Avalanche failed to sell out its first game after eleven straight years of sellouts in Denver (Bloom, 2006).

Like attendance, the response to the new rules, especially the increased enforcement of interference, hooking and holding, and the shootout as a way of ending the tie game, was mixed. The new standards of enforcement led to a steep rise in the number of penalties called during a game and this lasted for much of the first season after the lockout. The number of power play chances (when one team was penalized) leapt 35 percent during the first half of the season. People feared that hockey was becoming a game of special teams play only. Bill Watters, former executive of the Toronto Maple Leafs, said that the rules "have taken the physicality" out of hockey (Manly, 2005). Many journalists, however, expressed a more positive view. Lorne Manly, writing for the *New York Times*, suggested that the rules could "overcome years of borderline thuggish behavior" (Manly, 2005).

The rule changes did have an immediate effect on scoring, which was one of the league's top priorities coming out of the lockout. If you look again at Table 19.2 you can see that during the first post-lockout year, scoring jumped from 5.14 to 6.17 goals per game. The goals per game in each year after the lockout were higher than any of the five years prior to the lockout. Lead changes and come from behind victories were much more common after the lockout, and although many fans objected to the gimmicky nature of the shootout, it did produce a winner for every game.

In November of 2005, *Sports Illustrated* writer E. M. Swift nominated Gary Bettman as Sportsman of the Year. Raising a question almost every reader was sure to ask, Swift wrote: "Why should we bequeath an award to a man who so unapologetically places business ahead of sport, and is willing to smother his sport for an entire year? Because the new NHL, the post-lockout league of 2005-06 is better as a result" (Swift, 2005). Swift went on to cite lower ticket prices and the changes to the game as his reasons. Unfortunately for Bettman, such compliments were few and far between. The commissioner was now being castigated for his cable rights deal and the league's continued poor ratings. The rest of this section will examine those criticisms, and Bettman's image repair responses.

One of the most critical early post-lockout reactions regarded the NHL's decision to sign a cable rights agreement with the little-known and lightly regarded Outdoor Life Network (OLN), later rebranded as Versus. ESPN had an option to pick up the rights for the first post-lockout season at a price of $60 million, but declined that option, seeking the same revenue-sharing agreement (with no upfront money) that the NHL had given to NBC. The league refused this offer and went to Versus, whose primary sports properties were the Tour de France and professional bull riding. At that time, Versus and its owner, Comcast, were seeking to shed the network's image as a hunting and fishing channel and build a competitor to mighty ESPN. Acquiring NHL rights was the first step in this direction and the network offered $65 million, $70 million, and $72.5 million for a three-year cable rights deal. George Bodenheimer, the president of ESPN and ABC Sports, refused to match the Versus offer and said that "given the prolonged work stoppage and the league's TV ratings history, no financial model even remotely supports the contract terms offered" (Sandomir, 2005). Most fans and commentators felt that the NHL could not survive and thrive without its games on ESPN and criticism of the Versus deal was fierce and continuous.

Howard Bloom at *Sports Business News* repeatedly criticized the new cable arrangement, along with a number of other Bettman decisions, and called for Bettman's ouster as commissioner. Bloom argued that because Versus had no cache among sports fans and was in only 65 million homes, against 90 million for ESPN and ESPN2, and had no experience covering a major team sport, that the league's money grab would consign hockey to ratings oblivion (Bloom, 2006a). Indeed, Versus ratings for the 2005-2006 regular season games actually declined from ESPN's low levels prior to the lockout. Versus recorded a miniscule 0.2 rating, compared to 0.47 for games on ESPN and 0.24 for games on ESPN2 in the final year of the contract. Paul Swangard, managing director of the Warsaw Sports Marketing Center at the University of Oregon, said, "ESPN provides the sort of Good Housekeeping stamp of approval," and that the NHL would be "better off finding a working partnership between themselves and ESPN. If it were my decision . . . this league needs as many symbolic attachments to maintain their position as a major professional sport" (Bloom, 2006b).

Howard Bloom suggested that ESPN was mocking the post-lockout NHL when it refused to accept paid advertising from the league:

> Ask any ESPN sales representative—there's always room at the inn for any-one willing to buy advertising, except the pariah better known as the National Hockey League. . . . It's almost as if ESPN is mocking the National Hockey League. When was the first time any advertising driven media (ESPN or any media outlet) suggested an organization's money wasn't good enough. (Bloom, 2006b)

According to Mike Chen (2007) at FoxSports.com,

> In terms of pure exposure, the Versus experiment is a failure on the long-term and short-term. The short-term is out of sight, out of mind, and the game stalls. The long-term is that the longer the NHL stays out of the mainstream, the further it gets pushed back on the sports landscape. If games were on ESPN, don't you think they'd try marketing the league by showing highlights and commercials to much bigger audiences than, say, Professional Bull Riding?

In an article written a year and a half after the lockout (December 2006), sportswriter Howard Bloom had this to say of Gary Bettman's leadership,

> Clearly the National Hockey League is suffering from a terrible lack of leader-ship at its highest levels, its most important people are no longer leaders capable of moving the National Hockey League forward. It's time the NHL Board of Governors cleaned house and hired new and focused leadership capable of moving the NHL forward. The alternative is even scarier—the collapse of the NHL. (Bloom, 2006b)

The author spoke for many who were critical of the NHL and its business practices.

And Versus wasn't the only concern. Ratings on the regional sports networks (e.g., Comcast or one of the Fox Sports Network regionals) had fallen from pre-lockout levels. Florida Panthers ratings were down 77 percent from expectations and Atlanta Thrashers ratings were 70 percent below expectations. Even in Detroit, America's self-anointed Hockeytown USA, ratings were down (Gallagher, 2006). Clearly, while attendance had improved, national ratings continued their precipitous slide. The criticism of the NHL's ratings continued throughout 2007, when Chen said that "The media and blogosphere is having a field day with the NHL's TV ratings" (Chen, 2007).

The NHL's Attempt to Restore Its Image Regarding Its Television Problems

During the two years after the lockout, Gary Bettman was criticized regarding the new rules and attacked about the contract with Versus and the league's poor ratings. In response, the league relied extensively on transcendence, bolstering, and minimization.

Transcendence

Like in his response to the lockout itself, Gary Bettman relied heavily on transcendence to respond to criticism regarding the new rules and the cable contract with Versus. First, critics said the new rules were creating too many penalties that slowed the game to a crawl. Speaking for the league, Brendan Shanahan, a member of the new Competition Committee, said that physical hockey would increase and penalties would decrease as players got more used to the rules. "I get frustrated during games sometimes, but I have to remind myself it's only been a few months," he said. "We're not there yet, but it's getting better" (Manly, 2005). The NHL consistently claimed that the sacrifice being made during these early stages of the new rules would eventually pay off in a better, faster, more high scoring game and they asked fans to be patient through the adjustment period.

Transcendence was also a common theme in Bettman's response to criticisms regarding the Versus contract. Bettman defended the contract by directing attention to higher, more important values, in this case the quality of coverage that Versus provided over ESPN. Several comments clearly illustrate this appeal to higher values. "We gave up some distribution, but the coverage they have given us is the coverage we have always craved . . . doubleheaders. Old hockey movies. And they are continuing to grow" (Allen, 2006).

Although Bettman never criticized ESPN directly, he sometimes compared the treatment the league received on ESPN to its new partner. "ESPN was a good partner . . . but they didn't have the ability to promote us or give us the type of attention that OLN can, because we're important to OLN. During intermissions, OLN stays with hockey. After the game, they don't go off somewhere else. They stick around for half an hour and give you a studio show" (Gaventa, 2005).

Bettman frequently argued that the sacrifice of some distribution was worth it to gain improved coverage quality from Versus:

> We knowingly gave up some distribution in the short term for better coverage on our games. The treatment that Versus gives us is phenomenal. Last year in the playoffs, every night was all NHL. There was wall-to-wall coverage, with double-headers. There was ancillary hockey programming and movies. The intermissions were devoted to hockey. There was extended post-game coverage every night. So in terms of how we were treated, we couldn't be happier. We knew, at least in the short term, that while Versus was growing, we were going to have to give up some distribution to get that. (Penaccio, 2006)

When criticism was leveled at the league regarding the new rules and the Versus contract, the commissioner and the league frequently employed transcendence as a response.

Bolstering

Bettman also used bolstering to defend the Versus deal. He said that the network's distribution had already grown during the first year of the lockout from 64 million to 70 million homes, and that the league would continue to grow its ratings as Versus itself grew. Before game one of the Stanley Cup finals in June 2006, Bettman said that he expected Versus' growth to follow that of Rogers Sportsnet in Canada, which was a young network when it signed a deal with the NHL in 2000, and had nowhere near the cache of Canada's version of ESPN, Total Sports Network. By 2006 Rogers had grown to be one of the country's largest cable entities (Biggane, 2006). Bettman continually stressed patience and that Versus' distribution and brand recognition would continue to improve.

Minimization

The NHL frequently responded to criticism of its low ratings with minimization. The essence of this strategy was to claim that almost all sports TV ratings were in decline and that the NHL was no different than most other sports properties. For example, in February 2006, Bettman said that the Nielsen rating for the first NBC broadcast that year was a 1.5, "and the NBA is in the low 2's now. So that isn't bad" (Boyle, 2006).

In January 2007, Bettman responded to low ratings by saying, "No when you look around at the sports ratings landscape, most sports, all sports are in decline, and that's a function of fragmentation, both with respect to other programming and the new technology. So, I think you have to look at it in context. But other than the NHL, I'm not sure anybody has a great ratings story to tell" (Bloom, 2007).

These minimization tactics were not likely to be effective. Although Bettman's point about declining sports ratings was generally true, it wasn't very convincing given the already dismal NHL ratings. Whereas a loss to NBA or MLB ratings might be bad, a drop in the NHL's ratings could lead to total obscurity.

To summarize, the reaction to the NHL during the early post-lockout phase (July 2005 to June 2007) was mixed. Attendance at games increased, and early criticism of the rule changes quickly diminished. Unfortunately, criticism of Bettman and the NHL's business on TV was enormous. The NHL's various attempts to repair its image regarding the Versus TV contract and the ratings have to be judged a failure. Criticism continued well past the early post-lockout period.

LATE POST-LOCKOUT PERIOD: RESURGENCE AND GROWTH

The late post-lockout phase lasts from August 2007 through the Stanley Cup playoffs in 2010, when this research was completed. During this time, changes to the game began to be fully appreciated, the improved product began generating increased TV ratings, and the NHL came to be seen by many as a "hot" property. Only late during this phase did criticism regarding the league's TV deals subside. By 2010, the NHL had completed its transition from a joke to a league experiencing resurgence and growth, despite the "Great Recession."

As the NHL's game became more exciting and its TV ratings began to climb, people came to share a view of the lockout similar to the one Bettman promulgated in his repeated transcendence messages. The lockout came to be seen as a necessary tool that not only allowed the NHL to get its financial house in order, but to fix the game and its marketing strategies. Writing in the *Orange County Register*, Marcia C. Smith said, "The lost season that was once entirely perceived as a blot in sports history has turned out to be the NHL's saving grace. It led to a radical restructuring of the NHL" (Smith, 2009). Sportswriter Jack Todd wrote an article admitting he was wrong about Bettman and the lockout: "The bottom line is that Bettman did it his way and it worked. The National Hockey League that was on display here this weekend [January 2009] is a far happier, healthier place than it was in the fall of 2004 when Bettman locked out the NHLPA" (Todd, 2009). What created this turnaround among sportswriters?

First, by the late post-lockout phase, most of the complaints about the new rules of play had dissipated and it was widely acknowledged that the quality of the game had vastly improved. Mac Engel, writing in the *Dallas Star-Telegram*, said that the new rules, including limiting goaltenders' ability to play the puck and shrinking their equipment, had shifted the balance of the game to offense (Engel, 2010). Ken Campbell, a writer for the *Hockey News* and frequent critic of both the NHL and Bettman, said, "Yes, the NHL deserves credit for making the playoffs fun again. When it decided to open up the game after the lockout season, it was with the intention of making the game more watchable and it has hit a home run on that one" (Campbell, 2010). By the late post-lockout phase, the claims the league had made about the rules in its appeals to transcendence were vindicated by the play on the ice, and this was recognized by most hockey commentators and fans. For some, this change alone justified the lockout.

Other commentators took note of the improved competitiveness across the league's thirty teams, something Bettman promised many times in his transcendence-based justifications for the lockout. Final post-season playoff berths were being decided in the last week, or in some cases, the last day, of the regular season. For example, during the spring of 2008, the Washington Capitals needed to win their last game of the regular season to make the playoffs (they succeeded). In 2009, the New York Rangers were in a similar situation, winning their final game of the season to edge their way into the last open playoff spot. The Rangers found themselves in a same situation in 2010, needing to win their final game against the Philadelphia Flyers to claim the final East playoff spot. This time, the Flyers won in a shootout and not only slipped into the playoffs, but made it all the way to the finals.

In the 2009-2010 playoffs, the first two games of every first-round series ended in a 1-1 split. The Eastern conference finals featured the eight-seed Montreal Canadiens against the seven-seed Philadelphia Flyers. The Canadiens got there by upsetting the number one seed Washington Capitals with their superstar Alexander Ovechkin, and then went on to upset the highly favored Pittsburgh Penguins and their superstar Sidney Crosby. Before meeting the Canadiens, Philadelphia defeated the Boston Bruins after going down 0-3, a comeback that has only happened twice in NHL history, only once in baseball (Red Sox over the Yankees in 2004), and never in the NBA. By 2010, competitiveness meant that any team could win at any time and against any odds, precisely what the NHL promised in its image repair messages during the lockout. The 2010 playoffs were also the highest scoring playoffs since 1996 (Moulton, 2010).

Writing in the *Detroit Free Press*, Drew Sharp (2010) commented on the competitiveness that in 2010 matched the Detroit Red Wings against the Phoenix Coyotes in the first round of the Western Conference playoffs. The Wings, a perennial Stanley Cup contender, were playing a Coyotes team that was in bankruptcy and being run by the league while it searched for a new owner.

> The Wings no longer instantly intimidate the opposition like they once did from the sheer force of their vast numbers. They could put 20-goal scorers like Mikael Samuelsson and Jiri Hudler on the third and fourth lines, guys who would make the difference in a playoff game because opposing teams had no alternative but to concentrate defensively on containing the Wings' top two lines. The salary cap killed that.

The money-losing Coyotes eventually extended the Wings to seven games before succumbing. Sharp wrote, "Somewhere a vindicated Gary Bettman is smirking. The personality of these playoffs, barely a week old, is precisely why the NHL commissioner steered hockey into a ten-month work stoppage nearly six years ago when the league owners demanded fiscal certainty" (Sharp, 2010). Notice that this commentator accepts and legitimizes the appeals to transcendence that Bettman made throughout the lockout.

Attendance and ratings numbers continued upward for the league, especially during the 2008-2009 and 2009-2010 seasons. At the end of 2009, the league achieved its fourth consecutive season of record attendance. On January 1, 2008, the first signs of a TV ratings resurgence came in the form of the Winter Classic, a regular season game between the Pittsburgh Penguins and the Buffalo Sabres, played outdoors in Ralph Wilson Stadium in Buffalo. In this case, the NHL capitalized on an idea first tried with incredible success by the Edmonton Oilers. Hockey was born outdoors in the cold climates in Canada and migrated to the northern tier of the United States where almost every kid who played the game has fond memories of pick-up games on ponds, sloughs, and backyard rinks. The Winter Classic played perfectly on all these memories, highlighting players with million-dollar contracts using snow shovels to clean the ice during TV timeouts. A snow-globe-look was created by the weather as Sidney Crosby won the game in a shootout. The event played beautifully on television and was a huge ratings success. The Classic has become an annual event and was held in Wrigley Field in Chicago in 2009 and Fenway Park in Boston in 2010. For 2011, two outdoor games were held, one in Pittsburgh, featuring the Penguins and Sidney Crosby against Alexander Ovechkin and the Washington Capitals. A second game was held in Calgary between the Flames and the Montreal Canadiens. The outdoor events represent the quintessential post-lockout NHL marketing device. The sights and sounds of the game in its natural surroundings play on the memories of committed hockey fanatics, while the hype and venue (revered stadiums) attract casual fans.

Television ratings for regular season games were also on the increase, vindicating Bettman's television deals with Versus and NBC. Table 19.3 illustrates Nielsen ratings for Versus and NBC, regular season and playoff games, from the first season after the lockout through the 2010 Stanley Cup playoffs. These figures were collated by the first author from over twenty individual blogs and news articles between 2005 and 2010. Most figures have at least two sources of support.

Table 19.3.   Post-Lockout Regular Season and Stanley Cup Finals Ratings for Versus and NBC

	Versus		NBC	
	Regular Season	Stanley Cup Finals	Regular Season	Stanley Cup Finals
2005-06	0.2	0.9	1.0	2.3
2006-07	0.2	0.7	1.0	1.6
2007-08	0.3	1.3	1.0	3.1
2008-09	0.3	1.8	1.1	3.1
2009-10	0.3*	1.9	0.9	3.4

*For much of the 2009-10 season, Versus was taken off of the DirectTV satellite system because of a carriage dispute between the two firms. Once Versus was restored, late in the regular season, ratings for the remaining regular season games were 28 percent above those of the 2008-2009 season.

As you can see, ratings growth was slow or nonexistent for the early postlockout phase. However, by the 2007-2008 season larger gains were being posted. Some other figures attest to the ratings growth during the playoffs. For example, the early-round playoffs on NBC in 2009 averaged a 1.3 share, but for 2010 they had moved up to a 1.4 (Lepore, 2010a). In 2010, the conference quarterfinal matchups on Versus were 0.6, up 25 percent from 2009 ("Versus attracting," 2010). In May 2009, based largely on its NHL playoff numbers, Versus was the number 21 cable network in prime time ("Bettman pleased with TV," 2010), by the spring of 2010 Versus was a top ten cable network in viewership of adults 18-49 and 25-54, and a top five network in the coveted demographic of men 18-49 and 25-54 (Lepore, 2010b). The 2010 conference quarterfinal and semifinal rounds on Versus were the most-watched first two rounds on cable television since NHL playoff viewership became available by Nielsen in 1993-1994 ("Stanley Cup Playoffs," 2010).

The 2010 Stanley Cup final pitted two large market, storied franchises, the Philadelphia Flyers and the Chicago Blackhawks, against one another in a series that created some of the best NHL TV ratings ever seen in the United States. Philadelphia, a hugely popular team with a national following, had not won the Cup since its back-to-back championships in 1973-1974 and 1974-1975. The long-moribund Blackhawks, having failed to win a Stanley Cup since 1961, had recently emerged from sporting purgatory and were revitalized under new president Rocky Wirtz. Chicago (and its enormous market) had come to matter again in hockey circles and legions of local and national fans were ready to follow the team into the finals. In baseball, basketball, and hockey, finals matchups strongly determine national TV ratings. Large market teams with big national followings almost always draw better TV ratings than smaller market teams with little or no history. The NHL was perfectly positioned to take advantage of the Flyer/Blackhawk matchup.

Game three of the Stanley Cup final was Versus' highest-rated and most-watched telecast in network history (3.1 rating) and Versus was the most-watched cable network in the country that night ("Stanley Cup Playoffs," 2010). According to *Sports Business Daily*, game six on NBC averaged a final rating of 4.7 and 8.28 million viewers, marking the highest-rated and most-viewed NHL game since 1974. The rating was 38 percent higher than the 3.4 for the previous year's game six between the Penguins and Detroit Red Wings ("Cup Final Game Six," 2010).

It's important to keep in mind that although the NHL's ratings were spiking upward, this came from a very poor foundation. The NHL's ratings were still well below those of the NBA and MLB. However, that they were rising, and dramatically, did put the NHL in an enviable position, especially against other sports and entertainment properties, whose ratings were in decline. For example, NASCAR, once the heavily courted sports darling among the cable and network TV executives, saw its ratings among men 18-34 years old drop by 29 percent between 2009 and 2010 ("Fox' David Hill," 2010). The NHL was looking pretty good by comparison.

The NHL news from the local TV markets or RSNs (regional sports networks) was also good. During the 2008-2009 season, ratings on the RSNs rose in fifteen of the twenty-two markets (Mickle, 2009a). And in January 2010, more than 70 percent of the RSNs were reporting flat or increased ratings. Two interesting ratings stand out among the RSNs, both of which come from the 2010 playoffs. During game one of the Chicago Blackhawks conference final series against the San Jose Sharks, Comcast Sports Net Chicago garnered an 11.2 share, beating the combined ratings from the Cubs, White Sox, and Boston-Orlando NBA game ("Fox' David Hill," 2010). In May 2010, Pittsburgh's game 7 match-up against the upstart Canadiens (a game the Canadiens would go on to win), garnered a Nielsen rating of 26.4 and at one time during the game 43 percent of all households in Pittsburgh were tuned in ("Fox's David Hill," 2010).

Finally, the NHL's digital media strategy was also paying dividends. In 2010, hits to the NHL.com website were up 148 percent over the previous year, unique visitors increased by 35 percent, and page views were up 54 percent. Mobile page views (cell phones) were up 203 percent (Lepore, 2010c).

Throughout the early post-lockout period, Bettman's appeals to transcendence and bolstering promised that the quality of coverage they were getting from Versus and the ability of that network to grow would eventually pay off in improved ratings. These persuasive appeals were borne out during the late post-lockout period. In 2009, Versus brand awareness jumped to 60 percent from 16 percent in 2006, and distribution jumped to eighty million households, largely on the back of the NHL ("NHL ratings on Versus," 2009). Christine Merrifield, senior vice president and director of video investment at MediaVest said, "There is a good, healthy buzz about the NHL. From an advertiser perspective, it's priced fairly. And being able to combine broadcast and cable buys is good" (Consoli, 2010b). After the 2010 Stanley Cup finals ended, Steve Lepore (2010d) of Puck the Media blog said of Versus:

> It has built itself into a better partner in all aspects [than] ESPN was during its' 12 years with the league before the lockout. Especially this season, with the ramped up coverage and the additional studio content and the best playoff ratings on cable ever. . . . It is time for every MSM columnist, every "pundit", every commentator, every Chicago Blackhawks owner, every blogger, every commenter and every fan to admit that they were wrong on this. 3.6 million people on a cable network that couldn't draw flies before the NHL got here (and couldn't even for two years into the deal) can't be wrong.

Consistent to his core, Bettman reminded audiences of his transcendence arguments regarding competitive balance when he discussed Versus' improved ratings:

> The game never has been better, and we've never had better competitive balance. Our ratings are up across the board, and it's more than just the series the Blackhawks are playing in . The style of hockey is perhaps the most competitive, more entertaining, and most skilled-laden, and the fastest we've ever seen. And while the fans in Boston aren't too happy about it, that a team came back for the third time in our history . . . all of that tells you that the game is vibrant and what you're seeing on the ice is compelling. That's what's underlying (the ratings). The hockey has been really good. (Sherman, 2010)

Bettman continued his tactic of transcendence, claiming as he did that the changes to the league and the game made during the lockout created the current game, which is both exciting and successful. In this same interview, Bettman justified his commitment to Versus over the years: "Nobody gives their sport the type of coverage they give us. We're their most important sports property. They started from scratch with us. They built their distribution close to 80 million homes. And the way they cover the game, they've constantly improved to where it is better than first-rate" (Sherman, 2010). Bettman continued to use transcendence to justify his actions, but this time it rang more true, given the success the strategy had created. Once again, the eventual success of the league on Versus came to vindicate the appeals to transcendence made right after the lockout.

Evidence of the final triumph of Bettman's television strategy, his focus on quality coverage with Versus and his willingness to swallow pride and go with a no-upfront-money deal with NBC, occurred when John Skipper, executive vice president at ESPN, indicated he wanted hockey to return to ESPN and ABC (Consoli, 2010a). Jim Kelley (2009), a sports commentator with Sportsnet.ca in Canada, echoed Bettman's own appeals to transcendence:

> But Bettman saw a different truth. He saw that ESPN hadn't been all that great a partner to begin with and that from the moment the network acquired NBA rights the league began losing a great deal of promotion time. The network canceled shows like Hockey Tonight. The games themselves were moved from ESPN to ESPN 2 (which in the last year of the contract with the league was significantly smaller in size) and the games that were shown were pretty much treated as filler, something to be sandwiched in between one college basketball game and another. . . . Meanwhile Versus offered the league real money, primetime slots and dedicated programming. True it wasn't on par with ESPN, but then ESPN wasn't exactly giving the league all that it had.

Kelley went on to state that Bettman was correct when he said it was better to have a partner that wants you and is willing to help grow you than one that doesn't.

Ken Campbell (2009), writing in the *Hockey News*, stated that it was likely that when the current broadcast and cable deals come up in 2011, the "free lunch for NBC is over." The NHL itself believed that the negotiation of both its cable and broadcast deal would double its current $75 million a year from Versus and lead to $500 million over several years for the league and teams (Shoalts, 2010).

Ed Willes (2010), writing in the *Province* (Vancouver), made the following grudging admissions regarding the current state of the NHL and its leader, Gary Bettman:

As painful as this is to write—believe me, I'd rather vacation in Kabul than sympathize with Gary Bettman—you can understand the wee commissioner's frustration with his critics and their preoccupation with some of the NHL's recurring problems. Bettman, in case you missed it, is currently overseeing a stunning, virtually unprecedented rise in the league's fortunes. This year's Stanley Cup final, which features two of the game's most important markets in Philadelphia and Chicago . . . has delivered knockout TV ratings in Canada, and more importantly, south of the border. . . . Add it all up, then, and you can make the case the NHL is in the process of reclaiming all the ground it lost following its high-water mark in the 1993-94 season; that once again it's on the verge of establishing itself as the fourth major professional league in North America. The game has never been better. It has personality and star appeal. And, for the first time in almost two decades, it has momentum.

Despite his reluctance to do so, Willes is forced to agree with Bettman's transcendence arguments—that the game is better than it has ever been and that the league is seeing an unprecedented resurgence.

A bright picture of the NHL's finances was painted by Ted Leonsis, who in the spring of 2010 purchased the NBA's Washington Wizards. Leonsis said that the NHL is in better financial shape than the NBA because of a salary cap "that protects owners from taking stupid pills." He said that the hard cap in the NHL was far better protection from overzealous owners than the soft-cap/luxury tax combination employed in the NBA contract with its players ("Leonsis: No stupid pills," 2010). In part because player costs were finally under control, NHL team valuations were again rising, albeit unevenly, given the recession. See Table 19.1 again for the post-lockout team valuations for 2008 and 2009.

IMPLICATIONS

Although it was a long time in the making, the NHL was able to restore its image after years of financial mismanagement, poor product quality, and ineffective marketing. By themselves, the image repair tactics employed both during and immediately after the lockout were ineffectual. The NHL's image only improved when the changes to the on-ice product and marketing strategies began to show real results. These results legitimized the league's image repair tactics and only then were the tactics accepted by fans and commentators. Although there is still plenty of room for improvement, all significant business indicators were growing by the spring of 2010. This was all the more impressive given that the U.S. was still emerging from the worst recession since the Great Depression. This section will focus on the relative effectiveness of the NHL's image restoration strategies, and then look at the interaction between the league's image restoration strategies and its product and marketing changes.

The NHL's image restoration strategies during the lockout focused on transcendence, shifting the blame, bolstering, and some mortification. The transcendence tactics justified the lockout by appealing to the higher values of financial stability and improved competitiveness. These claims were logically supported with evidence from the Leavitt report. At the same time, they shifted the blame for the lockout to the NHLPA, whom they consistently excoriated for not responding to its initiatives. Finally, the league bolstered their case by saying that they were willing to meet at any time. Two Canadian opinion polls suggested that these tactics did effectively pin much of the blame for the lockout on the NHLPA, but this did not translate into much positive credibility for the NHL or its commissioner. Fans and commentators did not appear to respond positively to the appeals to transcendence that the NHL repeatedly made and there were many calls for Bettman's resignation both during and immediately after the lockout. It's possible that in a complex crisis with many contributing factors, one may succeed in shifting some blame to another party, but this doesn't automatically translate into a better image for oneself.

The league's image restoration strategies after the lockout focused on responding to criticisms of the cable contract with Versus and low TV ratings. The league responded with transcendence, bolstering, and minimization. In terms of transcendence, Gary Bettman put the deal within a new context, emphasizing that the sacrifice in distribution was more than offset by the high-quality treatment the game received on Versus. Bettman also bolstered by saying that Versus' distribution had grown during the first year of the contract and would continue to grow. He used minimization when he claimed that all sports ratings were in decline. These strategies did little to quell the criticism, which continued unabated until the spring of 2010.

What we see in this case study are largely failed attempts to repair the NHL's image during and immediately after the lockout. This occurred despite the fact that the tactics selected had a number of things in their favor. First, previous research suggests that the tactics under the reducing the offensiveness label tend to improve audience attitude toward an organization better than any of the other strategies (denial, reducing responsibility, corrective action, or mortification). Also, the tactics under reducing offensiveness tend to improve an organization's reputation, and perceptions of the organization's ability, credibility and positioning better than tactics under the other five strategies (Dardis & Haigh, 2008). During the lockout, two of the four NHL image repair tactics fell within the reducing offensiveness category.

During the early post-lockout phase, all of the NHL's image tactics fell within the reducing offensiveness category. Despite this, the NHL experienced little success in restoring its image.

Second, the tactics the NHL deployed also showed remarkable internal consistency. Previous research on the Firestone tire crisis demonstrated that mortification and bolstering were undermined by denial and corrective action. The authors suggested that some tactics simply do not work well together because they undermine one another (Blaney, Benoit, & Brazeal, 2002). This was clearly not the case with the NHL. During the lockout, the NHL justified its actions using transcendence, shifted the blame, and bolstered. The first two tactics would have been contradicted had the NHL used extensive mortification, which accepts blame for the problem. However, the NHL only engaged in the minimum mortification necessary to avoid appearing uncaring and callous toward fans and employees.

Third, previous research shows that the image repair rhetoric must be consistent across time and consistent with the image and personality of the person delivering the message. In a study of Tonya Harding's response to charges that she was involved in the attack on Nancy Kerrigan, her closest rival, Harding painted herself as a victim of child abuse and abuse by her estranged husband and then alleged co-conspirator, Jeff Gillooly. However, this new image was not consistent with the brash, outspoken, "bad girl of figure skating" image that Harding had ridden to fame. In their research, Benoit and Hanczor (1994), concluded that it was counterproductive for Harding to attempt to portray a new and different impression of herself in the middle of a crisis. However, this was not a problem in the NHL case. The NHL's leader, Gary Bettman, is often described as combative, testy, even prickly. He is known for never backing down from decisions and often criticized for refusing to admit errors or even admitting that the league has problems. These personality characteristics were perfectly represented in image repair tactics that rarely apologized, justified his decisions, and shifted the blame. Of all the things he was accused of during the lockout, changing his own approach was never one of them. In addition, Bettman was incredibly consistent in his tactical choices throughout the lockout and in the immediate aftermath—transcendence, shifting the blame, and bolstering during the lockout, and transcendence and bolstering (primarily) after the lockout.

So, why did the NHL's image repair efforts largely fail? According to Seeger (2010), "More often than not, efforts to respond to a crisis and restore the corporation's image are not successful, such as the EXXON Valdez oil spill or the sex scandal in the Catholic Church" (p. 1). Seeger's examples in this quote are illustrative because both crises are huge in terms of the damage done and largely self-inflicted. Although the NHL's lockout didn't kill anyone and did not damage the environment, it was a "near death" experience for the NHL, and the sport of hockey at the adult and minor league levels was severely damaged across North America. In this kind of a serious and long-term crisis, it's probably true that no amount of image repair work, by itself, will work, no matter how consistent and well executed the rhetoric. Something else must happen, in addition to image rhetoric, to restore the organization.

Organizations whose crises are "near death" experiences, or whose crises are massively damaging to innocents and/or largely self-inflicted, need, in addition to image repair messages, a total makeover in every element of their business and marketing to have any hope of returning to viability. By 2010, the NHL had made enormous strides in restoring its image. This was accomplished only by a combination of effectively conceived and delivered image repair strategies during the crisis, and most important, a completely new product and marketing campaign after the crisis. This worked for the NHL because its transcendence messages promised a particular future and the changes to the product and the marketing helped bring about this future. And, as the NHL case shows, the new makeover must succeed before image improvement will occur. In other words, the future promised by the image repair strategies must come to fruition before the NHL's image was restored.

What happened in the NHL's case is an unusual shift in the relationship between an organization's image repair strategies and the actions employed by the organization to resolve the crisis. Image restoration strategies are typically thought to justify, explain, and account for practices that the organization is using to resolve the crisis. For example, in a normal organizational crisis, effective attempts to resolve the problem can be trumpeted in the organization's image restoration discourse as proof that it's doing its part. According to Benoit (1995), when an organization's actions are fitting, defensive discourse can emphasize and exploit them on the organization's behalf.

In the NHL's case, things worked the other way around—the actions the league took to fulfill the promise of its appeals to transcendence ended up justifying those messages years later. Bettman's use of transcendence justified the lockout by picturing a future league that would be better (more financially stable and more competitive with better TV coverage) if they held firm during the lockout. These transcendence messages were only minimally persuasive at the time because that future was contingent. The NHL's actions regarding its product and marketing were the steps it took to assure that this future would occur, but nothing is certain and had the future pictured in the transcendence messages (those during and after the lockout) not come to pass, it's doubtful the NHL would have succeeded in restoring its image. Once the future did begin to resemble the one Bettman pictured, commentators began to laud the NHL, sometimes parroting Bettman's own justifications.

Although the NHL is still image-challenged in many areas, especially among Canadians, where Bettman is perceived as not wanting more teams in Canada, the league did largely repair its image and improve its business after the lockout. But this return only came with a combination of solid image repair strategies and a complete restructuring of its on-ice product and marketing. When these various elements were successfully combined, it validated the future depicted by the commissioner and started the league back on the road to return.

REFERENCES

Allen, K. (2006, June 27). NHL makes save in return to ice. *USA Today*, Retrieved from http://www.usatoday.com/sports/hockey/nhl/2006 06 27 league report_x.htm.

Anderson, S. (2006, October 4). The NHL bounced back last season after a year-long lockout, but what's next?*post-gazette.com*, Retrieved from http://www.post-gazette.com/pg/06277/727161-61.stm.

Average save percentage of NHL goalies between 1982/83 - 2009/10. (2008, November 15). Retrieved from http://quanthockey.com/TS/TS_SavePercentage.php.

Belson, K. (2009, December 2). Currency rise helps Canadian N.H.L. teams. *nytimes.com*, Retrieved from http://www.nytimes.com/2009/12/02/sports/hockey/02hockey.html.

Benoit, W.L. (1995). *Accounts, excuses, and apologies.* Albany, NY: State Unuversity of New York Press.

Benoit, W. L., & Brinson, S. L. (1994). AT&T: "Apologies are not enough". *Communication Quarterly, 42*, 75-88.

Benoit, W. L., & Hanczor, R. S. (1994). The Tonya Harding controversy: An analysis of image restoration strategies. *Communication Quarterly*, 42, 416-433.

Berri, D. J., Schmidt, M. B., & Brook, S. L. (2007). *The wages of wins.* Stanford: Stanford University Press.

Bettman intends to make counterproposal. (2004, December 9). *ESPN.com*, Retrieved from http://sports.espn.go.com/nhl/news/story?id=1942746.

Bettman: NHL won't contract teams. (2004, October 14). *TSN.ca*, Retrieved from http://www.tsn.ca/nhl/story/?id=101711&hubname=nhl.

Bettman pleased with TV partners but expects additional interest. (2010, May 27). *Sports Business Daily*, Retrieved from http://www.sportsbusinessdaioly.com/article/139625.

Bettman rejects proposal; counteroffer turned down. (2004, December 14). *ESPN.com*, Retrieved from http://sports.espn.go.com/nhl/news/story?id=1946330.

Biggane, B. (2006, June 6). Bettman defends OLN decision. *Palm Beach Post*, Retrieved from http://findarticles.com/p/news-articles/palm-beach-psost/mi_8163/is_20060/bettman-defends-oln-decision/ai_n51920995/.

Blaney, J. R., Benoit, W. L., & Brazeal, L. M. (2002). Blowout!: Firestone's image restoration campaign. *Public Relations Review, 28*, 379-392.

Bloom, H. (2006a, October 18). Just another day at the office for Gary Bettman and the National Hockey League. *sportsbusinessnews.com*, Retrieved from http://sportsbusinessnews.com/_news/news_352219.php.

Bloom, H. (2006b, December 12). Memo to the NHL - time to wave the white towel.*sportsbusinessnews.com*, Retrieved from http://www.sportsbusinessnews.com/_news/news_355147.php.

Bloom, H. (2007, January 24). Time to fire Gary Bettman. *sportsbusinessnews.com*, Retrieved from http://www.sportsbusiness.com/_news/news_357276.php.

Boyle, M. (2006, February 6). Ending hockey's biggest fight. *Fortune*, 153(2), 32.

Brehm, M. (2004, February 12). Study backs NHL's claim of major financial losses. *USA Today*, Retrieved from http://www.usatoday.com/sports/hockey/nhl/2004-02-12-finances-study_x.htm.

Burnside, S. (2004, June 25). Commish states league's case in CBA clash. *ESPN.com*, Retrieved fromhttp://sports.espn.go.com/nhl/news/story?id=1829690.

Campbell, K. (2009, January 25). Campbell's cuts: making new friends.*thehockeynews.com*, Retrieved from http://www.thehockeynews.com/articles/22727-Campbells-Cuts-Making-new-friends.html.

Campbell, K. (2010, April 19). Campbell's cuts: fantastic first round all thanks to rule changes. *thehockeynews.com*, Retrieved from http://www.thehockeynews.com/articles/33069-Campbells-Cuts-.

Chen, M. (2007, January 26). We Don't need no stinkin' tv ratings.*FoxSports.com*, (URL unavailable).

Consoli, J. (2010a, April 25). NHL: National hot league.*MEDIAWEEK*, Retrieved from http://www.mediaweek/">http://www.mediaweek   .com/mw/content_display/news/cable-tv/e3ieae2fa145a)5b6f7f039 aa91bab73b7c.

Consoli, J. (2010b, April 26). NHL ratings, ad revenue growing. *The Hollywood Reporter*, Retrieved from http://www.hollywoodreporter.com/hr/content_display/news/e3i30743ee7ced09867615aeb0f110430f0.

Collective bargaining agreement. (2005, July 22). *NHL.com*, Retrieved from http://www.nhl.com/ice/page.htm?id=26391.

Counsel presents league's position. (2004, February 12). *ESPN.com*, Retrieved from http://sports.espn.go.com/nhl/news/story?id=1720436.

Cup final game six earns most viewers, best rating since '74. (2010, June 11). *Sports Business Daily*, Retrieved from http://www.sportsbusinessdaily.com/index.cfm?fuseaction=sbd.main&articleID=139959.

Dardis F. & Heigh M. (2008, May). Prescribing versus describing: An original test of all image-restoration strategies within a single crisis situation . Unpublished paper presented at the International Communication Association Conference.

Doors locked on NHL opening day. (2004, October 14). *CBC.ca Sports*, Retrieved from http://www.cbc.ca/sports/story/2004/10/13/nhldark041013.

Egan, M.E. (2006, November 27). Sharp Sabres. *Forbes.com*, Retrieved from http://www.forbes.com/forbes/2006/1127/106.html.

Engel, M. (2010, April 30). NHL goalie era officially gone.*star-telegram.com*, Retrieved from http://www.star-telegram.com/2010/04/30/2155861/nhl-goalie-era-officially-gone.html.

Farber, M. (2004, June 14). Dark days ahead: A labor stalemate shadows playoff glory. *SI-Vault*, Retrieved from http://sportsillustrated.cnn.com/vault/article/magazine/MAG1032258/index.htm.

Fox's David Hill voices concern over NASCAR ratings, demo drops. (2010, May 27). *Sports-Business Daily*, Retrieved from http://www.sportsbusinessdaily.com/article/139640.

Gallagher, T. (2006, December 10). TV ratings going south: It keeps getting worse in big U.S. markets. *The Vancouver Province*, Retrieved from http://www.canada.com/theprovince/news/sports/story.html?id=4becf13b-d02a-45f2-b58e-2cb9e263c496.

Garrioch, B. (2005, July 6). NHL's 'bitter pill to swallow'. *Toronto Sun*, Retrieved from http://torsun.canoe.ca/Sports/Hockey/2005/07/04/pf-1116370.html.

Gary Bettman's letter to fans. (2005, February 16). *TSN.ca*, Retrieved from http://www.tsn.ca/nhl/story/?id=115169&hubname.

Gaventa, M. (2005, December 13). Your dog watches more hockey than you do.*Sports Media Watch*, (URLunavailable)

Karl, W. (2003, September 14). CBA understanding the issues. *ESPN.com*, (URL unavailable).

Kelley, J. (2009, June 11). Bettman praiseworthy? *sportsnet.ca*, Retrieved from http://www.sportsnet.ca/hockey/2009/06/11/kelley_column_.

Klein, J.Z., & Reif, K.E. (1995). *The death of hockey*. Toronto: Macmillan.

Labor talks shift to general league discussion. (2004, August 17). (URL unavailable).

Leggio, J. (2009, January 22). NHL digital roll-out drumbeats to all star game. *ZDNet*, Retrieved from http://www.zdnet.com/blog/feeds/nhl-digital-roll-out-drumbeats-to-all-star-game/405.

Leonsis: no 'stupid pills' in NHL. (2010, May 21). *ESPN.com*, Retrieved from http://sports.espn.go.com/nhl/news/story?id=5208536.

Lepore, S. (2010a, March 8). Breaking: NBC draws 1.7 rating for Blackhawks/Sharks, down from 2009.*Puck the Media*, Retrieved from http://puckthemedia.wordpress.com/2010/05/18/exclusive-nbc-draws-1-7-rating-for-blackhawkssharks-down-from-2009/.

Lepore, S. (2010b, May 18). More numbers from the NHL on versus, TSN.*Puck the Media*, Retrieved from http://puckthemedia/wordpress.com/2010/05/18/more-numbers-from-the-nhl-on-versus-tsn/#respond.

Lepore, S. (2010c, May 4).More Good NHL ratings news as San Jose-Detroit game 2 is most-watch round 2 game in a decade.*Puck the Media*, Retrieved from http://puckthemedia.wordpress.com/2010/05/04/more-good-nhl-ratings-news-as-san-jose-detroit-game-2-is-most-watch-round-2-game-in-a-decade/.

Lepore, S. (2010d, June 7). It's time for VERSUS to get the credit it deserves.*Puck the Media,* Retrieved fromhttp://puckthemedia.wordpress.com/.

A look at the NHL's new rules. (2005). *NBC Sports*, Retrieved from http://nbcsports.msnbc.com/id/8672777/.

Maney, K. (2005, March 20). Amid canceled season, NHL faces financial meltdown. *USA Today*, Retrieved from http://www.usatoday.com/sports/hockey/nhl/2005-03-20-nhl-financial-trouble_x.htm.

Manly, L. (2005, December 20). Putting the skill back into the N.H.L. *nytimes.com*, Retrieved from   http://query.nytimes.com/gst/fullpage.html?res=9C05E3D81730F933A15751C1A9639C8B63&pagewanted=all.

Mickle, T. (2009a, January 19). NHL's attendance, TV ratings both showing increases.*Sports Business Journal*, Retrieved from http://www.sportsbusinessjournal.com/article/61172.

Mickle, T. (2006b, November 13). NHL's Shannon takes his broadcast manifesto to the markets. *Sports Business Journal*, Retrieved from http://www.sportsbusinessjournal.com/article/52743.

Moulton, D. (2010, May 13). David Moulton: Folks, it's time to talk about hockey. *naplesnews.com*, Retrieved from http://www.naplesnews.com/news/2010/may/13/david-moulton-folks-its-time-talk-nhl-hockey/.

NHL allowance draws criticism. (2004, October 20). *ESPN.com*, Retrieved from http://sports.espn.go.com/nhl/news/story?id1905938.

NHL average goals per game. (2005). Retrieved from http://www.dropyourgloves.com/Stat/LeagueGoals.aspx.

NHL enacts rules changes. (2005, July 22). *NHL.com*, Retrieved from http://www.nhl.com/nhlhq/cba/rules_changes072205.html.

NHL exec accuses union of conducting 'charade'. (2004, August 26). *NBC Sports*, Retrieved fromhttp://nbcsports.msnbc.com/id/5822070/.

NHL owners vote to lock out players. (2004, September 15). *TSN.ca*, Retrieved from http://www.tsn.ca/nhl/story/?id=98791&hubname=nhl.

NHL ratings on Versus increasing, viewer complaints decreasing. (2009, January 23). *Sports Business Daily*, Retrieved from http://www.sportsbusinessdaily.com/aricle/127171.

Panaccio, T. (2006, October 11). Wall Street Journal talks to the commish. *HockeyBuzz.com*. Retrieved from http://www.hockeybuzz.com/blog.php?post_id=3184.

Players blamed for lockout of Canada's game: Survey. (2004, October 14). Retrieved from http://www.tns-cf.com/news/04.10.14-nhl_lockout.pdf.

Podell, I. (2005, March 17). Players' association mulling over two offers from NHL. *USA Today*, Retrieved from http://www.usatoday.com/sports/hockey/nhl/2005-03-17-labor-talks_x.htm.

Sandomir, R. (2005, August 18). ESPN passes on N.H.L. television rights, ending 21-year relationship with league.*nytimes.com*, Retrieved from http://www.nytimes.com/2005/08/18/sports/hockey/18sandomir.html.

Seeger, M.W. (2010). Image restoration and the Toyota recall. *Communication Currents*, 5(2).

Sharp, D. (2010, April 22). NHL commissioner Gary Bettman has been the big winner so far in playoffs. *Freep.com*, Retrieved from http://www.freep.com/article/20100422/COL08/4220334/NHL-commissioner-Gary-Bettman-has-been-the-big-winner-so-far-in-playoffs.

Sherman, E. (2010, May 26). Bettman: The hockey has been really good. *Chicago Business.com*, Retrieved from http://www.chicagobusiness.com/cgi-bin/blogs/sherman.pl?plckController=Blog&plckScript=blogScript&plckElementId=blogDest&plckBlogPage=BlogViewPost&plckPostId=Blog%3Af5555513-c950-4657-a93a-80db16fdf4adPost%3Ae757b7d8-69d4-42a1-9793-dce0d509803f&sid=sitelife.chicagobusiness.com.

Shoalts, D. (2010, March 31). Bettman pitches NHL as must-see TV.*The Globe and Mail*, Retrieved from http://www.theglobeandmail.com/sports/hockey/bettman-pitches-nhl-as-must-see-tv/article1519366/.

Smith, M.C. (2009, March 30). NHL's story of survival for the little guy. *ocregister.com*, Retrieved fromhttp://ocregister.com/articles/bettman-nhl-season-2349798-hockey-sports.

Stanley Cup Playoffs attract largest audience ever. (2010, June 14). *NHL.com*, Retrieved from http://www.nhl.com/ice/news.htm?id=531630.

Stepneski, M. (2008, June 29). *NHLU.S. television ratings*. Retrieved from http://www.andrewsstarspage.com/index.php/site/comments/nhl_us_television_ratings/.

Sullivan, E.A. (2008, October 1). Power play. *Marketing News*, *42*(16), 12-17.

Swift, E.M. (1994, June 20). Hot not: while the NBA's image has cooled, the NHL has ignited surprising new interest. *SIVault*, Retrieved from http://sportsillustrated.cnn.com/vault/article/magazine/MAG1005307/index.htm.

Swift, E.M. (2005, November 3). My sportsman choice: Gary Bettman.*SI.com*, Retrieved from http://sportsillustrated.cnn.com/vault/article/web/COM1039786/index.htm.

Todd, J. (2009, January 26). Bettman hits mark on many counts.*The Gazette (Montreal)*, Retrieved from http://www.canada.com/topics/sports/hockey/canadiens/story.html?id=fdfd2f09-402b-4f70-8f18-df93991c0da2.

Versus attracting key demographics. (2010, April 27). Retrieved from http://www.kuklaskorner.com/index.php/hockey/.

Watzlawick, P., Beavin, J.H., & Jackson, D.D. (1967). *Pragmatics of human communication*. New York: Norton.

Willes, E. (2010, June 10). NHL's at the top of its game--so don't blow it this time. *The Vancouver Province*,Retrieved from http://www.theprovince.com/sports/game+blow+this+time/3134803/story.html.

Wilstein, Steve. (2005, February 18). Time for Bettman to go. *FoxSports.com*, (URL Unavailable).

Chapter Twenty

Celebrating Spectator Sports in America: The Centrality of Press Conferences and Media Interviews to Sports Image Repair

Peter M. Smudde and Jeffrey L. Courtright, Illinois State University

The spectator sports industry, which comprises leagues, sports teams, and individual athletes, spans the globe in a wide variety of sports and games. When not watching a game in person or on television, and when reporting on the performance of a team or athlete through a news source (e.g., newspapers, local and national news, and ESPN), perhaps the two most prominent ways sports teams and individual athletes manage and, especially, repair their respective images are press conferences and media interviews.

Whether the news is good or bad, sports garners a sizable amount of attention in our culture in the United States. Today's athletes are to us what the gladiators were in ancient Rome. The business of "major league" professional sports in the United States (e.g., auto racing, baseball, basketball, bowling, boxing, football, golf, hockey, jai-alai, motorcycle racing, rodeo, skiing, soccer, tennis, wrestling), according to Kopylovsky (2010) and IBIS World (2010), brings in nearly $26 billion in revenue annually. This result includes the minor league professional and semiprofessonal sports portion of the industry, which are usually training grounds for athletes who want to get into the major leagues and tend to garner great community support at very local levels. (Add national collegiate sports, and the annual industry revenue is much greater.) With so much money on the line in the overall business of spectator sports in America, effective image management (and repair, when necessary) is absolutely essential, and its foundation is sound public relations.

Sports public relations has as its sharpest focus the fans for every sport, team, and athlete. Fans, after all, support sports enterprises by buying tickets, gear, and much more. Some spectator sports organizations devote more to their public relations efforts than others, but the ultimate objective is the same: to maintain a strong team image that builds the base of fans. Athletes, too, hire people to help them manage their relationships with and educate them in relating well to fans and the general public. Media training, for example, is one of the single most important areas athletes, coaches, managers, and organization executives must master because they are the literal public faces of the sports and sports organizations for which they work. Effective press conferences and interviews, then, are the payoffs on media training that manages and, when necessary, repairs image.

Spectator sports, while an intensely competitive industry, is more an entertainment industry. To that end, the promotion and coverage of sporting events and athletes is much more *epideictic* than anything. That is, sports public relations hinges on the value of sports as an inherent social good. Moreover, sports public relations is a matter of inviting people to join the celebration about a sport, team, or athlete. After all, true fans are those who support "their" teams (and individual athletes) all the time, not just when they win. Witness "diehard" Cubs fans.

The celebration of a sport, team, or athlete relies on the engagement of athletes, the coaching staff, team management and owners, and others showcased in sporting events. The *epideictic* character of sports public relations rests largely on two central public relations genres: press conferences and media interviews. It is in these two genres—out of the thirty-nine any public relations professional could use (see Smudde & Courtright, 2010)—where the message design and, most important, public relations strategy are employed to repair image effectively.

This chapter examines the discourse conventions for press conferences and media interviews through Smudde and Courtright's (in press) *epideictic* genre perspective, drawing upon examples of sports apologiae. We extend the application of this genre perspective to prescribe better strategic use of them in spectator sports—in strategically *epideictic* and proactive ways for the repair of sport, team, or athlete images.

PRESS CONFERENCES AND INTERVIEWS AS EPIDEICTIC DISCOURSE

Although a sports figure may issue written statements or have lawyers or other surrogates (e.g., a coach, team owner, or league official) speak on her or his behalf, press conferences and interviews are central to what Hearit (2006) has called the ritual of *apologia*. The discourse conventions of these genres function to repair image and, hopefully, resolve a crisis of confidence. They also function as image maintenance, "bolstering organizational values, denying intent to create harm, and preventing recurrence by seeking the cause of the problem" (Rowland & Jerome, 2004, pp. 207-208). We argue that sports *apologiae* employ the *epideictic* functions of public relations discourse (Smudde & Courtright, in press), especially press conferences and interviews, to repair and maintain a sports figure's corporate image. What is important is not that public relations professionals merely follow the rules for effective press conferences or interviews, but, most important, they understand and apply the principles of effective epideictic discourse. In this section we explain the four *epideictic* functions that govern these and other public relations genres. This material is necessary as a prelude to their application to selected examples of sports *apologiae*.

There is no exact translation of the Greek word *epideictic*, but its origins are found in the games and festivals of ancient Athens, when part of the event's program included public speaking and written composition (Perelman & Olbrechts-Tyteca, 1969). Confined to such situations, scholars typically explain to students that *epideictic* messages are ceremonial in character, focused on "praise" and "blame" (i.e., extolling the virtues that the community holds dear, and sometimes vilifying what it does not stand for, at times even casting aspersions on enemies). Thus funerals are *epideictic* situations that invite eulogies of praise for the deceased. Today, all sorts of celebrations provide opportunities for *epideictic* discourse: a ribbon cutting, an award ceremony, all sorts of organizational events. Its utility for organizations, however, is far greater and untapped (pragmatically and academically).

As Perelman and Olbrechts-Tyteca (1969) assert, the *epideictic* genre forms "a central part of the art of persuasion, and the lack of understanding shown toward it results from a false conception of the effects of argumentation" (p. 49). As such, we argue that much of what public relations does stems from its celebratory nature (see also Crable & Vibbert, 1983). Scholarship has moved well beyond viewing epideictic messages as opportunities for speakers to display rhetorical skill and audiences to appreciate it. From this scholarship, we have determined epideictic's four core functions: celebratory, performative, epistemic (i.e., knowledge producing), and preservative. These functions are not simplistic, unidimensional terms. Each has specific components that make public relations key not only to organizational success, but also to a more enlightened view of publics as audiences and how organizations seek to inspire cooperation with them.

Celebratory Function

The celebratory function of epideictic discourse includes ritualistic and axiological dimensions. Ritualistic dimensions concern how a special occasion is particularly memorialized. This means that speakers make a special point to follow established, accepted patterns of language and behaviors for exalting or decrying something. Public relations discourse in this case need not be as dramatic as that sounds. In public relations, the ritualistic dimension is obvious in new product unveilings, statements of self-defense, and press conferences, but it also is subtle in news genres, in which the writer should temper word choices so that the message conforms to the journalistic standard of objectivity. The other dimension of the celebratory function is axiological, which focuses on values-oriented statements that address something in terms of praise and blame. Public relations' axiological function is seen at its best when organizations explicitly or implicitly communicate values that the organization stands for, values that its products or services represent, or, through issue advocacy, values associated with the corporate position regarding the issue at hand. Simultaneously, the values expressed through the discourse also should reflect those held by target publics. Public relations influences society through invocation of organizational core values, but must be a reflection of the environment in which their clients operate as well. Values appeals, therefore, work best when they are shared by the organization and its publics.

Performative Function

The performative function of epideictic discourse is chiefly concerned with *ethos*, and, in the case of public relations, performative epideictic discourse establishes who the organization is and how it develops a relationship with the audience (Black, 1970; McMillan, 1987). There are three components to the performative function. First, the political component sees the speaker as a leader who is acting as a member of a community. In this social role, the speaker has a bardic (i.e., grand promoter or evangelist) and/or prophetic voice (Lessl, 1989), both of which mean the speaker "sings the praises" of the organization and the past, present, and future value the community derives from it, although the prophet also might cast aspersions on enemies or chastise a community for not living up to its values. By the same token, audiences have the role of observer, judge, and participant as they experience the speaker and the message, evaluate what is said, and choose to take action or not. In public relations the political component of its discourse is evident in feature articles and annual reports, for example. Second, the identity management component concerns reputation building through *ethos* (see Sullivan, 1993) so that audiences acknowledge and embrace a speaker's credibility and authority. In public relations, fact sheets and corporate social responsibility reports, for example, can fulfill this need to manage an organization's identity. Third, the rhetorical (or symbolic) component of performative epideictic discourse involves the creation of consubstantiality between an audience and the speaker. The discourse in this vein is designed to influence audiences immediately and over the long term, defining their roles and relationship to each other. In public relations, Lindeman's (2006) view of outputs, outtakes, outcomes and outgrowths as dimensions of the range of results sought to inspire cooperation between an organization and its publics.

Epistemic Function

The epistemic function of epideictic discourse focuses on the knowledge-building capacity it has for speakers and, especially, audiences. This function covers two dimensions: educational and explanatory. The educational dimension features messages that inculcate values and encourages the imitation and buy-in to certain virtues that are established through socialization. Public relations practitioners exercise this dimension, for example, when they publish advertorials or public service announcements. The second epistemic dimension is explanatory, which involves defining or otherwise facilitating audience understanding of something. This dimension can be realized when discourse addresses what the audience already knows as the basis for connecting it with something new they do not know and should embrace, and that new knowledge balances audience and organizational needs. It also can be realized as discourse, which

> refers to the power of epideictic to explain the social world. Audiences actively seek and invite speech that performs this epideictic function when some event, person, group, or object is troubling. The speaker will explain the troubling issue in terms of the audience's key values and beliefs. (Condit, 1985, p. 288)

Thus the epistemic and celebratory functions work in tandem. The celebratory function reflects the worldview that the organization and its publics share; the epistemic function attempts to influence how audiences think about the world and what they believe to be true.

Preservative Function

The preservative function of epideictic discourse conserves and reinforces the community values that may be celebrated or vilified through messages (see Cherwitz & Hikins, 1982; Perelman & Olbrechts-Tyteca, 1969). There are three important components to this function. The first is coherence, which concerns how the language and the very structure of the discourse itself helps everything work together within the text and, especially, among all other epideictic functions. Public relations discourse must always cohere with other corporate discourse on many levels, at the very least to "stay on message." The second preservative component is reflexive: Rhetoric functions for the organization as a means of self-persuasion (see Burks, 1970). Discourse becomes part of the public record and, therefore, influences how the organization and its members perceive themselves in relationship to their surroundings. Rhetoric thus becomes a historical record of what the organization says and does—a repository of organizational memory from which anyone may draw ideas for new discourse. Finally, epideictic preserves messages for future usage. The most obvious way this occurs is repurposing, in which practitioners create premises for future communication to inspire cooperation (even forensic or deliberative discourse; see Cheney & Vibbert, 1987) and for other epideictic situations. In the practice of public relations, discourse is regularly reused for multiple purposes, and that can include the reapplication of text from one document or occasion to another, like information from a fact sheet to a news release to a speech. However, the public availability of organizational discourse allows others—publics, opinion leaders, the news media, activists—to quote, paraphrase, or recast ideas as they see fit. This futuristic dimension can be quite far-reaching, because public discourse may be invoked long after its original moment of communication (see Courtright, 1991). For example, what an organization's founder said or wrote becomes fodder for press kits, speeches, annual reports, and advocacy advertising. Also, what an organization says in its financial discourse about its past performance has implications for people's perceptions of its potential future performance (e.g., whether investments in a publicly traded company may be prudent).

All epideictic functions are important, and depending on the type of discourse genre chosen, the importance of epideictic functions (and their individual dimensions) varies in ways that explain why they work so differently and potently. In fact, the balance among organization, message topic, and audience is a key to making the most of the four epideictic functions. Wayne Booth (1963), in an oft-cited article in the field, argued that a *rhetorical stance* occurs when speakers address audiences in such a way that a message does not overemphasize one element more than another: "the available arguments about the subject itself, the interests and peculiarities of the audience, and the voice, the implied character, of the speaker" (p. 141). Applied to public relations message design, no topic is so intrinsically interesting that it needs not relate to organizational or audience interests. Likewise, the message should not feature the organization's credibility at the expense of the other elements any more than should the audience's wants and desires.

GENERAL EPIDEICTIC CHARACTERISTICS FOR THE TWO GENRES

Taken together, the four functions of epideictic discourse provide us with a usable and useful view of public relations that can be used at the tactical level, but they are especially potent at the strategic business level. All four functions are always present and always work together (or work against each other when used poorly) but in various ways for different discourse genres. This view represents an untouched and powerful way to plan, act, and evaluate public relations. Because celebratory rhetoric showcases community (or societal) values, much of what passes for newsworthy information is focused on those values that organizations and their publics share. Corporate officials must take into consideration their constituents', stakeholders', customers', markets', and other audiences' viewpoints, needs, and expectations when making *epideictic* arguments about what is going on. (This approach is no different than it would be with forensic or deliberative discourse.) Epideictic arguments are not only about the news or other matters, although that is important. The arguments are invitations to participate, even if it is only momentary or intellectually if not ultimately behaviorally, in the dramatic celebration of what is going on within, for, and about an organization that also concerns its publics. The invitations also include claims, backed by evidence and reasoning (see Toulmin, 1958), that participation would be good. When the news is good, bad, or neither, the invitation to the celebration is relevant. For image management and repair in professional sports, the two key genres on which we are focused are press conferences and media interviews.

Press Conferences

Press conferences are a display of rhetorical expertise in the context of one speaker addressing a live audience. Indeed, press conferences (also known as news conferences) in general are among the more celebratory of the two genres covered in this chapter, so we concentrate on that function first. Because press conferences are part of the public record, their preservative function is second. Next follows the epistemic function because press conferences deal with focused matters. This is not to say that the relationship between speaker and audience, the genre's performative function, is much less important because it is placed last. Rather, all four functions are extremely important to the success of press conferences, but those functions are fulfilled in a priority order (see Textbox 20.1), which we will explain.

Textbox 20.1

Epideictic functions' priorities for press conferences.

1. Celebratory — [1] ritualistic; [2] axiological
2. Preservative — cohesion; reflexivity; repurposing [these three characteristics are ever-present]
3. Epistemic — [1] educational; [2] explanatory
4. Performative — [1] rhetorical; [2] identity management; [3] political

In terms of their celebratory function, press conferences primarily feature the ritualistic dimension of epideictic celebration. Secondarily, its axiological dimension is of concern for, as Perelman and Olbrechts-Tyteca (1969) point out, epideictic discourse focuses chiefly on values—in this case, the values of the organization *and* those of its publics. Formal patterns are the stuff of ritual, and press conferences follow certain patterns, such as their opening, the formal statement or presentation, and question-and-answer period with reporters. Press conferences particularly highlight the core values of their messages, which forms the basis for all reasoning about the subject of the press conference, the organization overall, and specific people where needed.

Given the assorted media tactics that may be used during press confer-
ences, its dominant preservative dimension is cohesion. Press releases, for example, are a media tactic that facilitates repurposing of messages, but self-persuasion should occur primarily for the audience, not the organization. A good press conference includes a key message platform with strong proof points to support it. Press conferences provide a public record of the organization's perspective on a given situation. As such, organizations hope that the key message, or at least some of its evidence, becomes part of media reports of the press conference, thereby becoming preserved through news retrieval and perhaps through audience memory.

For their epistemic functionality, press conferences have both educational and explanatory dimensions; whereas effective use of the epistemic func-
tion's educational and explanatory dimensions balances concerns for the message with attention to an organization's position and the interests of the audience. When crafting messages to educate publics, the values implied in them should be those that will resonate with audiences and also reflect positively on the organization in ways consistent with its reputation and actual business practices. This, of course, ties in to press conferences' primary function of celebration and the axiological dimension. When building explanations, message designers must pay attention to audience perceptions of fact as a basis for extending knowledge.

When enacting epideictic's performative function, as Booth (1963) pre-scribes, its rhetorical and identity-management dimensions always should be balanced in message design. However, even in organizational crisis communication, with its emphasis on image repair and frequent use of press conferences to accomplish it, concerns for audience adaptation are paramount. We, therefore, place the rhetorical dimension first in importance under press conferences' performative function, with identity management close behind and then the political dimension, which depends a great deal on the nature of the situation and the issue being addressed.

Interviews

In this section we address how public relations officials should think about interviews so they can maximize the effectiveness of their language (verbal and nonverbal) to inspire cooperation between a sports organization or athlete and its publics. Such effectiveness is driven by the epideictic functions for interviews (see Textbox 20.2), with the celebratory and performative functions providing the foundation for the epistemic and preservative functions. The first two functions work in tandem to capitalize on the value-centered, ritualistic, rhetorical, and identity management dimensions native to two-way communication.

Textbox 20.2

Epideictic functions' priorities for interviews

1. Celebratory — [1] ritualistic; [2] axiological
2. Performative — [1] rhetorical; [2] identity management; [3] political
3. Epistemic — [1] explanatory; [2] educationa
4. Preservative — cohesion; reflexivity; repurposing [these three charac-teristics are ever-present]

For celebratory messages, attention to style, organizational patterns, and commonly shared, ritualized behaviors and values become the "music" of conversational genres in public relations message design. Hearit (2006) has noted the importance of ritual in corporate *apologiae*. It comes as no surprise, then, that interviews, speeches, and corporate blogs have become important components to crisis communication plans. Certainly the celebratory qualities of interviews invite vividness (see Pratkanis & Aronson, 2001), but not to the point of letting the characterization of themes or core values overwhelm the main point of the message. Beyond vividness, the deliberate choice of words or phrases that evoke particular mental images can be powerful, particularly as they resonate with publics.

The communication between an organization and its publics can be said to be an interaction with the words and symbols chosen and used in such a way as to increase perceptions of identification and relationship quality. Interviews focus heavily on the identity-management and rhetorical dimensions of the performative function. For message design, some of these conventions invite opportunities to engage the political dimension, but practitioners must use the proper steps to avoid appearing fully engaged in policy advocacy (or coach spokespeople to follow the proper "dance" pattern). Interviews can build upon celebration and performance to explain and educate publics about an organization, its positions on issues, and its attitudes toward publics.

Interviews can build upon the celebratory and performative functions through the epistemic function—to explain and educate publics about an organization, its positions on issues, and its attitudes toward publics. For epistemic message design, interviews may place explanation first, although education may be a close second. In a sense, interviews' celebratory song and performative dance are followed by the display of explanations and knowledge organizations deem important for their publics

Interviews serve functions beyond those meant for their immediate audiences. Communicators can use interviews to bring coherence to seemingly disparate messages, especially with social media, which give varying degrees of control over what is shared in the media. Putting organizational messages in other forms (e.g., press releases, news stories, blog posts, YouTube) that can be referred to by organizational members, media contacts, and other interested individuals makes for a rhetorical storehouse of discourse preserved for future use.

As textboxes 20.1 and 20.2 show, it is apparent that press conferences and interviews share similar priorities but important differences. Both genres make the celebratory function of epideictic rhetoric paramount. After all, both genres are inviting people to join in the cause that is the focus for a sports figure or group. In that celebration, even if it is in self-defense, the ritual of *apologia* and the values at stake must be established if the other epideictic functions are to be used effectively. Both genres utilize the epistemic function to inform audiences of the facts from the apologist's viewpoint and to capitalize on what audiences already know and believe, but this function is subordinate to either the preservative or performative functions of epideictic. Press conferences make the preservative function second in importance because the apologist's statements are for the public record. Interviews, on the other hand, place the performative second, for reasons that will become evident in the next section.

APPLICATION OF EPIDEICTIC PRINCIPLES TO SPORTS *APOLOGIAE*

Press conferences are a principal concern in sports *apologiae*. They are the prime opportunity for the apologist to establish his or her core values, view of the facts, position on the issue(s) in question, and personal character. The press conference thus serves as a touchstone for the apologist, the media, and others to refer to when interviews and other rhetorical opportunities arise. After the apologist uses a press conference to frame the situation, interviews serve the important performative function of *epideictic* discourse because of their dialogic nature (between interviewer and interviewee): to rebuild image, foster favorable relationships with multiple audiences, and capitalize on the political dimension of a controversy or depoliticize it. We therefore offer in this section examples of the epideictic functions of sports press conferences in action first, followed by sports *apologia* examples of interviews.

Sports Press Conferences

As the ideal opportunity to assert a sports figure's or sports organization's response to accusations and begin image repair, our epideictic typology for press conferences in textbox 20.1 might at first appear counterintuitive. Shouldn't the communication advisor to the accused focus primarily on the performative function, with its concerns for identity management, rhetorical adaptation to audiences, and addressing the crux of the matter, that is, the politics of the situation? The examples we offer in this chapter suggest that advisors to sports apologists would be wise to think first of the other three functions—celebratory, preservative, and epistemic—as essential to give performative strategies in press conferences a strong foundation.

Celebratory function

As noted earlier, epideictic's celebratory function has two dimensions: ritualistic and axiological. Press conference strategy for sports image repair purposes should begin with the ritualistic first, for apologists must pay attention to the formalized conventions of the genre as part of corporate apology (see Hearit, 2006) and, quite often, atonement (Jerome, 2008; see also Koesten & Rowland, 2004). In such cases, reporters expect to have opportunity to ask questions of the accused after his or her formal statement. Being prepared for those questions is part of the game, just as in interviews (see Smudde, 2004). For example, when Augusta National Golf Club chairman Hootie Johnson defended the organization against criticism from the National Council of Women's Organizations that it omitted women, he addressed the issue in the Masters tournament's annual prematch press conference with obvious apprehension. Although he concluded his opening statement with "I will have nothing further to add about our membership or related issues" (Juliano, 2003, p. E01), the Q&A (question and answer) period of course was focused on the controversy. Although he defended the organization's position in response to each question, he thanked a reporter who asked about any special care needed for golf balls due to weather and course conditions ("Masters Chairman Johnson," 2003). The *Melbourne Age* in Australia noted an even more telling response to questions: referring to his own athletic background as a football defenseman, "I don't think I've experienced anything like this assault" (Hinds, 2003, p. 13). Whether planned or "cajoled" into answering questions, as was Johnson, Q&A after an opening statement is a must. When Tiger Woods not only confined his press conference about his "personal transgressions" in his marriage and off-the-course behavior to a 13-minute statement but limited journalists' live attendance to three media representatives, sports journalists were critical (e.g., Sobel, 2010; see also Benoit chapter).

The axiological dimension for athletes in need of image repair requires them to extol the values at stake in the situation— at personal, professional, and societal levels. Michael Vick, for example, focuses on maturity and self-improvement in his press conference:

> I wanna apologize to all the young kids out there for my immature acts. And what I did was—what I did was—very immature. So that means I need to grow up. I totally ask for forgiveness and understanding as I move forward to better Michael Vick the person, not the football player. (Van Susteren, 2007, para. 2-3; corrected, based on Vick, 2007)

Bobby Knight also emphasizes personal values but focuses on the values that have guided his coaching throughout his career: politeness and respect— reminding young autograph hounds to say "thank you," never allowing students to be familiar by calling him "Bobby," and keeping interactions with other people in a conversational tone (Woodruff, 2000). His personal values were the issue because he had tried to correct an Indiana University student who allegedly had said to him, "Hi, Knight." Knight's version of the subsequent discussion denied physically harming the student and cussing him out.

Many sports press conferences, of course, emphasize the athletic values the apologist wishes to associate with him or herself and the respective organization and/or sport profession involved. For example, Tonya Harding stressed the value of competition when she asserted regret over (but ignorance of) the attack on fellow skater Nancy Kerrigan: "I was disappointed not to have the opportunity to compete against Nancy at Nationals. I have a great deal of respect for Nancy. My victory at Nationals was unfulfilling without the challenge of skating against Nancy" (Cable News Network, 1994, para. 4). She went on to emphasize sportsmanship:

> I still want to represent my country in Lillehammer, Norway next month. Despite my mistakes and my rough edges, I have nothing—have done nothing to violate the standards and excellence of sportsmanship that are expected in an Olympic athlete. (para. 5)

Unifying professional and organizational ethics occur quite naturally, too, when a coach or league official introduces the athlete at a press conference (e.g., Vick, 2007) or when the organization's reputation itself is under attack and the organization's head is the spokesperson (e.g., Hootie Johnson and Augusta National Golf Club; see Juliano, 2003). In the case of the Duke University lacrosse team alleged rape scandal, statements at various times were issued by the university's senior vice-president for public affairs and government relations, the athletics director, and the executive committee of the Academic Council, as well as the captains of the lacrosse team; however, press conferences and interviews were handled principally by Duke University president Richard Brodhead. In suspending the team from play until the matter was fully investigated, he invoked the university's values as a whole: "A majority of the team members attended the party, which included underage drinking and the hiring of private party dancers. This conduct was wholly inappropriate to the values of our athletics program and the university" (Duke University, 2006a, para. 4).

The previous examples, of course, have their societal dimension. Yet many values invoked through sports image repair transcend personal, professional, and organizational issues. In short, societal values at stake in sports image repair situations make them newsworthy. Athletes and their advisors are well aware of this. Mike Tyson, after biting Evander Holyfield's ear in a boxing match, acknowledged the rule of law to the press: "I'm proud of the— of— to the living up to the terms of my probation" (CBS News, 1997a, para. 4). Likewise, Tonya Harding's desire to represent her country at the Olympic games in Lillehammer (Cable News Network, 1994) implies respect for society's values, in this case, patriotism—and perhaps tenacity, the push for achievement and success (see Steele & Redding, 1962, for an introductory list of quintessential American values). Terrell Owens (2005) illustrates this desire well:

> When I got hurt last year and everyone said my season was over, I fought hard to prove the world was wrong and do everything possible, includin' riskin' my career, and to help the Eagles win the Super Bowl. . . . I'm a fighter, I've always been, and I'll always be. I fight for what I think is right.

Preservative function

Like any other public relations campaign, crises of reputation necessitate attention to message consistency. This is not only important for credibility during image repair, but for the public record for the present and for posterity. Sports figures must pay attention to reputation over the long haul. To that end, the three dimensions of epideictic's preservative function, cohesion, repurposing, and self-persuasion, must be attended to in conducting press conferences.

Most important is cohesion, which, simply put, means staying on message. In the case of press conferences, certainly any deviation in later messages suggests that the initial statement was an attempt to deceive. (We'll discuss this more when we discuss the preservative function as applied to interviews.) Among more convincing sports image repair efforts, we find that press conference statements flow in terms of legal concerns, narrative, or both. Tiger Woods's (2010) statement avoids admission of criminal guilt but takes responsibility for what he considers to be the facts:

> I have a lot to atone for, but there is one issue I really want to discuss. Some people have speculated that Elin somehow hurt or attacked me on Thanksgiving night. It angers me that people would fabricate a story like that. Elin never hit me that night or any other night. There has never been an episode of domestic violence in our marriage, ever. Elin has shown enormous grace and poise throughout this ordeal. Elin deserves praise, not blame. The issue involved here was my repeated irresponsible behavior. I was unfaithful. I had affairs. I cheated. What I did is not acceptable, and I am the only person to blame. (para. 10-11)

In contrast, Bobby Knight relies on narrative in his self-defense:

> And I remember one Sunday morning at church—much to the disbelief of some, I went to church a lot—and we had a coach who had played football and baseball at Ohio State. He was an excellent baseball player. And he coached all three sports in a small school. And his name was Bill Coyer (ph). And I later—long after he had retired—got to know him. And his mother and step-father became very close friends of mine. But as a fifth- or sixth-grader in church this morning, I happened to beside Coyer. And his nickname—he was a stocky-built guy—and his nickname was Chub. And I said: "Chub, how are you?" He put his hand on my shoulder and he said: "Son my name, my name Mr. Coyer, or coach Coyer." I never forgot that. (Woodruff, 2000, para. 10-11)

Such narratives must hang together and ring true for the audience (W. R. Fisher, 1987). Duke University (2006a) president Brodhead similarly and quite naturally recounts a narrative of what the lacrosse team is accused of and then articulates the university's legal position.

Establishing cohesion is essential for the other two dimensions of the preservative function. First, the sports figure (and his or her advisors) must consider how quotes from the press conference statement and answers to questions may be used. The athlete may refer to something said in interviews or any other media use that follows the press conference. For example, the night before an accusation of drug doping regarding Lance Armstrong's 1999 Tour de France win was to be published in the French sports periodical *L'Equipe*, the cyclist posted on his website the denial he had made in response to allegations over the years: "I will simply re-state [*sic*] what I have said many times. . . . I have never taken performance-enhancing drugs" (Lindsey, 2005, para. 16). Excerpts from press conferences also may be used in court (e.g., Tiger Woods in a possible divorce, Duke University, Tonya Harding, and Bobby Knight in civil suits). The preservative function also suggests that these words "for the record" may become part of public memory, to be used by journalists and other commentators in stories during the image repair process, in retrospective reports, and in books written later on. Indeed, a television writer and producer paid over $10,000 to the Humane Society for what were allegedly Michael Vick's notes for his press conference ("TV Producer Pays," 2007).

Ideally, the final dimension of epideictic's preservative function, self-persuasion, should occur within the audience. That is, the audience becomes convinced of the speaker's arguments by supplying the values and beliefs they already hold, thus identifying with the speaker. (More about this when we discuss the remaining epideictic functions for press conferences.) However, the examples we survey here indicate that press conference statements and subsequent Q&A may function to reinforce the athlete's view of the facts and communicate them with conviction. After Terrell Owens provided his opening statement to apologize for criticizing his coach and teammates, for instance, agent Drew Rosenhaus conducted the Q&A in dramatic terms. According to Brazeal (2008), Rosenhaus insisted repeatedly that Owens was sorry for what happened.

Epistemic function

The preservative function thus builds upon what is said in the press conference. In conjunction with it, the epistemic function connects with audience values and helps to frame a perspective on the accusation and the speaker's response. Audience values are the focus of the epistemic function's educational dimension. Tiger Woods refers to community standards, such as the right to privacy between a husband and wife, in working out differences and his upbringing as a Buddhist. Sometimes such appeals draw attention away from the issue and focus on the speaker's character. Hootie Johnson's appeal to the constitutional right of association may strike many readers as ineffective:

> Single-gender is an important fabric on the American scene. . . . There are thousands and thousands [of clubs] all across America, both genders—health clubs, sewing circles, Junior League, Shriners. . . . We're not discriminating, and we resent it very much when that accusation is made against us. (Juliano, 2003, p. E01)

Through invocation of values, the educational function ought to work to get the audience on the apologist's side. Such efforts provide a context for the facts of the case.

The epistemic function's explanatory dimension therefore accounts for the behavior and circumstances surrounding the immediate situation. How the speaker frames the facts in the epistemic function's educational dimension builds on the values addressed through epideictic's celebratory function. Bobby Knight's view of what happened provides a good case in point, because the press conference also includes a student athlete witness to the event, Mike Davis, who backs up Knight's story (Woodruff, 2000). After Terrell Owens issued his apologetic statement to his coach and his fellow Philadelphia Eagles, Drew Rosenhaus used the Q&A session to redefine what was going on:

> The bottom line is, I don't believe the media's been fair to him. There are players . . . in the NFL who are arrested, who violated the program when it comes to drugs or substance abuse, and they are not punished as severely as he has been. (Brazeal, 2008, p. 148)

Unfortunately, Owens's agent was too much of a contrast with his client's apology: "Rosenhaus' contempt destroyed any goodwill his client had created" (p. 149). Similarly, Tonya Harding's attempts to excuse herself from blame in the attack on Nancy Kerrigan fell flat because of the varied denials of foreknowledge she had made in interviews.

Performative function

Having provided the foundation for image repair, the first three functions now lead to what, for most practitioners, would be the main point—to repair image. Press conferences provide an important first opportunity to assert *ethos* and seek to identify with audiences from whom the apologist hopes for support. The need for apologia thus requires a balancing act between the performative function's rhetorical and identity-management dimensions. Subordinate to these, the apologist must address the political dimension of the situation.

Each of the press conferences in this analysis attempts to rebuild image and connect with audiences. They do so in at least four ways. The first two relate to the identity-management dimension of rhetoric. The athlete, celebrity, or spokesperson acknowledges the potential damage and often leans on his or her prior credibility. Duke president Richard Brodhead also illustrates recognition of the situation:

> As we move past the period of the two [game] forfeitures, the question arises what to do now. This afternoon the captains of the Duke lacrosse team notified Mr. [Joe] Alleva [Director of Athletics] and me that the team wished to suspend competitive play until the DNA results come back. (Duke University, 2006a, para. 5)

In addition to recognizing the need for image repair, agent Drew Rosenhaus reinforces Terrell Owens' statement and reminds his audience of his past reputation: "His goal this year was to win a Superbowl [*sic*] as a member of the Philadelphia Eagles" (Brazeal, 2008, p. 148). Such efforts of recognizing the need for image repair and reliance on past credibility then lead to two rhetorical strategies to identify with the audience: role modeling and appeals that contextualize ethos within the larger athletic association or professional sport.

The concern for the example the athlete provides, along with what her or his reputation does for the sport, stands in stark contrast to what the person is accused of. Because many such appeals imply values at stake, the rhetorical dimension of epideictic's performative function builds upon the celebratory function. Michael Vick apologizes "to all the young kids out there for my immature acts" (Van Susteren, 2007, para. 3). Such appeals to identification most likely are more effective than the weak appeals to the larger sport or professional association. Tiger Woods (2010) thanks "the PGA Tour, Commissioner Finchem and the players for their patience and understanding while I work on my private life" (para. 26) and also "my friends at Accenture and the players in the field this week for understanding why I'm making these remarks today" (para. 22). Tonya Harding's references to the Olympics look forward to competition: "But I still want to represent my country in Lillehammer, Norway next month. . . . I have devoted my entire life to one objective—winning an Olympic gold medal for my country" (Cable News Network, 1994, para. 5).

Interestingly, sports image repair examples modify slightly Cheney and Vibbert's (1987) dictum that, with the political dimension, organizations should only make broad statements of issues in order to make political statements without appearing to act politically. Clearly, sports apologists must address the issue at hand and make a stand with regard to it. Such appeals play better with genuine contrition than with combativeness, as the Owens-Rosenhaus press conference illustrates. Hootie Johnson did little to help Augusta National with his line in the sand attitude:

> Single gender is an important fabric of the American scene. . . . There are thousands and thousands (of single-gender clubs) all across America. Both genders. Health clubs, sewing circles, Junior League, Shriners . . . and we're not discriminating. And we resent it very much when that accusation is made against us. (Wagner, 2003, p. C7)

In contrast, Michael Vick acknowledges, "Dogfighting is a terrible thing and I did reject it" (Van Susteren, para. 6). Likewise, Duke's president acknowledges the issues involved in accusations against lacrosse team members:

> While we await the results of the investigation, I remind everyone that under our system of law, people are presumed innocent until proven guilty. One deep value the university is committed to is protecting us all from coercion and assault. An equally central value is that we must not judge each other on the basis of opinion or strong feeling rather than evidence of actual conduct. (Duke University, 2006, para. 9)

It is worth noting, however, that Barnett (2008) argues that Duke University failed to address the issue of rape itself.

The interactions among all three dimensions of epideictic's performative function, then, combine in the stance toward the situation, the speaker's resources to build credibility, and efforts to identify with audiences. The performative function of press conferences, however, relies on the framework provided by the genre's celebratory, preservative, and epistemic functions *first*. To not do so is akin to making bricks without straw. Likewise, to engage in interviews before doing a press conference when sports image repair is required is like building a house upon sand.

Sports Interviews

As a complement and important follow-up tactic to press conferences, preparation for interviews should focus first on the celebratory function of epideictic. Each interview a sports figure does extends an image repair effort through adaptation to multiple audiences. After this is attended to through the performative function, the focus should be on the epistemic: to build on the information the audience already knows, and offer new information to expand what has been said in press conferences, other interviews, and other public relations discourse genres. Interviews thus build off the key message platform used in the press conference. Interviews, then, become the fodder for the public record and what audiences may remember most about the sports figure and the controversy.

Celebratory function

The ritualistic dimension of interviews is somewhat different from that of press conferences. The latter is based on the expectations of journalists and other audiences, but it provides an overarching statement communicated to a mass audience. Therefore the press conference is much more conducive to managing messages—a one-to-many context—instead of one on one. In the case of interviews, journalistic conventions set constraints on the interviewer but much more so on the interviewee. Interviews are structured interpersonal conversations that are designed for a mass-mediated audience to "overhear." It is important to note that the interviewer has control over the final product. The sports apologist seeks to get his or her main ideas across without saying something to detract from the message; the interviewer is looking for a good story to present with an interesting angle and gets to edit it for that purpose. The interplay of questions and answers thus can become a contest of motives and skill—skill at asking questions and answering them.

Theoretically, the degree to which an interviewer's questions are open or closed should shape the scope of the answers given (Stewart & Cash, 2007); however, the contest of wills in today's media interviews often becomes a ritual of yes-no questions with far-reaching answers, broad questions that lead to brief answers, and redirecting when the interviewee reframes a question to return to key talking points. The interviews we examined for this chapter tended to be very focused. Duke University president John Brodhead's interview on CBS's *60 Minutes* conforms to the ideal: Ed Bradley asks fairly narrow questions, but they allow Brodhead to address particular issues and expand briefly on them (Duke University, 2006b). Connie Chung asked even more specific questions, such as why Tonya Harding did not go to the authorities when she learned that her trainer and husband had planned the attack on Nancy Kerrigan (CBS News, 1994). In a later interview at the Olympics, Harding ended an interview with Chung, saying, "I'm not answering that. . . . O.K. I'm done. This is over," in response to a statement that two Czech judges would be influenced by the fact that Harding failed to report what she knew about the attack ("Winter Olympics," 1994). Failure to complete the interview ritual merely compounded Harding's image problems.

As is central to epideictic, interviews' axiological dimension allows speakers to celebrate and reinforce the values they stand for. One of the best examples of this is Hootie Johnson's stand on Augusta National's right of association to limit club membership to men: "When [Martha Burk] throws out 'bigotry' and 'discriminatory' if we're discriminating, then all [the] other single-gender organizations are discriminating. . . . And they're not. It's a terrible thing if they're accused of that also" (E. Fisher, 2002, p. C01). In contrast, as mentioned earlier, cyclist Lance Armstrong has used interviews to assert his opposition to performance-enhancing drugs (e.g., Lindsey, 2005).

Performative function

Attention to ritual and values frames efforts to identify with audiences, repair image, and address issues head on. Rhetorically, poor interviewee behavior clearly plays poorly with audiences (e.g., Olympians Tonya Harding and Bode Miller; see Jenkins, 2006). Tiger Woods seems to fare better when he states, "I owe a lot of people an apology. I hurt a lot of people, not just my wife: my friends, my colleagues, the public, kids who looked up to me" (Rinaldi, 2010). Less contrite, baseball player Barry Bonds attempts to identify with fans but discounts media assertions of drug use:

> From all the places I've ever gone, and I've traveled all over the place and gone places: "Barry, keep your head up, we're behind you." . . . And I mean, coming over to me—the things that I've always wanted, to come over to me and just shake my hand and say, "You know what? Who cares. You're a good ballplayer. You proved it. You know, you've done this, you've done that. We're all supporting you." I've never heard that before. ("Bonds Doesn't Pull Punches," 2005, para. 34).

These examples of the performative function's rhetorical dimension also reflect on the apologists' efforts at identity management. The two dimensions work in tandem. In this regard, Olympians Tonya Harding and Bode Miller both failed to connect with audiences because they continued to say things in interviews that intensified character issues rather than allay them. Harding continually revised her story until she set the record straight in her press conference. Miller continued to harm his image during the 2006 Winter Olympics, even though he had apologized for saying, "If you ever tried to ski when you're wasted, it's not easy" ("U.S. Skier," 2006, para. 2; see also Jenkins, 2006; Schorn, 2006). In the 2010 Winter Olympics, Miller finally showed maturity in his interviews along with better performance in his events (Abrahamson, 2010).

Most sport interviewees we selected for this chapter made positive identity-management efforts through audience identification in their interviews. It is best to do this as soon as an image repair effort has begun. Olympic swimmer Michael Phelps, like Terrell Owens and Mike Tyson in their press conferences, managed his image with genuine contrition over a photo that showed him smoking pot:

> Seeing my mom reminded me of how it was the day after I got my DUI, and I swore to myself I'd never do that again. . . . This is just a stupid thing of mine that I did, and I have to live with it. (Van Valkenburg, 2009, para. 7)

Audiences who hold that civility is needed in today's society may have viewed Bobby Knight as a holder of traditional values (Fasbender, 2000) when he said, "What I did with that student was simply try to teach him something about manners" (para. 5). Similarly, although he had denied steroid use in testimony before Congress in 2005, Mark McGwire came clean with *USA Today* (Antonen, 2010) and in other interviews, finally beginning a true identity-management process.

Similar to press conferences, interviews in sports image repair may address the politics of the issues in question head-on. However, interviews also provide the opportunity to begin the transition to organizational renewal (see Ulmer, Seeger & Sellnow, 2007) or, in most cases, to a long-term, positive image for the athlete. In so doing, apologists engage in Cheney and Vibbert's (1987) explanation of the political dimension, to make political statements without appearing to do so directly.

The latter is what Tiger Woods did successfully through interviews prior to the Masters tournament. He separated the private from the public in his first interview, a little over a month after his press conference in which he asserted the same thing. When asked about what happened when he crashed his truck, Woods replied, "Well, it's all in the police report. Beyond that everything's between [wife] Elin and myself and that's private" (Rinaldi, 2010). He also asserted what his treatment entailed between the press conference and the interview as between his wife and him. In short, Woods implicitly invoked his right to privacy. He emerged from the personal crisis with his professional reputation intact.

Similarly, Duke president John Brodhead spoke to key principles behind the university's affirmative-action policy without referring to that contentious legal concept:

> We have a wonderful history of African American alumni who've come out of this school. I could tell you lots of examples. Current students here—really impressive, serious, gifted people. Faculty . . . you tell me a field and I'll tell you a distinguished African American faculty member we have in that field. (Duke University, 2006b, para. 18)

In contrast, as earlier examples from his press conference illustrate, Hootie Johnson maintained a firm stance in interviews regarding the constitutional rights of exclusive clubs (e.g., Fisher, 2002).

Epistemic function

Our observation about interviews at the beginning of this section prompts yet another: that the same messages directed to the interviewer may serve the epistemic function's explanatory dimension while also serving the educational dimension with mediated audiences. The explanatory dimension builds on what the interviewer—and/or other audiences—already knows. Close on the heels of this dimension is the educational dimension, whose purpose is to give the interviewer and her or his audiences new information. In this way, the epistemic function takes on a dramatic character because the interview ostensibly is just between the immediate parties, but it also appeals to and is designed for other audiences. This is most important when the interview participants are at odds. The mediated audience becomes the one to win over (Van de Vate, 1965).

At an elementary level, however, the interviewer usually knows more background for a story than the mediated audience. The sports apologist must do her or his homework (see Smudde, 2004) to therefore be prepared to build an explanation on what the interviewer and, to perhaps a lesser degree, audiences already know. Most likely, reporters and swimming fans knew the back story when NBC's Matt Lauer interviewed Michael Phelps after a picture of him, with marijuana pipe in hand, appeared in a tabloid. Note Lauer's prior knowledge:

> Then the weeks kept going on and we started to get about a month out, and we started to hear some other stories circulating about you. And these were more stories about women you were seen with and parties you were seen at and clubs you were frequenting. Was it a case of blowing off some steam? (NBC News, 2009, para. 9)

Phelps confirmed it with this explanation: "I was just blowing off steam and relaxing and having fun. And just doing what I. . . ." Lauer filled in, "Enjoying the some of the spoils of the victory?" Phelps responded, "And definitely enjoying. Celebrating, yes" (para. 10-12). For some audience members, this interchange would have been news and therefore would satisfy the educational dimension of epideictic's epistemic function. As well, it seems an interviewer can appear supportive of the interviewee's image repair efforts—the two are seeking parallel ends. The converse is possible, like Tonya Harding. In both cases, the interview becomes personal and then part of the image repair's success or failure, thereby complementing or undermining the epideictic celebratory and performative functions.

This is not to say that an interview appeal might not serve the same function for both interviewer and particular audiences. Hootie Johnson's interviews make the point. In one, he said:

> When [National Council of Women's Organization's Martha Burk] throws out "bigotry" and "discriminatory" if we're discriminating then all [the] other single-gender organizations are discriminating. . . . And they're not. It's a terrible thing if they're accused of that also. (E. Fisher, 2002, para. 7)

Many interviewers, plus many feminists in the audience, would reject Johnson's position. In that case, Johnson's use of the explanatory dimension fails to build on what those audiences consider to be true. Johnson's explanation might have been successful with some audiences, because a poll found that 70 percent of Americans favored the right to association (E. Fisher, 2002).

Preservative function

Last but not least, the preservative function of interviews furthers an image repair effort through cohesion, the self-persuasion of the speaker and his or her audiences, and repurposing messages for immediate needs and for the public record.

As noted earlier, interviews should cohere with the initial press conference. Based on the previous examples, it is clear that Bobby Knight, Hootie Johnson, and Michael Phelps, among others, were successful in this regard. Those who did not either were lying (e.g., Harding, McGwire) or did not seem to care (e.g., Bode Miller). The latter examples support the classic public relations advice in crisis: If you are in the wrong, admit it with appropriate contrition and move on.

Regardless of public opinion, interviews may reinforce perceptions for some audiences, certainly for the athlete or spokesperson, and for the interviewer as well. The interviewee, by maintaining consistency through adherence to a key message platform, theoretically will become more confident in his or her position the more often it is asserted. Hootie Johnson's resistance to change approaches extreme dogmatism, but, again, audiences with similar viewpoints likely would seek out such self-confirming messages. Likewise, the interviewer comes to the situation with particular objectives in mind and is likely to pursue those based on her or his reputation as a journalist. Matt Lauer, for example, represents the sympathetic, perhaps even empathic, questioner and listener. Connie Chung became identified with an aggressive persona that she clearly maintained in her questioning of Tonya Harding. How our examples relate self-persuasion to the performative function's identity-management function demonstrates the importance of self-persuasion and self-assurance for the interviewer as well as for the interviewee.

Finally, repurposing of interview messages may occur in several ways. First, there is the ease of using other genres to repeat the message (thus supporting a cohesive campaign) by taking advantage of journalism's intertextuality.

Hootie Johnson's (2002) op-ed in the *Wall Street Journal* echoes his numerous statements in press conferences as well as interviews:

> For men of all backgrounds to seek a place and time for camaraderie with other men is as constitutionally and morally proper as it is for women to seek the same with women. Men and women have always occasionally sought out

single-sex spheres in certain corners of their social lives, a habit that has always been a positive trapping of civil society. Women gather in book groups to study literature, in investment clubs to discuss the markets, or in fitness clubs to exercise. That they are able to make those choices is a fundamental freedom that most Americans believe is proper and important. (para. 3)

Finally, the importance of sports and celebrity in this country makes it a given that journalists will refer to the public record from times of image repair. Bode Miller's poor image from the 2006 Olympics was referred to by the press four years later (Vinton, 2010). When an athlete has tried to change public perceptions, someone like Tonya Harding may reframe what was said and done. As she told Larry King six years after the Kerrigan incident:

. . . you go through life on a roller coaster, it has its ups and down, and I'm human, and I'm going to make mistakes and I'm probably continue to make mistakes. But as long as I learn from them, then I think that it makes me a better person. . . . (CNN, 2000, para. 103)

Harding later reframed what occurred in a book (Prouse, 2008).

One final point about interviews is important to make as we conclude this section. Interviews are used *during* sporting events to get players' reactions to and feelings about the contest in which they are engaged. For example, during the 2010 Winter Olympics NBC featured interviews with athletes before and after their events, especially in-depth interviews in the studio. Also, during the 2010 Stanley Cup playoffs, the television organizations broadcasting the games not only featured customary interviews with players before and after the games, but also included interviews with players between periods and interviews with the head coaches during the first and second periods. Interviews of this sort can be seen easily during all mass-mediated sporting events. This use of interviews, then, raises the question, "Do these kinds of routine interviews have relevance to sports image repair?" The answer is an emphatic yes.

Whether things are going well for a sports figure or organization, or whether a sports figure or organization has come out of an image repair effort, these routine, in situ interviews enact all the epideictic functions we explained above and are essential for image maintenance (see Jerome & Rowland, 2009; Rowland & Jerome, 2004). Indeed, these in situ interviews do precisely what they are supposed to do to maintain image: give "a particular response involving a limited set of message strategies that reinforce a positive image for the organization if [it] has any hope of maintaining credibility and retaining a positive image" (Rowland & Jerome, 2004, p. 200) at any time, whether there is a crisis or not. Sports organizations help their players and representatives be "media savvy" by providing them with training to handle reporters and their questions so that the players best represent their organizations and themselves. In situ interviews of sports figures, then, showcase them at their discursive best (or worst) as they often wax philosophical about the contest, their performance, the opponent, and the specter of success or failure.

DISCUSSION OF SPORTS *APOLOGIAE* FOR IMAGE REPAIR

Because professional sports are entertainment, audiences live vicariously through sports figures, facilitating identification between fans and sports figures. That identification is possible largely through the performative function's rhetorical dimension and the epistemic function's educational dimension. All the cases we covered lean on pre-issue celebrity/athlete ethos, which means that there is a large shared context among all audiences about each of the people and sports organizations involved. At the same time, however, there are weak or implied appeals in each case to their respective larger sports (e.g., NFL, PGA, Olympics, NCAA) or teams because of their employment (in the case of professionals) or official involvement (in the case of amateurs) with them. All athletes to some degree (some more than others) recognize their responsibility as role models, and in this way they also recognize (again, some better than others) the potential damage *and* need to repair image when it is at risk.

Both the press conference and interview genres emphasize the importance of epideictic's celebratory function in sports *apologiae*. This is particularly important: first to fulfill the ritualistic character of going before the public to defend one's reputation and/or accept responsibility of wrongdoing; second, to provide the axiological foundation for identity management (i.e., image maintenance, as Rowland and Jerome [2004] put it) and the other dimensions of the epideictic functions. These purposes prescribe a particular order for using these genres: First hold a press conference, and do so early with definitive and impeccable information; then do interviews.

Generally speaking, the cases we address in this chapter indicate that there are advantages to following this prescription that hinge on the very conventions for each discourse. Leading any sports image repair effort with a press conference allows for a sports figure or organization to have one on-the-record opportunity to present the case to all media, and thereby fans and other publics, at one time. This one-to-many approach inherent in press conferences enables the sports figure or organization to reasonably control key messages through a formal statement and then use them further during a question-and-answer (Q&A) period with journalists immediately after the statement. To exclude a Q&A period after a formal statement—even to the extreme of not allowing journalists in the room during the statement, similar to what Tiger Woods did—is seen as an important breach of etiquette that could likely result in (1) unwanted negative coverage in addition to analysis of the situation itself and (2) additional negative attitudes cultivated toward the sports figure or organization. Notice in press conferences that a sports figure or organizational representative has a fair amount of control over message consistency while, at the same time, fulfilling the expectation for some level of dialogue. Press conferences, then, work as the foundation for any future public discourse to repair an image.

The natural follow-up genre to a press conference is interviews. The reason is simple: The key messages that were presented at the press conference (and any new information that may have emerged since then) can be more personally addressed in a truly dialogic way between a sports figure and a journalist, which is then shared broadly through the mass media. The discourse of a press conference, having been made available to news organizations (and their audiences), serves as common ground for any interviews. In this way, too, key messages articulated during the press conference can be reinforced and, if necessary, augmented if significant new information comes to light. If more than one interview is held after a press conference, the preceding interviews may also serve as part of the common ground for the case, but the press conference is still primary. Notice that sequential interviews require fastidious attention to message consistency based on the content of the press conference and preceding interviews because each dialog happens in a different place and time with a different journalist.

It is also important to note that beginning sports image repair with one or more interviews runs a great risk of losing message consistency and image management because there is no foundation from which to work. Because of the competitive nature of the news business, each journalist and his or her news organization wants to put the story into a new context; otherwise, it is not news. Indeed, each interview exists in its own news outlet and is subject to a different agenda from each interviewer. So, if another news outlet wants to cover the story, it must come up with a new angle to differentiate the story from other media stories. These factors for interviews make message consistency—and, thereby, image management—very difficult for a sports figure to control, if the lead discourse consists of interviews rather than a press conference. The reason is that a sports figure effectively gives up control of what their key messages are, allowing multiple views of a situation to develop *first* instead of presenting as early as possible one definitive and ethical view of it from the start—and to do so at a press conference for everyone to experience. And, of course, leading a sports image repair effort with a press conference that is later shown to have been based on erroneous and/or false information, like Tonya Harding's, makes it virtually impossible to turn around a negative image over any number of interviews.

What we see, then, between the two genres is serious complementarity because of the overlap in the agendas and motives of the sports figures/ organizations and journalists/news organizations. In both genres the celebratory function comes first, and this is vital because both the sports figure/ organization and journalists have a vested interest in participating in the mystique and appeal of the sport, sports organization, and even individual sports people. The key reason for this shared interest is a large, shared context that, until an image repair situation emerges, dominates everyone's view. When a negative situation occurs, the context is, in effect, polluted, and the sports figure/organization must deal with the responsibility issue—who or what is the cause or holds the blame for the situation that undermines the established context and causes disorder. Given the very public nature of spectator sports, responsibility very easily becomes a public issue that is analyzed in the mass media. This public analysis largely fuels alliances of those in support of the sports figure/organization *and* those against it. Eventually one view about the cause or blame for the situation tends to dominate, principally because of the preponderance of evidence and effective reasoning. In this way the sports figure/organization can be its own best or worst enemy, as purification for the pollution of the order of things is gradually achieved over time through media coverage. In the end, a new order is established—for better or for worse—for the sports figure/organization. That new order ideally should be a better, stronger image, which must be dealt with accordingly and appropriately. This sequence of evolutionary phases for sports image repair is shown in figure 20.1, and it applies equally well to individual sports people as it does to whole sports organizations.

Notice in figure 20.1 that the focus is the sports figure/organization, and the role of journalists and the mass media generally occurs throughout, as they help facilitate communication, perpetuate images, and stimulate dialogue about sports news. When it comes to image repair matters, the mass media comes into greater play in Phase 2, when a situation is announced and blame or cause is assigned. The mass media are especially important in Phase 3 as things are sorted out publicly and, eventually, a new order—a new image (positive or negative)—is established in Phase 4 about the subject sports person or sports organization. This final phase is the essence of image renewal, which Ulmer, Seeger and Sellnow (2007) describe as "a fresh sense of purpose and direction an organization discovers after it emerges from a crisis" (p. 177) and enacts key messages in various discourse types that focus attention on the new order of things, thereby facilitating image maintenance.

Also notice in Figure 20.1 how the epideictic functions for press conferences and interviews work most effectively in the evolutionary process of sports image repair. There are additional reasons for following our prescription to hold a press conference with definitive and impeccable information first and early on, and then do interviews. Remember that, between the two

PHASE 1: Order	PHASE 2: Pollution & Assignment of Guilt	PHASE 3: Purification	PHASE 4: Redemption
The state of things about and for an organization, what it stands for, and what it offers is stable.	Something from within, without or both upsets or significantly changes the stability of things, and blame or responsibility must be assigned for it on the public stage.	Efforts to make things right gradually secure the public's approval, where the success of one side over the other becomes increasingly apparent, especially as an organization accepts responsibility of its own accord or is saddled with responsibility by others.	• For an organization that secures the public's favor, final vindication of it is given & a new order is created, which would bolster its image and credibility. • For an organization that does not secure the public's favor, it must cope with the new order, which (adversely) affects the organization's reputation, and credibility.

Figure 20.1.   Four-phase evolution of image repair (Smudde, 2010)

genres, the first and third epideictic functions—celebratory and epistemic—
are consistent in their order of priority among all epideictic functions. It is the
other two functions—preservative and performative—that switch places as
either second or fourth between press conferences and interviews (see textboxes 20.1 and 20.2). Specifically, press conferences make the preservative
function second in importance because the apologist's statements are showcased for the public record. The preservative function's secondary role for
press conferences indicates why it is a natural fit for being the first step in an
effective image repair effort—and to do so in Phase 2 in figure 20.1 so that
one, definitive, and impeccable view of the situation is established. Interviews, on the other hand, place the performative function second because
both interviewer and interviewee are motivated to make the genre work best
for their respective agendas. Here the performative function's secondary role
for interviews reveals why it is so potent for the latter phases of an image
repair effort in Figure 20.1—to engage in dialogue through the mass media
based on a firm foundation of key messages and analysis about the situation
that can allow a sports figure's or sports organization's image to be ultimately repaired or even renewed.

CONCLUSION: AUTHENTICITY AS KEY

Sports image repair, as we have argued, is principally conducted through the strategic use of two genres of public relations discourse—press conferences and interviews. These genres, like all public relations genres, are epideictic in nature and thus form the ritual of apology in sports image repair. The particular sequences of epideictic functions for press conferences and for interviews must be followed to ensure their effectiveness on both the micro level (i.e., the discourse itself) and on the macro level (i.e., the repair or renewal of a sports figure's/organization's image). The micro level of effectiveness is most immediately measurable because of people's responses to the discourse and the messages in it soon after it is shared publicly. The macro level of effectiveness is more laboriously measurable because of the evolution of the image repair effort, as shown by figure 20.1.

Indeed, if there is one concept that binds all the epideictic functions together for sports image repair it is authenticity, and components of it have been illustrated throughout this chapter. In contemporary society, authenticity is vital from interpersonal interactions (physical and virtual) to organizational public statements. But what is authenticity? Simply put, authenticity is someone using verbal and nonverbal language to be him-/herself (or represent an organization) without putting on airs, trying to appear to be something he/she (or an organization) is not, or masking things from what they truly are from one's own perspective *and* the audience's perspective. All this assumes that the apologist shares a similar view of and value for authenticity as others. As our analysis of several case examples show, there are many points at which sports image repair can be won or lost because of poor choices in the use of press conferences and interviews. To the degree that an apologist applies the epideictic functions of public relations discourse, authenticity should be established and maintained well for the duration of an image repair effort.

Ultimately, such authenticity throughout the evolution of the image repair situation should lead to forgiveness and reconciliation—a new order of things where the sports figure or sports organization enjoys a repaired or renewed image. If a sports figure or organization emerges from an image repair effort after having satisfactorily lived up to terms for punishment, like Michael Vick did by serving time in jail and performing hundreds of hours of community service (e.g., McGlone, 2009; Humane Society, 2009), the debt has been paid and atonement for the sin has been achieved. Such atonement usually opens doors for new opportunities, as Vick was offered and accepted a position as a backup quarterback for the Philadelphia Eagles in 2009. Such new opportunities, in turn, open new problems for the affiliated sports organ-ization as it must explain its decision to hire an athlete with a tarnished image, which the Eagles had to do with Vick.

Public forgiveness seems a tenuous thing that depends on the nature of the sin and the sinner's authenticity as a communicator, which is conveyed by the mass media. Public forgetfulness about the sin may be impossible with the historical records of media stories, but public memory and attitude can be tempered by authentic communication. As long as sports figures and organ-izations "do the right thing" at all times (a kind of sportsmanship with the media and the public), which means the ethical and effective use of the epideictic functions of press conferences and interviews in that order, their image repair efforts should be successful and result in redemption.

REFERENCES

Abrahamson, A. (2010, February 22). Miller changes perceptions with amazing Games. *NBC Sports* [Online]. Retrieved June 17, 2010, from http://www.nbcolympics.com/news-fea-tures/news/newsid=437181.html.
Antonen, M. (2010, January 12). *USA Today* interview: McGwire details steroid use. *USA Today* [Online]. Retrieved June 17, 2010, from http://www.usatoday.com/sports/baseball/2010-01-11-mcgwire-steroids_N.htm.
Barnett, B. (2008). Framing rape: An examination of public relations strategies in the Duke University lacrosse case. *Communication, Culture & Critique, 1,* 179-202.
Black, E. (1970). The second persona. *Quarterly Journal of Speech, 56,* 109-119.
Bonds doesn't pull punches with media. (2005, February 23). *ESPN* [Broadcast transcript]. Retrieved June 14, 2010, from http://sports.espn.go.com/mlb/news/story?id=1997605.
Booth, W. C. (1963). The rhetorical stance. *College Composition and Communication, 14,* 139-145.
Brazeal, L. M. (2008). The image repair strategies of Terrell Owens. *Public Relations Review, 34,* 145-150.
Burks, D. M. (1970). Persuasion, self-persuasion and rhetorical discourse. *Philosophy & Rheto-ric, 3,* 109-119.
Cable News Network. (1994, January 27). Tonya Harding says she had no prior knowledge of attack. *CNN News* [Broadcast transcript]. Retrieved May 11, 2010, from Academic Universe (Lexis-Nexis) database.
CBS News. (1994, February 10). *Eye to eye with Connie Chung.* [Broadcast transcript]. Re-trieved May 11, 2010, from Academic Universe (Lexis-Nexis) database.
CBS News. (1997a, July 1). Boxer Mike Tyson apologizes after the ear biting incident during a boxing match with Evander Holyfield. *CBS This Morning* [Broadcast transcript]. Retrieved May 11, 2010, from Academic Universe (Lexis-Nexis) database.
CBS News. (1997b, July 1). Boxer Mike Tyson apologizes for biting opponent Evander Holy-field's ear. *CBS Morning News* [Broadcast transcript]. Retrieved May 11, 2010, from Aca-demic Universe (Lexis-Nexis) database.
Cheney, G., & Vibbert, S. L. (1987). Corporate discourse: Public relations and issue manage-ment. In F. M. Jablin, L. L. Putnam, K. H. Roberts, & L. W. Porter (eds.), *Handbook of organizational communication,* (165-194). Newbury Park, CA: Sage.
Cherwitz, R. A., & Hikins, J. W. (1982). Toward a rhetorical epistemology. *Southern Speech Communication Journal, 47,* 135-162.
Condit, C. M. (1985). The functions of epideictic: The Boston Massacre orations as exemplar. *Communication Quarterly, 33,* 284-298.

Courtright, J. L. (1991). "Tactics" and "trajectories": The argumentative resources of Supreme Court dissenting opinions. Ph.D. dissertation, Purdue University, Indiana. Retrieved January 15, 2009, from Dissertations & Theses: Full Text database. (Publication No. AAT 9215536).

Crable, R. E., & Vibbert, S. L. (1983). Mobil's epideictic advocacy: "Observations" of Prometheus-bound. *Communication Monographs, 50*, 380-394.

Culler, J. (1975). *Structuralist poetics: Structuralism, linguistics, and the study of literature.* Ithaca, NY: Cornell University Press.

Duke University Office of News & Communications. (2006, March 28). Duke suspends men's lacrosse games pending clearer resolution of legal situation. [News release]. Retrieved May 11, 2010, from http://news.duke.edu/2006/03/lacrossestatement.html

Fasbender, R. (Executive Producer). (2000, September 12). Firing of Bobby Knight of Indiana University. *Cable News Network: Rivera Live* [Broadcast transcript]. Retrieved May 12, 2010, from Academic Universe (Lexis-Nexis) database.

Fisher, E. (2002, November 13). Augusta's Johnson using PR campaign. *Washington Times*, p. C01. Retrieved May 14, 2010, from Academic Universe (Lexis-Nexis) database.

Fisher, W. R. (1987). *Human communication as narration. Toward a philosophy of reason, value, and action.* Columbia: University of South Carolina Press.

Fortunato, J. A. (2008). Restoring a reputation: The Duke University lacrosse scandal. *Public Relations Review, 34*, 116-123.

Hearit, K. M. (2006). *Crisis management by apology: Corporate responses to allegations of wrongdoing.* Mahwah, NJ: Erlbaum.

IBISWorld. (2010, April 17). *IBISWorld risk rating report: Sports franchises in the US: 71121a.* Santa Monica, CA: Author. Retrieved May 24, 2010, from http://www.ibisworld.com/reports/reportdownload.aspx?cid=1&rtid=10&e=1628&ft=pdf.

Jenkins, S. (2006, February 26). Only medal for Bode Miller is fool's gold. *Washington Post* [Online]. Retrieved June 14, 2010, from http://www.washingtonpost.com/wp-dyn/content/article/2006/02/25/AR2006022501546.html.

Jerome, A. M. (2008). Toward prescription: Testing the rhetoric of atonement's applicability in the athletic arena. *Public Relations Review, 34*, 124-134.

Jerome, A., & Rowland, R. (2009). The rhetoric of interorganizational conflict: A subgenre of organizational apologia. *Western Journal of Communication, 73*, 395-417.

Johnson, H. (2002, November 12). Why I'm teed off: The chairman of the Augusta National Golf Club weighs in. [Editorial]. *Wall Street Journal* [Online]. Retrieved June 17, 2010, from http://www.opinionjournal.com/extra/?id=110002611

Juliano, J. (2003, April 10). A defiant Johnson defends Augusta's men-only policy. *Philadelphia Inquirer*, p. E01. Retrieved May 14, 2010, from Academic Universe (Lexis-Nexis) database.

Koesten, J., & Rowland, R. C. (2004). The rhetoric of atonement. *Communication Studies, 55*, 68-87.

Kopylovsky, D. (2010, March). *IBISWorld industry report: Racing & other spectator sports in the US: 71121b.* Santa Monica, CA: IBISWorld. Retrieved May 24, 2010, from http://www.ibisworld.com/reports/reportdownload.aspx?cid=1&rtid=1&e=1629&ft=pdf&beta=y

Kristiva, J. (1984). *Revolution in poetic language* (L. S. Roudiez, Trans.). New York: Columbia University Press. (Original work published in 1974)

Lessl, T. M. (1989). The priestly voice. *Quarterly Journal of Speech, 75*, 183-197.

Lindemann, W. K. (2006). *Public relations research for planning and evaluation.* Gainesville, FL: Institute for Public Relations Research. Retrieved June 15, 2007, from http://www.instituteforpr.org/research_single/relations_research_planning/

Lindsey, J. (2005, December). J'accuse. *Outside Magazine* [Online]. Retrieved May 12, 2010, from http://outside.away.com/outside/features/200512/lance-armstrong-1.html.

Masters Chairman Johnson doesn't give a hoot about protesters. (2003, April 10). *Alameda (CA) Times Star.* Retrieved May 14, 2010, from Academic Universe (Lexis-Nexis) database.

McGlone, T. (2009, July 1). Michael Vick now working for Peninsula Boys & Girls Clubs. *Virginian-Pilot* [Online]. Retrieved June 17, 2010, from http://hamptonroads.com/2009/06/michael-vick-now-working-peninsula-boys-girls-clubs.

McMillan, J. J. (1987). In search of the organizational persona: A rationale for studying organizations rhetorically. In L. Thayer (Ed.), *Organization↔communication: Emerging perspectives II* (pp. 21-45). Norwood, NJ: Ablex.

Humane Society of the United States. (2009). *Michael Vick's participation in the HSUS' End Dogfighting Program.* [Online Frequently Asked Questions page]. Retrieved June 17, 2010, from http://www.hsus.org/acf/fighting/dogfight/vick_faq.html.

Owens, T. (2005, November 14). Terrell Owens apology—11.08.05. [Video file]. Retrieved May 11, 2010, from Owens_TO_press_apology_11-08005.wmv at http://blog.mccannta.com/mccannta/video/

Perelman, C., and Olbrechts-Tyteca, L. (1969).*The new rhetoric: A treatise on argumentation* (J. Wilkinson and P. Weaver, Trans.). Notre Dame, IN: Notre Dame University Press.

Prouse, J. D. (2008). *The Tonya tapes: The Tonya Harding story in her own words.* New York: World Audience.

Rinaldi, T. (2010, March 22). Woods gives first interview since crash. *ESPN* [Online]. Retrieved June 14, 2010, from http://sports.espn.go.com/golf/news/story?id=5016125

Rowland, R. C., & Jerome, A. M. (2004). On organizational apologia: A reconceptualization. *Communication Theory, 14,* 191-211.

Schorn, D. (2006, January 12). Bode Miller apologizes for comments:Ski champ's comments on *60 Minutes* stirred up controversy. *CBS News: 60 Minutes* [Online]. Retrieved June 17, 2010, from http://www.cbsnews.com/stories/2006/01/12/60minutes/main1203734.shtml

Smudde, P. M. (2004a). Implications on the practice and study of Kenneth Burke's idea of a "public relations counsel with a heart." *Communication Quarterly, 52,* 420-432.

Smudde, P. M. (2004b). The five Ps for media interviews: Fundamentals for newbies, veterans and everyone in between. *Public Relations Quarterly, 49*(2), 29-36.

Smudde, P. M. (2010). *Public relations as dramatistic organizing: A case study bridging theory and practice.* Cresskill, NJ: Hampton Press.

Sobel, J. (2010, February 20). Still waiting for answers from Tiger Woods. *ESPN* [Online]. Retrieved May 24, 2010, from http://sports.espn.go.com/golf/columns/story?columnist=sobel_jason&id=4930736

Steele, E. D., & Redding, W. C. (1962). The American value system: Premises for persuasion. *Western Speech, 26,* 83-91.

Stewart, C. J., & Cash, W. B., Jr. (2007). *Interviewing: Principles and practices* (12th ed.). New York: McGraw-Hill

Sullivan, D. L. (1993). The ethos of epideictic encounter. *Philosophy and Rhetoric, 26,* 113-133.

Toulmin, S. E. (1958). *The uses of argument.* New York: Cambridge University Press.

TV producer pays $10,200 for notes to Vicks apology. Retrieved June 2, 2010, from http://sports.espn.go.com/nfl/news/story?id=3020177

U.S. skier Bode Miller upset over 60 Minutes *interview.*(2006, January). Retrieved June 17, 2010, from http://www.shortnews.com/start.cfm?id=52126

Van de Vate, D., Jr. (1965). Disagreement as a dramatic event. *The Monist, 49,* 248-261.

Van Susteren, G. (2007, August 27). Michael Vick cops plea. [Broadcast transcript]. *Fox on the Record.* Fox News Network. Retrieved May 12, 2010, from Academic Universe (Lexis-Nexis) database.

Van Valkenburg, K. (2009, February 5). Intense scrutiny has Phelps weighing whether he will swim in 2012 Games. *Baltimore* (MD) *Sun* [Online]. Retrieved June 17, 2010, from http://www.baltimoresun.com/sports/olympics/bal-te.sp.phelps05feb05,0,3171313.story

Vick, M. (2007, August 27). Michael Vick's press conference and statement. [Video]. Retrieved May 12, 2010, from http://www.youtube.com/watch?v=I2V9Mo9WX-Y.

Vinton, N. (2010, February 6). Bode's a powder keg: Four years after Turin blowup, Bode Miller racing toward revival at Vancouver Games. *New York Daily News* [Online]. Retrieved June 17, 2010, from http://www.nydailynews.com/sports/more_sports/2010/02/06/2010-02-06_bode_miller_olympics_powder_keg.html#ixzz0r7uFwD13.

Wagner, C. (2003, April 10). Hootie stands firm; Augusta National chairman re-emphasizes stance on all-male membership.*Syracuse* (NY) *Post-Standard,* p. C7. Retrieved May 12, 2010, from Academic Universe (Lexis-Nexis) database.

Winter Olympics; Harding walks out of interview. (1994, February 21). *New York Times* [Online]. Retrieved May 11, 2010, from http://www.nytimes.com/1994/02/21/sports/winter-olympics-harding-walks-out-of-interview.html

Woodruff, J. (2000, September 8). Coach Bobby Knight denies mistreating Indiana University student. [Broadcast transcript]. *CNN Headline News.* Retrieved May 12, 2010, from Academic Universe (Lexis-Nexis) database.

Woods, T. (2010, February 19). Tiger Woods press conference transcript: Full text of apology. *New York Daily News* [Online]. Retrieved May 12, 2010, from http://www.nydailynews.com/news/2010/02/19/2010-02-19_tiger_woods_press_conference_transcript_full_text_of_apology_given_during_public.html?page=2#ixzz0nkDUneKn.

VI

Research in Brief

Reputation Differences between Mortification-Only and Mortification/ Corrective Action Strategies Following a Transgression by a Professional Athlete

John Twork and Joseph Blaney, Illinois State University

Background: Image Restoration Theory case studies since 1995 have asserted that various public figures (e.g., Bill Clinton, Pope John Paul II, Hugh Grant) used mortification effectively in their attempts to repair image following accusations of wrongdoing, but surmised that mortification would be more effective when combined with promises of corrective action. No empirical tests ever confirmed these claims, so we hypothesize:

H: Mortification plus corrective action will provide greater repair of reputation than mortification only for athletes following an accusation of a transgression.

Method: Subjects (300 students and community members solicited via e-lists and social networking sites) were exposed to one of four groups: (1) male transgression+mortification only, (2) male transgression+mortification + corrective action, (3) female transgression + mortification only and (4) female transgression + corrective action + corrective action. The transgression was proffered as a newspaper article about an unprovoked act of physical aggression (punching an athletic rival) during a competition. The varying image repair strategies were offered as a standard-format press release from the athlete. Data were entered into SPSS and two t-tests were run, first for the variance in the male category and then in the female category. The reputation measure was adapted from:

Coombs, W. T., and Holladay, S. J. (1996). Communication and attributions in a crisis: An experimental study in crisis communication. *Journal of Public Relations Research, 8,* 279-295.

1. The athlete is concerned with the integrity of the sport.
2. The athlete is basically unsportsmanlike.
3. I do not trust the athlete to play fair.
4. Under most circumstances, I would be likely to expect the athlete to play fair.
5. The athlete is not concerned with the integrity of the sport.

Results: There were no significant differences for either t-test.

Test 1 (Male Moritification Only/Male Mortification Plus Corrective Action)
$t(-.708, d.f.=133), p=.48$

Test 2 (Female Mortification Only/Female Mortification Plus Corrective Action)
$t(.264, d.f.=123), p=.79$

Secondary t-tests showed no significant difference between males/females.

IMPLICATIONS/LIMITATIONS

This calls into question the assumption of the many case studies (some included in this volume) that argue for more effective image repair by coupling corrective action with mortification. These findings (or lack thereof) also have implications for the promises that athletes will need to make when charged with excessive and overt aggression on the playing field. Should athletes promise to enter therapy after such untoward events? We will leave that to mental health professionals. However, our study suggests that such promises do not add to reputational outcome. While these findings call into question assumptions about these corrective action promises, our claims should be considered tentative as we did not run a manipulation check assessing perceived differences in messages with/without the statement, "I will also be enrolled in an anger management class."

Finally, we must raise the possibility of perceptual differences between readers of text and watchers of video. Significant findings could result from the same statement of corrective action if proffered by the athlete televisually. Such research should be conducted.

CONDITION EXAMPLES

MORTIFICATION ONLY CONDITION

Smith out for season after altercation

MILWAUKEE–The National Athletic League (NAL) has suspended Kevin Smith for the remainder of the season following his role in last week's physical altercation with Jerome Williams. Smith might also be forced to sit out during the beginning of next season, pending a league ruling.

Smith, 29, repeatedly punched Williams after a verbal dispute between the two escalated during last week's Las Vegas versus Milwaukee game at Lake Stadium. Williams, who was knocked to the ground and did not retaliate during the exchange, was transported to the hospital with multiple minor injuries. Williams said he is not pressing charges against Smith. The verbal dispute began when a referee made a controversial call.

"The National Athletic League is extremely disappointed in the actions taken by Kevin Smith," NAL commissioner Patricia Martinez said in a prepared statement. "Kevin engaged in unacceptable behavior that clearly violated league rules. Sportsmanship is of utmost concern to the NAL, which is why we are suspending Kevin for at least the remainder of this season."

Prior to the suspension, Smith was statistically on-pace for a career-best year. Without Smith in the lineup, Milwaukee will be forced to start a rookie in Smith's former position.

FOR IMMEDIATE RELEASE

Kevin Smith has released the following statement in response to his altercation with Jerome Williams.

"I am deeply sorry for the physically aggressive actions I took against Jerome Williams during last week's scuffle. I should not have hit Jerome. I accept full responsibility for my actions, and I willingly accept my suspension by the league office. I am sorry for my transgression, and grateful for your support."

On a scale from 1 to 5, with 1 representing disagree strongly, 2 disagree somewhat, 3 unsure, 4 agree somewhat, and 5 agree strongly, please indicate your level of agreement with the following statements.

MORTIFICATION PLUS CORRECTIVE ACTION CONDITION

Smith out for season after altercation

MILWAUKEE–The National Athletic League (NAL) has suspended Kevin Smith for the remainder of the season following his role in last week's physical altercation with Jerome Williams. Smith might also be forced to sit out during the beginning of next season, pending a league ruling.

Smith, 29, repeatedly punched Williams after a verbal dispute between the two escalated during last week's Las Vegas versus Milwaukee game at Lake Stadium. Williams, who was knocked to the ground and did not retaliate during the exchange, was transported to the hospital with multiple minor injuries. Williams said he is not pressing charges against Smith. The verbal dispute began when a referee made a controversial call.

"The National Athletic League is extremely disappointed in the actions taken by Kevin Smith," NAL commissioner Patricia Martinez said in a prepared statement. "Kevin engaged in unacceptable behavior that clearly violated league rules. Sportsmanship is of utmost concern to the NAL, which is why we are suspending Kevin for at least the remainder of this season."

Prior to the suspension, Smith was statistically on-pace for a career-best year. Without Smith in the lineup, Milwaukee will be forced to start a rookie in Smith's former position.

FOR IMMEDIATE RELEASE

Kevin Smith has released the following statement in response to his altercation with Jerome Williams.

"I am deeply sorry for the physically aggressive actions I took against Jerome Williams during last week's scuffle. I should not have hit Jerome. I promise this will never happen again. I accept full responsibility for my actions, and as I serve my suspension for the remainder of the season, I will also be enrolled in an anger management class. If I become involved in a future verbal altercation, I promise I will not use physical violence to express my anger. I am sorry for my transgression, and grateful for your support."

On a scale from 1 to 5, with 1 representing disagree strongly, 2 disagree somewhat, 3 unsure, 4 agree somewhat, and 5 agree strongly, please indicate your level of agreement with the following statements.

Conclusion

Joseph R. Blaney

Hopefully the purpose of this book became more and more obvious as you proceeded from chapter to chapter. What is at stake when an athlete's or athletic organization's reputations is sullied? Consider the list: hundreds of millions of dollars in endorsements, ticket sales, and contracts; goodwill necessary for fans to remain spectators; personal freedom (prison life versus civilian life); and merely the maintenance of a favorable reputation, which remains a primary goal of all communicators (Clark and Delia, 1979).

The value of reputation clearly understood, sports communicators (and their surrogates) have rhetorical choices to make. We have seen in these chapters both examples of prodigious, excellent repair of reputations and absolute communicative malpractice.

We are confident that the reader now has much context from which to draw when crafting messages for clients, friends, and even oneself. Communicating in relationships, groups, organizations, and with the public requires our very best on behalf of all stakeholders: athletes, fans, investors . . . and the very integrity of the sports we love.

REFERENCE

Clark, R. A., & Delia, J. G. (1979). *Topoi* and rhetorical competence. *Quarterly Journal of Speech, 65,* 187-206.

Index

60 Minutes, 11, 13, 14, 20, 22, 24, 42, 45, 377

accident, 2, 91, 192, 198, 226
all-star game, 106, 272, 275
amateurism and education, 283, 284, 285, 286, 287, 289, 294n2
Andro. *See* androstenedione
Androstenedione, 20, 29
anger management, 4, 224, 227, 232, 396, 398
anger management counseling, 4
answering questions with questions, 242, 248, 250
antapologia, 59, 60, 62–63, 66–67, 69, 204, 207, 208, 209, 210, 216, 217, 218–219
anti-doping rules, 75
apologia, 60, 61, 66, 68, 69, 188, 198, 204, 207–208, 209, 210, 215, 216, 219, 226, 229, 250, 267, 268, 269, 275, 276, 277, 278, 279, 301, 360, 361, 367, 368, 369, 374, 383
apology, 33, 38, 47, 49, 52, 74, 75, 77, 79, 80, 89, 92, 102, 114, 117n19, 123, 133, 134, 158, 159, 163–164, 165, 166, 174, 179, 181, 204, 207, 208, 216, 226, 229, 230, 232, 243, 244, 245, 246, 248, 249, 258, 279, 328, 333, 369, 374, 378, 387
Arenas, Gilbert, 169–171, 172, 173, 183n1
ARF. *See* Australian Rules Football
Associated Press, 29, 42, 53, 54, 73, 105

Association Football. *See* Soccer
Atlanta Journal-Constitution, 152, 162, 165
attack strategy, 212, 213, 214, 217
attacking the accuser, 2, 3, 4, 91, 195, 198, 210, 219, 226
Australian Rules Football, 228
Authenticity, 17, 78, 82, 83, 136, 216, 247, 383, 387, 388

B-12 vitamin, 13, 19, 20
BALCO. *See* Bay Area Lab Co-operative
band-aid approach, 71, 76, 81, 82, 84
Baseball Writers Association of America, 44, 54
Bay Area Lab Co-operative, 9, 41, 42, 46, 47, 49, 60
BBC. *See* British Broadcast Corporation
BBWAA. *See* Baseball Writers Association of America
Beckham, David, 126–127, 128, 144n3
Benoit, William, 1, 4, 28, 33, 38, 45, 61, 62, 78–84, 152, 170, 207, 209, 214, 225, 240, 257, 270
Bettman, Gary, 320, 321, 324, 326, 327, 328, 329–330, 333, 336, 337, 339–340, 340–341, 341–342, 342–343, 343–346, 348, 349–350, 351, 353, 354
Bloomberg, Michael, 187, 189, 195, 198
Bolstering, 2, 3, 10, 12, 15, 21, 36, 46, 50, 53, 60, 63, 64, 66, 68, 69, 79, 91, 107,

156–162, 226, 242, 243, 246, 247, 248, 258, 262, 268, 276, 327, 333, 342, 351, 361

Bonds, Barry, 9, 11, 20, 41–55, 56n1–56n4, 378

brand image, 72, 76, 78, 82, 127, 129, 132, 140, 227, 336, 342, 348

Brand, Myles, 224, 230

British Broadcast Corporation, 126

broadcast contracts, 287, 319, 323, 324, 326, 340, 341, 345

Brown v. Board of Education, 104

Bryant, Kobe, 97, 97–100, 103–104, 104–108, 108–115, 116n1–116n11, 117n18, 117n19

Burke, Kenneth, 2, 71, 76, 78, 79, 84, 90, 188, 283, 284, 286, 293

Burress, Plaxico, 187–199

Bush Russert exchange, 61

business of major league professional sports, 359

Caminiti, Ken, 20

Canseco, Jose, 18, 23, 28, 29, 32, 33, 36, 38, 42, 45, 47, 48, 51

celebrity, 37, 63, 64, 69, 77, 83, 97, 105, 106, 107, 110, 115, 123, 124, 126, 134, 136, 229, 239, 253, 375, 382, 383

character attack, 214, 219

Chelsea, Premier League Club, 123, 137, 127–128, 129–130, 131, 134–135, 139, 140, 143

Clemens, Roger, 9–25, 44, 45, 55

Clijsters, Kim, 240, 245, 246

Clinton, William, 22, 74, 80, 209, 395

Collective bargaining agreement, 158, 164, 169, 178, 270, 272, 274, 275, 320, 321, 326, 327, 328, 330, 332, 337

communication strategies, 72, 81

compensation, 2, 91

congress. *See* congressional hearings

congressional hearings, 15, 22, 23, 24, 54, 227

Constitution, 172, 373, 379, 381

Conte, Victor, 41

contrition, 64, 133, 165, 241, 269, 375, 378, 381

corporate sponsorship, 126, 132, 272

corrective action, 3, 4, 32, 35, 36, 39, 78, 80, 89, 91–93, 153, 154, 158–162, 170, 174, 178, 182, 242–249, 258, 259, 262, 277, 352, 395, 396, 397

counterattack, 207, 219, 226, 307

court of law, 30, 61, 102, 104, 105, 116n7, 116n12, 123, 130, 131, 132, 142, 156, 158, 162, 172, 175, 181, 203, 212, 311, 373

credibility, 12, 13, 14, 15, 17, 20, 21, 22, 23, 47, 48, 51, 91, 109, 112, 136, 160, 163, 195, 217, 233, 269, 319, 329, 351, 362, 372, 375, 376, 382

crisis, 117n14, 142, 226, 228, 229, 269, 300, 301, 314, 351, 352, 353

crisis communication, 1, 2, 367, 396

crisis communication discourse, 2

Critical Race Theory, 103, 104

CRT. *See* critical race theory

Cuban, Mark, 107

cultural lag, NCAA, 283, 284, 285, 286, 287, 289, 291, 293

Dale Earnhardt, Inc., 297–299, 300, 301, 301–302, 303, 304, 305, 307, 308–309, 311–315

The Death of Hockey, 324

defensibility, 2, 15, 19, 36, 41, 91, 153, 160, 162, 246, 260

DEI. *See* Dale Earnhardt, Inc.

denial, 2, 3, 4, 10, 13, 15, 20, 22, 24, 32, 35, 37, 41, 46, 49, 52, 55, 65, 78, 83, 91, 153, 157, 160, 163, 170, 182, 198, 210, 226, 242, 243, 248, 268, 276, 351, 373

Denmark women's handball team, 229

Differentiation, 2, 10, 60, 63, 64, 67, 68, 91, 191, 193, 198, 226, 268, 276–277

dog fighting, 158, 164

dramaturgical model, 124

drug testing, 9, 47, 50–51

Duke lacrosse team, 228, 371, 372, 373, 375

Earnhardt, Dale Jr., 297–298, 299, 302, 304, 305, 306, 307, 308, 309, 310, 311, 313, 314

Earnhardt, Dale Sr., 297, 302, 303, 304, 306, 311, 313, 314, 315, 315n2

Earnhardt, Teresa, 298, 299, 300, 301, 301–302, 303, 305, 308, 310, 311, 314, 315

Earnhardt-Ganassi Racing, 312–313

endorsements, 28, 46, 72, 78, 83, 84, 93, 106, 107, 117n18, 127, 128, 308, 334, 401

epideictic, 360, 361, 363, 387

epideictic argument, 365

epideictic core functions, 361, 363, 364, 385, 387, 388; celebratory function, 361, 362, 363, 365, 366, 367, 368, 369, 374, 375, 376, 377, 380, 385; performative function, 361, 362, 365, 367, 368, 369, 374, 375, 376, 378, 380, 381, 383, 385; epistemic function, 361, 363, 365, 366, 367, 368, 369, 373, 374, 376, 379, 380, 383, 385; preservative function, 361, 363, 365, 366, 367, 368, 369, 372, 373, 376, 381, 385

epideictic discourse, 360, 361, 362, 363, 366, 360, 361, 365

epideictic genre, 360, 361, 363

epideictic messages, 361, 363

epideictic situation, 361, 363

ESPN, 20, 89, 155, 165, 191, 193, 194, 195, 197, 198, 205, 206, 208, 210, 211, 213, 214, 217, 218, 225, 229, 230, 231, 241, 244, 254, 255, 310, 319, 324–325, 326, 339, 340, 341, 348, 349

facework, 2, 123, 124, 128, 131, 133

Fainaru-Wada, Mark, 41, 55

fan base, 107, 159, 270, 274, 321, 336, 337

faux pas, 226

Federation Internationale de Football Association, 125

Fehr, Donald, 274

FIFA. *See* Federation Internationale de Football Association

forgiveness, 3, 64, 66, 77, 79, 91, 92, 93, 133, 139, 160, 199, 226, 229, 244, 248, 301, 370, 387

Formula One racing, 227

Foudy, Julie, 255

four phase evolution of image repair, 385

gambling, 128, 154, 156, 158, 159, 163, 164, 167, 173, 177, 228

Game of Shadows, 9, 55

Gender, 110, 112, 98, 101, 102, 104, 113, 138, 241, 250, 255, 257, 259–260, 262, 374, 376, 377

gender violence, 97, 98, 99, 106, 111, 112, 115

Giambi, Jason, 9, 42, 47, 49, 52

gladiator analogy, 359

Goffman, Erving, 2, 124, 129, 136, 138, 140

good Black man, 108, 109, 110

good intentions, 2, 15, 34, 36, 91, 225

Goodell, Roger, 158, 159, 161, 163, 166

grand narrative, 98

gun crime, 171, 173, 178, 181, 182, 188, 191, 192, 194, 195

gun culture, NBA, 177, 180

gun laws, 169, 172, 174, 178, 180

Hall of Fame, 24, 27, 30, 54, 313, 325

hand/eye coordination argument, 52

Harding, Tonya, 3–4, 207, 352, 370, 371, 373, 374, 375, 377, 378, 380, 381, 382

Hendrick Motorsports, 298, 303, 304, 311

HGH. *See* human growth hormone

higher education, 285, 286, 292

human growth hormone, 9, 10–19, 20–22, 23, 24, 27, 56n2, 227

Humane Society, 151, 155, 373, 387

Humility, 165, 247

humor, media, 176, 187, 223, 254

identity, 55, 72, 110, 125, 128, 138, 284, 288, 362, 367, 368

identity management, 362, 367, 368, 369, 374, 378, 379, 381, 383

image (definition), 1, 72

Image Repair Theory, 1–2, 3, 4–5, 28, 36, 90, 257, 267, 268, 270, 277, 278, 279, 395

immediate antapologia, 59, 60, 66, 68, 69

impression management, 123

Indiana University, 223, 224, 229, 230, 370

infidelity, 1, 82, 89, 91, 93, 97, 190, 209

intercollegiate athletics, 285, 290

interest convergence, 97, 103, 104–106, 107, 109, 112, 113

International Olympic Committee, 60

IRT. *See* Image Repair Theory

James, Adam, 205, 206, 208, 209, 210, 211, 212, 213, 214, 218
Johnson, Hootie, 369, 371, 373, 375, 377, 379, 380, 381
Jones, Marion, 59–70
Juiced, 29, 42, 48, 51

kategoria, 62, 69, 188, 204, 207, 208, 209, 210, 219, 276
Kerrigan, Nancy, 3–4, 207, 352, 370, 374, 377, 382
Knight School reality TV show, 224, 225, 231
Knight, Bob, 223–233, 370, 372, 373, 374, 379, 381
Kornheiser, Tony, 21, 22, 23, 24, 165, 166

labor agreement, 268, 272, 274, 275, 278
labor dispute, 267, 268, 270, 274, 279, 319, 330, 332, 337, 338
labor lockout, 272, 319–321, 322, 324, 326, 327, 329, 330, 331, 333–334, 335, 344, 349, 351
labor negotiations, 267, 270, 271, 272, 273, 274, 276, 277, 278, 279
labor negotiations, 267, 270, 271, 272, 273, 276, 277, 279
Lambert, Elizabeth, 253–254, 254–257, 258–260, 260–254
large market teams, 329, 347
Leach, Mike, 203, 204, 205–207, 208–209, 210, 211–219
league revenue, 320, 322, 327, 333, 338
Leyland, Jim, 43
Lil Wayne, 193
Linkugel, W., 2, 170, 207, 268, 276
Los Angeles Lakers, 106, 107
luxury tax, 271, 275, 321–322, 350

Major League Baseball, 9, 28, 29, 42, 47, 51, 267, 268, 271, 272, 273, 274, 275, 276, 277, 278, 279, 321, 323, 338, 343
Major League Baseball Players Association, 267, 268, 271, 273, 274, 277, 278
Major League Baseball Players Association, 267, 268, 271, 273, 274, 276, 277, 278, 279
Marijuana, 71, 74, 77, 80, 151, 152, 380
marketing plan, 28, 74, 127, 128, 142, 225, 273, 320, 327, 334, 335, 336, 337, 340, 343, 350, 353, 354
McGwire, Mark, 11, 20, 27–30, 31, 32–33, 33–34, 34, 35, 36–39, 42, 44, 45, 54, 55, 379, 381
McNamee, Brian, 9–10, 10–11, 12, 12–15, 16, 17, 18, 20, 21, 22–23, 24
media contextualization, 170
media interview, epideictic function, 367, 368, 369, 376, 377
media interviews, 59, 61, 62, 70, 359, 360, 365, 377
media opinion, 20, 54
media reaction, 254
membership report, NCAA, 289, 291, 293, 294n5
micropolitics of power, 298, 300, 301, 303
Miller, Bode, 378, 381, 382
minimization, 2, 28, 36, 91, 244, 248, 262, 310, 341, 343, 351
Mitchell Report, 9, 10–11, 12, 15, 20–25
MLB. *See* Major League Baseball
MLBPA. *See* Major League Baseball Players Association
mortification, 3, 4, 33, 36, 37, 55, 77–79, 89, 91–94, 158–166, 170, 174, 178, 180–182, 188, 198, 226, 244–249, 258–262, 277, 327, 336, 352, 395, 396
mortification-corrective action couplet, 4
Most Valuable Player, 20, 43, 44, 54
Mountain West Conference, 253, 256–254, 257, 261
MVP. *See* Most Valuable Player

narrative theory, 124
NASCAR. *See* National Association for Stock Car Auto Racing
National Association for Stock Car Auto Racing, 225, 227, 297, 298, 300, 301, 302, 303–304, 305, 308, 310, 311, 312, 313, 314, 315n1–315n3, 319, 347
National Basketball Association, 106, 107–108, 112, 113, 169, 170, 171, 172, 174–175, 175, 177, 178, 179, 180, 182, 183n1, 290, 321, 338, 342, 344, 347, 349, 350

National Collegiate Athletic Association, 203, 214, 224, 253, 256, 257, 261, 283, 284, 285, 285–293, 293n1–294n6, 383

National Football League, 97, 151, 152, 153, 155, 158, 159, 162, 164, 165, 166, 167, 188, 190, 194, 195, 198, 205, 290, 324, 335, 338, 383

National Hockey League, 319–322, 323, 324, 325, 326, 327, 328, 329, 330, 331–338, 338–340, 342, 342–345, 347–348, 349–354

National Hockey League Players Association, 319, 320, 321, 327, 329, 330, 332, 333, 343, 351

NBA. *See* National Basketball Association

NCAA financial situation, 292

NCAA. *See* National Collegiate Athletic Association

neo-Aristotelian paradigm, 270

news cycle, 71, 74, 83, 83, 84

News of the World, 73, 74, 130

NFL. *See* National Football League

NHL. *See* National Hockey League

NHLPA. *See* National Hockey League Players Association

Nixon, Richard, 22, 132

no pay for play rule, 288

Nordegren, Elin, 89

NY Giants, 187, 188, 189, 190, 193, 195, 196, 197

Obama, Barrack, 116n9

officiating, 229, 263

Olympics, 3, 4, 59, 60, 61, 71, 72, 73, 74, 75, 80, 82, 207, 371, 375, 377, 378, 382, 383

oppression, 99, 108, 299

The Oprah Winfrey Show, 59, 60, 61, 63

organization image, 319

organizational apologia, 269, 279

Owens, Terrell, 37, 227, 371, 373, 374, 375, 378

Pardon the Interruption, 20, 21, 23, 155, 165, 255

patriarchy, 97, 105, 109, 113

People for the Ethical Treatment of Animals, 151

perceived responsibility, 209

performance-enhancing drugs, 11, 14, 20, 25, 31, 35, 41, 45, 53, 60, 373, 377

perjury, 13, 15, 41, 55, 56n2

personal lives, 84, 97, 254, 288

persuasion, 199, 361, 363, 366, 372, 373, 381

PETA. *See* People for the Ethical Treatment of Animals

Pettitte, Andy, 10, 12, 13–14, 14–15, 16, 19, 20, 22, 24

Phelps, Michael, 71–84, 378

player strikes, 270

polling data, 24, 37, 163, 166, 333

post-labor lockout, 337, 338, 339, 340, 341, 343, 344, 345, 346, 348, 350, 351, 352–354

press conference, 14, 28, 42, 46, 47, 48, 49, 52, 153, 162, 163, 164, 191, 227, 242, 243, 244, 245, 246, 249, 268, 274, 276, 279, 328, 359, 360–361, 362, 365, 366–367, 368, 369, 369, 370, 371, 372, 373, 374, 376, 379, 381, 383, 384, 385, 387

press conference, epideictic function, 369, 372, 373, 374, 375, 376, 380, 382, 385

priesthood function, 283

privilege-class and celebrity, 97, 99, 101, 105, 106, 107, 108, 110, 112, 114, 115

product improvements, 320, 334

provocation, 2, 91, 191, 194, 244, 246, 262, 258, 262

PSA. *See* Public Service Announcement

psychologically reformative, 268, 276, 277, 279

psychologically transformative, 268, 276, 277, 279

PTI. See Pardon the Interruption

public image, 37, 61, 94, 97, 115, 123, 124, 131, 141, 198, 239, 249, 284, 302

public opinion, 20, 30, 37, 80, 82, 244, 311, 381

public pedagogy, 97, 104, 105, 111, 115

public relations, 30, 177, 207, 226, 227, 228, 229, 231, 233, 239, 250, 256, 308, 359, 360, 361, 362, 363, 365, 367, 372, 376, 381

public relations discourse, 361, 362, 363, 376, 387

public relations professional, 1, 4, 227, 245, 360, 361
public scrutiny, 20, 98, 189, 219
Public Service Announcement, 30, 289

race, 97, 100–101, 103, 104, 110, 113, 171, 172, 177, 241, 250
rape, 99, 101–103, 105, 106, 107, 108, 110–113, 115, 116n5–116n7, 223, 228, 256, 371, 376
reputation, 5, 10, 18, 22, 24, 28, 44, 45, 46, 47, 49, 51, 53, 54, 72, 76, 77, 78, 80, 83, 84, 90, 109, 117n18, 129, 156, 157, 166, 190, 199, 215, 224, 225, 226, 228–229, 268, 278, 351, 362, 366, 371, 375, 381, 383, 395, 396
retaliation, 258, 262, 397, 398
rhetoric of rebirth, 77; pollution, 77, 385; purification, 2, 77, 188, 385; redemption, 65, 69, 77, 78, 165, 188, 198, 388
rhetorical posture, 268; absolution, 268, 269; vindication, 268, 269; explanation, 268, 269; justification, 268, 269
rhetorical situation, 51, 163, 166, 207, 208, 215, 219, 276
rhetorical strategy, 67, 78, 84, 166, 188, 190, 191, 192, 193, 209, 226, 243, 248, 268, 293, 301, 302, 361, 362, 364, 367, 369, 375
Ruth, Babe, 50, 56n3, 310
Ryan, Bob, 43

salary, 28, 106, 205, 228, 271, 275, 278, 308, 319, 320, 321–322, 324, 326, 327, 329, 332, 345, 350
salary cap, 271, 319, 320, 321, 321–322, 324, 326, 327, 329, 332, 333, 350
San Francisco Chronicle, 41, 42, 45, 46, 47, 53, 55
Sanford and Son, 47, 52
Schaap, Jeremy, 191, 192, 193, 194, 196, 197, 198
self-defense, 59, 62, 68, 69, 204, 268, 276, 362, 368, 372
self-monitors, 250
self-sacrificing, 50
self-fulfilling prophecy, 133

Selig, Bud, 9, 33, 37, 51, 271, 272, 273, 274, 275
Semiotics, 124, 140
sense-making, 124
sexual assault, 97, 99, 106, 107, 110, 112
sexual contact, race, 102–103
sexual misconduct, 1
Sheffield, Gary, 42, 227
shifting the blame, 2, 15, 77, 161, 162, 225, 327, 331, 333, 351
silence, 82, 123, 124, 131, 132, 133, 134, 142, 143, 216, 300
sincerity, 37, 79, 117n19, 216, 247, 249
slander, 174, 212
small market teams, 271, 321, 323
soccer, 125, 123, 124, 125, 126, 130, 132, 133, 135, 137, 139, 253–254, 256, 258, 259, 261, 262, 263, 325, 359
social media, 83, 169, 173, 174, 175, 241, 245, 253, 255, 256, 294n3, 294n6, 299, 368, 395
Sosa, Sammy, 11, 20, 28, 29
Soviet Union, 62, 209
spectator sports, 359, 360, 385
speech set, 69, 204, 207, 208, 210, 217, 219, 276
sponsors, 28, 72, 74, 79–80, 89, 112, 126, 128, 129, 131, 132, 133, 228, 229, 272, 275, 298, 301, 311–312, 319, 320, 327
sport apologists, 269
sports commentators, 170, 175
sports communication, 1, 30
Sports Illustrated, 20, 28, 55, 308, 321, 339
sports organizations, 269, 360, 382, 383, 385
sportsmanship, 255, 370, 371, 388, 396, 397, 398
Stanley Cup finals, 321, 324, 325, 326, 342, 343, 345, 346, 347, 350
state of the great address, 42, 45, 46, 49, 51–52, 53, 54, 55
Stein's typology of antapologia, 62, 66, 68, 69, 204, 209
Stern, David, 113, 169, 172, 174, 175, 175–176, 178, 179–180, 181, 321
steroid abuse, 12
steroid era, 9, 11, 20, 44, 51, 53, 55
steroids, 9–12, 13–25, 27, 29, 30, 31, 32–39, 41–45, 47–55, 59–64, 227

Stewart, Tony, 227, 301, 308
student athlete, 224, 260, 283, 284, 285–293, 374
Super Bowl, 190, 197, 198, 375
synecdoche, 283–285, 286, 287–289, 290, 292, 293

tabloids, 47, 73, 74, 116n6, 123, 126, 135, 139–140, 141, 142, 143, 380
team sport, 129, 132, 137, 250, 269, 278, 301, 319
team sport ethic, 269
television ratings, 273, 324, 325, 326, 330, 337, 339, 340, 341, 342, 342–343, 343, 346, 347, 348–349, 350, 351
Terry, John, 123–125, 127–130, 130–135, 136, 137–138, 139–141, 141–143, 144n2; Terry's expressive display, 124; the armband, 124, 131, 133, 135; the handshake, 124, 131, 137; the kiss, 124, 131
Texas Tech University, 203, 204, 205, 206, 210, 211, 212, 214, 215, 217, 218, 224, 225, 229, 231, 233
textual analysis, 66, 124
Thomas, Frank, 12
Tierney, John, 15, 16, 17, 22, 23
Title IX, 263
Toradol, 12, 13
transcendence, 2, 32, 46, 47, 50, 55, 60, 63, 64, 65, 68, 69, 89, 91, 93, 164, 191, 192, 193, 198, 226, 268, 276, 327, 328, 330, 333, 336, 341, 343, 345, 348, 349, 350, 351, 353
transgressions, 65, 91, 135, 138, 171, 226, 227, 230, 250, 91, 370, 395
Tyson, Mike, 106, 108, 109, 115, 371, 378

universe of silence, 189
University of New Mexico, 253, 254, 256–257, 258, 260, 261

USA Swimming Organization, 75
USA Today, 24, 43, 73, 79, 177, 379

Vecsey, George, 22
The View, 164, 241
Vick, Michael, 151–167, 370, 371, 373, 375, 376, 387

WAG. *See* Wives and Girlfriends of sports stars
Wall Street Journal, 305, 381
Wallace, Mike, 10, 11, 12, 13, 15, 21, 22, 42
Walruip, Michael, 297–298, 310, 313
Ware, B., 2, 207, 268, 276, 279
Washington Post, 37, 109, 169, 176–177, 180, 181
Washington Wizards, 169, 170, 171, 173, 174, 175, 178, 179, 181, 350
wicked stepmother spiral, 299, 315
Wilbon, Michael, 21, 22, 23, 155, 165, 166, 177, 181
Williams, Lance, 41, 55
Williams, Serena, 239–251
Winfrey-Jones interview, 60
Winslow, Kellen, 228
Wives and Girlfriends of sports stars, 137, 144n5
women's soccer, 253, 254, 255, 257, 258, 259, 261, 263
women's tennis, 239, 240
Woods, Tiger, 37, 81–82, 84, 89–94, 110, 123, 127, 130, 133, 167, 190, 209, 239, 369, 372, 373, 375, 378, 379, 383
World Cup, 123, 125, 126, 127, 128, 127, 135, 136, 143, 209
World Series, 12, 21, 28, 29, 56n4, 268, 270, 275, 319
written statements, 174, 175, 191, 242, 245, 246, 247, 248, 249, 361

About the Authors

H. R. Allen (B.A. BYU-Idaho) is a graduate student in the Department of Communication and Rhetorical Studies at Idaho State University. His research interests are in corporate and sports image repair strategies.

Matthew Barton (Ph.D., University of Nebraska) is associate professor of communication at Southern Utah University.

William L. Benoit (Ph.D., Wayne State University) is professor of communication at Ohio University. He publishes on image repair discourse and political campaign discourse. He served as editor of *Communication Studies* and *Journal of Communication.*

Joseph R. Blaney (Ph.D., University of Missouri) is associate dean of the College of Arts and Sciences and professor of communication at Illinois State University. His research interests are repair of public image and media education. He also serves as editor of the *Journal of Radio and Audio Media* which is published by the Broadcast Education Association.

LeAnn M. Brazeal (Ph.D., University of Missouri) is associate professor and director of graduate studies in the Department of Communication Studies at Kansas State University.

Jordan L. Compton (M.A., Missouri State University) is a second-year Ph.D. student in communication studies at Ohio University. His research interests include image repair, functional theory of political communication, and sports rhetoric.

Jeffrey L. Courtright (Ph.D, Purdue University) is associate professor of public relations in Illinois State University's School of Communication. His research focus is on how message design communicates the preferred image of organizations across a variety of contexts: environmental communication, community relations, and international public relations. He has published two books with Dr. Peter Smudde, as well as several book chapters and journal articles.

Craig W. Cutbirth (Ph.D., Bowling Green State University) is an emeritus associate professor in the School of Communication at Illinois State University. He continues to teach political communication at the Osher Lifelong Learning Institute at the University of Illinois.

James R. DiSanza (Ph.D., Penn State University) is chair of two departments—Communication & Rhetorical Studies and the James E. Rogers Department of Mass Communication—at Idaho State University. He conducts research on organizational image management and is co-founder of the journal *Relevant Rhetoric: A New Journal of Rhetorical Studies.*

Mark Glantz (Ph.D., University of Missouri) is assistant professor of communication at St. Norbert College.

Rachel Alicia Griffin (Ph.D., University of Denver) is assistant professor in the Department of Speech Communication at Southern Illinois University at Carbondale. Her research interests span critical intercultural communication, critical race theory, Black feminist thought, popular culture, and gender violence. All of her publications and projects speak strongly to notions of power, privilege, and voice, which she has presented at national conferences, keynote addresses, and social justice workshops.

John Huxford (Ph.D., University of Pennsylvania) is a former reporter, feature writer, and editor from Britain and currently an associate professor of communication at Illinois State University. His research interests include the visual and textual construction of news.

Ric Jensen (Ph.D., Texas A & M University) is assistant professor of marketing at Montclair State University. Ric has been widely published about sports communication issues, mainly about how sports organizations have used public relations to manage crises.

Angela M. Jerome (Ph.D., University of Kansas) is associate professor of communication at Western Kentucky University. Her scholarly interests are in crisis communication.

Lindsay Johns (B.A. Penn State Erie, The Behrend College) is a recent communication graduate of Penn State Erie where she was an active member of Lambda Pi Eta the national undergraduate communication honor society, and is currently working in sales and marketing.

Michael R. Kramer (Ph.D., University of Minnesota) is associate professor of communication studies and Chair of the Department of Communication Studies, Dance, & Theatre at Saint Mary's College. His research interests are political rhetoric, public memory, and image repair. He also writes *Club Apologia*, a blog about image repair and apologia case studies.

Nancy J. Legge (Ph.D., Penn State University) teaches in the Communication & Rhetorical Studies Department at Idaho State University. Her research interests focus on rhetoric and popular culture. She is co-founder and the Editor of the journal *Relevant Rhetoric: A New Journal of Rhetorical Studies*.

Lance R. Lippert (Ph.D., Southern Illinois University, Carbondale), is associate professor of communication at Illinois State University. His research interests include organizational communication, leadership, and instructional communication. He also directs the University's interdisciplinary Civic Engagement and Responsibility Minor.

John McGuire (Ph.D., University of Missouri) is associate professor and graduate coordinator in the School of Media and Strategic Communicationsat Oklahoma State University. His research interests include sports journalism practices, sports announcing, and political journalism.

Lori Melton McKinnon (Ph.D., University of Oklahoma) is associate professor in the School of Media and Strategic Communications at Oklahoma State University. Her research focuses on political and strategic communications, especially regarding ethical issues. The Arthur W. Page Center for Integrity in Public Communication has named McKinnon a Page Legacy Scholar.

Kevin R. Meyer (Ph.D., Ohio University) is assistant professor of communication and director of forensics at Illinois State University. His research interests include student silence and participation grades, instructional communication, the basic communication course, sports apologia, and health communication.

Mike Milford (Ph.D., University of Kansas) is assistant professor at Auburn University. His research interests include allegory in popular discourse and the rhetoric of sports.

Theodore F. Sheckels (Ph.D., Pennsylvania State University) is professor of English and communication studies at Randolph-Macon College. His research interests are campaign communication and Presidential public address. He has published on political topics as varied as Congress, gender, South Africa, and the state of Maryland.

J. Scott Smith (M.S., Illinois State University) is a Ph.D. student at the University of Missouri. His research interests include political rhetoric, mythic criticism, repair of public image, and popular media.

Peter M. Smudde (Ph.D., Wayne State University) is associate professor of public relations in Illinois State University's School of Communication. After sixteen years in industry, he moved to higher education full time in 2002. He is accredited in public relations (APR) through the Public Relations Society of America. Pete has published numerous articles and four books (multiple articles and two books with Dr. Jeffrey Courtright) that explore areas of public relations' synergy with corporate strategy, public relations discourse, and pedagogical approaches to public relations.

Kevin A. Stein (Ph.D., University of Missouri) is associate professor in the Department of Communication at Southern Utah University. His research interests include the rhetoric of attack (*kategoria*), defense (*apologia*), and responses to defense (*antapologia*). He also examines political campaign communication.

Rod L. Troester (PH.D. Southern Illinois University) is associate professor of communication studies at Penn State Erie, The Behrend College. His research interests are in the areas of civility and communication and grassroots environmental organizing.

Paul Turman (Ph.D., University of Nebraska) is associate vice-president for academic affairs, South Dakota Board of Regents. His research interests include communication and sport.

John Twork (M.S., Illinois State University) is a professional sports play-by-play announcer covering college baseball, football, softball, and volleyball games in the Midwest.

Wayne Wanta (Ph.D., University of Texas) is professor and chair of the Department of Journalism at the University of Florida. He is a past president of AEJMC, and twice represented AEJMC as a delegate to the World Journalism Education Congress. He has lectured and presented papers in 40 different countries, including recently as a Fulbright Scholar in Iceland, and has written more than 150 research articles and papers, many in the area of sports, political and visual communication.

James T. Wilde (B.A. BYU-Idaho) is a graduate student in the Department of Communication and Rhetorical Studies at Idaho State University. His current research interests are image restoration, training and development, and business communication.